Criminality and Crime

Criminality and Crime

A Social-Cognitive-Developmental Theory of Delinquent and Criminal Behavior

Glenn D. Walters

LEXINGTON BOOKS
Lanham • Boulder • New York • London

Published by Lexington Books
An imprint of The Rowman & Littlefield Publishing Group, Inc.
4501 Forbes Boulevard, Suite 200, Lanham, Maryland 20706
www.rowman.com

86-90 Paul Street, London EC2A 4NE, United Kingdom

British Library Cataloguing in Publication Information Available

Library of Congress Cataloging-in-Publication Data

Names: Walters, Glenn D., author.
Title: Criminality and crime : a social-cognitive-developmental theory of delinquent and criminal behavior / Glenn D. Walters.
Description: Lanham : Lexington Books, [2022] | Includes bibliographical references and index. | Summary: "Criminality and Crime integrates criminality and participation in a specific criminal event. Although criminality and crime are normally considered separate entities, this book treats them as part of the same process, connected by their common association with criminal thinking"—Provided by publisher.
Identifiers: LCCN 2021057406 (print) | LCCN 2021057407 (ebook) | ISBN 9781666904420 (cloth) | ISBN 9781666904437 (epub) Subjects: LCSH:
Criminal behavior. | Criminal psychology. | Juvenile delinquency. | Crime—Sociological aspects.
Classification: LCC HV6080.W253 2022 (print) | LCC HV6080 (ebook) | DDC 364.3—dc23/eng/20220104
LC record available at https://lccn.loc.gov/2021057406
LC ebook record available at https://lccn.loc.gov/2021057407

Contents

Introduction 1

SECTION I

1 On Not Missing the Forest for the Trees 5

2 Crime, Criminality, and Human Nature 21

3 Social Foundations of a Criminal Lifestyle 33

4 Cognitive Foundations of a Criminal Lifestyle 55

5 Developmental Foundations of a Criminal Lifestyle 79

SECTION II

6 The Moral Model of Lifestyle Criminality 103

7 The Control Model of Lifestyle Criminality 127

8 The Decision-Making Model of Crime 151

SECTION III

9 Managing Criminality: Part I. Reducing Risk by Building Competencies 175

10 Managing Criminality: Part II. Reducing Risk by Changing Environments 199

11 Crime Prevention: Limiting Opportunities, Altering Incentives, and Addressing Aggravating and Mitigating Conditions 223

12 Returning to the Forest 247

References 255

Index 305

About the Author 311

Introduction

This book elaborates on the criminal lifestyle, a topic that I began researching in the late 1980s. Because I have already published three books on the criminal lifestyle (*The Criminal Lifestyle*, 1990; *Criminal Belief Systems*, 2002; *Modelling the Criminal Lifestyle*, 2017), a fair question would be, what makes this effort different from the previous three? This question can be answered in several ways. First, traditional criminological theories address either criminality (the propensity to commit crime) or crime (involvement in a specific criminal event), but not both. The current book introduces the reader to the three models that comprise criminal lifestyle theory—two of which are designed to explain criminality (moral and control) and one of which is designed to explain crime (decision-making)—and illustrates how they can be integrated. Second, much of my prior work has focused on adult offenders. The current book, which is based primarily on research I have conducted over the past six to eight years, focuses more heavily on delinquency and the transition from childhood to adolescence, in an effort to better understand the developmental origins of a criminal lifestyle. Third, this book introduces the reader to an entirely new concept in the form of the antisocial spectrum. As described in the opening chapter of this book, the antisocial spectrum is comprised of behaviors that not only lead to delinquency and crime (school bullying, animal cruelty, firesetting), but which may also help clarify the developmental origins of a criminal lifestyle.

Before moving into chapter 1, it is imperative that the reader understand that this book is designed to contribute to the study of criminal behavior by taking a holistic approach to the interrelated concepts of criminality and crime. Criminological theory has traditionally focused either on the criminal act (crime) or the overall propensity to commit crime (criminality). Both are important in explaining criminal behavior, but neither is complete in and of itself. Criminology began as the study of crime based on the philosophical writings of Italian jurist Cesare Beccaria and English philosopher Jeremy Bentham, but eventually shifted to the study of criminality with the advent of positivistic criminology and the work of Italian physician Cesare Lombroso. Thus, while crime and criminality are distinct concepts, one or the other of which serves as the foundation for nearly every contemporary theory of crime, they are rarely viewed as part of the same process. The parts have thus been given precedence over the whole. It is the integration of the parts, however, rather than the parts themselves that holds the most promise of answering the questions that have plagued criminology and puzzled criminologists for centuries. In the opening chapter of this book, the goal of developing a holistic understanding of crime by merging the interrelated concepts of criminality and crime is discussed using the analogy of not missing the forest for the trees. This theme will then carry over to the remainder of the book as we search for a more integrated and holistic perspective on crime.

This book is broken down into three sections. In the first section (chapters 1–5), the focus is on the trees or more accurately, groups or types of trees that go into criminological theory. Following an introduction to the overlapping concepts of criminality and crime in chapter 1, the reader is taken on a tour of the types of trees that make up the forest that is criminal behavior. These include biological factors (chapter 2), social factors from parents and peers to the larger social structure (chapter 3), cognitive and emotional factors (chapter 4), and developmental factors (chapter 5). In each of these four chapters, the objective is to elaborate on how these different factors contribute to both criminality and crime. In the second section of this book, the relationship between criminality and crime is developed further by introducing three models, two of which are designed to explain criminality and the third of which provides an interpretation of crime. The two criminality models are based on morality (chapter 6) and control (chapter 7), whereas the crime model addresses criminal decision-making (chapter 8). In the third and final section of this book, the focus shifts to application and integration and the goal of constructing a holistic view of delinquent and criminal behavior. Here, the emphasis is on managing criminality (chapter 9), preventing crime (chapter 10), using a holistic model to alter the criminal justice system (chapter 11), and the inherent compatibility of criminality and crime (chapter 12). We begin, then, with a discussion on the importance of not overlooking the forest for the trees in our efforts to understand as much as possible about the different types of trees that fill the forest.

Section I

Chapter 1

On Not Missing the Forest for the Trees

"The Journey Begins"

Whether one considers it a clever idiom or a simple proverb, the phrase "missing the forest for the trees" encourages us to keep an eye on the object of our investigation as we go about testing the finer aspects of the theory that we have created to explain the object. These finer aspects are remnants of the scientific tests we use to validate our theories, but they are not the theories themselves. Whether theories evolve over time, through a process of falsification and refinement (Popper, 1999), or progress by leaps and bounds as part of an intellectual revolution or paradigm shift (Kuhn, 1962/2012), they are more than the empirical tests used to verify their utility. The theory, then, is the forest and the individual constructs, tenets, and principles the trees. In science, we test hypotheses derived from theories using operationally defined indicators designed to represent major theoretical concepts (Earman, 1984). The key to validating a theory is to avoid losing sight of the larger picture as we work to reduce complex phenomenon to more manageable units in order to test the theory. There can be times when we get so wrapped up in the details that we miss the big picture. The same goes for theories of crime, which more often than not center on isolated variables instead of variable relationships. Variable relationships, it should be pointed out, provide a theory with mechanisms (mediation) and context (moderation). Before discussing variable relationships, however, my overall objective in writing this book requires clarification.

CRIMINALITY AND CRIME

Criminality can be defined as a person's propensity to engage in criminal conduct, whereas crime is a person's involvement in a specific criminal act. Criminality is the focus of positivistic criminology as put forth by Cesare Lombroso (1835–1909); crime is the product of classical criminology and the deterrence doctrines of Cesare Beccaria (1738–1794) and Jeremy Bentham (1748–1832). Most theories in criminology adopt either a classical or positivistic perspective, but very few emphasize both. My purpose in writing this book is to illustrate how criminality and crime are compatible, complementary, and integratable. Conceptualizing criminality as the forest and specific crimes as trees, we can see how focusing on one or the other can lead to a less-than-adequate understanding of criminal behavior, though this is precisely what many theories in criminology do. As a means of reversing this trend, the present book will demonstrate how criminality and crime can be integrated to provide a holistic understanding of criminal behavior. In the next three subsections, three different criminological theories will be examined. In each case, the theory, despite being popular, appears to miss the mark when it comes to the forest-and-tree issue.

Gottfredson and Hirschi's General Theory of Crime

In their general theory of crime, Gottfredson and Hirschi (1990) contend that low self-control is the principal cause of crime. Although they also discuss the role of opportunity in the decision to commit crime, the theory rests almost exclusively on the shoulders of low self-control, so much so that many criminologists refer to the model as low self-control theory. There is an impressive body of evidence showing that low self-control is a reliable and consistent correlate, if not predictor, of delinquency, crime, and general antisocial behavior (Donner et al., 2014; Ha & Beauregard, 2016; Pratt & Cullen, 2000; Siegfried & Woessner, 2016). Criticisms have nonetheless been leveled against the theory, alleging that low self-control is just another term for crime and that the low self-control–crime relationship is nothing more than a tautology (Akers et al., 2021). It has also been found that factors other than parental discipline, from biology to neighborhood context, contribute as much to low self-control as weak parenting (Buker, 2011), that low self-control is not nearly as stable as Gottfredson and Hirschi make it out to be (Burt et al., 2006), and that low self-control does a relatively poor job of explaining certain forms of crime, such as white-collar offending (Benson & Moore, 1992). The general theory of crime, in fact, is a prime example of a single variable theory.

As a one-variable theory, Gottfredson and Hirschi's general theory of crime could be considered as a theory that misses the forest for the trees. In effect, it focuses on one type of tree (low self-control), while ignoring the rest of the forest. Although low self-control may be a prominent tree in the antisocial forest, it is still just one of the several types of tree found in the forest. Moreover, the theory does not distinguish between two subspecies of low self-control. In elaborating on their theory, Hirschi and Gottfredson (1993) assert that low self-control is a behavioral construct that should be assessed with behavioral ratings, preferably made by an outside observer, such as a parent or teacher, and in situations where self-reports are used, the instrument should reference specific behaviors and not attitudes. Self-control, however, may be more complex than this, with the position of this book being that low self-control can be divided into two dimensions: behavioral impulsivity and cognitive impulsivity. The rationale for and significance of treating cognitive and behavioral impulsivity separately is discussed at length in chapter 7, and research indicates that when they are assessed separately both correlate with delinquent and criminal behavior (Evans et al., 1997; White et al., 1994). Distinguishing between cognitive and behavioral impulsivity offers a better view of the forest, but it is still a forest in which many of the trees are missing.

Moffitt's Developmental Taxonomy

Three years after Gottfredson and Hirschi (1990) unveiled their general theory of crime, Moffitt (1993) published an influential paper on a three-trajectory taxonomy of delinquent development. The first trajectory in Moffitt's model was the "life-course-persistent" pattern. This particular trajectory was believed to have its onset in late childhood and to persist well into adulthood. Moffitt postulated that of the three trajectories in her theory, the "life-course-persistent" pattern was the one most likely to lead to future adult offending. A second trajectory proposed by Moffitt had an age of onset in early to mid-adolescence and normally terminated a few years later in mid- to late adolescence. She labeled this the "adolescence-limited" pattern. Individuals in this pattern almost always had a shorter criminal career than those in the "life-course-persistent" pattern and usually desisted from crime by late adolescence or early adulthood. Moffitt held that this pattern had significantly more members than the "life-course-persistent" pattern but presented significantly fewer long-term problems because of a relatively short lifespan. The largest trajectory was a pattern Moffitt referred to as "non-delinquency." Youth in this pattern engaged in minimal levels of offending from childhood to adulthood. Studies provide general support for Moffitt's model, although the number of trajectories identified in these studies often includes more than the three from Moffitt's model (Jennings & Reingle, 2012).

Whereas Gottfredson and Hirschi (1990) miss the forest for the trees by focusing on a specific type of tree (low self-control), Moffitt's (1993) theory may have stymied the study of trees by creating two distinct forests: a life-course-persistent (LCP) forest and an adolescence-limited (AL) forest. I would argue, in line with Sampson and Laub (1997), that there is but one forest and that all individual differences are subsumed under this one forest. Despite the support Moffitt's theory has garnered in several studies (Barnes et al., 2011; Eme, 2020; Leaw et al., 2015), her developmental taxonomy suffers from a serious conceptual problem. The statistical procedures that are used to identify trajectories do an effective job of identifying the number of classes in a distribution, but they do a poor job of determining latent structure type or whether the construct under evaluation is continuous (dimensional) or categorical (taxonic). The latter requires a statistical procedure like Meehl's (2004) taxometric method. When the taxometric method has been applied to parental ratings of antisocial behavior, the results usually indicate that the latent structure type is dimensional rather than taxonic (Walters, 2011a; Walters & Ruscio, 2013). This would seem to imply, contrary to Moffitt's original premise, that the difference between LCP and AL antisocial behavior is quantitative rather than qualitative. As such, individual differences on measures comparing LCP and AL offending are a matter of degree (quantitative) rather than a difference in kind (qualitative), which is inconsistent with Moffitt's notion of a developmental taxonomy.

Cohen and Felson's Routine Activity Theory

Whereas Gottfredson and Hirschi (1990) and Moffitt (1993) sought to explain how individual differences in criminality account for criminal offending, Cohen and Felson (1979) developed a theory designed to explain how crimes occur. In their routine activity theory of crime, Cohen and Felson argued that crime is a function of three factors: a motivated offender, a suitable target, and the absence of capable guardians against crime. A motivated offender is someone with a moderate to high proclivity for crime. A suitable target is an object, asset, or person the offender is interested in victimizing. Capable guardians are situational factors that increase the likelihood that the offender will be deterred from committing the crime by virtue of an increased probability of detection and arrest. Guardians may include a police patrol, guard dog, increased neighborhood lighting, or the fact that a house is occupied rather than unoccupied. The goal of routine activity theory is to reduce target suitability and achieve maximum guardianship as a means of deterring a motivated offender from acting on a criminal opportunity.

At first blush, it would seem that routine activity theory, unlike most traditional theories of crime, addresses both criminality and crime. After all, the first element of routine activity theory, a motivated offender, is in line with criminality and the notion of divergent propensities for delinquency and crime. The problem is that Cohen and Felson (1979) largely ignore the motived offender element of their model in favor of the suitable target and capable guardian elements when discussing how to manage crime through environment engineering. Gottfredson and Hirschi's (1990) general theory of crime would also appear to integrate criminality (low self-control) and crime (opportunity) but still suffers from myopia by virtue of only examining one type of tree. Moffitt's (1993) oversight has been to act as if there is more than one forest. As was previously mentioned, however, there is no justification for assuming a categorical difference between the "life-course-persistent" and "adolescence-limited" patterns when the correct statistical procedures are employed (Walters, 2011a; Walters & Ruscio, 2013).

VARIABLES VERSUS VARIABLE RELATIONSHIPS

One of the principal arguments made in this book is that criminological theory is better served by an emphasis on variable relationships than by an emphasis on single variables and by a focus on multivariate relationships than by a focus on bivariate associations. Whereas multivariate relationships encompass three or more variables, bivariate relationships cover only two. And because a measure of crime, delinquency, or antisocial behavior is normally included in most criminological studies, bivariate relationships linking an independent variable to crime, delinquency, or antisocial behavior is standard practice in criminology. If our goal is to understand crime in all of its complexity, however, relationships involving three or more variables are required. The basic three-variable model is called a triad, and multiple triads, it has been argued, can be combined to form variable clusters (Walters, 2020a). This process, referred to as elaboration, is one avenue by which theories are constructed; incidentally, this is why variable relationships are emphasized over the variables themselves. The fact that elaboration does not appear to have been practiced extensively in the field of criminology may be one reason why there are so many single variable theories of crime. A secondary objective in writing this book is to illustrate how variable relationships can be used to clarify and change serious criminal conduct.

Categories of Variable Relationship

There are three categories of variable relationships central to criminal lifestyle theory. These are presented as dualities, but each duality has as many similarities as they do differences. The three dualities are unidirectional and bidirectional effects, moderation and mediation, and confounding and suppressor variables.

Unidirectional and Bidirectional Effects

When it comes to bivariate relationships, the effect can travel in one direction, from one variable to the next (unidirectional), or in both directions, from one variable to the next and then back again (bidirectional). Bidirectional or reciprocal effects are the cornerstone of Thornberry's (1987) interactional theory of crime, in which constructs from social control and social learning theories are organized into reciprocally related pairs over early, middle, and late adolescence. Peer delinquency and participant delinquency, for instance, are held to be bidirectionally related, such that delinquent behavior on the part of a youth may lead them to seek contact with other delinquents (peer selection effect) and association with delinquent peers may lead an individual into further delinquency as they learn attitudes and techniques conducive to crime (peer influence effect). Belief in conventional values and commitment to school likewise form a bidirectional relationship, as do weak attachment to parents and adoption of delinquent beliefs by the child. Outside of Thornberry's theory, strong reciprocal relationships have been observed between parental control/support and child delinquency (Abar et al., 2014; Zhang et al., 2020) and between antisocial attitudes and emotions like guilt and anger (Walters, 2020k; Walters & Espelage, 2021).

The best way to test for bidirectional relationships is with cross-lagged correlations. To calculate a cross-lagged correlation, one must measure the variables of interest twice, with a reasonable amount of time between the two assessments. In the Walters (2020k) investigation, for instance, neutralization beliefs and guilt were measured at Time 1 and then again 12 months later at Time 2. The two cross-lagged coefficients (from neutralization at Time 1 to guilt at Time 2 and from guilt at Time 1 to neutralization at Time 2) were then calculated and compared, the results of which showed that both correlations were statistically significant and of comparable size. This led to the conclusion that neutralization and guilt are reciprocally related, to the point where a rise in neutralization may reduce guilt and a rise in guilt may impede neutralization. Bidirectionality, rather than being assumed, should be tested in each relevant situation. For those relationships that are clearly bidirectional, there is both a conceptual and practical benefit. The conceptual benefit is further knowledge. The practical benefit is that interventions effective with one pole of the bidirectional association (e.g., guilt) should also be of assistance in treating the other pole (e.g., neutralization) and vice versa given the reciprocal nature of the relationship. The world, it would seem, is made up of both unidirectional and bidirectional associations; it is the job of the scientist to determine how relevant variables fit into these two pathways.

Moderation and Mediation

Moderation and mediation are sometimes mistaken for one another, but they are two distinct processes. Moderation is tested by gauging the effect of the interaction between an independent variable (X) and a moderator variable (W) on a dependent variable (Y). When appended to a bivariate correlation, a moderating variable forms a triad (see figure 1.1, panel a). The triad created with the addition of a moderating variable provides context to a relationship. Defoe et al. (2020) tested a peer presence × sex interaction by having early adolescent boys and girls complete a risky decision-making task under one of two sets of conditions: alone or with two same-sex peers. A significant peer presence × sex interaction revealed that while boys and girls engaged equally in risk-taking when completing the task alone, boys were significantly more likely than girls to engage in risk-taking when completing the task with two same-sex peers. This indicates that risky decision-making was similar for boys and girls in one context (alone) but not in another context (with peers).

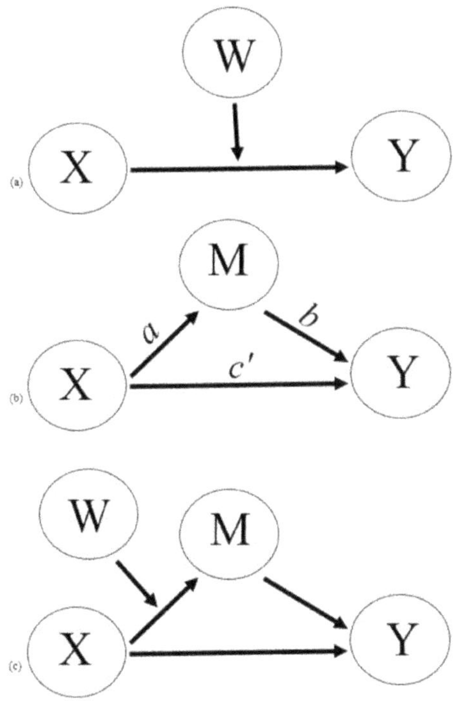

Figure 1.1 Moderation (panel a), Mediation (panel b), and Moderated Mediation (panel c). Note: X = independent variable, Y = dependent variable, W = moderator variable, M = mediator variable, *a* = a path of indirect effect, *b* = b path of indirect effect, *c′* = direct effect. *Source:* Created by author.

One way to interpret this finding is that peer pressure—operationally defined as completing a task with peers—has a significantly stronger impact on risky decision-making in boys than in girls.

Whereas moderation requires the construction and testing of an interaction effect, mediation entails performing a path analysis with at least three nonoverlapping waves of prospective data. In the case of mediation, the third variable in the triad, rather than providing a context for the independent-dependent variable relationship, as is the case with moderation, provides a mechanism by creating a link between the independent and dependent variables in what is commonly referred to as an indirect effect (see figure 1.1, panel b). In a study by Stylianou et al. (2019), victimization and bullying mediated the relationship between psychopathic personality traits and delinquency. The indirect effect, which ran from psychopathic traits to victimization or bullying (*a* path) and from victimization or bullying to delinquency (*b* path), was significant, according to model fit statistics from a structured equation modeling analysis. Unfortunately, as will be discussed in chapter 4, this is not how causal mediation analysis is currently conducted. State of the art mediation analysis tests the significance of the total indirect effect (*ab*) with nonparametric bootstrapped confidence intervals. The direct effect of psychopathic traits on delinquency is measured along the *c'* path and should also be reported.

Confounding and Suppressor Variables

There is a broad coalition of variables that can be used to challenge the causal status of a research finding. This coalition consists of confounding, suppressor, and collider variables. Confounding occurs when an unobserved variable correlates with both the measured outcome (Y) and one or more independent variables (X). Unobserved in this context means that the variable is not included in the current research design. In a study where maternal awareness correlated with future child delinquency, neighborhood disorganization would be considered a confounding variable if it correlated with both maternal awareness and child delinquency and in so doing altered the relationship between these two variables. Confounding variables violate the sequential ignorability assumption of path and regression analysis, which holds that all relevant covariates have been accounted for in one's model (Imai et al., 2010). The degree to which a study violates this assumption can be considered an estimate of omitted variable bias. The best way to control for omitted variable bias is to include the confounding variable in the research design as a control variable, although it is not always possible to identify or measure all potential confounding variables. That is why researchers often perform a sensitivity analysis designed to determine the likelihood of a confounding variable affecting the results of one's study. Kenny's (2013) "failsafe ef" procedure, for instance, generates a coefficient that indicates how strongly an unobserved covariate confounder would need to correlate with the mediating and dependent variables in a mediational analysis to lower to zero the coefficient along the *b* path of a significant indirect effect.

While confounding variables create problems that are best handled by including them in the research design, suppressor variables create problems that are best dealt with by removing them from the study. A suppressor variable, by definition, is a variable that when added to a regression equation increases the predictive validity of one or more predictor variables, even though the suppressor itself may be unrelated to the outcome (Conger, 1974). Thus, if adding a measure of verbal intelligence to a regression equation succeeds in increasing the overall regression coefficient as well as the individual coefficients for age, older sibling delinquency, and fighting in school, then verbal intelligence could be considered a suppressor variable. As a consequence of selection bias, irrelevant variance (i.e., variance unrelated to the outcome measure) in each predictor variable is "purified" by removing or partialling out the variance it shares with the suppressor variable. Suppressor effects are quite common and once identified, are best handled by combining the suppressor variable with the variable it is suppressing or eliminating one of the two variables from the regression equation (Maassen & Bakker, 2001). Suppression also illustrates the value of restricting control variables to only those that are most relevant to the research question and avoiding the dangerous but unfortunately not-uncommon practice of "throwing everything but the kitchen sink" into a regression equation.

A collider variable is a special case of the broader suppressor variable classification. A collider effect occurs when a researcher conditions on a prior measure of a predicted variable. Collider effects are most likely to occur when a researcher uses a lagged outcome measure in which a precursor measure of the outcome is included as a covariate in an equation predicting that particular outcome. It should be noted that when one is conducting a mediation analysis, it is imperative that the temporal order and direction of the variables be established. Temporal order is achieved by using prospective data in which the X variable precedes the M (mediator) variable, which, in turn, precedes the Y variable. Temporal direction is attained by controlling for a prior or precursor measure of the predicted variable (i.e., M in the equation predicting M, and Y in the equation predicting Y). The most common way to accomplish this is by using a lagged outcome variable. Conditioning on a precursor measure, however, can potentially introduce endogenous selection bias or a collider effect into the analysis (Elwert & Winship, 2014). This is best handled by conducting a secondary analysis in which all of the precursor measures are removed. Should the path coefficients increase or remain the same with removal of the precursor measures, then there is minimal support for a collider effect. But if a path coefficient were to demonstrate a substantial drop with removal of a precursor measure, particularly if it went from significant to nonsignificant, then a collider effect needs to be entertained as a possible explanation for the results.

Combining Categories

Some of the relationship patterns described in this section can be combined, with combinations occurring across and within categories. Moderation and mediation, for instance, can be merged into a single statistical procedure known as moderated mediation (Hayes, 2018). Walters (2018k) performed a moderated mediation analysis of the peer resistance–future delinquency relationship using moral disengagement as the mediator variable and peer delinquency as the moderator variable. Results indicated that while moral disengagement mediated the peer resistance–future delinquency relationship, this mediated relationship was moderated by peer delinquency, such that peer resistance inhibited future delinquency via reduced moral disengagement more reliably in youth with fewer delinquent friends. When peer delinquency was high, peer resistance was only weakly correlated with future delinquency by way of reduced moral disengagement. Hence, a mediated relationship (peer resistance → low moral disengagement → decreased delinquency) was moderated by the youth's level of peer delinquency (see figure 1.1, panel c). Although panel c of figure 1.1 restricts moderation to the *a* path of the mediated relationship, any combination of the three paths (*a*, *b*, *c'*) could be moderated, depending on the model. A mediated moderation analysis is also possible using the same exact statistical approach, but with a different objective: that is, explaining a moderated relationship (peer resistance × peer delinquency → delinquency) with a mediational mechanism (moral disengagement).

Because most studies in criminology employ a unidirectional approach to causation, unidirectional moderation and mediation are common cross-category combinations. Still, there is no reason why moderation and mediation cannot be combined with a bidirectional approach. Two previously mentioned studies on the relationship between cognition and emotion did just that. Walters (2020k) used bidirectional mediation to demonstrate how guilt mediates the neutralization–delinquency relationship and neutralization mediates the guilt–delinquency relationship. In this antagonistic bidirectional nexus, guilt and neutralization (cognitive insensitivity) inhibited one another: neutralization led to reduced levels of guilt which, in turn, led to increased delinquency and guilt engendered reduced neutralization which was then followed by decreased levels of delinquency. Walters and Espelage (2021) subsequently examined the complementary bidirectional nexus that exists between anger and cognitive impulsivity and discovered that anger produced higher levels of cognitive impulsivity which, in turn, precipitated a rise in bullying, and that cognitive impulsivity encouraged higher levels of anger which also led to increased bullying. Combinations involving confounding and suppressor variables and relationships are more difficult to envision but both should be routinely evaluated when conducting regression and path analysis.

THE CRIMINAL LIFESTYLE

My view of the criminal lifestyle has gradually changed in the 30+ years since I helped coin the term (Walters & White, 1989b) and wrote a book on the concept based on my experiences as a psychologist running treatment groups at the U.S. Penitentiary in Leavenworth, Kansas (Walters, 1990). Since then, I have come to realize that the criminal lifestyle is a fiction you approach rather than a reality you achieve. As I envision it, there is no such thing as a lifestyle criminal, even though I have unfortunately used this term in the past. Two advantages of labeling the lifestyle instead of the person are that it reduces labeling effects while emphasizing the prospect of change in response to either internal (maturity) or external (situational) forces. Behavioral patterns of a criminal lifestyle listed in my 1990 book are still as relevant today as they were 30 years ago: irresponsibility or lack of accountability, self-indulgence or the pursuit of immediate gratification, interpersonal intrusiveness or infringing on the rights and personal space of others, and social rule breaking or violating accepted standards of conduct. The degree to which a person embodies these four behavioral styles can be used to assess how fully they embody the negative ideal of a criminal lifestyle.

An instrument designed to assess the four behavioral styles of a criminal lifestyle was developed years ago as the Lifestyle Criminality Screening Form (LCSF: Walters et al., 1991). The LCSF was created as a chart audit procedure and its items were selected based on their availability in most federal pre-sentence investigation (PSI) reports. There are limitations to using the LCSF to estimate the four behavioral styles, however. First, it requires a PSI and thus is not appropriate for individuals who have never been convicted of a crime. Second, it is a static measure based on historical information and so does not reflect the change that is believed to occur with respect to a person's ongoing relationship with the criminal lifestyle. Third, the items were selected because of their availability in a standard PSI and so some are weak indicators of the behavioral dimensions they are designed to represent. For instance, quitting or being fired from a job was included on the irresponsibility subscale even though it did a less-than-adequate job of assessing irresponsibility at work, and prior divorces were included on the self-indulgence subscale even though they were a poor substitute for sexual promiscuity. In short, we need to find a better way to assess a person's degree of engagement in a criminal lifestyle than is possible with the LCSF.

THE ANTISOCIAL SPECTRUM

Spectrums of disorders have been introduced in psychiatry and psychology in an effort to group certain mental disorders that share a common symptomology, etiology, or treatment response. The schizophrenia spectrum, for instance, encompasses a range of disorders believed to stem from a genetically based subtle neurointegrative deficit referred to by Meehl (1989) as schizotaxia. This subtle neurointegrative deficit purportedly leaves a person vulnerable to a range of psychiatric disorders of moderate to high severity in which periodic or sustained loss of contact with reality, flat or inappropriate affect, and disturbances in movement up to and including catatonia are observed. The disorders found along the schizophrenia spectrum include schizophrenic disorder, schizoaffective disorder, schizophreniform disorder, delusional disorder, brief psychotic disorder, and schizotypal personality disorder. The antisocial spectrum, on the other hand, is composed of a series of behavioral patterns linked not by a genetically based neurointegrative deficit, but by the four characteristics of a criminal lifestyle: irresponsibility, self-indulgence, interpersonal intrusiveness, and social rule breaking (Walters, 1990). Patterns of behavior that display a moderate degree of one or more of these behavioral styles are awarded a place on the antisocial spectrum (for related views, see Krueger et al., 2000, and Frick & Viding, 2009).

Behavioral patterns like chronic adult criminality and psychopathy can be found at the upper or right end of the antisocial spectrum, expressive (reactive) and instrumental (proactive) delinquency fall into the middle section, and such developmental antecedent behaviors as animal cruelty, school bullying, early drug use, and firesetting fill out the lower or left end of the antisocial spectrum. Membership on the antisocial spectrum requires evidence of moderate to high involvement in one or more of the four previously mentioned behavioral styles (i.e., irresponsibility, self-indulgence, interpersonal intrusiveness, and social rule breaking). Animal cruelty and school bullying, for instance, earn their place on the antisocial spectrum by highlighting interpersonal intrusiveness (with animal cruelty extending the intrusion to a person's treatment of animals), whereas early substance use and firesetting pull for self-indulgence and irresponsibility. Support for bullying and animal cruelty's positions on the antisocial spectrum and their potential role as developmental antecedents to delinquency can be found in a study by Walters (2019a) whereby these two behavioral patterns exerted a robust indirect effect on future delinquency via moral disengagement (cognitive insensitivity). In addition, a process known as psychological inertia, whereby continuity in delinquency is mediated by reactive criminal thinking (RCT)/cognitive impulsivity but not proactive criminal thinking (PCT)/cognitive insensitivity (Walters, 2016h, 2019h), may also help explain bullying continuity (Walters & Espelage, 2018a).

The antisocial spectrum is conceptualized as a horizontal hierarchy organized into three columns. The first or left-most column contains the developmental antecedents, the second or middle column houses expressive and instrumental delinquency, and the third or right-most column encompasses adult criminality. Adjacent columns are connected by strands of antisocial cognition/criminal thinking, either cognitive insensitivity/PCT or cognitive impulsivity/RCT. Cognitive insensitivity is believed to link such antecedent behaviors as animal cruelty and school bullying to instrumental delinquency, whereas cognitive impulsivity is believed to link such antecedents as firesetting and drug use to expressive delinquency, PCT (an advanced form of cognitive insensitivity) is believed to link instrumental delinquency to adult criminality, and RCT (an advanced form of cognitive impulsivity) is believed to link expressive delinquency to adult criminality. In this way, the thinking that supports antisocial behavior is mild and unintegrated (either cognitive insensitivity or cognitive impulsivity) at first but becomes more powerful and integrated (both PCT and RCT) over time. The main sections of the antisocial spectrum, along with the temperamental (fearlessness and disinhibition) and behavioral (callous-unemotional traits and low self-control) precursors to the antecedents and the connecting cognitive mediators are depicted in figure 1.2.

Criteria from the fifth edition of the Diagnostic and Statistical Manual of Mental Disorders (DSM-5: American Psychiatric Association, 2013) apply to the antisocial spectrum in two ways. First, they help identify potential antecedents to crime and delinquency like animal cruelty, school bullying, and firesetting, all of which are listed as criteria for conduct disorder under Section A of the manual. Based on these criteria, additional behaviors that might qualify as developmental antecedents to delinquency would include cruelty to people, lying and conning others, chronic truancy from school, and running away from home. Second, the seven Section A DSM-5 criteria for antisocial personality disorder fit the four behavioral styles of a criminal lifestyle: irresponsibility (blatant disregard for the safety of self and others; pattern of irresponsibility), self-indulgence (lying, deception, and manipulation for profit or self-amusement; impulsive behavior), interpersonal intrusiveness (irritability and aggression, assaults on others, or regular fighting; lack of remorse for actions), and social rule breaking (failure to obey laws and norms

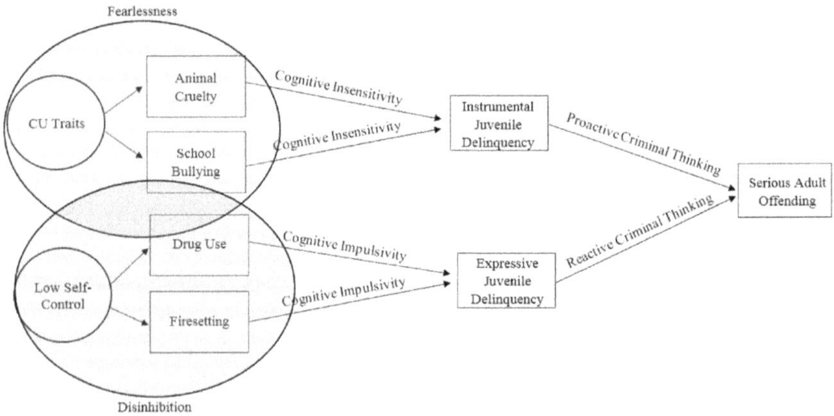

Figure 1.2 The Horizontal Hierarchical Organization of the Antisocial Spectrum, Showing the Behavioral Styles of CU Traits and Low Self-Control in the Left-Most Column, Developmental Antecedents in the Second Column, Juvenile Delinquency in Its Instrumental and Expressive Forms in the Third Column, Serious Adult Offending in the Right-Most Column, and Specific Antisocial/Criminal Thinking Dimensions Connecting Adjacent Columns. *Source:* Created by author.

by engaging in behaviors that result in or would warrant criminal arrest). The antisocial spectrum captures what the social-cognitive-developmental model described in this book seeks to predict, explain, and change. This book will not focus on a single behavioral entity, but rather on a range or spectrum of antisocial behavior, from serious crime and delinquency to less serious forms of antisocial behavior. Consequently, studies cited in the next 11 chapters will consider a range of antisocial behaviors believed to be members of the antisocial spectrum, although the focus remains on serious delinquency and adult criminality.

MARKING THE TREES AS WE MOVE THROUGH THE FOREST

As we set out on our journey to understand as much as possible about the trees in the forest of a criminal lifestyle, it is crucial that we not lose sight of the forest in which these trees are located. In order to successfully complete our journey, we must keep one eye on the forest and the other eye on the individual trees we have decided to examine. Keeping one eye on the forest is a theme that will be played out repeatedly as we move through the chapters of this book. This recurring theme also helps shape some of the principal tenets and assumptions of lifestyle theory, 10 of which are presented and discussed in the next 10 chapters (chapters 2 through 11), starting with the assumption "man is a biological organism," which underpins chapter 2. These 10 assumptions will help guide us through the major constructs, principles, postulates, and tenets of lifestyle theory, while reminding us not to forget the forest as defined in this opening chapter for the many trees we will be exploring in subsequent chapters.

Chapter 2

Crime, Criminality, and Human Nature

"Criminals Are Made, Not Born"

The purpose of this chapter is to review some of the contributions biological variables make to our understanding of criminality and crime. There are two statements, that, while they may seem incompatible or counterintuitive at first, underpin the current chapter. First, there is the assumption upon which the current chapter is based, namely, that criminals are made, not born. Second, there is the premise that humans are biological organisms. Being a biological organism means that biological factors play more than a negligible role in human behavior, including criminal behavior, but it does not mean that biology determines either one. Factors other than biology also contribute to criminal behavior, either in conjunction with or independent of biology. Many of these moderating and mediating influences are examined in this book. For the purposes of the current discussion, however, it should be noted that while biological factors play a fairly substantial role in criminality, they do not normally determine a person's involvement in specific criminal events. This, among other things, illustrates the importance of differentiating between crime and criminality.

CRIME AND CRIMINALITY REVISITED

As previously stated, biological factors may be more relevant to criminality than they are to crime. Crime is narrower in scope than criminality and can be construed as the natural consequence of a person's decision to capitalize on salient criminal opportunities and participate in specific criminal acts. These decisions, while they can be influenced and shaped by biological factors, are never the exclusive province of genetics, physiology, or biochemistry. Therefore, while biology can shape the overall tendency to engage in crime (criminality), its effect on a person's decision to commit a specific criminal act is indirect, nondeterministic, and more limited than its influence on criminality. Social and physical environmental factors likewise contribute more to the propensity to commit crime than to involvement in specific criminal acts. Even so, there are isolated instances where a social environmental factor, like pressure from peers to participate in an ongoing antisocial act, a physical environmental factor, like a particularly hot and humid day, or a biological factor, like heavy intoxication, can help precipitate a specific criminal event. In the holistic spirit in which this book was written, different factors may play a more salient role in criminality than in crime and vice versa, but all factors, whether biological, social, psychological, or developmental, influence both criminality and crime to some extent, making criminality and crime inseparable to a large extent.

As shown in table 2.1, crime can be defined as an act performed in violation of a law prohibiting it (robbery) or neglected in violation of a law requiring it (paying taxes). Criminality, on the other hand, is defined as the propensity to commit crime and is measured along a continuum. Also, the variables involved in crime are proximal in the sense that they occur close in time and space to the criminal act. Variables for criminality tend to be more distal, both temporally and spatially. Similarly, while crime is more heavily influenced by situational factors, criminality is more clearly influenced by dispositional factors, whether they be biological, psychological, or sociological in nature. It should be pointed out that most criminological theories are theories of criminality designed to explain differences in people's propensity to commit crime (these include such major theories as social control, social learning, and general and classic strain theory). There are several theories, however, such as deterrence (Nagin, 1998), rational choice (Cornish & Clarke, 1986), and routine activities (Cohen & Felson, 1979) theories, that attempt to explain crime or the factors that lead to a person's decision to commit crime. Finally,

Table 2.1 Comparing Crime and Criminality

Crime	*Criminality*
Act committed in violation of a law prohibiting it or neglected in violation of a law requiring it (based on a dichotomous decision)	Propensity to commit crime (measured along a continuum that ranges from low to high)
Proximal	Distal
Situational	Dispositional
Classical criminology	Positivistic criminology
Aggravating and mitigating conditions	Risk, promotive, and protective factors

Source: Table created by author.

crime is a function of aggravating (making it more likely that a crime will be committed) and mitigating (making it less likely that a crime will be committed) factors and conditions. Criminality, by contrast, is assessed with risk factors (increase the propensity for crime), promotive factors (decrease the propensity for crime), and protective factors (decrease the propensity for crime by neutralizing a risk factor).

BIOLOGICAL BASES OF CRIMINAL BEHAVIOR

Some of the earliest philosophers of crime viewed biological factors as quintessential in explaining antisocial behavior. These early theorists not only proposed that biological variables increased risk for future offending, they also believed that biological variables accounted for a person's involvement in specific criminal events. Hence, these early theories of crime, delinquency, and general antisocial behavior held that biological factors exerted both an indirect and direct effect on antisocial activity as exemplified by their presumed facility in explaining both the propensity to commit crime (criminality) and a person's decision to become involved in a specific criminal act (crime). Hence, some of the earliest theories in criminology sought to explain both criminality and crime. This is true, for instance, of Goddard's (1914/1972) feebleminded theory of crime. The individuals who composed these theories may have been overambitious in their assertions and in some cases the data they used to support their claims were misinterpreted to promote reprehensible public policies, like eugenics and compulsory sterilization, yet this is all part of criminology's past and should not be ignored. Another of these early theories was Lombroso's atavistic theory in which he proposed the existence of a "born criminal."

LOMBROSO'S BORN CRIMINAL

Cesare Lombroso (1835–1909) borrowed a concept from Charles Darwin's theory of evolution in an effort to develop an atavistic theory of crime. Darwin postulated that some organisms revert back to an earlier stage of development as part of a counter-evolutionary process. The born criminal, according to Lombroso (1876/2008), was an atavism or throwback characterized by physical and neurological abnormalities that placed the individual at increased risk for criminality due to low morality and weak personal control. Lombroso, who was trained as a physician, measured physical traits in military service members and prison inmates and reviewed postmortem test results obtained from autopsies of convicted criminal defendants to create a diagnostic system he used to identify the born criminal. Among the physical signs and attributes Lombroso believed identified the born criminal, a small, large, or misshapen skull, brain asymmetries, facial irregularities, a sloping forehead, a large protruding jaw, a receding chin, unusually large or small ears, and long ape-like arms were among some of the more noteworthy characteristics. These physical traits were considered markers of an atavistic process that interfered with the individual's ability to conform their behavior to the requirements of the law.

Although there is more to Lombroso's theory than born criminals, this facet of his theory has received the greatest amount of attention from modern-day criminologists. It is also the facet for which he has received the most criticism. Over the years, Lombroso's born criminal concept has been employed as a "straw man" to discredit biologically informed theories of crime (Wolfgang, 1961). Yet, Lombroso adopted a much broader view of crime than many criminologists apparently realize. Besides the born criminal, Lombroso also theorized about the epileptic criminal, the insane criminal, and several forms of occasional criminal, including the criminaloid. Criminaloids were viewed by Lombroso as having none of the physical abnormalities of the born criminal but engaging in crime as a result of environmental factors and opportunity (Gibson, 2002). Of the various groups in Lombroso's theory, the criminaloids were the largest. Thus, rather than using Lombroso's theory to cast aspersions on biological interpretations of crime, we should celebrate Lombroso's role as the father of positivistic criminology and the scientific study of criminality. His contributions to the field of criminology are immense despite the conceptual and methodological shortcomings of his approach (Gatti & Berde, 2012).

BIOLOGICAL AND SOCIOLOGICAL THEORIES OF CRIME

Most theories of crime are sociologically based and most criminologists, at least in the United States, are trained in sociologically oriented departments of criminology or criminal justice. As such, most criminologists adopt a sociological perspective on crime and have traditionally been less interested in the biological, psychological, and economic features of criminality and crime than in the sociology of crime. Studies testing biologically based hypotheses may be particularly anathema to criminologists who have been trained to adopt a sociological perspective on crime where, contrary to biologically and psychologically trained scholars, equality of individuals is held to be more important than the study of individual differences (Walsh & Wright, 2015). It has also been suggested that the editors of some of the more prestigious journals in criminology and criminal justice have a built-in bias against biological theories of crime and that this has led to a dearth of biologically oriented articles in criminology and criminal justice journals (Beaver et al., 2015). Focusing on sociological factors while downplaying and ignoring biological, psychological, and economic factors restricts and limits our ability to construct a complete picture of crime. Consequently, while there is no evidence to support the existence of a Lombrosian's born criminal, it would be a mistake to exclude biologically based indicators from a discussion of the causes and correlates of crime and delinquency.

One of the earliest papers I ever published in a criminology/criminal justice journal was on genetics and crime (Walters & White, 1989a). I followed this up three years later with a meta-analysis of genetic studies on crime (Walters, 1992b). The review article critiqued the methodology and conclusions of early genetic studies on crime, whereas the meta-analysis disclosed evidence of a small but significant genetic effect for criminal offending. The meta-analysis has been cited over one hundred times in psychology and criminology journals and in most cases where it has been cited in a criminology journal it has been used as a foil for the possibility that genetics or biology contribute meaningfully to crime. But that is not what the results of the meta-analysis revealed. Instead, the results showed that genetics played a significant role in crime and delinquency, although compared to environmental factors, the role was small. When estimates of heritability, shared environment, and nonshared environment from this meta-analysis were compared to estimates of heritability, shared environment, and nonshared environment from a meta-analysis of genetic studies on alcohol abuse (Walters, 2002), the outcome revealed that heritability for crime was half that of alcohol abuse and shared environment (i.e., growing up in the same household) accounted for three-and-one-half times the variance in crime as it did in alcohol abuse (see figure 2.1). It is highly misleading, however, to conclude that the genetic effect for crime is insignificant based on these results.

Acknowledging the role that biological factors play in research and theory on crime does not mean accepting biological determinism. The biosocial theory of crime, as a case in point, offers a number of interesting possibilities but requires careful study and thoughtful deliberation to avoid falling into a deterministic or reductionistic trap. Several studies indicate that such well-known environmental correlates of crime as parental criminality (De Lisi et al., 2009), neighborhood disadvantage (Beaver et al., 2012), peer delinquency, and low self-control (Beaver et al., 2009) interact with genetic abnormalities, usually involving one of the dopamine genes, to increase a person's propensity for crime and delinquency, though it should be noted that all three studies employed a twin methodology and failed to test the equal environments assumption. Twin studies compare identical and fraternal twins (100% versus

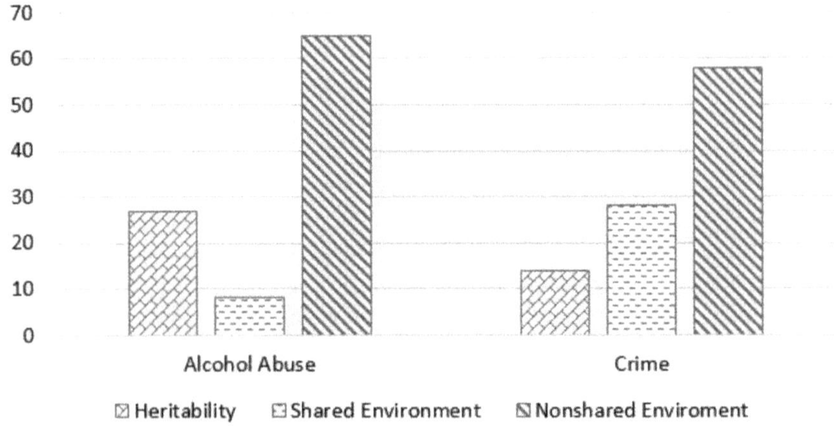

Figure 2.1 Comparing the Heritability, Shared Environment, and Nonshared Environment Breakdowns for Alcohol Abuse (Walters, 2002) and Crime (Walters, 1992b). *Source*: Created by author based on own data.

50% genetic similarity, respectively) in an effort to determine whether there is greater concordance (agreement) for crime/delinquency in identical twins. The validity of this approach, however, rests on the equal environments assumption, which holds that the environments of identical twins are no more alike than the environments of fraternal twins (Plomin et al., 1976). Because this assumption is rarely satisfied, it can lead to inflated heritability estimates, although to be fair, the bias created by violations of the equal environments assumption is often only modest (Felson, 2014; LoParo & Waldman, 2014). As such, interpreting a biological (genetic) effect based on twin data should be accompanied by support for the equal environments assumption.

RISK AND PROTECTIVE FACTORS

If, as stated previously, biological factors do not normally cause crime directly, then we need to figure out if and how they do cause crime. According to criminal lifestyle theory, biological factors, along with psychological and sociological factors, serve as risk factors for criminality. The higher the risk, the greater the propensity for future criminal involvement. Hence, biological risk factors, like psychological and sociological risk factors, can have an impact on one's future propensity to commit crime (criminality) but may have little direct bearing on a person's involvement in specific criminal events (crime). Once again, this underscores the advisability of differentiating between criminality and crime. Risk factors are variables capable of predicting some future outcome, which in the current context would be behaviors on the antisocial spectrum. Bonta and Andrews (2017) have identified three categories of risk factor: static (historical, unchanging), stable dynamic (slow changing), and acute dynamic (fast changing). Biological risk factors fit into all three categories. Intoxication serves as an example of an acute dynamic biological risk factor, while the genetically related variable of intelligence represents a stable dynamic biological risk factor. Biological risk factors can also fall into the static category by virtue of their historical significance and role in the human limbic system. This is explored further in the next section of this chapter.

It should also be noted that a variable can serve as a risk factor for itself and that two variables can serve as risk factors for each other in a pattern known as reciprocal risk. Crime and substance misuse serve as an example of how reciprocal risk works in a pattern that has come to be called the "worst of both worlds" (WBW) effect. For those who display this pattern, criminality and substance misuse serve as risk factors for each other. The WBW hypothesis states that a prior history of substance use/misuse and criminality predicts future substance use/misuse and criminality better than either a prior history of substance use/misuse or criminality alone, a supposition that has received a fair amount of research attention and support (Walters, 2014a, 2015b, 2015f, 2016a, 2016b, 2017b; Walters & Magaletta, 2015). A WBW effect was also observed when school bullying and alcohol experimentation served as the predictor variables and delinquency and substance use served as the outcome measures (Walters, 2021f). This, like studies in which bullying has been shown to exhibit a pattern of psychological inertia similar to what has been observed with delinquency (Walters & Espelage, 2018a), suggests that bullying belongs on the antisocial spectrum along with crime and delinquency.

Whereas risk factors predict an increased likelihood of future criminal involvement, promotive and protective factors predict a decreased likelihood of future criminal involvement. Promotive factors predict better outcomes by stimulating the functional end of a risk dimension (Farrington et al., 2016). Thus, while low intelligence may serve as a risk factor for delinquency by predicting elevated levels of future offending, high intelligence may serve as a promotive factor for non-delinquency by predicting lower levels of future offending. A protective effect, on the other hand, predicts better future outcomes by interacting with and neutralizing the effect of a risk factor. If the interaction between female gender and a low resting autonomic response, a stable dynamic biological risk factor capable of predicting future antisocial behavior (Glenn et al., 2007), were to predict low future delinquency, we might conclude that the static characteristic of female gender served as a protective factor against a low resting autonomic response by reducing a person's odds of engaging in future delinquency. This would seem to suggest that it is the interplay of biological, psychological, and sociological risk, promotive, and protective factors that gives rise to individual differences in criminality.

A TWO-DIMENSIONAL MODEL OF CRIMINALITY

In outlining the role of biology in a comprehensive theory of criminality, the limbic system would appear to be a good place to start. Anatomically, the limbic system is composed primarily of subcortical structures that connect the midbrain to the cerebral cortex, although certain areas of the cortex are also considered part of the limbic system. Whereas the limbic system is capable of affecting a wide range of human activities, it has its greatest impact on motivation, emotion, learning, and memory. Among the structures normally identified as being part of the limbic system, we can list the thalamus, hypothalamus, amygdala, hippocampus, fornix, mamillary bodies, nucleus accumbens, orbitofrontal cortex, and anterior cingulate cortex. What needs to be understood is that the various functions attributed to the limbic system are not seated in any one particular area or structure, but are instead a reflection of a complex network of structures and pathways that join various limbic structures to other parts of the central nervous system. The amygdala and orbitofrontal cortex, for instance, are extensively involved in the learning and coding of emotion, but they have no meaning without sensory input from the temporal and occipital lobes and corresponding output to higher cortical areas such as the anterior cingulate cortex (Rolls, 2015).

The limbic system may be particularly noteworthy in advancing our understanding of antisocial behavior based on its ability to identify the origins of two temperament dimensions that appear to give rise to antisocial behavior and cognition. Walters (2008) originally proposed that the temperament dimensions of fearlessness (Lykken, 1957) and disinhibition (Krueger et al., 2007) were at the heart of antisocial spectrum disorders. These two temperament dimensions, it was argued, offer insight into how the study of individual differences can help clarify diversities in criminality. Some children, by virtue of their lack of fear and poor impulse control, were said to be at increased risk for future criminal involvement because they had a more difficult time conditioning to punishment (fearlessness) and controlling their impulses (disinhibition). In looking for a biologically informed explanation for these individual differences, Walters and Kiehl (2015) cited research showing that lesions in the amygdala, two almond-shaped structures, each about the size of a walnut, found near the thalamus, led to weak and inconsistent fear conditioning (Phelps et al., 2001; Sah et al., 2003), whereas lesions in the hippocampus, an elongated structure located anterior to the amygdala, resulted in poor behavioral control (Cherbuin et al., 2008; Shechner et al., 2014).

Walters and Kiehl (2015) tested their model in a sample of 191 incarcerated male juvenile delinquents, ages 13–19. In this study, gray matter volumes (GMV) from a magnetic resonance imaging (MRI) analysis of the amygdala and hippocampus served as the independent variables, fearlessness and disinhibition, assessed with items from the Psychopathy Checklist: Youth Version (PCL: YV: Forth et al., 2003), served as the dependent variables, and age, IQ, regular substance use, and total brain volume served as control variables. It was predicted that amygdaloid GMV would correlate negatively with fearlessness and hippocampal GMV would correlate negatively with disinhibition. Consistent with predictions, results from a regression analysis revealed that lower levels of gray matter in the amygdala were associated with higher levels of fearlessness but not disinhibition along the two temperament dimensions, whereas lower levels of gray matter in the hippocampus were associated with higher levels of disinhibition but not fearlessness. Based on these findings it could be inferred that reduced activity in the amygdala, as indicated by a below-average level of amygdaloid gray matter, corresponds with a fearless temperament, whereas reduced activity in the hippocampus, as indicated by a below-average level of hippocampal gray matter, corresponds with a disinhibited temperament.

While the results of the Walters and Kiehl (2015) study suggest that a poverty of cell bodies in the amygdala correlates with a pattern of fearlessness that then interferes with a person's ability to learn from punishment and that a poverty of cell bodies in the hippocampus correlates with a pattern of disinhibition and weak behavioral control, it should be noted that these structures, in all likelihood, function as part of a larger system of interconnected structures and pathways. The amygdala, for instance, receives sensory input from the temporal and occipital lobes, as well as information from the hippocampus, anterior cingulate cortex, and orbitofrontal cortex, which is then directed as output to various subcortical and cortical brain structures, especially the basal and accessory-basal nuclei (Hammond, 2014). In all probability, it is these systems that are responsible for weak fear conditioning. There is also evidence that certain areas of the amygdala are more central than other areas in promoting fear conditioning, with the middle region of the amygdala being particularly critical in this regard (Li et al., 2013). Finally, there is ample evidence that structures other than the amygdala also play a role in fear conditioning and that threat assessment and a "fearless" temperament may derive from more than one system or neural network (Fiddick, 2011; Sacchetti et al., 2005).

NEUROTRANSMITTERS AND THE LIFE INSTINCT

In the previous section, we discussed the structural nature of biological risk as represented by neurological sites and pathways that increase the risk of future offending. Biological risk also has a functional side. This is most evident at the cellular level. The neuron, which serves as the basic building block of the central nervous system, communicates with other neurons by means of an electrochemical process (Hammond, 2014). The resting potential of a neuron is negative, usually around −70 mV, depending on where in the central nervous system the neuron is located. Neurons provide either excitatory (making the receiving neuron less negative and bringing it closer to firing) or inhibitory (making the receiving neuron more negative and taking it further from firing) input to other cells by sending chemical messages to the dendrites (tree-like structures) and/or cell body of a receiving neuron. If the summed input raises the threshold potential of the receiving neuron to around −55 mV, the receiving neuron depolarizes or fires (i.e., rapidly goes from negative to positive). This creates an electrical impulse or action potential that then travels down the length of the neuron's axon to the terminal buttons where chemical substances known as neurotransmitters are stored. The electrical impulse stimulates the release of the neurotransmitter into the synapse or space between neurons. The neurotransmitter then attaches itself to the wall of the receiving neuron, altering the permeability of the receiving cell's membrane to positively and negatively charged ions. Changes in the ratio of intercellular positive to negative ions either increase (excitatory) or decrease (inhibitory) the receiving neuron's likelihood of depolarizing.

Two of the most extensively studied neurotransmitters are dopamine and serotonin. Dopamine is an excitatory neurotransmitter that finds its greatest concentrations in the nigrostriatal and mesocorticolimbic pathways of the brain, the latter of which begins in the ventral tegmental area (VTA) and projects to the nucleus accumbens and frontal cortex. The mesocorticolimbic projection is particularly relevant to antisocial behavior given its role as a "reward" center and ability to produce pleasure through the release of dopamine (Hammond, 2014). Serotonin can serve as either an excitatory or inhibitory neurotransmitter, although in the area that will serve as the focus here (projections from the hippocampus to the nucleus accumbens, striatum, and frontal cortex), it acts as an inhibitory neurotransmitter. Research indicates that while higher dopamine levels are positively associated with aggression, impulsivity, and risky decision-making, higher serotonin levels are negatively associated with these same behaviors (Cupaioli et al., 2021; Narvaes & de Almeida, 2014). From this, it could be surmised that serotonin moderates or modulates the crime-promoting effects of dopamine. Seo et al. (2008), in fact, note that when serotonin fails to regulate dopamine, aggressive impulsivity often results. Accordingly, finding ways to reduce dopamine and increase serotonin could potentially aid efforts to reduce a person's propensity for crime, although none of these relationships are simple and are complicated further by the fact that multiple neurotransmitters interact with one another. The inhibitory neurotransmitter γ-Aminobutyric Acid (GABA), for instance, appears to moderate the effects of serotonin on dopamine (Takahashi et al., 2010).

As described in the previous paragraph, dopamine and serotonin seem to achieve opposing or contrary outcomes when it comes to promoting behaviors within the antisocial spectrum. This could imply a system of biological checks and balances similar to how the sympathetic and parasympathetic branches of the autonomic nervous system balance each other. There are also points of similarity between dopamine and serotonin. Both, in fact, may have far-reaching implications for human survival. Dopamine, it could be argued, supports survival by directing the organism toward appetitive activities that produce pleasure and offer the organism nourishment and vivacity. Serotonin, on the other hand, promotes survival by protecting and restoring these resources as they are consumed, thus promoting sleep, relaxation, and digestion (Di Giovanni et al., 2008). Given their success in supporting survival, these neurotransmitters have grown in importance in concert with evolution of the human genome. Together, they form what is known in lifestyle theory as the life instinct. A constantly changing environment that threatens the organism's survival and challenges its life instinct gives rise to a reaction referred to in lifestyle theory as existential fear. There are several ways to cope with existential fear, one of which is to adopt a routinized pattern of behavior like a criminal lifestyle. This process will be discussed in more detail in chapter 12 of this book. The purpose of the current discussion was to define the life instinct as the product of an evolutionary process in which dopamine and serotonin became part of the natural selection process through their ability to support survival.

CONCLUSION

The main takeaway from this chapter is that biological factors need to be accounted for in a comprehensive theory of crime and criminality. Contrary to the assertions of some sociologically minded criminologists (see Burt & Simons, 2014, for an example) there is value to be found in studying the biological foundations of antisocial behavior. In fact, it is important to acknowledge that people are not born equal. Each of us inherits divergent traits, abilities, and proclivities, including the propensity to commit crime. Although these biological factors do not determine whether one does or does not engage in a particular criminal act, they do increase or decrease a person's propensity or risk of future criminal involvement. Biological influences, such as reduced gray matter in the amygdala or a predominance of dopamine in the pathways of the mesolimbic system, can be considered primordial risk factors for crime. These influences no more preclude environmental effects than they support the notion of a born criminal. In fact, they are modified, shaped, and altered by subsequent sociological, psychological, and developmental factors. This can be seen in the evolution of temperament. A disinhibited temperament may have its origins in genetically based anatomical and neurochemical abnormalities in the hippocampus and its various neural pathways, but these tendencies are altered, sometimes drastically, by the sociological, psychological, and developmental influences that accumulate over the course of a person's life. As risk factors, these biological anomalies and tendencies help explain criminality but do nothing to explain crime. And while biologically based variables like alcohol intoxication and drug withdrawal can affect criminal decision-making and crime, biological variables contribute primarily to our understanding of criminality and need to be recognized for their ability to interface with environmental factors. In the next chapter of this book, we will consider two additional classes of risk factor—social environmental and physical environmental variables.

Chapter 3

Social Foundations of a Criminal Lifestyle

"Criminal Behavior Is Constructed from Social Interaction"

As postulated in chapter 2, people are biological organisms, and for this reason, behavior is at least partially a function of genetic, neurological, and physiological factors. A similar argument is advanced in the current chapter, although this time the focus is on social environmental factors instead of biological factors. The assumption that underpinned chapter 2 was that criminals are made, not born, even though biological variables do contribute to a person's propensity to commit crime. The assumption that guides the current chapter takes this one step further by asserting that criminality is a function of social interaction, even though physical environmental factors are also important and receive some attention near the end of this chapter (i.e., neighborhood disorder and ambient temperature). A commonality shared by endogenous biologic risk factors and exogenous social environmental risk factors is that their effect is more often distal and indirect than it is proximal and direct. Hence, the effect of biological and sociological influences, whether we are talking about a weak autonomic nervous system response or a weak parent-child relationship, on the criminal actions of an individual is indirect and can take anywhere from several weeks to several years to materialize. Moreover, the role of most social and physical environmental factors, like biological factors, is to augment a person's propensity to commit crime (criminality) rather than precipitate a specific criminal event (crime).

Three principal paradigms are commonly used to explain how organisms learn: respondent conditioning, operant conditioning, and observational or social learning. Respondent or classical conditioning was initially mapped out by Pavlov (1927) who discovered that dogs would salivate to a bell that had been paired with meat powder even after the meat powder was no longer presented. Later, Skinner (1938) introduced the paradigm for operant conditioning, whereby organisms are motivated to engage in behaviors that meet with pleasure (reinforcement) and refrain from behaviors that are followed by pain (punishment). Bandura (1986) is the psychologist most closely aligned with the social learning framework, although he later retitled his approach "social cognitive theory." One of the most important insights to be gleaned from Bandura's work is the notion of observational learning, whereby the individual learns by observing and modeling the behavior of others. As important as modeling is to social learning, it is not the sum total of social learning influence. Some rewards are more reinforcing than others. A child will find praise from a higher status peer more reinforcing than praise from a lower status peer (Dijksta et al., 2013) and will probably derive more pleasure from interacting with a parent they trust than with a parent they don't trust (Simonen et al., 2017). Learning, it would seem, takes place in a social context, not in a social vacuum.

The social factors described in this chapter, like the biological ones described in chapter 2, are most accurately classified as risk, promotive, and protective factors. As risk, promotive, and protective factors, social variables serve as independent variables (X) in equations that connect directly to crime or delinquency (Y). In subsequent chapters, we will examine cognitive

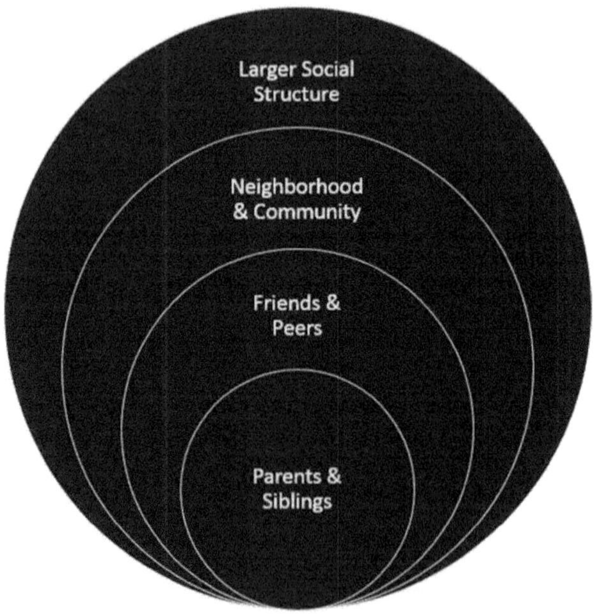

Figure 3.1 Layers of Social Environmental Variable That Potentially Exert Risk, Promotive, and Protective Effects. *Source:* Created by author.

and affective variables that mediate the relationship between X and Y and developmental variables that moderate the associations between these same variables. The focus of the present chapter will be on four levels of social variable: parents and siblings, peers and friends, neighborhoods and communities, and the larger social structure. These four levels of social variable are depicted in figure 3.1 and are represented by increasingly larger concentric circles, each embedded in the one it follows. The smallest circle is reserved for influences within the home (parents and siblings). This is encased in the next largest circle, the one signifying peers and friends. The next largest circle embodies social relationships outside the home and one's circle of friends and peers in the form one's neighborhood and community. The largest and most encompassing circle symbolizes the larger social structure consisting of the norms, culture, and society in which the child and their parents, friends, and neighbors must function. The overriding objective of this chapter is to illustrate how social factors contribute to criminality, while acknowledging the indivisibility of criminality and crime.

PARENTS

Of all the social environmental risk factors that have been studied as potential causes and correlates of delinquency, successful parenting may provide one of the strongest promotive effects. Unsuccessful parenting and certain deviant parental behaviors (e.g., parental criminality), on the other hand, increase the risk for delinquency and crime. Parenting, because it is normally in place long before some of the other social environmental influences described in this chapter, such as peers, neighborhoods, and school, occupies a unique position in the study of crime, delinquency, and general antisocial behavior. The three categories of parenting to be discussed in this section are parental control, parental support, and parental deviance.

Parental Control

In a meta-analysis of the parenting-delinquency relationship, Hoeve et al. (2009) ascertained that parental control and support achieved modest to moderate inverse correlations with delinquency of roughly equal magnitude. Parenting behaviors classified under the heading parental control in the Hoeve et al. meta-analysis included parental supervision, rule-setting, inductive discipline, authoritative parenting, and parental monitoring. From a theoretical standpoint, parental control has always been stressed by control theorists interested in explaining the origins of crime (Nye, 1958; Reiss, 1951; Toby, 1957). Its greatest expression, however, can be found in Gottfredson and

Hirschi's (1990) general theory of crime where parental discipline and control are said to give rise to low child self-control, which, in turn, is viewed by Gottfredson and Hirschi as the principal cause of crime and delinquency. Research indicates that even though low self-control correlates well with criminal offending (Pratt & Cullen, 2000; Tehrani & Yamini, 2020), there is evidence that it is not caused exclusively by parental discipline (McCartan & Gunnison, 2007), nor is it necessarily a better correlate of offending than parental discipline itself (Muftić & Updegrove, 2018; Wright & Beaver, 2005). Coupled with the fact that the low self-control–delinquency relationship has been criticized as tautological (Akers et al., 2021), it could be argued that weak parental discipline and not low self-control is the key risk factor in the general theory of crime.

Controversy surrounds one particular element of parental control—namely, parental monitoring. Active surveillance and solicitation of information may be less important than a child's willingness to self-disclose information to their parents in determining how much a parent knows about their child's activities, whereabouts, and associations. Kerr and Stattin (2000; Kerr et al., 2010) have argued that what has traditionally been attributed to parental monitoring may actually be the result of passive knowledge obtained through child self-disclosure. If true, this would mean that parental knowledge is as much a function of parental support as it is of parental control given that a child is unlikely to volunteer information to a parent they do not trust and to whom they are poorly attached. There is research, in fact, showing that active surveillance and solicitation may be interpreted by a child, particularly a child in mid- to late adolescence, as invasive. This in turn can lead to higher rather than lower levels of future delinquency (Hawk et al., 2008; Laird et al., 2018). Others have noted that strong parental knowledge predicts decreased future delinquency, even after controlling for child self-disclosure (Lahey et al., 2008; Lippold et al., 2014). The issue at hand is not whether parental knowledge is negatively associated with child delinquency—because research has consistently demonstrated that it is (Racz & McMahon, 2011)—but rather, to what can we attribute the success of parental knowledge as a correlate and predictor of delinquency. In other words, is parental knowledge primarily a function of parental control or is it the combined result of parental control and support?

Like any risk factor, parental control can exert risk, promotive, and protective effects. Low levels of parental control in the form of parental neglect or overindulgence and excessive parental control in the form of abuse or invasiveness can produce a risk effect capable of increasing a child's propensity for future criminal activity. This suggests that a curvilinear relationship exists between parental control and child delinquency, and that either too much or too little parental control can be problematic. Widom's work on the "cycle of violence" likewise demonstrates that children who have been victimized by physical and psychological abuse are at increased risk of abusing their own children and engaging in delinquency, crime, and other behaviors found on the antisocial spectrum like intimate partner violence (IPV) (Milaniak & Widom, 2015; Widom & Maxfield, 2001). A moderate amount of parental control, on the other hand, should promote positive behavior and protect individuals who are at risk for antisocial involvement. The results of a recent meta-analysis revealed that parental knowledge and rule-setting promoted prosocial behavior, although the effect was stronger for parental knowledge than it was for rule-setting (Flanagan et al., 2019). There is no consistent evidence, however, that parental control is capable of protecting youth at risk for delinquency by virtue of delinquent peer associations (Trucco et al., 2011; Walters, 2019b).

If, as was suggested earlier, social environmental risk, promotive, and protective factors owe their existence to a learning process, then what specifically does parental control teach the child? The answer boils down to learning the skills required to control one's behavior. As indicated in chapter 2, a major assumption of criminal lifestyle theory, not to mention Gottfredson and Hirschi's (1990) general theory of crime, is that people are born impulsive and self-serving and must learn to control their behavior by delaying gratification and anticipating the consequences of their actions. A principal way the child acquires self-discipline is by interacting with a benevolent parenting figure. Walters (2020l) observed this when conducting a secondary analysis of data from the Gang Resistance and Education Training (GREAT) study. According to the results of the Walters investigation, parental monitoring and knowledge served as a stimulus for youth control by reducing the cognitive impulsivity that gives rise to behavioral impulsivity. Without this stimulus, the child would remain in their natural state of high cognitive and behavioral impulsivity. In this instance, it is not learning but rather lack of learning (more specifically, lack of learning self-control) that puts a child at risk for ongoing delinquent and criminal behavior. Through such learning, or lack of learning, a bidirectional association forms between parental control and child behavior where weak or ineffective parental control leads to child misbehavior and lack of self-disclosure, while child misbehavior and lack of self-disclosure lead to even more extreme, inconsistent, and ineffective parental control (Kapetanovic et al., 2019).

Parental Support

The general theory of crime is not the only criminological theory for which Hirschi is known. He was also instrumental in the development of one of the earliest parental support-related social control theories of crime, in which it is argued that people learn how not to commit crime by bonding to institutions of conventional society, such as schools, work, and family (Hirschi, 1969). Individuals exhibiting strong bonds to conventional society were seen as more likely to follow societal rules and avoid criminal activity than persons displaying weak bonds to conventional society. The most important social bonds were those that the child formed with their parents. As such, parental support can be considered an extension of the social bonding process. Children who feel close to their parents believe that their parents have their best interests in mind and are willing to share their thoughts and feelings with their parents. These types of children are unlikely to engage in criminal activity. Parents who demonstrate warmth, caring, and concern in their interactions with the child and are appropriately involved in the child's life are parents whose children are unlikely to act on antisocial, delinquent, and criminal opportunities. Parental support may therefore be as critical as parental control in preventing delinquency in at-risk youth.

Lack of parental affection and support have long been considered risk factors for child delinquency (Saner & Ellickson, 1996). Strong parental affection and support, on the other hand, may serve as promotive or protective factors in preventing or reducing future delinquency. Many studies bear this out, several of which have been published in the last several years. Examining longitudinal associations in a group of early to mid-adolescents, Padilla-Walker and Son (2019) determined that child self-disclosure predicted parental support, which, in turn, predicted prosocial behavior on the part of the child. Following a slightly older sample of participants, Hill et al. (2018) discovered that parental social support predicted reduced levels of delinquent activity in a group of emerging adults. Kramer-Kuhn and Farrell (2016) also observed a promotive effect for positive parenting, parental involvement, and family cohesion on subsequent delinquency but very little evidence of a protective effect in adolescents placed at risk for future delinquency by delinquent peer associations or community violence. This illustrates the importance of differentiating between promotive and protective effects and the necessity of finding family variables that protect at-risk children from the effects of risk factors in the child's environment.

Whereas parental control is designed to teach the child how to control their behavior, parental support teaches the child how to feel good about themselves, get along with others, and differentiate between right and wrong. Morality or conscience is a function of three principal factors: empathy, guilt, and moral reasoning. Lack of empathy can be viewed as an interpersonal deficit that correlates moderately with offending behavior (Jolliffe & Farrington, 2004). On the other hand, youth who suffer from an emotional deficit characterized by a general inability to experience self-conscious emotions like guilt, remorse, and shame are at increased risk for delinquent and criminal behavior (Spruit et al., 2016). Accompanying the interpersonal deficit of low empathy and the emotional deficit of inadequate remorse for bad behavior is the cognitive deficit of weak moral reasoning (Romeral et al., 2018). Early attachment relationships between the child and parent, particularly the mother (Ainsworth, 1989; Bowlby, 1969/1982), are instrumental in the development of empathy, self-conscious emotions, and moral reasoning. One of the principal consequences of a good attachment relationship is the ability to empathize with others (Stern & Cassidy, 2018). Moreover, experiencing guilt and remorse requires an authority figure capable of generating respect and eliciting self-conscious emotion in the child (dos Santos, 2020). Finally, moral reasoning is often acquired by modeling the behavior of a supportive and nurturing role model (Batool & Shehzad, 2019). Consequently, children with weak parental attachments are usually lacking a functional conscience or system of effective moral judgment.

There is growing consensus that parental control and support may interface. What this means is that one may moderate or mediate the effect of the other. Micalizzi et al. (2019), for instance, ascertained that parental knowledge and subsequent delinquency were negatively correlated, but only when parental support was high. A significant parental knowledge × parental support interaction was also observed in a series of studies by Walters and colleagues (Walters, 2021h; Walters et al., 2020) marking the temporal relationship between bullying and delinquency. Whereas both the parental knowledge and support main effects predicted lower levels of future delinquency, their interaction was also instrumental in preventing youth from moving up the antisocial spectrum from bullying to delinquency. As it turns out, a high level of parental support coupled with a low level of parental knowledge was the only combination in which bullying did not lead to delinquency. Because parental knowledge is sometimes acquired through active surveillance, something youth may find intrusive (Hawk et al., 2008; Laird et al., 2018), these results suggest that parents who are supportive yet nonintrusive are the ones least likely to have children who progress from bullying to delinquency. Moderation is one way parental control and support interface, mediation is another. Take, for instance, a study by Walters (2021d) in which parental control self-efficacy mediated the relationship between parental support/warmth and delinquency, corroborating a premise from social cognitive learning theory that performance accomplishments (parental warmth) precede and lead to increased self-efficacy (Bandura, 1986).

Parental Deviance

Whereas absent parental control and support are the two most common parental risk factors for offspring antisocial behavior, the presence of parental deviance can also serve as a risk factor for antisocial spectrum disorders, whether it be crime, delinquency, psychopathy, bullying, or animal cruelty. Studies indicate that parental arrest and incarceration correlate significantly with offending behavior in both male (Murray & Farrington, 2005) and female (Leve & Chamberlain, 2004) offspring. Genetics is one possible explanation for these results. The genetic argument would go something like this: children follow in the footsteps of their parents regarding delinquency, crime, and arrest because they inherit a biologically based predisposition to engage in antisocial behavior from their parents. Family, twin, and adoption studies support this assertion, although the effect is relatively small, particularly when adoption studies are examined (Rhee & Waldman, 2002; Walters, 1992b). In chapter 2 of the present book it was argued that purely genetic interpretations of criminal behavior are overly simplistic and potentially misleading, but that genes and other biological factors are, in fact, part of the larger system of interlocking biological, psychological, and environmental influences that give rise to antisocial spectrum disorders. One of the more important environmental influences would appear to be parenting.

Several studies have sought to identify the mechanism responsible for the parental deviance–child delinquency relationship. One possibility is that the irresponsibility, unreliability, deceitfulness, and aggression inherent in a criminal lifestyle traumatizes the child and disrupts the parent-child relationship to the point where the affected child uses antisocial behavior to cope with the resulting negative affect (Torry & Billick, 2011). It is also possible that the intergenerational transmission of criminality is, in part, a labeling effect. The parent develops a reputation as a chronic lawbreaker, a label that then generalizes to all offspring who may have run-ins with the law (Augustyn et al., 2019). A third possibility is that a dynamic interaction takes place between the child and parent, which over time gives rise to observational learning or modeling effects (Johnson et al., 2016). A fourth possibility is that certain characteristics of the child interact with parental deviance to increase a child's propensity to engage in illegal activity. Li and Ang (2019), for instance, detected an interaction between parental arrest, on the one hand, and child narcissism and callous-unemotional traits, on the other hand, such that parental arrest correlated with self-reported child delinquency, but only when the child displayed strong evidence of narcissism and callous-unemotional traits.

SIBLINGS

Although genetic factors may explain a portion of sibling similarity in delinquency and crime, shared environment is an even more likely explanation (see figure 2.1). Like parenting, this particular form of shared environmental influence originates from the home. This influence is difficult to chart theoretically, however, because it shares features in common with both parenting (social control) and peers (social learning) and is not discussed at great length by any of the major theories of criminology. Its influence is nonetheless important. Early studies revealed a positive correlation between family size and child delinquency that has been attributed to increased opportunity for interaction between adolescent siblings (Brownfield & Sorenson, 1994; Lauritsen, 1993). Yet, the sibling effect need not be negative to be relevant nor must it be restricted to adolescents to be active. The results of a study using the retrospective accounts of adults from the 1942 and 1949 Racine birth cohorts revealed that the effect of siblings on youth delinquency, like the impact of parents, peaked during childhood and was significantly more positive than negative (Walters, 2018i). The current section begins with a discussion of positive sibling effects before moving into a discussion of negative sibling effects.

Positive Sibling Effects

Positive sibling effects, like positive parenting effects, can be broken down into subcategories of control and support. Just as parents socialize children through control and support, so do siblings. Control is exercised when a child learns from a sibling, often an older sibling, the value of controlling their behavior. This can be achieved through instruction, observation, or programming. With respect to the latter, an after-school program entitled "Siblings Are Special" (SIBS) sought to improve sibling relationships and self-control in the younger siblings (grades 2–4) of a randomly selected group of fifth graders. Compared to families not enrolled in the SIBS program, families with a fifth grader who participated in the program experienced more sibling positivity, greater sibling social competence, better sibling academic performance, and higher sibling self-control (Feinberg et al., 2013). Investigating sibling social support, Widmer and Weiss (2000) determined that older sibling support had a positive effect on the adjustment of socially disadvantaged younger siblings, provided the younger sibling had a positive image of their older sibling. The results of this study suggest that propping up an older sibling in the eyes of a younger sibling by a parent, teacher, coach, or other adult authority figure may be helpful in achieving a significant positive sibling effect.

Although younger siblings may learn from older siblings through instruction and coaching, more often than not, a younger sibling learns by modeling the behavior of an older sibling. This may be why younger siblings had to have formed a positive impression of their older sibling before the older sibling could serve as a source of social support in the Widmer and Weiss (2000) study. Attention is the first step in the observational learning or modeling process (Bandura, 1986). In order for the child to pay attention to the model, the model must be relatable and respected. It also helps if there is resemblance between the model and observer, a process known as model-observer similarity (MOS: Bandura, 1994). Similarity based on sex (Bussey & Bandura, 1984; Gallupe et al., 2019) and age (Hoogerheide et al., 2016; Krebs et al., 2019) has produced mixed results. Still, it may be useful to test for similarity to see what effect it has on preventing sibling delinquency. If the MOS assumption is correct, then we should expect to find stronger modeling effects in same-sex siblings of the same general age than in opposite-sex siblings of widely disparate ages. These relationships were initially verified in studies conducted in the 1990s (Bank et al., 1996; Rowe & Farrington, 1997) and were recently corroborated by Mikkonen et al. (2020) using a large sample of Finnish siblings between the ages of 11 and 20.

Negative Sibling Effects

Whereas research on sibling delinquency has lagged behind research on parental and peer influences on criminality, several studies nonetheless indicate that siblings may serve as risk factors for delinquency. Early investigations showed evidence of good concordance for sibling delinquency, but many of these studies were cross-sectional in nature and did not control for important social environmental factors like parenting and peer associations (Lauritsen, 1993; Rowe & Gulley, 1992). Controlling for multiple child and family risk factors, Fagan and Najman (2003) observed a moderately strong correlation between juvenile offending in siblings. The study was limited, however, by the fact that sibling delinquency was measured concurrently instead of prospectively and peer delinquency was not controlled. Using longitudinal data, Defoe et al. (2013) noticed that externalizing problems in an older sibling predicted externalizing problems in a younger sibling, even when controlling for their best friend's externalizing behavior. Walters (20181) also found evidence of a sibling delinquency connection using a relatively long (five-year) follow-up and controlling for parental monitoring, parental disciplinary style, and peer delinquency. When the sample was divided into younger (sibling delinquency measured when participant was 9–12 years of age and participant delinquency measured when participant was 14–17 years of age) and older (sibling delinquency measured when participant was 13–17 years of age and participant delinquency measured when participant was 18–22 years of age) cohorts, sibling concordance for delinquency was confined to the older cohort. This suggests that the maximum effect of sibling delinquency may have to wait until after parental control and support have had their effect.

There are at least two ways in which sibling delinquency is transmitted: sibling conflict and sibling modeling. The sibling conflict explanation assumes that conflict with a sibling serves as a stimulus for aggression that is then generalized to other aspects of the child's social environment. A study by Garcia and colleagues (2000) disclosed that destructive sibling conflict moderated the nexus between parental rejection and mother- and teacher-rated aggression. In this study, aggression was at its height when prior sibling conflict and parental rejection were both elevated. Criss and Shaw (2005) also observed a prospective relationship between sibling conflict and participant delinquency, even after the effects of a negative mother-child relationship had been controlled. Walters and Espelage (2020a) have taken this research a step further by identifying a mechanism for the sibling conflict-aggression relationship. Assessing a group of early adolescents, they discovered that hostility but not anger or dominance mediated the relationship between an aggressive sibling relationship and fighting at school. Hence, aggression in the home may teach the child that violence is the best way to solve disagreements, which may then lead to a hostile attitude capable of linking aggression in the home to aggression outside the home. Modeling of sibling behavior has also been found to explain similarities in sibling behavior (Whiteman et al., 2007). Mediation of the sibling delinquency-participant delinquency relationship by proactive (planned, calculated) criminal thinking (PCT) may explain how delinquency and aggression are learned following exposure to a rule-breaking sibling (Walters, 2020r). This also appears to be what links peer and participant delinquency, the next social environmental risk factor to be discussed in this chapter.

PEERS

Whereas genetic factors very likely explain a portion of delinquency based on parental deviance and negative sibling relations, they play no role in peer associations unless the peers are also biological relatives. Consequently, any effects we can attribute to peers should be classified under shared environmental effects. Returning to the previously reviewed Walters (2018i) investigation in which the retrospective accounts of birth cohort members were analyzed, the reader may recall that parent and sibling effects peaked in late childhood. Peer effects, on the other hand, peaked several years later, in early to mid-adolescence. This finding denotes that peer effects follow rather than precede parent and sibling effects. It also provides indirect support for the notion that behaviors in the home set the stage for behaviors outside the home. In the previously mentioned Walters (2018i) investigation, there was also a large difference in the ratio of positive-to-negative influences attributed to parents, siblings, and peers (classmates). Where participants reported a ratio of positive-to-negative influences of 8:1 with parents and siblings, they reported a positive-to-negative ratio of 2:1 with classmates. Based on these results, it could be argued that peers exert an influence on early to mid-adolescents that is qualitatively distinct from the influences previously discussed with respect to parents and siblings. This influence will be discussed under the following three headings: negative peer effects, positive peer effects, and peer victimization.

Negative Peer Effects

Negative peer effects are one of the most frequently cited risk factors for delinquency (Warr, 2002). They also figure prominently in several major theories of crime. Social learning approaches to crime, such as Sutherland's (1947) differential association theory and Akers's (1998) differential reinforcement expansion of differential association theory, are based on a social learning model. Sutherland emphasized differential associations and definitions favorable and unfavorable to violation of the law in his differential association theory of crime. For those unfamiliar with the theory, differential association means that individuals who spend a significant amount of time interacting with those who violate the law normally often end up violating the law themselves. It is also asserted that the law-violators with whom the individual interacts are often peers. Through their associations with criminal others, youth develop thoughts or definitions favorable to violating the law. Those who differentially associate with law-violators tend to hold a greater proportion of definitions favorable to violation of the law than definitions unfavorable to violation of the law. Akers expanded Sutherland's differential association model by including ideas borrowed from major psychological theories of learning—modeling (Bandura, 1986) and operant conditioning (Skinner, 1938), in particular. According to Akers, youth learn crime by modeling the actions of criminal others and by receiving positive reinforcement for their criminal actions.

Peer delinquency is one of the most common and consistent correlates of crime (Hoeben et al., 2016; Pratt et al., 2010). There is disagreement, however, on the nature of the relationship. Social learning theorists contend that peers socialize non-offending youth into committing delinquent and criminal acts, in a pattern known as peer influence or socialization. Although there is evidence in support of a peer influence effect (Gifford-Smith et al., 2005; McGloin & Thomas, 2019), others have argued that the strong peer-participant delinquency correlation is the result of a peer selection or homophily effect (Gottfredson & Hirschi, 1990; Kiesner et al., 2003). Thus, while the peer influence explanation of the peer-delinquency relationship holds that associating with delinquent peers leads to increased participant delinquency (peer delinquency → participant delinquency), the peer selection explanation asserts that delinquent individuals seek similarly delinquent peers with whom to associate (participant delinquency → peer delinquency). Research conducted on both alcohol use (Leung et al., 2014) and delinquency (Jose et al., 2016) suggests that peer influence and peer selection are equally important components of the peer-delinquency relationship. There is a third interpretation of the peer-delinquency relationship in which peer similarity in delinquency is said to be the result of participants projecting their own level of delinquency onto their peers, given that most studies in this area rely on participant reports of peer delinquency (Young et al., 2013). When the prospective relationship between prior perceived peer delinquency and subsequent participant delinquency, controlling for prior participant delinquency, was evaluated in 22 samples, however, there were significant partial correlations in 21 of the samples (Walters, 2019f), a finding inconsistent with the projection bias hypothesis.

In searching for a mechanism that might explain the peer influence and selection effects, one need look no further than criminal thinking. Although the topic of criminal thinking is explored in much greater detail in chapter 4 of this book, a brief summary is required to provide the current discussion with context. Lifestyle theory proposes that criminal thinking can be divided into two categories: criminal thought content, or *what* a criminal thinks, and criminal thought process, or *how* a criminal thinks. Criminal thought process, the category most relevant to the peer influence and selection effects, is broken down further into two overlapping dimensions: proactive and reactive. PCT covers the planned, calculated, and amoral aspects of criminal thought process. Two of its principal facets are moral disengagement (Bandura et al., 1996) and neutralization beliefs (Sykes & Matza, 1957). Reactive criminal thinking (RCT) encompasses the impulsive, irresponsible, and emotional aspects of criminal thought process, two of its principal facets being hostile attribution biases (Dodge, 2006) and thrill/excitement seeking (Zuckerman, 2007). Research consistently demonstrates that the peer influence effect in juveniles is mediated by PCT, regardless of whether the peer variable is friend/peer delinquency (Walters, 2015e, 2016d), gang affiliation (Walters, 2019d; Walters, 2021c), or co-offending (Walters, 2020j) and the peer selection effect is mediated by RCT, although at the present time this pathway has only been verified in one study (Walters, 2016d). These results suggest that the definitions youth learn from their close contacts and associations with law-violating peers are designed to justify, excuse, and normalize law-violating behavior and distance them from the negative consequences of their antisocial actions.

There are peer-related factors other than peer associations and delinquency that can encourage antisocial behavior in youth. One such factor is unsupervised or unstructured routine activities. Unsupervised routine activities (Osgood et al., 1996) are youth undertakings in which there is little to no adult supervision. Examples include partying with friends, informal get-togethers, driving around in cars, and hanging out at the local mall. Haynie and Osgood (2005) discovered that unsupervised routine activities with friends predicted delinquency after controlling for the effects of peer delinquency. It would appear that involvement in unstructured peer activities with minimal adult supervision creates opportunities for reckless and destructive behavior in individuals who are less apt to consider the consequences of their actions than adults for reasons of incomplete frontal cortex development and limited life experience (Steinberg, 2008). Peer delinquency and unsupervised routine activities may also be of assistance in explaining why delinquency is more common in boys than in girls given that susceptibility to peer influence for risk-taking behavior (McCoy et al., 2019) and unsupervised routine activities (Novak & Crawford, 2010) are both more prevalent in boys. Finally, unsupervised routine activities were found to act as a mediating mechanism that linked parental knowledge to delinquency, such that youth reporting high perceived parental knowledge were less likely to engage in unsupervised routine activities than youth reporting low perceived parental knowledge. This, in turn, led to reduced levels of future offending (Walters, 2018m).

The Walters's (2018m) investigation reminds us that peers may interface with parents in determining a child's risk of future delinquent involvement. This would seem to suggest that parental control and support could potentially serve as protective factors in mitigating the risk presented by negative peer influence. This has generally not been the case, however. As indicated in the previously mentioned Kramer-Kuhn and Farrell (2016) study, positive parenting generated a promotive effect but failed to produce a protective effect. Studies examining the parent-peer interface have come to a similar conclusion. In a multigroup analysis of 10 longitudinal samples, Walters (2019b) detected a prospective relationship between the parent × peer interaction and delinquency in only one of the samples, but unearthed support for a cumulative effect (separate significant parent and peer effects) in 9 out of 10 samples. Studies using a mediation methodology, like the previously mentioned Walters (2018m) investigation and studies by de Vries et al. (2016) and Walters (2016g, 2020s), have documented a mediated relationship in pathways running from parental control/support to perceived peer delinquency to participant offending. Although moderating effects can be small and difficult to detect (McClelland & Judd, 1993), so can mediating effects (Kenny & Judd, 2014). The presence of a cumulative mediated effect instead of an interactive moderated effect for parenting and peers suggests that parenting has less of a protective effect on peer influence than an indirect promotive effect for low delinquency that operates through peer-related factors.

Positive Peer Effects

There has been a great deal more written about negative peer effects and delinquency than there has been about positive peer effects and pro-sociality. Unfortunately, this has left a large gap in the literature. If the reader will recall, there was a much higher proportion of positive-to-negative influences attributed to parents and siblings than to peers in the Walters (2018i) investigation, but in peers there were still twice as many positive as negative influences. As one might expect, no major criminological theory has taken, as its primary focus, positive peer effects. To find a theory that enthusiastically embraces the potential deterrent effect of prosocial peer relations and puts them on equal footing with negative peer relations, we need to consult Catalano and Hawkins's (1996) social development model. The founding premise of Catalano and Hawkins's social development model is that prosocial and antisocial behaviors are the result of similar developmental processes and so prosocial peers can have as much impact on youth behavior as antisocial peers. According to this model, interventions must be introduced that augment the protective effect of prosocial peers and lower the risk presented by antisocial peers. Whereas the social development model highlights the value of positive peer relations perhaps more than any other theory designed to explain crime, it should be noted that Sutherland's (1947) differential association theory (definitions unfavorable to violation of the law) and Sampson and Laub's (1993) age-graded theory (peer-related turning points) also call attention to positive peer associations as a means of preventing and desisting from crime, respectively.

Placing equal emphasis on positive and negative peer influence has been found to predict delinquency (Fleming et al., 2008) and substance misuse (Lonczak et al., 2001) at least as well as an isolated focus on negative peer influences. Romantic partner affiliations also break down along deviant and prosocial lines, such that youth who are involved with a prosocial partner engage in significantly less crime and delinquency than youth who are involved with a deviant partner (Lonardo et al., 2009). Studies such as these provide evidence of a promotive effect for prosocial peer relations but fail to clarify whether there is a protective effect. Even a promotive effect is not guaranteed when prosocial peer associations are investigated as part of studies on delinquent peer associations. Farrell and colleagues (2017), for instance, observed that having friends who immerse themselves in prosocial activities is a likely sign that the individual him- or herself will also participate in prosocial activities, although participant antisocial behavior was more closely connected to friend antisocial behavior than to friend prosocial behavior in this study. A longitudinal investigation uncovered a moderately strong prospective relationship between friend and participant substance use; support from friends, however, had no bearing on a participant's use of substances (Branstetter et al., 2011). Thus, while most studies offer modest to moderate support for the hypothesis that prosocial peer relations promote lower levels of concurrent and future delinquency, there is no clear evidence that prosocial peer relations protect against future delinquency by neutralizing the effects of delinquent peer associations.

Two recent studies have sought to evaluate the risk (a poverty of prosocial peer associations leading to high delinquency), promotive (an abundance of prosocial peer associations leading to low delinquency), and protective (interaction between more prosocial peer associations and delinquent peer associations leading to low delinquency) status of prosocial peers vis-à-vis subsequent participant delinquency. In the first study, Walters (2020p), analyzing longitudinal data from the GREAT study, reported that while prosocial peers achieved risk and promotive effects in early adolescents, there were no signs of a protective effect when prosocial peers and delinquent peer associations were entered into an interaction and regressed onto participant delinquency. In a second study, Walters (2020n) examined longitudinal data provided by adolescent youth from the Longitudinal Study of Australian Children (LSAC). The results of this study disclosed that positive peer associations moderated the mediated relationship that ran from peer delinquency at age 12/13 to low empathy at age 14/15 to participant delinquency at age 16/17, at two different points, age 12/13 and age 14/15. At age 12/13, positive peers reduced the effect of peer delinquency on empathy, and at age 14/15, positive peers protected youth with low empathy from engaging in delinquency. This is one of the few studies in which a cogent protective effect for prosocial peers was found.

Peer Victimization

In reviewing the literature on offending and victimization, Jennings and colleagues (2012) and Berg and Mulford (2020) identified some interesting trends in the literature and arrived at several important conclusions. Of the 37 studies reviewed in the Jennings et al. paper, 31 showed clear evidence of a relationship between offending and victimization or what is commonly referred to as victim-offender overlap. Not all of the victimizations reported in these studies were perpetrated by peers, although many were. In addition, not all victims offend and not all offenders experience victimization (Mustaine & Tewksbury, 2000), although a good portion do. Dual trajectory analyses performed on criminal offending and victimization data (Mulford et al., 2018) and bullying perpetration and victimization data (Walters, 2021m) denote that offender-victims and bully-victims are at least as common as pure perpetrators and pure victims. Furthermore, as the earlier reference to a bullying dual trajectory study suggests, victim-perpetrator overlap is not limited to crime and delinquency. It extends to other behaviors on the antisocial spectrum, from bullying, to child aggression, to IPV. A meta-analysis of the bullying literature, for instance, revealed significant overlap between bullying victimization and perpetration both concurrently and prospectively (Walters, 2020q). Research on child aggression (Park, 2006) and IPV (Muftić et al., 2015), on the other hand, indicates that the victims of these antisocial acts are sometimes also the perpetrators and that these victim-perpetrators often suffer worse outcomes than pure victims or pure perpetrators.

There is no consensus on which criminological theory best explains victim-offender overlap. Even so, a number of theories have been offered as explanations for the overlap. Among them are the general theory of crime (Gottfredson & Hirschi, 1990), social learning theory (Akers, 1998), general strain theory (GST) (Agnew, 1992), subcultural theory (Wolfgang & Ferracuti, 1967), and routine activities/lifestyles theory (Cohen & Felson, 1979; Hindelang et al., 1978). Given what appears to be a bidirectional relationship between criminal offending and victimization or bullying perpetration and victimization, it may well be that different mechanisms account for each of the pathways that operationalize victim-offender overlap. The pathway that runs from offending to victimization may best be explained as a case of person proximity in line with routine activities/lifestyle theory. In two separate studies, one on criminal offending (Walters, 2020i) and the other on bullying (Walters, 2020s), delinquent peer associations mediated the offending-victimization relationship. This would seem to suggest that offending can lead to negative peer associations, which, in turn, elevate one's likelihood of being victimized by these same associates. The pathway running from victimization to offending is better explained by the general theory of crime and GST. In three separate analyses, two on criminal offending (Walters, 2020f; Walters & Espelage, 2020b) and one on bullying (Walters & Espelage, 2018b), hostility and/or cognitive impulsivity (the developmental antecedent to RCT) mediated the victimization-offending pathway. This pathway denotes that victimization leads to the formation of negative affect/hostile attributions, and that these negative thoughts and feelings, in turn, encourage the individual to be aggressive toward others.

NEIGHBORHOOD AND COMMUNITY

Thus far, the focus has been on relatively small, circumscribed groups of individuals like parents, siblings, and peers. With the introduction of the next two sections, the focus shifts from the small group influences of parents, siblings, and peers to the community- and society-wide influences of neighborhoods, schools, and social structure. One of the earliest theoretical models in criminology was the theory of human ecology put forth by students and researchers in the department of sociology at the University of Chicago. Work on this theory began in 1915 and ended sometime in the 1950s. Using the city of Chicago as a social laboratory, researchers from the University of Chicago drew concentric circles or zones around the Chicago metro area, starting with center city Chicago and extending out into the suburbs. They used this natural experiment to illustrate the relationship between poverty, shifts in population density, social breakdowns in neighborhoods, physical deterioration in buildings, and crime, while demonstrating the ecological principles of invasion, dominance, and succession (Shaw & McKay, 1942). The early work of the Chicago school gave rise to two currently influential theories of crime: social disorganization theory and broken windows theory.

The fundamental premise behind social disorganization theory is that neighborhoods with high levels of social disorganization lack the social capital and collective efficacy to deal effectively with crime (Sampson et al., 1997). Whereas social capital refers to the network of relationships that promote common action and common goals (Coleman, 1988), collective efficacy refers to the ability of a neighborhood to maintain control over and monitor resident and nonresident activity in public spaces such as streets and parks (Sampson & Groves, 1989). Studies have consistently shown that when social capital and collective efficacy are high, neighborhood crime rates tend to be low (Blasius & Friedrichs, 2007; Valasik & Barton, 2018). A question that continues to plague social disorganization theory, however, is whether the relationship between social disorganization and crime is causal. It could be that crime leads to social disorganization or that crime and social disorganization are the result of some third variable (e.g., racial heterogeneity: Kubrin, 2000). Although this issue remains unresolved, there is evidence from at least one study that the relationship between collective efficacy and delinquency is limited and that it is no substitute for addressing individual needs when it comes to reducing youth antisocial behavior (Gearhart & Tucker, 2020).

Even as social disorganization theory focuses on neighborhood social relationships in an effort to reduce crime, broken windows theory (Wilson & Kelling, 1982) is more concerned with how physical decay in a neighborhood, as represented by graffiti, litter, and abandoned buildings, encourages crime. Such physical decay, it is reasoned, sends a signal to citizens and criminals alike that there is insufficient care, concern, and collective efficacy in the community to prevent crime. There are two principal consequences of physical decay, both of which have been confirmed through research. First, people who live in the neighborhood do not feel safe and so are less likely to engage in behaviors designed to protect the neighborhood from crime (Ren et al., 2019). Second, potential criminals feel emboldened to commit crime in the neighborhood based on the perception that local citizens are unwilling or unable to take care of and protect their streets, sidewalks, parks, and homes (Teixeira, 2016). Although programs designed to improve physical conditions in a neighborhood normally produce modest reductions in crime (Braga et al., 2015), criticisms have been leveled against the theory, including the criticism previously mentioned with respect to social disorganization theory—that it is difficult to establish the causal direction of the relationship between physical disorder and crime.

Schools are another segment of the community capable of creating a risk, promotive, or protective effect. A unique aspect of the school social environment is that it is often the first environment in which the child interacts regularly with adult authority figures outside the home. This includes both teachers and school administrators. The school environment is also the place where the child learns to compete and cooperate with peers. These peer interactions may inspire some of the positive and negative peer effects described earlier in this chapter. Research indicates that school failure and attachment may serve as risk and promotive factors for delinquency, respectively. Bersani and Chaple (2007), for instance, discovered that school failure served as a negative turning point for future delinquency and marijuana use. There were no significant interactions between positive and negative effects, however. Nearly a decade later, Chen et al. (2016) identified a promotive effect for school attachment on subsequent delinquency marked by a negative correlation whose magnitude was on par with family warmth and neighborhood cohesion. Although interactive effects were tested, there was no evidence that school attachment served as a protective factor by moderating the relationship between the risk factor of community violence exposure and delinquency.

LARGER SOCIAL STRUCTURE

Merton's (1957) classic strain theory is an example of a criminological theory that adopts a system-wide or macro-level perspective on crime. The principal argument made by classic strain theory is that society establishes goals for its members to pursue and then ascribes the means by which these goals are to be achieved. Merton believed that in the United States the principal goal was to accumulate material wealth by means of hard work, education, honesty, and delayed gratification. Some of those who are blocked in achieving the goal of material wealth due to their standing in society (classism, racism) find illegitimate or illegal means to achieving the goal of material wealth. This is why crime tends to be concentrated in the lower social classes, although it is clearly not restricted to these classes. There is another process at work in the United States that explains why crime can occur at any level of society.

The goal of material wealth, as promoted in American politics, social policy, and even the mass media, has become so central to definitions of personal success in the United States that it now eclipses the institutional means by which wealth is accumulated. Emphasis is placed on the goal, with very little consideration of the means. This, according to proponents of classic strain theory, has led to an explosion of greed and a breakdown in the moral fiber of society.

Classic strain theory has received mixed reviews since its inception in the late 1930s. The main premise of Merton's model, that crime results from a gap or disjunction between a person's aspirations for material wealth and expectations of obtaining that wealth, has received support when aspirations and expectations are measured in strictly monetary terms (Farnsworth & Leiber, 1989) or disjunction is measured as perceptions of blocked opportunities for economic success (Vowell & May, 2000). Yet, the theory lost adherents in the late 1970s after Kornhauser's (1978) reading of the literature suggested that delinquents suffer from both low aspirations and low expectations, thus precluding the possibility of strain. Five years later, Cullen (1983) offered a more nuanced interpretation of the literature on strain theory by proposing that Merton's theory contained two separate arguments. The first argument was made at the individual level and postulated that a disjunction between aspirations and expectations produced frustration that could then lead to delinquency. The second argument was rendered at the aggregate level, but rather than describing offenders as stressed or frustrated, it alleged that some offenders make a calculated decision to use illegitimate means to achieve societal goals. The first argument was developed further by Agnew (1992) into GST and is discussed in chapter 4. The second argument was molded into institutional anomie theory (IAT) by Messner and Rosenfeld (1994); it is discussed next.

In their IAT version of strain theory, Messner and Rosenfeld retained Merton's emphasis on material wealth as the cultural ethos responsible for elevated crime rates in the United States but added to this the idea that deifying material success made noneconomic institutions like families, churches, schools, and politics subservient to the economy. By placing a premium on material wealth, with little regard for how the wealth is acquired, and weakening the institutions that could provide moral leadership in controlling people's worst instincts, the market mentality cultural ethos could very well be considered criminogenic. Support for IAT has been obtained using aggregate-level (Maume & Lee, 2003; Savolainen, 2000) and aggregate- and individual-level (Karstedt & Farrall, 2006; Weld & Roche, 2017) variables. Analyzing data supplied by nearly 66,000 youth from 28 countries with a multilevel model, Walters (2021i) sought to determine whether a free market cultural ethos measured at the aggregate (macro) level interacted with criminal thinking and delinquent behavior measured at the individual (micro) level. Results revealed a stronger link between criminal thinking and delinquency in countries receiving higher scores on the Heritage Foundation's Index of Economic Freedom, after age, sex, peer delinquency, and individual-level measures of two noneconomic institutions (family and school) were controlled. This suggests that macro-level constructs and micro-level constructs do, in fact, interact.

A second multilevel analysis was performed on the same set of data used in the Walters (2021i) investigation—namely, the Second International Self-Reported Delinquency Study (ISRD-2). The macro-level variable in this case was ambient temperature. Prior research had shown that as the ambient temperature in an area rose, so too did interpersonal aggression (Anderson, 1987; Cotton, 1986). Subsequent research revealed that aggression and violent criminality increased during the warmer months and during warmer years, even after controlling for the increased opportunity for interaction that normally accompanies warmer weather (Carbone-Lopez & Lauritsen, 2013; Tiihonen et al., 2020). In the ISRD-2 study mentioned at the beginning of this paragraph, Walters (2021a) discovered that countries with higher average annual ambient temperatures displayed a significantly stronger link between RCT and violent offending than countries with lower average annual ambient temperatures. As predicted, there was no relationship between the average annual ambient temperature and PCT or property offending. There may be something about increased ambient temperature that gives rise to a stronger connection between the impulsive and reckless thinking of RCT and participation in violent crime. Thus, while the principal environmental risk factor for antisocial spectrum disorders is the social environment, aspects of the physical environment, as represented here by ambient temperature and in the previous section by physical neighborhood deterioration, can also serve as risk factors for antisocial behavior.

A third multilevel analysis was performed in an effort to test the cross-level interaction between a country's free market cultural ethos and the micro-level variable of perceived certainty of punishment (Walters, 2021b). Data for this study was provided by 52,458 individuals (average age = 48 years) from the fifth round of the 27-country European Social Survey (ESS). Free market cultural ethos was measured with the Heritage Foundation's Index of Economic Freedom, whereas offending and certainty of punishment were assessing using self-reported past five-year involvement in and perceived likelihood of getting caught and punished for three minor offenses (false insurance claim, buying stolen property, and traffic offenses). Findings from a two-level multilevel modeling analysis revealed a significant cross-level interaction between perceived certainty of punishment at Level 1 and a country's free market cultural ethos at Level 2, with participants living in countries marked by a stronger free market cultural ethos displaying more of a negative association between perceived certainty and minor offending than participants residing in countries marked by a weaker free market cultural ethos. According to the results of the first and third studies reviewed in this section, the effect of a free market cultural ethos on individual offending depends on the nature of the variables with which cultural ethos interacts. A strong free market cultural ethos may stimulate crime by enhancing the pro-offending effects of criminal thinking (Walters, 2021i) but it may also suppress crime by enhancing the anti-offending effects of perceived certainty of punishment (Walters, 2021b).

CONCLUSION

This chapter describes the social variables that serve as risk/promotive factors for criminality. Of cardinal significance when engaged in the practice of theory building is organizing variables into triads. Social variables are best suited to serving as the independent variables in these triads, but they can also serve as mediators (Walters, 2018m, 2020i) and in some cases, perhaps even dependent variables. As became increasingly apparent as we progressed through this chapter, social environmental variables only rarely serve as protective factors. This is not all that surprising given the results of taxometric research showing that the latent structure of most disorders on the antisocial spectrum is continuous/dimensional rather than categorical/taxonic (Haslam et al., 2020). As such, the variables involved in their genesis will more likely accumulate than interact (Ruscio et al., 2010) and the triads will more likely be mediating than moderating pathways. There will continue to be moderating relationships and even some protective relationships (see Walters, 2020n), but it is much more likely that variables involved in the formation of antisocial spectrum disorders sum their effect rather than interact. As indicated in the paragraph preceding this one, environmental risk/promotive factors can either be social or physical in nature. Although I would argue that social environmental factors are more central to a criminal lifestyle than physical environmental factors, physical environmental risk/promotive factors should not be ignored. Beyond the social and physical exogenous or environmental risk/promotive factors discussed in the current chapter, there are internal or endogenous risk/promotive factors that were first described in chapter 2 under the heading of biological, genetic, and physiological factors, and are discussed in greater detail in chapter 4 under the heading of cognition and affect.

Chapter 4

Cognitive Foundations of a Criminal Lifestyle

"Reality Is a Perception from Which Thought Flows"

The notion that serious crime is a consequence of thought and action patterns derived from a criminal lifestyle has been the principal focus of my research over the past 35 years. In writing about a criminal lifestyle, my initial goal was to describe the behavior and demonstrate how it is supported by a series of criminal thought patterns. From my interactions with prison inmates, many of whom were chronic violent offenders, and using data gathered from some of these same individuals, I began formulating and testing hypotheses based on my observations. Many of these hypotheses were falsified and discarded; a few, however, were retained. From these early efforts, I concluded that criminal thinking operated through a person's perceptions and served to justify, advance, and fortify criminal behavior. Moreover, it seemed to me that criminal thinking both followed and preceded criminal action. Not long after, I published these preliminary findings in a book entitled *The Criminal Lifestyle* (Walters, 1990). Since then, I have written over a hundred papers, articles, and books on the topic of criminal thinking. After retiring from prison work, I shifted my attention to at-risk children and adolescents in an effort to gain a better understanding of the developmental origins of the criminal thought patterns that I had come to believe were responsible for a criminal lifestyle. Unlike biological, social environmental, and physical environmental factors, all of which do a better job of explaining criminality than crime, criminal thinking is as relevant to crime as it is to criminality. The present chapter is the culmination of 35 years of study, the first section of which provides a review of the philosophical, psychological, and sociological underpinnings of a construct I have come to call criminal thinking.

THE PHILOSOPHICAL GENEALOGY OF THEORIES OF CRIMINAL THINKING

Historical treatises in areas of science often reference the ancient Greeks, which seemed as good a place as any to launch a discourse on the philosophical origins of theories of criminal thinking. Beginning with the philosophies of Plato (428–347 BC) and Aristotle (384–322 BC), we can see that concepts central to criminal thinking, among them association and rationalization, were being discussed hundreds of years before the birth of Christ. Plato contributed to our understanding of criminal belief systems by characterizing human beings as rational thinkers who seek knowledge by exploring ideas or what he called "forms." Each form was said to capture the essence of an object or quality. Plato was particularly interested in establishing universal forms, such as beauty, truth, and justice. Aristotle, a student of Plato, transformed the largely abstract Platonian concept of form into a more concrete construct, arguing that form and matter are interdependent and part of the same process. This gave rise to beliefs about the inseparability of mind and body and related views on the indivisibility of logic and ethics. Plato and Aristotle, like Socrates before them, were intrigued by the complexity of ethical principles and each in his own way set out to define the "good life." In so doing, they laid the groundwork for moral philosophy, another metaphysical stepping-stone to theories of criminal thinking. A cursory genealogical diagram of the intellectual lineages that have given rise to theories of criminal thinking is depicted in figure 4.1.

Saint Thomas Aquinas (1225–1274) was a Dominican friar, Catholic theologian, and Italian philosopher who built on the work of the ancient Greeks, particularly Aristotle, to create a more complete understanding of human cognition. In an attempt to match the teachings of Aristotle to the doctrines of the Holy Catholic Church, Aquinas sought to expound on the Aristotelian concept of human rationality. According to Aquinas, reason is composed of two parts: cognitive processes or intellect and appetitive processes or will. When cognitive errors confabulate the intellect or passions overwhelm the will, behaviors inconsistent with current moral-ethical standards often surface, he said. Nearly 400 years later, René Descartes (1596–1660) used the Aquinian notions of intellect and will to advance a mind-body duality which, in direct opposition to Aristotelian and Aquinian scholars, held that the senses were of the body rather than of the mind. Whereas mind-body dualism has long been rejected by philosophers of science, there are at least two ways in which mind-body dualism has facilitated the development of theories of criminal thinking. First, by creating a split between the mind and body, Cartesian metaphysics allotted more attention to human cognition than had previously been the case. Second, even though Descartes was not the first philosopher

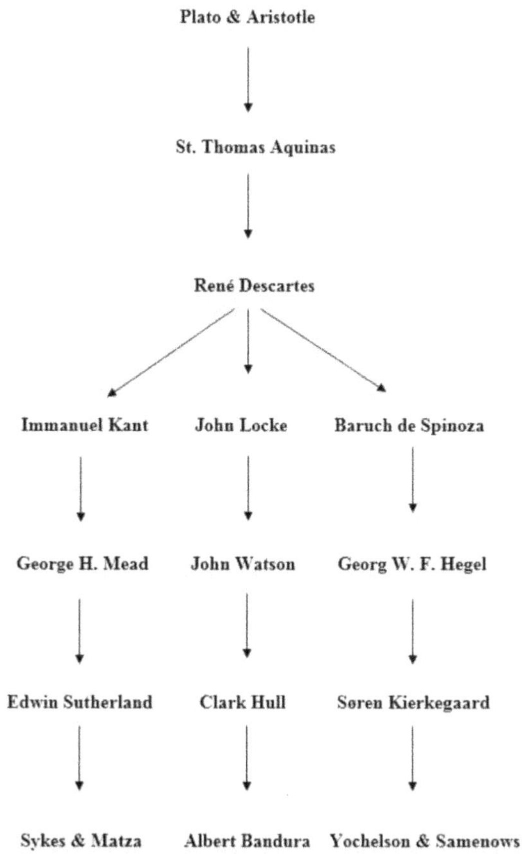

Figure 4.1 Philosophical Antecedents of the Cognitive Component of Criminal Lifestyle Theory. *Source*: Created by author.

to propose that cognition is centered in the brain, his early physiological research on aspects of brain function helped popularize this view.

Descartes' impact on theories of criminal thinking was nothing short of profound as indicated by his presence at the top of three major lineages of influence (see figure 4.1). In the first line of influence, his ideas bore on the work of Immanuel Kant (1724–1804), a major Enlightenment philosopher. Kant, in turn, contributed to theories of criminal thinking by asserting that reason was the greatest source of morality. Morality and social learning figure prominently in this opening line of influence, a line that appears to be social psychological in nature. Following Kant were groups of theorists and researchers whose investigative efforts were designed to explain how people learn to think criminally by observing, modeling, and interpreting the actions of others. The American sociologist and psychologist George Herbert Mead

(1863–1931) was inspired by the German idealism of Kant and Hagel to develop a model that emphasized symbolic interactionism and development of the self through reflected appraisals. From 1894 until his death in 1931, he taught at the University of Chicago, where he mentored students like Edwin Sutherland (1883–1950). Sutherland, who is best known for his studies on white-collar crime and the creation of differential association theory, proposed that definitions favorable and unfavorable to violations of the law helped shape criminal behavior. It should therefore be noted that Sutherland constructed one of the first cognitive theories of crime, a theory which Gresham Sykes (1922–2020) and David Matza (1930–2018) built upon in formulating their drift and neutralization theories of offending behavior.

A second line of influence that can be traced back to Descartes is the behavioral lineage. After Descartes, the line shifts to the British empiricist John Locke (1632–1704) who proposed that the human mind comes into the world as a blank slate (tabula rosa). Unlike Kant, who built largely on the ideas of Descartes, Locke sought to counter Descartes, adopting views that in many cases were the polar opposite of the Cartesian perspective. For instance, where Descartes believed that human reasoning was both intuitive and innate, Locke operated under the assumption that there was nothing innate about the human mind and that is was created exclusively from environmental experience. As the philosophical progenitor of behavioral psychology, Locke metaphorically encouraged the early investigative efforts of behaviorists like John B. Watson (1878–1958). Watson, in turn, influenced the first generation of behavioral psychologists, among them, Clark Hull (1884–1952). Working out of the department of psychology at Yale University, Hull developed a theory of behavior based on drives, needs, conditioned reflexes, and schedules of reinforcement. One of Hull's students, Kenneth Spence (1907–1967), contributed to this lineage by mentoring Albert Bandura (1925–2021), who eventually became a highly influential psychologist who devised popular social learning and cognitive social learning theories of human behavior.

A third line of influence that appears to have evolved from Descartes's philosophy of mind-body duality took shape under the Dutch Jewish philosopher Baruch de Spinoza (1632–1677) and is referred to as the existential lineage. Like Descartes, Spinoza was one of the great rationalists of the early modern era and played a leading role in the early years of the age of Enlightenment. Unlike Locke, Spinoza concurred with Descartes that there was such a thing as a priori knowledge, although he disagreed with Descartes's views on mind-body duality. Thus, while Descartes considered emotion a manifestation of the body that was separate from cognition, Spinoza believed that cognition and emotion were interrelated processes and that emotions derived from cognition. It was Descartes who wrote, "I think, therefore I am." We might paraphrase Spinoza as "I think, therefore I feel." Spinoza also believed that the labels we use to describe other people and various life situations (e.g., good versus evil) tell us more about ourselves than they do about the people and situations being described. Spinoza had a powerful influence on Georg Wilhelm Friedrich Hegel (1770–1831), a proponent of German idealism and the originator of the thesis-antithesis-synthesis triad. Hegel, in turn, influenced, in a negative or reactive way, early existential philosophers like Søren Kierkegaard (1813–1855), the latter of whom insisted that people make their own choices and that these choices often lead to despair, suffering, and irrationality. The idea that people choose to think irrationally rather than being forced to think irrationality is Kierkegaard's principal contribution to Samuel Yochelson (1906–1976) and Stanton Samenow's (b. 1941) work on the criminal personality, where criminal thinking is highlighted.

As will be discussed in the next section of this chapter, three manifestations of cognition are encompassed by the term "criminal thinking." Two of these manifestations reflect criminal thought process (*how* an offender thinks), whereas the third manifestation reflects criminal thought content (*what* an offender thinks). The first criminal thought process is proactive criminal thinking (PCT). PCT represents the planned, calculated, and amoral aspects of antisocial cognition. This form of antisocial cognition is reflected in the most recent progenitor of each line or lineage (found at the bottom of each line in figure 4.1): namely, Sykes and Matza (neutralization techniques), Bandura (moral disengagement), and Yochelson and Samenow (power thrust, superoptimism). The other criminal thought process is reactive criminal thinking (RCT) or the impulsive, irresponsible, and emotional aspects of antisocial cognition. RCT is reflected in several of Yochelson and Samenow's 52 thinking errors (i.e., cutoff, fragmentation) and overlaps with attitudinally measured low self-control (Gottfredson & Hirschi, 1990) but does not appear to borrow much from either Sykes and Matza or Bandura. Finally, a few of Yochelson and Samenow's thinking errors (e.g., criminal pride, victim stance) share features in common with criminal thought content, as do thought patterns learned through observation and modeling in Bandura's social cognitive learning theory (e.g., attributions, outcome expectancies).

THE HIERARCHICAL STRUCTURE OF CRIMINAL THINKING

Criminal thinking can be organized into a vertical hierarchy, with general criminal thinking (GCT) at the top and two clusters of individual thinking styles at the bottom. This vertical hierarchy contrasts sharply with the horizontal hierarchy into which the antisocial spectrum is organization. Initially, the hierarchy bifurcates into criminal thought process and criminal thought content (see figure 4.2). Criminal thought process represents *how* an offender thinks; the form or pattern of thought, whether it be organized and goal-directed or disorganized and affect-driven. Criminal thought content, by contrast, is more a matter of *what* an offender thinks than how they think. Instead of focusing on the form or pattern of thought, emphasis is placed on the content or substance of a person's cognitive constructions. Whether a person's criminal thinking is slow and methodical or fast and impulsive, we can infer that they are expressing an aspect of criminal thought process. If, on the other hand, the person was articulating their attitude toward crime or conventional behavior, then we can infer that they are airing aspects of criminal thought content. Criminal lifestyle theory assumes that criminal thought process and criminal thought content are equally important facets of criminal cognition, but this is an area of research that is still in its infancy, particularly since there have only been a handful of studies conducted on the relationship between criminal thought process and criminal thought content.

As previously stated, criminal thought process can be broken down into two overlapping dimensions: PCT and RCT. Whereas PCT represents the planned, calculated, and amoral aspects of antisocial cognition, RCT represents the impulsive, reckless, and emotional aspects. One observation that has been repeatedly made is that PCT and RCT are moderately to highly correlated, usually somewhere in the neighborhood of .40 to .75 (Walters, 2020a). This, despite the fact, PCT and RCT often correlate differentially with outside criteria. Thus, while PCT has been found to postdict instrumental crimes significantly better than expressive crimes (Walters et al., 2007), correlate with positive outcome expectancies for crime but not with hostile attribution biases (Walters, 2007b), predict failure to register as a sex offender but not general sex offender recidivism (Walters et al., 2015), and moderate the relationship between past and future intimate partner violence (Walters, 2020o),

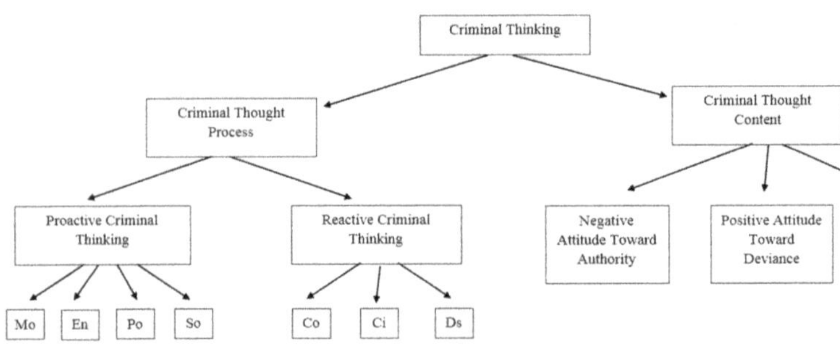

Figure 4.2 The Hierarchical Structure of Criminal Thinking Broken Down into Criminal Thought Process and Criminal Thought Content. Note: Mo = Mollification, En = Entitlement, Po = Power Orientation, So = Superoptimism, Co = Cutoff, Ci = Cognitive Indolence, Ds = Discontinuity. *Source*: Created by author.

RCT does the exact opposite. Therefore, while PCT and RCT often show similar levels of elevation when assessed in the same person, it is still important to take note of even relatively small differences in elevation between these two criminal thinking dimensions.

According to criminal lifestyle theory, criminal thought content is composed of three overlapping dimensions (inter-scale correlation = .51–.57). The first dimension of criminal thought content is a negative attitude toward authority. Someone involved in a criminal lifestyle will often express negative attitudes toward authority figures, whether it be parents, teachers, bosses, the police, probation officers, or judges. Attitudes toward a range of authority figures should therefore be gauged when evaluating this particular dimension of criminal thought content. The second dimension of criminal thought content in criminal lifestyle theory is a positive or accepting attitude toward deviance. This dimension can be assessed by asking the individual to rate the wrongfulness of various antisocial/unethical and criminal/illegal acts (e.g., cheating on a test, cheating on one's taxes, lying to parents, lying in court, getting into a fight, assaulting someone). Those who score high on this scale demonstrate an antagonistic attitude toward the rules of conventional society. The third dimension of criminal thought content, as put forth by criminal lifestyle theory, is a criminal identity. In assessing this dimension, questions are asked about how much the individual identifies with and feels comfortable around lawbreakers, attains satisfaction from their own breaking of the rules, and feels alienated from conventional people and activities. Someone who endorses these type items would be classified as having a strong criminal identity.

The final level of the left side of the criminal thinking hierarchy is occupied by a series of seven thinking styles, four of which are linked to PCT and three of which are associated with RCT. Mollification (Mo), Entitlement (En), Power Orientation (Po), and Superoptimism (So) fall under the PCT umbrella, whereas Cutoff (Co), Cognitive Indolence (Ci), and Discontinuity (Ds) are expressions of RCT. Table 4.1 defines each one of these thinking styles. Criminal lifestyle theory postulates that each thinking style starts out as a false premise. Technically, there are two parts to a false premise: denial and defense. Denial represents what it is about human nature, social relationships, or personal responsibility that is ignored, refuted, or trivialized. The defense in support of the denial is how the individual keeps from acknowledging the reality they have denied by making excuses, rationalizing their actions, and justifying their intentions. The belief system upon which the false premise is based acts to maintain, protect, and advance the evolving criminal lifestyle. Over time, these thoughts become automatic, making them even more difficult to identify, challenge, and change. Interventions must consequently be constructed that slow the progress and confront the validity

Table 4.1 Thinking Styles that Comprise the Proactive and Reactive Dimensions of Criminal Thought Process

Thinking Style	*Dimension*	*Description*	*Denial*	*Defense*
Mollification	PCT	Justifications and blaming attributions used to negate bad behavior	Denial of responsibility	Excuses and Rationalizations designed to minimize personal accountability
Entitlement	PCT	Belief in one's uniqueness, specialness, and prerogative	Denial of humility	Granting oneself permission to violate propriety out of a sense of privilege
Power Orientation	PCT	Controlling social situations and others through deception and intimidation	Denial of vulnerability	Putting others down in an effort to feel better about oneself
Superoptimism	PCT	Belief that one can indefinitely avoid the negative consequences of one's actions	Denial of truth	Assumption of immunity from the natural negative consequences of one's actions
Cutoff	RCT	Rapid elimination of deterrents to crime through a word, phrase, or use of drugs	Denial of self-control	Mechanisms designed to limit self-control
Cognitive Indolence	RCT	Failure to critically evaluate plans and ideas	Denial of industriousness	Ignoring the necessity of hard work
Discontinuity	RCT	Problems following through on initial intentions and commitments	Denial of consistency	Easy distractibility in the face of mounting environmental pressure and change

Note: Thinking Style = Psychological Inventory of Criminal Thinking Styles (PICTS) thinking style scale; Dimension = dimension of criminal thought process; PCT = proactive criminal thinking; RCT = reactive criminal thinking; Description = description of thinking style; Denial = form of denial that is at the core of the false premise; Defense = way in which the individual enacts the denial.
Source: Table created by author.

of these thought processes, given their role in the ongoing activities of someone committed to a criminal lifestyle.

ASSESSING CRIMINAL THINKING

Before we can change criminal thinking, we must be able to assess it. Because adults and juveniles think differently, it is imperative that we find ways to assess criminal thinking at different ages. This may entail using separate instruments and scales for adults and juveniles. The current section explores how this can be accomplished.

Assessing Criminal Thought Process and Content in Adults

Separate instruments have been devised to assess criminal thought process and criminal thought content, but I know of no instruments that are capable of doing both. Starting with criminal thought process, the How I Think scale (HIT; Barriga et al., 2000), TCU Criminal Thinking Scales (TCU CTS: Knight et al., 2006), Measure of Criminal Attitudes and Associates (MCAA: Mills et al., 2002), and Criminogenic Thinking Profile (CTP: Mitchell & Tafrate, 2012) all assess features of proactive criminal thought process, whereas the Measure of Offender Thinking Styles-Revised (MOTS-R: Mandracchia & Morgan, 2011), Criminal Cognitions Scale (CCS: Tangney et al., 2012), and Psychological Inventory of Criminal Thinking Styles (PICTS: Walters, 1995) assess features of both proactive and reactive criminal thought process. The Criminal Sentiments Scale–Modified (CSS–M: Gendreau et al., 1979; Simourd, 1997) and Criminal Thought Content Inventory (CTCI: Walters & Morgan, 2018), on the other hand, are designed to assess criminal thought content. Because the PICTS and CTCI were intended for use with the criminal lifestyle, these two instruments will receive the lion's share of attention in this section.

The PICTS is an 80-item self-report measure comprised of validity, thinking style, and higher order (PCT, RCT, and GCT) scales. This measure's reliability and validity are well-established and been found to be moderately strong (Walters, 2020). The PICTS has also become a major asset for research on criminal thinking and criminal lifestyle. For the purpose of interpreting the PICTS, raw scores are converted to T-scores, with T-scores ≥ 60 signaling areas of potential importance. If there are no more than 10 unanswered questions on the PICTS, the defensiveness validity scale is below a T-score of 70, and the confusion validity scale is below a T-score of 90, then the protocol is viewed as valid and amenable to review and interpretation. Starting at the top of the criminal thinking hierarchy, the GCT score is evaluated for significance ($T \geq 50$). If there is evidence of a GCT equal to or greater than a T-score of 50, then the next step is to determine the relative elevation of the PCT and RCT scores. A T-score difference of 10 or more points is considered significant. The final step of the interpretation process is to examine all individual thinking style scales that achieve a T-score of 60 or higher.

The CTCI is a 30-item inventory designed to assess criminal thought content. Three content areas are assessed by the CTCI, the results of which are conveyed in three subscale scores. Preliminary research on the reliability and validity of the CTCI subscales indicate that these scores possess adequate reliability and validity (Walters & Morgan, 2019), although more research is required. The three CTCI subscales are labeled Negative Attitude toward Authority (NAA), Positive Attitude toward Deviance (PAD), and Criminal Identity (CID). Because there have been no completed studies using the CTCI in a clinical sample, there is currently no way to meaningfully convert raw scores to T-scores. In the one college student sample where CTCI data are available, it is possible to compare the raw scores for each of the three subscales. Elevations on the NAA subscale reflect negative attitudes toward authority figures ranging from parents, to teachers, to clergy, to law enforcement. Above average scores on the PAD subscale of the CTCI are believed to reflect an attitude favorable to violation of family rules and societal laws. The CID subscale is designed to assess a respondent's self-view as it pertains to criminal offending. Items on this scale measure identification with criminal others, perceived similarity to law-violators, and pride in one's antisocial activities.

Assessing Criminal Thought Process and Content in Youth

Although a youth version of the PICTS is available, it has not received much research attention. Moreover, it is uncertain how well the thinking styles covered by the adult version of the PICTS represent the antisocial thinking of youth. For this reason, investigators might want to assess PCT and RCT with facets of each dimension appraised with scales that may be more applicable to adolescent respondents. In assessing youthful PCT or its juvenile antecedent, cognitive insensitivity, one could administer measures of neutralization (Huizinga & Jakob-Chien, 1998), moral disengagement (Bandura et al., 1996), or outcome expectancies for crime (Nickoletti & Taussig, 2006). It may be better to assess youthful RCT or its juvenile antecedent, cognitive impulsivity, with measures of thrill/sensation seeking (Zuckerman, 2007), hostile attribution biases (Dodge, 2006), or temporal discounting (Varghese et al., 2014) than with a juvenile PICTS. Similarly, the content dimension of criminal identity may be more appropriately assessed using measures of criminal self-efficacy (Brezina & Topali, 2012), feared possible selves

(Wainwright et al., 2018), and reflected appraisals (Matsueda, 1992) than with the CTCI.

Walters (2020b) conducted a meta-analysis of studies addressing the relationship between adolescent PCT, RCT, and criminal identity, on the one hand, and concurrent or subsequent antisocial, delinquent, and criminal outcomes, on the other hand. Three sets of findings were obtained. First, the PCT indicators (neutralization, moral disengagement, and positive outcome expectancies for crime) achieved a pooled effect size (r) of .34 (95% CI = .29, .40). The effect size dropped slightly but remained moderate when analyses were restricted to longitudinal data (r = .31, 95% CI = .24, .38). A modest to moderate effect size was obtained when RCT indicators (thrill/sensation seeking, hostile attribution biases, and temporal discounting) were analyzed (r = .25, 95% CI = .20, .30), which fell to .23 (95% CI = .10, .35) when only longitudinal studies were considered. A modest to moderate pooled effect size was also recorded when criminal identity indicators (criminal self-efficacy, future feared selves, and reflected appraisals) were evaluated as a group (r = .24, 95% CI = .13, .35), although this time the pooled effect size rose when analyses were restricted to longitudinal studies (r = .29, 95% CI = .10, .46).

ROLE OF CRIMINAL THINKING IN A CRIMINAL LIFESTYLE

Criminal thinking and its cognitive antecedents play multiple roles in a criminal lifestyle. Two such roles are as mediating and moderating variables in a triad. As was noted in chapter 1, a triad is a three-variable model comprised of a predictor variable, an outcome variable, and a mediating or moderating variable. In nearly all cases, the predictor or outcome variable is some form of offending and the corresponding outcome and predictor variables are a well-documented correlate of offending behavior. Hence, in explaining the relationship between harsh parental discipline and offspring delinquency, harsh parental discipline serves as the predictor variable and offspring delinquency serves as the outcome variable in the parent-initiated model, whereas offspring delinquency serves as the predictor variable and harsh parental discipline serves as the outcome variable in the child-initiated or evocative model. A third variable in the form of a mediator or moderator variable is then added to the bivariate relationship to complete the triad. This is how simple models are used to construct more complex models. Cognitive variables like criminal thinking are ideal mediators in that they are often sufficiently stable and robust to predict other variables (*b* path of the indirect effect), yet sufficiently malleable and plastic to be predicted by other variables (*a* path of the indirect effect). They are also effective as moderators in that they are sufficiently stable to meaningfully interact with other variables for the purpose of predicting future crime and delinquency.

Criminal Thinking as a Mediator of Other Variable Relationships

A partial list of the bivariate associations that have been found to be mediated by criminal thinking in my own research includes the relationship between past offending and future offending (Walters, 2016h), the relationship between past bullying and future bullying (Walters & Espelage, 2018a), the relationship between past substance abuse and future crime (Walters, 2016f), the relationship between past animal cruelty and future violent offending (Walters, 2014d), the relationship between early callous-unemotional traits and later peer influence (Walters, 2018a), the relationship between prior peer delinquency and subsequent participant delinquency (Walters, 2016d), the relationship between prior gang affiliation and subsequent participant delinquency (Walters, 2019d), the relationship between prior sibling delinquency and subsequent participant delinquency (Walters, 2020r), the relationship between earlier co-offending and later delinquency (Walters, 2020j), the relationship between the "big five" personality traits of low agreeableness/low conscientiousness and future offending (Walters, 2018h), the relationship between past criminal victimization and future criminal offending (Walters, 2020f), the relationship between past bullying victimization and future bullying perpetration (Walters & Espelage, 2018b), the relationship between past bullying victimization and future delinquency (Walters & Espelage, 2017), and the relationship between low empathy and subsequent bullying perpetration (Walters & Espelage, 2018c). These results clearly indicate that criminal thinking is a mechanism capable of linking important criminological variables and influences, although they do not tell us how the mechanism works. Additional research and theorizing are required to answer that question.

In explaining how criminal thinking and its cognitive antecedents act to mediate such well-known criminological relationships as crime continuity (past crime → future crime), drug-crime connectivity (drugs ↔ crime), peer influence (peer delinquency → participant delinquency), peer selection (participant delinquency → peer delinquency), and victim-offender overlap (criminal victimization ↔ criminal offending), it is imperative that we consider the role of additional factors like internalization. The social variables described in chapter 3 do not ordinarily cause crime directly. Instead, they are sensed by the individual (perception), after which they are incorporated into the individual's belief systems (cognition). It is this perceptual-cognitive process that is at the core of behavioral influence.

Two studies that illustrate the perceptual-cognitive process that gives rise to internalization are reviewed next. Using four waves of data and a sample of early to mid-adolescents from the National Youth Survey, Walters (2015d) discovered that parental appraisals of the wrongfulness of delinquent behavior predicted child-perceived parental appraisals of the wrongfulness of delinquent behavior. This, in turn, predicted the child's own attitude toward the wrongfulness of delinquency, which then predicted the child's subsequent involvement in offending behavior. Using a sample of mid- to late-adolescent youth from the Youths and Deterrence study, Walters (2021j) ascertained that the reflected appraisals of best friends' reactions to participant deviance predicted participant disapproval of their own involvement in delinquency, which then predicted participant involvement in delinquency two years later. In this second study, parental reflected appraisals had no effect on the child's attitude or behavior, perhaps because these participants were older than the participants from the earlier Walters (2015d) investigation.

The reader needs to understand that while the two previously reviewed studies focused on criminal thought content (i.e., positive attitudes toward deviance), criminal thought process is just as readily internalized as criminal thought content. Employing two separate samples of juvenile respondents, Walters (2015e, 2016d) determined that PCT mediated the peer influence effect which runs from peer delinquency to participant delinquency. In relating this finding to internalization, we need to take note of research on the projection hypothesis of peer-participant delinquency relationships. The projection hypothesis asserts that participants project their own level of delinquency onto that of their friends when asked to estimate how many of their friends engage in delinquent behavior (Young et al., 2013). From here, it is alleged that the projection bias artificially inflates the correlation between peer and participant delinquency, transforming a small and potentially nonsignificant relationship into a large and highly significant correlation. In a meta-analysis of 22 youth samples, however, participant-reported peer delinquency predicted subsequent participant delinquency in 21 out of the 22 samples after prior participant delinquency had been controlled. In fact, the resulting pooled effect size was significant and at least modest in magnitude ($r = .16$, 95% CI = .12, .19: Walters, 2019f). This, of course, does not preclude the possibility that projection or overestimation plays a limited role in the participant-peer delinquency relationship, especially since internalized representations of peer delinquency are likely to have a greater impact on participant delinquency than actual peer delinquency, just as internalized representations of peer drug use have been found to have a greater impact on participant drug use than actual peer drug use (McAlaney et al., 2015).

Criminal Thinking as a Moderator of Other Variable Relationships

The second major role criminal thinking plays in a triad is that of a moderator of important criminological relationships. It should be noted, however, that moderation is not as precise or as elegant as mediation. That is because it is procedurally impossible to differentiate between moderator and moderated variables. The differentiation must be made exclusively on theoretical grounds and then accepted at least partially on faith. To test moderation, one calculates the interaction between the moderator (W) and moderated or independent (X) variables. In the case of a study where family socioeconomic status (SES) is identified as the independent variable, neighborhood disorder is classified as the moderator variable, and child delinquency is positioned as the dependent variable, a significant interaction would be interpreted as evidence that the family SES-child delinquency relationship was moderated by or conditioned on neighborhood disorder. If we switch things around and make neighborhood disorder the X variable and family SES the W variable, the results would be exactly the same, yet they would be interpreted differently (i.e., that the neighborhood disorder-child delinquency relationship was moderated by or conditioned on family SES). With mediation, one can reverse the X and mediator (M) variables to test whether the pattern remains significant. Often when the X variable is a social factor and the M variable is a cognitive factor, the reverse pattern is nonsignificant. The same cannot be done with moderation and so we are left with a less precise outcome and a more ambiguous conclusion. Accordingly, while we get internalization with mediation, we get nothing more than a nonspecific interaction with moderation.

The aforementioned procedural and conceptual limitations of moderation aside, it is still a potentially useful methodology capable of contributing to the development of criminological theory. Studies such as the one performed by Caudy et al. (2015) sought to determine whether drug use moderated the ability of a criminal thinking measure, in this case the TCU CTS, to predict recidivism in 226 drug-involved probationers and 337 jail inmates. Bivariate correlations revealed a significant relationship between criminal thinking and recidivism in jail inmates only. Subjecting these data to logistic regression analysis, the authors discovered that criminal thinking only predicted self-reported arrests in jail inmates when substance use symptomatology was low. These results suggest that criminal thinking may not be predictive of recidivism in persons with serious substance use problems, although it should be noted that the measure of criminal thinking used in this study (TCU CTS) measures only PCT and that RCT is the dimension most closely associated with substance misuse (Walters, 2012). In a moderated mediation study on peer-resistance skills and delinquency in seriously antisocial youth, Walters (2018k) ascertained that peer-resistance skills had their greatest impact on the PCT-future delinquency relationship in situations where peer delinquency was low. In other words, the criminogenic effect of PCT was weakest when peer-resistance skills were high and peer delinquency was low and strongest when peer-resistance skills were low and peer delinquency was high.

Several studies have examined the possibility that criminal thinking may moderate the relationship between a core variable from deterrence theory, perceived certainty of punishment, and a person's stated willingness to commit an antisocial act. In a study by Walters and Morgan (2019), college students' willingness to cheat on a hypothetical exam was evaluated under different levels of certainty. The results of a repeated measures analysis of covariance revealed that students with moderate PCT scores and moderate to high RCT scores were significantly less likely to be deterred from cheating when the odds of getting caught were low. In a follow-up to this study, Walters et al. (2019) presented three antisocial scenarios (cheating on a test, stealing $50, and selling marijuana) to a different group of students. As in the previous study, the gap in stated willingness to participate in antisocial acts between students with higher and lower PCT and RCT scores grew as the probability of getting caught decreased. In a third study, Walters et al. (2021a) presented three scenarios (cheating on a test, property damage, and drunk driving) to a small group of probationers attending a dayreporting program and discovered that participants with above average PCT scores were significantly more likely to report a willingness to participate in an antisocial act as the perceived certainty of getting caught went down. These results indicate that the relationship between criminal thinking and stated willingness to participate in an antisocial act is conditional on the certainty of punishment or that the relationship between certainty of punishment and stated willingness to participate in an antisocial act is conditional on the level of criminal thinking.

Other Roles Assumed by Criminal Thinking in a Triad

There are three principal roles in a triad: the predictor or independent variable role, the outcome or dependent variable role, and the mediator or moderator role. Whereas the roles for which cognitive factors like criminal thinking are best suited are mediation and moderation, criminal thinking is capable of fulfilling the independent and dependent variable roles as well. Positioned as the independent variable in a moderating triad, GCT was found to predict recidivism in 1,101 males released from prison within 42 months of completing the PICTS, although the effect was restricted to inmates with a GED or 12-plus years of education (Walters, 2014c). This suggests that education may moderate the criminal thinking-recidivism relationship. When a developmental facet of PCT, narcissistic entitlement, was cited as the dependent variable in a mediation triad of 1,700 youthful members of the Fragile Families and Child Wellbeing Study, weak mother-child attachment, as assessed by the mother when the child was 3 years of age, indirectly predicted narcissistic entitlement in the child 12 years later, via maternal ratings of child peer delinquency at age 9 (Walters, 2019c). This suggests that attachment and peer factors may play significant roles in the formation of a key developmental facet of PCT.

A DOORWAY BETWEEN TWO REALITIES

The importance of addressing both crime and criminality in a field like criminology was underscored in chapters 1 and 2 of this book. In the present section, I discuss how criminal thinking may be able to facilitate a rapprochement of crime and criminality by furnishing a doorway through which these two realities can be accessed. As the reader may recall, crime refers to a specific act whose presence or absence violates the law in some way. Criminality, on the other hand, refers to a person's propensity to commit crime. Therefore, while crime references a single event, criminality estimates the person's future likelihood of engaging in one or more of these events. Criminal thinking, given its unique combination of stability and plasticity, is in a position to contribute to our understanding of crime, criminality, and their intersection. In fact, it is possible that a thought that serves as a risk factor for future criminal offending (criminality) could also stimulate a specific criminal event (crime). Like a doorway that connects two dimensions or two realities, criminal thinking contributes to our understanding of both crime and criminality and effectively bridges the gap that separates them, a gap that has been exacerbated by a field that has failed to effectively integrate its classical and positivist schools and which appears to be more focused on differences than similarities.

There are three principal models in criminal lifestyle theory: the moral model, the control model, and the decision-making model. The moral and control models seek to explain criminality, whereas the decision-making model seeks to explain crime. An example of how the moral and control models are used to assess a person's propensity for crime (criminality) can be found in studies investigating whether the PICTS scores of released prison inmates, probationers, and forensic patients predict recidivism over a period of several years. As outlined in table 4.2, there are nine studies to the author's knowledge that have used GCT, PCT, and RCT scores from the PICTS to predict recidivism in follow-ups ranging from two to five years.

Table 4.2 Predicting Recidivism with the PICTS GCT, PCT, and RCT Scores

Study	*Location*	N	*Sex*	*Description*	*FU*	*GCT*	*PCT*	*RCT*
Walters (1997b)	U.S.	63	M	Federal Inmates	27 mo.	.23 (.26)	.16 (.19)	.24 (.27)
Walters and Elliott (1999)	U.S.	118	F	State Inmates	60 mo.	.22	.18	.21
Palmer and Hollin (2004)	G.B.	174	M	Prisoners	24 mo.	.14	.15	.11
Walters (2006b)	U.S.	226	M	Federal Inmates	30 mo.	.27 (.24)	.21 (.19)	.27 (.26)
Gonsalves et al. (2009)	U.S.	117	M	Forensic Patients	49 mo.	.27	.29	.23
Walters (2011b)	U.S.	1,101	M	Federal Inmates	30 mo.	.19 (.16)	.16 (.12)	.16 (.13)
Walters, Deming et al. (2015)	U.S.	322	M	State Sex Offenders	38 mo.	.16 (.13)	.15 (.11)	.14 (.11)
Walters and Lowenkamp (2016)	U.S.	81,881	M	Federal Probationers	24 mo.	.25 (.14)	.20 (.10)	.26 (.17)
Walters and Lowenkamp (2016)	U.S.	14,519	F	Federal Probationers	24 mo.	.25 (.17)	.19 (.11)	.27 (.20)

Note: Location = country where the study was conducted; *N* = sample size; Sex = sex of participants, M = male, F = female; Description = description of sample, U.S. = United States, G.B. = Great Britain; FU = follow-up period in months; GCT = zero-order correlation between PICTS General Criminal Thinking scale and presence/absence of recidivism during follow-up (partial correlation controlling for age and prior offending in parentheses); PCT = zero-order correlation between PICTS Proactive Criminal Thinking scale and presence/absence of recidivism during follow-up (partial correlation controlling for age and prior offending in parentheses); RCT = zero-order correlation between PICTS Reactive Criminal Thinking scale and presence/absence of recidivism during follow-up (partial correlation controlling for age and prior offending in parentheses).
Source: Table created by author based on study data.

Effect sizes for individual studies range from the low .10s to the high .20s, with mean pooled effect sizes in the modest to moderate range: specifically, .25 (.23, .26), .20 (.19, .20), and .24 (.21, .26) for the GCT, PCT, and RCT, respectively. When partial correlations were computed between the PICTS and recidivism, controlling for two of the best predictors of future offending (i.e., age and criminal history: Gendreau et al., 1996), the mean pooled effect sizes fell to .16 (.13, .18), .10 (.10, .11), and .18 (.15, .20), respectively, but remained significant. Based on these results, it could be argued that the RCT predicts recidivism slightly better than the PCT and on par with the GCT.

Beyond its ability to assess criminality, the PICTS may also be capable of assisting with the prediction of specific crimes. In the three previously reviewed scenario studies (Walters & Morgan, 2019; Walters et al., 2019, 2021a), both the PICTS and the interaction between the PICTS and perceived certainty of punishment correlated significantly with a respondent's stated interest in engaging in an antisocial act. A fourth study also uncovered evidence that criminal thinking may moderate the connection between certainty of punishment and intention to offend, but this time a generic measure of perceived certainty was used instead of perceived certainty of getting caught for a specific criminal act and outcome was measured as self-reported offending occurring within the past year rather than stated willingness to participate in a single criminal event (Walters, 2020c). In this fourth study, participants from the Pathways to Desistance study were asked to rate their perceived likelihood of getting caught if they were to engage in a series of seven delinquent acts (e.g., fighting, robbery, breaking into a home). The average score across the seven acts was then multiplied by the GCT score, calculated as a combined score from a moral disengagement scale and an excitement/thrill-seeking measure. Results revealed that delinquent youth at age 21 who had higher GCT and lower certainty of apprehension scores were more likely to be involved in crime at age 22 than delinquent youth with lower GCT and higher certainty of apprehension scores. These findings paralleled those from the scenario studies, further reinforcing the idea that criminal thinking may serve as a doorway between the crime calculations of the scenario studies and the criminality estimates made by Walters (2020c).

THE ORIGINS OF CRIMINAL THOUGHT PROCESS AND CONTENT

Although PCT and RCT correlate highly, they have very different origins and display moderately divergent patterns of correlation with outside criteria. This makes their high level of intercorrelation all the more enigmatic. The current section explores the origins, not just of proactive and reactive criminal thought process but also of the three dimensions of criminal thought content: negative attitudes toward authority, positive attitudes toward deviance, and criminal identity.

Origins of Proactive Criminal Thinking

It should be noted that lifestyle theory assumes that children are born neither moral nor immoral; instead, they learn moral integrity or moral duplicity through their interactions with the environment, the social environment in particular. Morally, children enter the world with a behaviorist's blank slate. This does not mean, however, that there are no preexisting biological tendencies or differences that make moral integrity more attainable for one child than another. Of the three principle elements of conscience, at least two are vulnerable to individual differences in biology. Empathy, for instance, has its foundation in a child's early attachment relationships with parents, particularly the mother, and achievement of such vital developmental milestones as joint attention, theory of mind, and cognitive/affective perspective taking (Evans & Marsh, 2017; Stefan & Avram, 2019; Stephenson et al., 2021). Because a difficult temperament places a child at increased risk for problems with attachment and positive socialization (Javakhishvili & Vazsonyi, 2021), genetic/biological factors can stand in the way of a child's ability to empathize with others. Likewise, children who do not condition well to punishment by virtue of a weak resting and reactive autonomic response (Glenn et al., 2009; Raine et al., 1997) may also have difficulty experiencing guilt and remorse for their criminal and antisocial actions. In most cases, however, empathy, guilt, and moral reasoning are learned through a child's interactions with parents, teachers, siblings, peers, and other important figures in a child's life, with much of the influence occurring in the preschool and primary school years (Stern & Cassidy, 2018).

PCT stands in opposition to moral integrity. Consistent with social learning theories of crime (Akers, 1998; Sutherland, 1947), research demonstrates that novice inmates placed in a medium security prison displayed significant increments in PCT over the first six months of incarceration (Walters, 2003a). More recent studies also indicate that associating with more criminally sophisticated individuals leads to a rise in PCT and that PCT appears to mediate the peer influence effect (peer delinquency → participant delinquency). According to the results of this research, PCT is the intervening variable in a mediating triad where participant delinquency serves as the dependent variable and either peer delinquency (Walters, 2015e, 2016d), sibling delinquency (Walters, 2020r), gang affiliation (Walters, 2019d, 2021c), or co-offending (Walters, 2020j) serves as the independent variable. In each study, except for Walters (2015e), where RCT was unavailable, when RCT was positioned as a mediator of the peer influence effect it failed to achieve a significant effect, thereby suggesting that the mediating effect was specific to PCT. There are several different possibilities but the results of these six studies make a strong case for a social learning interpretation of PCT, whereby participants observe and then model the actions of delinquent peers, antisocial siblings, fellow gang members, or codefendants. There is also evidence that PCT or neutralization is less a technique for reducing guilt in drifting delinquents than it is an example of moral turpitude in dedicated delinquents (Walters et al., 2021b).

Origins of Reactive Criminal Thinking

Whereas PCT is believed to be learned, RCT is considered a reflection of the human organism's natural, unsocialized state at birth: impulsive, irresponsible, and self-centered. And while the origins of PCT are best understood using principles from social learning theory, the origins of RCT are best understood using principles from social control theory. According to two prominent social control theorists, Gottfredson and Hirschi (1990), humans are born antisocial and must learn to be law-abiding. This contrasts with social learning theory which holds that humans are born neutral and must learn through experience to be either law-abiding or antisocial. If RCT is a reflection of the natural impulsive/self-serving state of the human organism, then it is not learning that leads to crime but rather, lack of learning and uncontrolled expressions of human nature that leads to crime. This also suggests that PCT and RCT are both affected by parenting, but in different ways. PCT is shaped by early attachment problems and lack of parental support (empathy), inconsistent parental discipline (guilt), and weak inductive parenting (moral reasoning), not to mention exposure to antisocial peers and siblings. RCT, by contrast, is rectified by mechanisms of parental control and modeling of prosocial peer and sibling behavior.

There is at least one other factor that is important in the development of RCT. Unlike parental control and the calming influence of prosocial peers and siblings, however, this influence acts directly on RCT by stimulating it. The influence I am referring to here is offending behavior. As a self-fostering process, offending augments the impulsivity, irresponsibility, and self-centeredness that is inherent in RCT, something that has been observed in both crime continuity and the peer selection effect. Crime continuity refers to the fact that past offending begets future offending. Early studies on this issue unearthed strong evidence that criminal-thinking-mediated crime continuity or the past crime-future crime relationship (Walters, 2015a). Subsequent research, however, disclosed that it was RCT rather than PCT that was at the heart of crime continuity (Walters, 2016h, 2019h) and its bullying analog (Walters & Espelage, 2018a). In all three of these studies, the reason why PCT failed to mediate the past crime/bullying–future crime/bullying relationship was that prior crime or bullying failed to stimulate PCT, though it did an effective job of stimulating RCT. Research also indicates that the peer selection effect (participant delinquency → peer delinquency) is mediated by RCT but not PCT and that it does so for the same reason PCT does not mediate crime/bullying continuity—that is, prior offending inculcates a rise in RCT but not in PCT (Walters, 2016d, 2021c).

Origins of Criminal Thought Content

Although there is a paucity of research on the origins of criminal thought content, several studies have nonetheless examined specific topics relating to criminal thought content, particularly attitudes toward the police (negative attitude toward authority) and perceived acceptability of criminal behavior (positive attitude toward deviance). Research indicates, for instance, that attitudes toward the police are shaped by attitudes of family members and friends (Miller & Davis, 2008), exposure to mass media and social media accounts of police behavior (Intravia et al., 2018), and direct and vicarious experiences with the police (Harris & Jones, 2020). Research conducted on youth attitudes toward crime, on the other hand, indicates that while such attitudes appear to be learned in association with others, particularly peers (Megens & Weerman, 2012), these attitudes form a multidimensional construct that is best assessed by sampling attitudes toward a cross-section of criminal and antisocial activities (Thomas, 2018). The third dimension of criminal thought content, criminal identity, given its centrality to a person's self-view is formidably complex, although reflected appraisals of how the individual believes peers and family members view them and how this initiates the internalization process previously described may play a particularly salient role in the development of this dimension of criminal thought content (Brownfield & Thompson, 2005).

RELATIONSHIP BETWEEN CRIMINAL THOUGHT CONTENT AND PROCESS

Whereas data on the CTCI continue to be collected, the only sample for which there is complete data is the original CTCI validation sample (Walters & Morgan, 2018). This sample of 791 college students (mean age = 19.05 years, 64% female) completed the CTCI and had scores on all three subscales—NAA, PAD, and CID—completed the PICTS, and rated themselves on a 15-item delinquency measure modeled after Huizinga et al.'s (1991) Self-Reported Offending (SRO) scale. The CTCI total score and GCT were found to correlate highly ($r = .62$) and each of the CTCI scales correlated slightly better with the PICTS PCT scale than with the PICTS RCT scale

(NAA = .44 versus .37, PAD = .50 versus .43, CID = .62 versus .51). A two-step regression analysis revealed that the CTCI correlated significantly with the SRO, $F(8, 780) = 75.20$, $p < .001$, even after age, sex, race, PCT, and RCT had been controlled, although only the PAD and CID scales achieved individual-level significance ($p < .05$). Further analysis revealed a significant GCT × CTCI interaction in which substantially higher levels of offending were reported by participants who produced elevated scores on both the GCT and CTCI. These results indicate that the CTCI, despite being slightly better aligned with PCT than RCT, provides useful information above and beyond a measure of criminal thought process (i.e., PICTS).

Several studies have also investigated whether criminal thought content, as assessed with measures of the perceived wrongfulness of antisocial behavior or negative attitudes toward the police, and criminal thought process, as assessed with a neutralization scale, might complement one another. Conducting a secondary analysis of data from the National Youth Survey, Walters (2016c) determined that both criminal thought content (attitudes toward deviance) and criminal thought process (neutralization) mediated the peer influence effect (peer delinquency → participant delinquency). Based on these preliminary findings, it could be argued that criminal thought content and criminal thought process are equally capable of mediating the peer influence effect and that both manifestations of criminal thought are learned in association with delinquent peers. Several years later, another secondary analysis was performed (Walters, 2020h), this time using data from the Gang Resistance Education and Training (GREAT) survey. In this study, criminal thought content was represented by negative attitudes toward the police and criminal thought process was represented by a neutralization scale similar to the one used in Walters (2016c). Employing four waves of data instead of three, it was discovered that the pathway running from peer delinquency to negative attitudes toward the police to neutralization to delinquency was significant whereas the pathway running from peer delinquency to neutralization to negative attitudes toward the police to delinquency was not. In this study, the order of the two cognitive mediators made a difference because only criminal thought content was effectively predicted by peer delinquency and only neutralization effectively predicted delinquency. At least where this study is concerned, criminal thought content made a better first-stage mediator and criminal thought process made a better second-stage mediator.

THOUGHT AND EMOTION

In studies that have pitted cognitive variables like RCT and cognitive-affective variables like hostility against purely emotional variables like anger, the cognitive and cognitive-affective variables have usually been found to serve as effective mediators of crime-relevant relationships, whereas emotional variables like anger have not (Walters & Espelage, 2017, 2018b). These results are inconsistent with predictions from general strain theory, which holds that anger is of paramount importance when it comes to mediating crime-relevant relationships (Agnew, 1992; Broidy, 2001). It is still possible, however, that like criminal thought process and criminal thought content, criminal thinking and emotion are in some ways collective, interactive, or reciprocal. Thornberry (1987) has long emphasized the salience of reciprocity in criminological research. Although reciprocity does not occur in all situations, it has been found to exist in a wide variety of criminological contexts (Andrews et al., 2017; Gearhart & Tucker, 2020; Yoo, 2017). Consequently, it may explain how emotions are able to alter variable relationships in some contexts but not others. As was reported in an earlier chapter, reciprocity has already proven its utility in charting the bidirectional relationship believed to exist between parenting and child misbehavior whereby negative parenting encourages child misbehavior and child misbehavior evokes or elicits negative parenting (Abar et al., 2014; Zhang et al., 2020).

There are at least two ways in which criminal thinking and emotion may be linked reciprocally; one is through an antagonistic process that places thought and emotion at cross-purposes. Walters (2020k) detected an antagonistic process in a secondary analysis of data from the previously mentioned GREAT study. According to the results of this study, anticipated guilt for engaging in antisocial behavior inhibited future PCT, as measured with a neutralization scale, and PCT deactivated guilt. The key finding was that emotion was just as effective in neutralizing cognition as cognition was in neutralizing emotion. Guilt and PCT represent two of the three elements of conscience—self-conscious emotions and moral reasoning, respectively. Self-conscious emotions like guilt, remorse, and regret can lead to change by allowing the individual an introspective glimpse into their behavior. PCT does just the opposite. Regardless of which PCT style the individual enacts—mollification, entitlement, power orientation, or superoptimism—the end result is an externalization of responsibility where other people, outside circumstances, or fate is blamed for one's bad decisions and destructive behavior. Guilt and remorse are opposites of PCT, entailing awareness of having violated accepted norms and moral values. It therefore makes sense that guilt would inhibit the false premise of PCT, and that PCT would impede the corrective action of guilt.

A second way criminal thought and emotion may be linked is through a complementary process. This is illustrated in a recent study by Walters and Espelage (2021) in which RCT (cognitive impulsivity) and anger were found to complement one another. In this study, RCT and anger were crossed at

Waves 1 and 2 of the Illinois Study of Bullying and Sexual Violence (ISBSV) and correlated with bullying perpetration at Wave 3. Results indicated that both cross-lagged correlations were significant and the second variable in each sequence predicted a change in bullying behavior. Thus, while both PCT-guilt cross-lags predicted a change in delinquency in Walters (2020k), both RCT-anger cross-lags predicted a change in bullying in Walters and Espelage (2021). The main difference between the two studies was that the cross-lagged variables in Walters (2020k) countered one another, whereas the cross-lagged variables in Walters and Espelage (2021) complemented one another. More to the point, there was reciprocity between variables and this reciprocity appeared to benefit the overall relationship, making all four cross-lags significant predictors of their respective outcomes. Hence, while emotions like anger may not be the principal mediators of criminological relationships, in part because they are less stable and enduring than cognitive and cognitive-affective variables, they may still play a role in criminological relationships because of the reciprocal bonds they form with cognition.

CONCLUSION

From Plato to Bandura and from Aristotle to Sykes and Matza, cognitive variables have a storied history in science, and as such, a great deal to offer the field of criminology in terms of explaining both crime and criminality. Their value can be traced to the fact that they are able to assume any one of the four roles in a triad—independent variable, dependent variable, mediator variable, and moderator variable—because they are sufficiently stable to predict most variables and sufficiently malleable to be predicted by these same and other variables. Flexibility aside, cognition's greatest contribution to the study of criminality may be as an intervening variable in a mediating triad, whereas its greatest contribution to the study of crime may be its ability to moderate the certainty-offending relationship. The social variables described in chapter 3 often initiate the criminality process by serving as independent variables in a triad. Cognitive and some affective variables take over from here by connecting the social variables to crime-related outcomes like delinquency and adult offending. Developmental variables, in turn, promote a moderation effect by exposing the development roots of these relationships and clarifying the context under which the resulting triads flourish. These developmental variables may be even more important when it comes to explaining crime. It is no coincidence, then, that development serves as the chief topic of discussion in the next chapter of this book.

Chapter 5

Developmental Foundations of a Criminal Lifestyle

"Growth and Change Are Inherently Human"

The essence of development is growth and change. Whether we are studying a single-celled organism or a 30 trillion-celled human, there is no getting around the fact that all living organisms, no matter how simple or complex, grow, change, and develop over time. A criminal lifestyle also demonstrates growth and change over regular intervals and time periods, and so in no small way shares features in common with a living organism. Several of these features are examined in this chapter as part of a more general discussion on development. One goal of this chapter, then, is to illustrate how the structure and function of a criminal lifestyle can be described in developmental terms. A second goal is to clarify the role of antecedent conditions like bullying, animal cruelty, and firesetting in shaping and promoting a criminal lifestyle through the context of developmental change. The initial emphasis of this chapter, however, will be on the change-stability paradox and how we can go about resolving this paradox. As a secondary objective, we might also be able gain insight into the developmental origins of a criminal lifestyle in the process.

THE CHANGE-STABILITY PARADOX

Most traditional positivist theories favor stability over change when it comes to explaining crime and criminality; when a change does occur, these theories usually ascribe it to environmental factors like differential opportunity and situational strain. With the rise of developmental and lifespan theories of crime, however, there has been increased awareness and acceptance of change as a fundamental part of the process that gives rise to serious antisocial behavior. Such theories hold that criminal behavior changes in both the long and short term. Even advocates of crime stability acknowledge that crime rates vary widely over the life course, as exemplified by the age-crime curve. It is noteworthy that Hirschi and Gottfredson (1983), two of the staunchest proponents of crime stability, characterize the age-crime connection as one of the few brute facts in criminology. In this opening section, we will examine change and stability in criminal offending, with an eye toward integrating these two interpretations into a single perspective capable of advancing our understanding of crime and criminality, with a particular emphasis on crime.

Change in Crime: The Age-Crime Curve

Recognition of the age-crime connection goes back nearly 200 years to the Belgian astronomer, mathematician, and sociologist Adolphe Quetelet (1796–1874). In 1831, Quetelet, a pioneer in crime statistics, discovered that crime differed significantly by age in what is known today as the age-crime curve. Using statistics that were revolutionary at the time, he was able to show that crime grew rapidly during early adolescence, peaked in mid- to late adolescence, and gradually declined as the individual moved through adulthood. Although not really known at the time, the effect has since been found to be invariant across sex, race, time, country, offense type, and measurement strategy (self-report versus official data). This is what Hirschi and Gottfredson (1983) meant when they said that the age-crime curve was a brute fact of criminology. Figure 5.1 depicts the age-crime curve in a moderately sized sample of London working-class males using official data (Farrington, 2005) and figure 5.2 models the age-crime curve in a small-sized sample of American female delinquents using self-report data (Mulvey, 2012). Although the two curves are not identical, they both display a noticeable peak around age 16 or 17 and a clear drop-off in early adulthood. In both cases, the age-crime curve consists of two legs: an ascending leg on the left and a descending leg on the right.

The left or ascending leg of the age-crime curve starts when there is little crime (late childhood) and follows a sharp upward trajectory which then peaks in mid- to late adolescence. This leg of the age-crime curve indicates that early to mid-adolescence is when delinquency often begins, or at least accelerates in frequency and severity. Using data from the Seattle Social Development Project, Farrington and colleagues (2003) observed a significant increase in the prevalence and frequency of official and self-reported offending between the ages of 11 and 12 and then again between the ages of 12 and 13. This study does not explain, however, why offending jumps during the transition from childhood to adolescence. What may be behind this sudden increase in criminality that shows up as a rapidly upwardly sloping

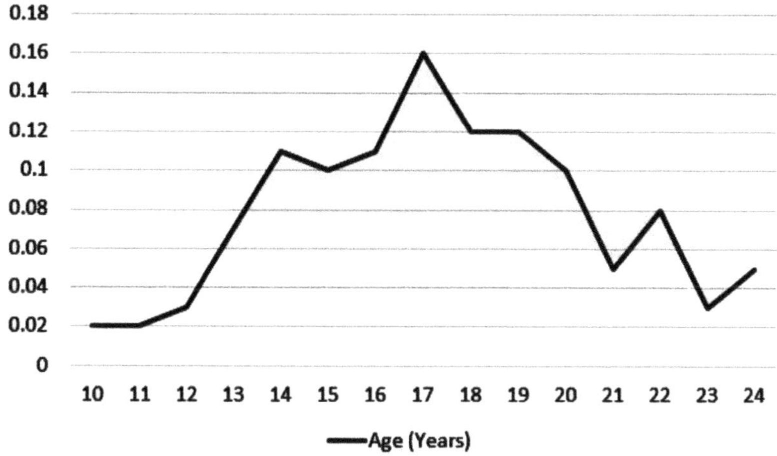

Figure 5.1 Average Number of Convictions in Boys from the Cambridge Study of Delinquent Development between the Ages of 10 and 24 (*N* = 411; Farrington, 2005). *Source*: Created by author using data from Cambridge Study of Delinquent Development, Farrington, 2005.

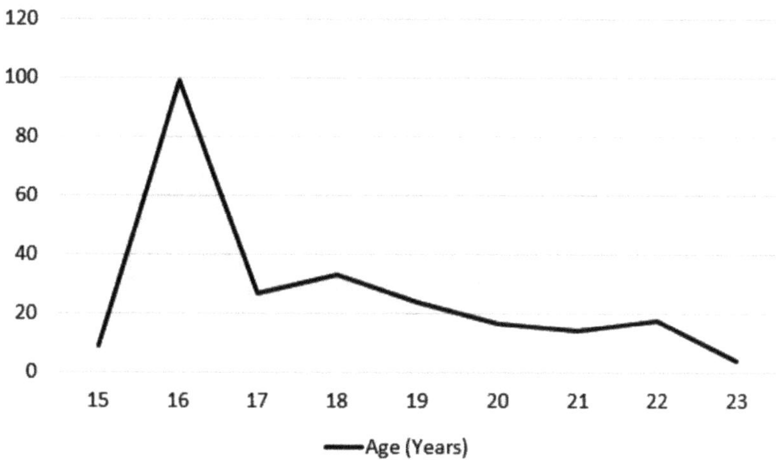

Figure 5.2 Average Number of Self-Reported Offenses in Girls from the Pathways to Desistance Study between the Ages of 15 and 23 (*N* = 184; Mulvey, 2012). *Source*: Created by author using data from Pathways to Desistance Study, Mulvey, 2012.

left side of the age-crime curve? Early adolescence is a period of growing independence and rebellion. Although parents continue to exert a powerful influence over their early adolescent offspring, peers begin to exert an equally important influence, and this influence is usually more negative than that of the parents (Brown & Bakan, 2011; Walters, 2020s). It is also during early adolescence that children begin to rebel against parental control and assert their independence. Rebellion, it is now known, can raise the odds of future delinquency by interfering with parental supervision (Le Blanc et al., 1998). The change, I would argue, is mediated by a change in cognition.

The right or descending leg of the age-crime curve starts at the peak age of offending (mid- to late adolescence) and gradually declines as the individual nears adulthood. This part of the age-crime curve implies that criminality may respond to internal and external exigencies. Internally, most individuals show signs of increased psychosocial maturity as they make their way through adolescence into adulthood; this can then lead to reduced antisocial behavior of either a callous-unemotional (Simmons et al., 2020) or impulsive (Riggs Romaine, 2019) nature. Externally, reduced opportunities for antisocial behavior and increased opportunities for prosocial behavior (Ayers et al., 1999), as well as a rise in the perceived certainty of getting caught (Walters, 2018b), have all been found to predict crime deceleration and desistance in late adolescence. Gottfredson and Hirschi (1990), in their general theory of crime, assert that relative self-control does not change after age 8 or 9, but absolute self-control does, improving as the youth's thinking matures and opportunities for crime dry up. Reduced opportunities for crime and a growing awareness of the more serious consequences the person faces should they get caught for adult criminality are part of the cognitive changes that occur during emerging adulthood that lead to a significant drop in offending.

Stability in Crime: Crime Continuity and Psychological Inertia

Crime stability has been championed by a large cross-section of criminologists. Some of the earliest theories of crime, in fact, made strong stability assumptions. Early biological theories of crime, such as Lombroso's (1876/2008) born criminal and Goring's (1913) mathematical-statistical model, and more recent efforts to develop genetic theories of crime (Mednick et al., 1984) and models that combine the effects of biology and sociology (Beaver et al., 2015) have treated crime as a stable concept. Models based on personality trait theory likewise make strong stability assumptions. Researchers applying the five-factor model to criminality report that offenders consistently demonstrate low levels of agreeableness and conscientiousness (Jones et al., 2011; Ruiz et al., 2008). Such traits, by definition, should remain stable. The crime stability argument has even been advanced by a few sociologists. Gottfredson and Hirschi (1987), as a case in point, have argued against widespread use of longitudinal research designs in criminology based, in part, on the belief that criminality is sufficiently stable to be adequately studied using less expensive cross-sectional designs. Nearly all of the arguments made in support of crime stability, whether originating from biologists, psychologists, or sociologists, assume crime continuity.

Crime continuity is based on the assumption that past crime is a strong predictor of future crime. As such, those who have committed crime in the past are at greatest risk of committing crime in the future. This is an assumption that has received an impressive array of empirical support (Farrington, 1998; McCord & Ensminger, 1997). The main question surrounding crime continuity is not whether it exists but why it exists. Nagin and Paternoster (2000) contend that the two most likely explanations for crime continuity are population heterogeneity and state dependence. The population heterogeneity interpretation of crime continuity holds that some individuals have a greater propensity for crime than other individuals and that this time-stable propensity makes it more likely that those with the propensity will engage in past, present, and future crime. Gottfredson and Hirschi's (1990) general theory of crime adopts a population heterogeneity interpretation of crime continuity, with low self-control serving as the propensity variable. The state dependence interpretation of crime continuity maintains that committing a crime early on transforms the individual's life circumstances, creating a contagion effect that places the individual at increased risk for future offending and arrest. Labeling theory (Lemert, 1967) would be an example of a theory that adopts a state dependence interpretation of crime continuity.

Without dismissing the population heterogeneity and state dependence interpretations of crime continuity, Walters offered a third interpretation, which he referred to as psychological inertia. According to this interpretation of the past crime-future crime relationship, certain thinking patterns, stimulated by criminal activity, serve as the source of future offending. Testing this supposition in a group of 673 mid- to late-adolescent British youth, Walters (2016h) determined that reactive criminal thinking (RCT), but not proactive criminal thinking (PCT), mediated the past offending-future offending relationship. It was theorized that the effect would be limited to RCT because RCT is seen as more responsive to criminal offending than PCT. In other words, RCT, being an innate feature of human cognition and the product of disinhibition, should be more easily stimulated by crime participation than PCT, a cognitive process that is learned through one's interactions with others, particularly peers. These results were replicated in a sample of 1,354 adjudicated delinquents (Walters, 2019h) and 1,161 early adolescents (Walters & Espelage, 2018a). In the latter study, the past bullying-future bullying relationship was mediated by cognitive impulsivity, the developmental antecedent to RCT, but not by cognitive insensitivity, the developmental antecedent to PCT. In all three studies the difference, as predicted, was that initial offending predicted RCT/cognitive impulsivity but not PCT/cognitive insensitivity (see also, Morris & Cope, 2012). Although PCT does not appear to be involved in psychological inertia, another cognitive variable central to the PCT-mediated moral model of lifestyle criminality is, that being, low self-efficacy for a conventional lifestyle (Walters, 2018f, 2018g).

Integrating Change and Stability

As previously noted, Gottfredson and Hirschi (1990) accept the age-crime curve as a brute fact of criminology despite espousing a population heterogeneity interpretation of crime stability. They reason that while absolute self-control improves as youth transition from adolescence to adulthood, there is little change in self-control relative to one's age-mates once the individual reaches the age of 8 or 9. The reason why youth and adults with low relative self-control do not continuously commit crime, according to Gottfredson and Hirschi, is that crime requires opportunity and not all situations provide adequate opportunities for crime, particularly as the individual grows older. Aging consequently decreases but does not eliminate offending in those predisposed to crime by virtue of a latent trait like low self-control. Terrence Thornberry's (1987) interactive theory, by comparison, emphasizes development and change rather than stability and opportunity. As laid out by Thornberry, the factors binding the individual to conventional society shift as the youth moves through adolescence. In early adolescence, the family is the most important factor tying the child to conventional society and shielding them from delinquency. During middle adolescence, delinquency is prevented by immersing oneself in positive peer associations, school, and youth culture. By the time the youth has reached late adolescence or early adulthood the emphasis changes once again, this time to a person's belief in conventional values and commitment to conventional activities. Sampson and Laub (1993), on the other hand, account for stability in development using the concept of cumulative disadvantage in which prior offending knifes off opportunities for a conventional lifestyle.

When attempting to understand how change and stability can be incorporated into a criminal lifestyle, it is helpful to remember that criminal thinking and antisocial attitudes serve as stable dynamic risk factors (Bonta & Andrews, 2017). What that means is that while these processes change, the change is usually slow and gradual, although there are times when it can be more rapid. For instance, the rise in delinquency that occurs in early adolescence and is part of the left or ascending leg of the age-crime curve is relatively swift. During early adolescence, the drive for independence, identity, and peer acceptance leads to risk-taking behavior on the part of many youth (Karaman, 2013). This, in turn, can give rise to antiauthority, if not antisocial, thinking. It is the growth of this type of thinking that could serve as further impetus for crime acceleration at this age. Crime deceleration and desistance are usually more gradual and extended processes, with roots in both late adolescence and early adulthood. Even so, cognitive factors are viewed as playing a vital role here as well. Reductions in criminal thinking, brought on by increased awareness of the certainty of punishment for crimes committed as an adult, may be particularly instrumental in promoting deceleration and desistance (Walters, 2020c). As a stable dynamic risk factor, criminal thinking is both stable and dynamic. It is the dynamic part that helps explain the age-crime curve and the developmental transitions described by Thornberry (1987), and it is the stable part that gives rise to crime continuity by way of psychological inertia.

STRUCTURE AND FUNCTION OF A CRIMINAL LIFESTYLE

Structure

The structure of a criminal lifestyle can be broken down into two parts: the behavioral styles used to define the lifestyle and the developmental stages that mark changes in the lifestyle. In the case of a criminal lifestyle there are four behavioral styles and four developmental stages, all eight of which are described next.

Behavioral Styles

The behavioral styles that define a criminal lifestyle are irresponsibility, self-indulgence, interpersonal intrusiveness, and social rule breaking. With irresponsibility, comes failure to meet personal and social obligations and a strong sense of unaccountability at school, at work, and in the home. Personal relationships are strained and sometimes lost as a result of this style. Self-indulgence drives the individual to seek immediate gratification, which is temporarily satisfied with substance use, sexual promiscuity, and compulsive gambling, but never fully sated. Interpersonal intrusiveness concerns the violation of the rights and personal space of others. This can be expressed in a number of ways, two of the more popular being charges of domestic violence and convictions for various forms of aggressive criminality. Finally, social rule breaking is marked by early and frequent violation of the rules and laws of society. These four behavioral styles can be assessed along a continuum of increasing or decreasing lifestyle involvement, commitment, and identification. These styles, like the thinking styles, that support them, are both stable and dynamic.

The four behavioral styles that define a criminal lifestyle can be assessed with the Lifestyle Criminality Screening Form (LCSF: Walters et al., 1991), a 14-item chart audit procedure that can be completed in 10 minutes provided there is a pre-sentence investigation (PSI) report available on which to base the ratings. A confirmatory factor analysis revealed that a four-factor model organized around the four LCSF subsections (irresponsibility, self-indulgence, interpersonal intrusiveness, social rule breaking) achieved a significantly better fit than a one-factor model in which all 14 items were loaded onto a single factor (Walters, 1997a). The inter-rater reliability of the LCSF is good, the internal consistency moderate, and the test-retest reliability excellent (Walters, 1998a). Validity studies have produced mixed results, however. While the LCSF may not be particularly effective in predicting institutional adjustment (Walters, 2005, 2007c), it does an adequate to good job of predicting re-offense in community supervised parolees and probationers (Walters, 2021k; Walters et al., 1990; Walters & McDonough, 1998) and recidivism in released prison inmates (Kroner & Mills, 2001; Walters, 2011b; Walters & Chlumsky, 1993).

Although the four behavioral styles that mark a criminal lifestyle are operationally defined by specific behaviors found in a PSI, they were originally derived from the thinking styles identified when criminal lifestyle theory was first formulated back in the late 1980s (Walters & White, 1989b). These thinking styles were either borrowed from Yochelson and Samenow's (1977) criminal personality model or were adopted from the author's clinical work with maximum security federal prison inmates at the United States Penitentiary in Leavenworth, Kansas. Shortly after being identified, the thinking styles were paired and analyzed for the purpose of creating behavioral styles that might be useful in defining the parameters of a criminal lifestyle. The erratic thinking styles of cognitive indolence and discontinuity, for instance, gave rise to the behavioral style of impulsivity. The egoistic thinking styles of sentimentality and superoptimism were merged to create self-indulgence. The aggressive thinking styles of entitlement and power orientation were used to craft the interpersonal intrusiveness behavioral style. Finally, the rebellious thinking styles of mollification and cutoff were instrumental in constructing the social rule breaking behavioral style. In each case, the behavioral styles were a function of previously identified criminal thinking styles (see figure 5.3).

Stages of a Criminal Lifestyle

Criminal lifestyle theory divides a criminal lifestyle into four stages: the pre-criminal stage, the early criminal stage, the advanced criminal stage, and the stage of burnout and maturity. Transitions taking place between stages illustrate the dynamic and developmental nature of a criminal lifestyle and personify the role of cognition in the unfolding antisocial behavior. Like the

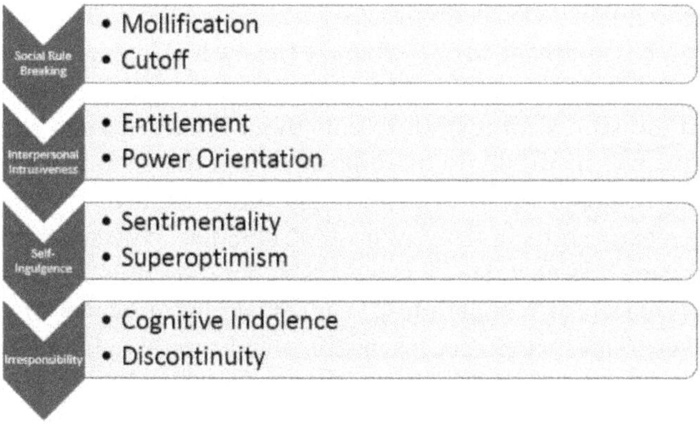

Figure 5.3 The Relationship Originally Proposed to Exist between Criminal Thinking and Criminal Behavior. *Source*: Created by author using data from Walters and White, 1989b.

behavioral styles used to define a criminal lifestyle, the four stages of lifestyle development are grounded in behavior, although it should be noted that it is the underlying thought patterns and processes that are of utmost importance when investigating the criminal lifestyle, because they drive the transitions and give rise to the developmental progressions that lifestyle theory partitions into four stages. In describing each stage, both the behaviors and supporting cognitions will be discussed as part of the developmental context of a criminal lifestyle.

The main theme of the pre-criminal stage of criminal lifestyle development is experimentation. It is during this stage that the individual tries out and tests antisocial behavior as a means of dealing with a constantly changing environment. These antisocial behaviors and their supporting cognitions are usually learned through interaction with friends, neighbors, schoolmates, and older siblings who have previously been involved in committing various antisocial, delinquent, and criminal acts. Motives for offending at this stage of a criminal lifestyle derive from excitement, control, rebellion, and the desire to assert one's independence from adults, particularly parents. There are no clear age guidelines for any of the stages, although individuals usually enter the pre-criminal stage in early to mid-adolescence. The most important cognitive development during this stage is the ascension of developmental antecedents to PCT and RCT, cognitive insensitivity and cognitive impulsivity, respectively. These pre-criminal thinking patterns lay the foundation for later cognitive changes that will then transition to a second and more criminally involved stage of criminal lifestyle development.

Whereas the main theme of the first or pre-criminal stage of a criminal lifestyle is experimentation, the principal theme of the second or early criminal stage is commitment. The defining characteristic of the early criminal stage is a growing commitment to the criminal lifestyle. Although the frequency and severity of criminal involvement often rise during this stage, the greatest changes are seen with respect to cognition. First, outcome expectancies for crime become increasingly more positive and outcome expectancies for conventional behavior become increasingly more negative. In other words, the balance clearly shifts in favor of positive outcome expectancies for crime. Second, efficacy expectancies for crime ("I'm good at crime") increase, while efficacy expectancies for noncrime ("I cannot imagine ever working a regular job") decrease. Third, cognitive insensitivity and cognitive impulsivity begin to evolve into the criminal thinking patterns of PCT and RCT, respectively. As commitment to a criminal lifestyle grows, so too do PCT and RCT.

The third stage of a criminal lifestyle is marked by near total commitment to a criminal lifestyle in what is commonly referred to as the maintenance or advanced stage of criminal lifestyle involvement. Maintenance means that most of the individual's thoughts and actions are geared toward defending, reinforcing, and advancing the criminal lifestyle. The word that best describes the advanced stage of criminal lifestyle development is compulsive. Hirschi (1969) has argued that crime is least likely when attachment, commitment, involvement, and belief in a conventional lifestyle are strong. Instead of emphasizing attachment, commitment, involvement, and belief in conventional relationships and institutions, criminal lifestyle theory stresses attachment, commitment, involvement, and belief in a criminal lifestyle. As the lifestyle progresses, the thinking behind the behavior becomes progressively more automatic, ingrained, and crystalized. Positive outcome expectancies for crime predominate over negative outcome expectancies, self-efficacy for crime exceeds self-efficacy for conventional behavior, and both the process and content of criminal cognition are at peak levels. Periodic doubts about the wisdom of continuing in the lifestyle are quickly dismissed as fear of change replaces fear of consequences in the minds of those most heavily committed to and obsessed with a criminal lifestyle.

Desistance is common during the pre-criminal stage, less common during the early criminal stage, and exceedingly rare during the advanced criminal stage. Dropping out of crime during the pre- or early criminal stages can be the result of maturity, increased opportunities for conventional behavior, decreased opportunities for crime, and changing perceptions of the certainty or severity of punishment (Rocque, 2017). By the time the individual reaches the advanced stage of criminal development, however, desistance may require an additional boost. More often than not, that boost comes from burnout, which can be defined as the physical and psychological drain of dealing with the accumulating negative consequences of a criminal lifestyle (Cusson & Pinsonneault, 1986; Paternoster & Bushway, 2009; Shover, 1983). Most of the research that has been done on burnout in the criminal justice field addresses burnout among police, correctional, and parole/probation officers (see Rhineberger-Dunn et al., 2017), but the lifestyle can also serve as a source of burnout for chronic offenders. This, in combination with maturity and changing perceptions of one's chances of getting caught and punished, leads to a significant reduction in offending in long-term follow-ups like the one conducted by Sampson and Laub (2003). This is referred to as the stage of burnout and maturity.

Function

The criminal lifestyle serves a variety of functions. Chief among these are meaning, continuity, predictability, and pleasure. In this chapter we explore each of these functions in an effort to gain a better understanding of the different roles a criminal lifestyle can play in a person's life.

Meaning

Viktor Frankl—psychiatrist, existential philosopher, author, and holocaust survivor—is best remembered for his work on logotherapy and his belief in meaning as the prime motive for human survival. Frankl viewed "will to sex" as Freud's principal contribution to psychiatry and "will to power" as Adler's principal contribution. In considering his own contribution, Frankl would often point to "will to meaning." Finding meaning in a situation, even if that situation is as dire as internment in a Nazi concentration camp, frees the person from their existential condition and affords them hope and a chance at survival (Frankl, 2000). The type of meaning a criminal lifestyle provides an individual is nothing like the meaning Frankl used to survive Auschwitz, Dachau, and a half dozen other Nazi concentration camps. The meaning provided by a criminal lifestyle is shallow, superficial, and contrived but at least it partially satisfies the human need for "will to meaning." It does so by funneling information to two belief systems that serve as the primary sources of life meaning: a person's self-view, followed by their world-view.

As described by Walters (2006a), the self-view is composed of five core elements: reflected appraisals, social comparisons, self-representations, role identities, and possible selves. Reflected appraisals are a person's perception of how they are viewed by others; these reflected appraisals can then give rise to self-appraisals or how the person perceives themselves. Social comparisons entail making upward, downward, or parallel comparisons with people and groups the individual aspires to, feels superior to, or considers their equal, respectively. Self-representations are the personal qualities or environmental artifacts with which a person identifies. The roles a person enacts are also key elements of a person's self-view. Finally, possible selves are the goals, values, and behaviors a person sees themselves actualizing sometime in the future. A criminal lifestyle provides the ingredients for the self-view, but in the case of a criminal lifestyle the self-view is primarily negative, constrained, and self-destructive. A criminal lifestyle is likely to be characterized by reflected appraisals as a delinquent or criminal, upward comparisons with notorious criminals and downward comparisons with noncriminals, self-representations that highlight past criminal exploits, role identities that focus on self to the exclusion of others, and possible selves as a successful criminal and source of fear to others.

Like the self-view, a person's world-view offers insight into the meaning they attach to their experience. Lifestyle theory proposes that a person's world-view is composed of four bipolar dimensions. The first dimension mechanicism versus organicism contrasts a mechanistic world-view with one that is integrated and holistic. The second dimension agenticism versus fatalism positions a world filled with options, possibilities, and choices against one dominated by forces outside the person's control. The third dimension fairness versus inequity juxtaposes a view of the world as fair versus one that sees the world as unjust, unfair, and biased against them. The fourth dimension malevolence versus benevolence balances a view where people's worst impulses are emphasized with one in which people's best impulses are highlighted. There is no single world-view common to all or even most individuals functioning in a criminal lifestyle, yet some patterns are more likely than others. Given the unyielding and manipulative nature of a criminal lifestyle, mechanistic, fatalistic, inequitable, and malevolent themes are more likely to be expressed than organic, agentic, fairness, and benevolent themes. In fact, high scores on mechanicism, inequity, and malevalence have been found to correlate with criminal thinking (Walters, 2007a). Moreover, the cognitive schemes that comprise the self- and world-views of offenders tend to be rigid, inflexible, and poorly integrated.

Continuity

A second function of a criminal lifestyle is continuity. By emphasizing cross-temporal stability, the criminal lifestyle provides the individual with reassurance that current knowledge and relationships will endure beyond the present moment. Earlier, in a discussion on the change-stability paradox, it was argued that change and stability not only coexist, they may actually complement one another. In the current section, we examine the importance of stability in protecting a person's psychological well-being. The reassurance provided by stability has the power to reduce negative affect (Sandstrom & Huerta, 2013). Fear of change is one expression of negative affect that can be effectively managed by integrating continuity and stability. A fear of change scale has been developed for the Psychological Inventory of Criminal Thinking Styles (PICTS) which has been found to possess adequate internal consistency (Walters, 2001a) and good construct validity (Walters & Geyer, 2007). In further analyzing their data, Walters and Geyer discovered that inmates dropping out of a cognitive behavioral intervention scored significantly higher on the PICTS fear of change scale than inmates who completed the intervention.

The cognitive underpinnings of continuity can be observed in the relationships that form between the three temporally ordered belief systems of past-view, present-view, and future-view. The past-view encompasses a person's attitude toward the past, their own past as well as the historical past. The present-view, on the other hand, is the belief system that interacts most directly with the environment through its sensory-perceptual and executive functions. The future-view is what the individual anticipates in both the immediate and distant future. Consistency between the three temporally ordered belief systems is what gives rise to continuity. The past is viewed through the lens of present perceptions and decisions, whereas the future is anticipated in light of both the past and the present. Consistency between the temporally ordered belief systems is sought because it is reassuring, even if it means distorting the past, present, or future to achieve such consistency. Cognitive consistency theories maintain that inconsistencies, whether between thoughts and behavior or between different thoughts, create imbalance and tension, which, in turn, motivate the individual to resolve the inconsistency by changing the thought, the behavior, or both (Brehm, 2007; Festinger, 1957). The same thing occurs when there are inconsistencies between the past-, present-, and future-views.

Predictability

Like continuity, predictability provides a person with a sense of security and reassurance. Another similarity between continuity and predictability is that each is balanced by an opposing force: change in the case of continuity and novelty in the case of predictability. The predictability-novelty tension or dialectic has been studied most extensively with interpersonal relationships where the parties to a relationship negotiate the degree to which they want the relationship to be new and spontaneous or old and familiar (Graham, 2003). Predictability-novelty also applies to lifestyles, in that all lifestyles provide a person with predictability but very little novelty. Even when someone in a criminal lifestyle attempts to create excitement by seeking out stimulating, exciting, and unfamiliar situations, a hallmark sign of novelty seeking, the unpredictability they exhibit is highly predictable. What I mean by this is that the excitement-seeking tendencies observed in a criminal lifestyle are not designed to expand the boundaries of a person's knowledge of self or others, but rather to stir things up as a means of achieving momentary gratification and sensory stimulation.

The imbalance observed between predictability and novelty in a criminal lifestyle, like the imbalance between continuity and change and the poorly integrated schemes that mark the self- and world-views, can be traced back to antisocial cognition. Criminal behavior is predictable because the thoughts behind it are rigid, inflexible, and overly simplistic. Instead of gathering information and advancing knowledge, its overriding purpose is to protect and defend the lifestyle against anything that may threaten it. Predictability is vital, however, to human survival. Homo sapiens have survived because they learned how to predict and manage their environment (Roberts & Stewart, 2018). Without being able to predict which plants were edible, which strangers were harmless, and which path led home, humankind would have gone extinct centuries ago. This said, there are two paths by which predictability is achieved: science and lifestyle. Scientific or empirical thinking uses systematic observation and testing to make sense of the world; lifestyle thinking imposes a preconceived cognitive map on the world and attempts to force the world to conform to the map. It is not difficult to see which approach has the greatest likelihood of supporting long-term survival.

Pleasure

While a case could be made for predictability's prominence in promoting survival, an explanatory mechanism is required. In searching for a mechanism there are certain questions that require answers. The first question that needs to be answered is how does predictability support survival? The answer to this question can be found in research on the neurophysiological foundations of reward and reinforcement. The philosophical underpinnings of this research go back several centuries to London, England, and the pioneering work of British philosopher and jurist Jeremy Bentham (1748–1832). The philosophical system that Bentham created is called "utilitarianism" and the central premise of utilitarianism is that people seek to maximize pleasure and minimize pain. Based on the prior writings of such luminaries as Francis Bacon, John Locke, and David Hume, Bentham's system sought to answer the age-old question of what drives people's behavior. In deciding whether to take a particular course of action a person, according to Bentham, weighs the anticipated pleasures against the anticipated pains and selects the option that they anticipate will provide them with the most pleasure and the least pain.

Bentham predated modern neurophysiology by more than a century, but his influence is still felt today. In determining how pleasure is represented neurophysiologically, scientists point to the excitatory neurotransmitter dopamine (DA). Research clearly indicates that subjective feelings of pleasure are associated with a rise in the release of DA from pathways projecting from the meso-limbic region of the brain to the prefrontal cortex (Hammond, 2014). DA is released whenever we engage in personal and species survival-enhancing activities like eating, drinking, fornication, and discovery, but it may be released in even greater amounts in response to such lifestyle-supporting activities as crime, gambling, and drug use (Buckholtz et al., 2010; Di Chiara & Imperato, 1988). Several interpretations of the DA-reward relationship have been offered, but the one that appears to have received the most support is the one that hypothesizes that DA creates a "wanting response" by focusing the organism's attention on reward-related stimuli (Berridge, 2007). Evolution has apparently equipped mammals and other vertebrates with a mechanism that connects survival-enhancing activities to pleasure and offers the organism, particularly the human organism, the opportunity to build new associations over time. Some of these associations involve the thinking behind the behavior and so criminal thinking may be just as rewarding as criminal behavior.

The pleasure created by the release of DA into the synapse can be highly reinforcing and a source of human survival. Left unchecked, however, the vigorous pursuit of pleasure and DA release can deplete natural stores of DA and make it difficult for the organism to cease the rewarding activity to the point of exhaustion, injury, or even death (Zald et al., 2009). Evolution, it would appear, has equipped the organism not only with an incentive system built around DA but also a disincentive or counter-control system built around the inhibitory neurotransmitter serotonin (5-hydroxytryptamine: 5-HT). Research indicates that 5-HT and DA have opposing effects on certain brain structures and the behaviors they control (Cupaioli et al., 2021; Narvaes & de Almeida, 2014). As such, 5-HT may be capable of balancing the excitatory effects of DA and along with DA, protect the organism's survival. A central concept in lifestyle theory, the life instinct, which when strained or challenged gives rise to existential fear, embodies aspects of both DA and 5-HT. DA aids the organism's survival by alerting the organism to survival-enhancing stimuli and encouraging survival-supporting behaviors; 5-HT aids the organism's survival by modulating excessive involvement in DA-driven activities. Hence, it is the dynamic balance of DA and 5-HT that is the key to survival, not DA alone. The criminal lifestyle does only the first part (pursuit of DA-enhancing stimuli and behaviors). In the absence of the second part (modulation by 5-HT), the lifestyle paradoxically puts the organism's survival at risk by virtue of its preoccupation with DA-enhancing activities.

DEVELOPMENTAL ANTECEDENTS

When exploring the developmental roots of a criminal lifestyle, it is imperative that we acknowledge, document, and discuss the childhood and early adolescent patterns that precede the lifestyle. Some of these patterns have been discussed previously as falling within the antisocial spectrum. In a very real sense, they can also be viewed as developmental antecedents to the criminal lifestyle. Three major developmental antecedents to a criminal lifestyle are reviewed in this section: school bullying, animal cruelty, and firesetting.

School Bullying

Our discussion on the developmental antecedents of a criminal lifestyle begins with school bullying. Ttofi et al. (2011) performed a meta-analysis using data from 28 longitudinal studies in which school bullying served as a predictor of delinquency, with a gap of several months to 11 years between predictor and outcome. Ttofi and colleagues observed a pooled odds ratio effect size of 2.50 (95% CI = 2.03, 3.08) when major childhood risk factors were not controlled and a pooled odds ratio effect size of 1.82 (95% CI = 1.55, 2.14) when major childhood risk factors were controlled. It was also noted that the effect was stronger in older youth than in younger youth. Prospective studies conducted since the Ttofi et al. meta-analysis have supported the general conclusion that bullying perpetration predicts future delinquency. Lösel and Bender (2014), for instance, detected a relationship between bullying at 9 years of age and self-reported aggression/violent offending at 13.7 years of age. Of particular note, the relationship was mitigated by several factors: to include consistent parental discipline and child intelligence, positive attitudes toward school, and prosocial behavior. In a more recent study, early adolescent school bullying was found to predict delinquency one year later, after controlling for the effects of age, sex, race, social support, bullying victimization, probullying attitudes, parental knowledge, child impulsivity, and peer delinquency (Walters & Espelage, 2019).

To serve as a causal or developmental antecedent to delinquency and crime, a variable must do more than correlate with and predict delinquent and criminal behavior. It should also fit within a nomological net of variables that have previously been found to support delinquency and crime. Of the two pathways proposed by lifestyle theory for delinquency and crime development, the proactive path would appear to be the one most relevant to bullying. Fearlessness, callous/unemotional traits, and low empathy are all considered key elements of early proactive criminal lifestyle development (Walters, 2017e). These same three factors have also been observed in school bullying, with bullying perpetration correlating positively with fearlessness (Panayiotou et al., 2015), callous-unemotional traits (Vaughn et al., 2011), and low empathy (Farrell & Vaillancourt, 2020). Given the perceived role of proactive factors in bullying, it is noteworthy that Walters (2019a) ascertained that the bullying-delinquency relationship was mediated by cognitive insensitivity (pro-bullying beliefs), the cognitive antecedent to PCT, but not cognitive impulsivity (self-reported impulsivity), the cognitive antecedent to RCT. On the other hand, cognitive impulsivity but not cognitive insensitivity has been found to mediate bullying continuity through psychological inertia (Walters & Espelage, 2018a), just as RCT but not PCT has been found to mediate crime continuity through psychological inertia (Walters, 2016h, 2019h).

Another parallel that can be drawn between delinquency and bullying is the existence of a bidirectional association between perpetration and victimization for both delinquency and bullying. Jennings et al. (2012) conducted a review of the literature on the relationship between crime victimization and perpetration, a pattern commonly referred to as victim-offender overlap. Of the 37 studies they reviewed, 31 offered robust support for victim-offender overlap and the other 6 reported weak or mixed results. In a meta-analysis of the literature on bullying victimization and perpetration, Walters (2020q) recorded a large pooled effect size ($r = .40$, 95% CI = .34, .45) for the concurrent relationship between bullying victimization and perpetration, and modest to moderate pooled effect sizes for the prospective victimization-perpetration ($r = .20$, 95% CI = .17, .24) and perpetration-victimization ($r = .21$, 95% CI = .17, .24) relationships. Other studies indicate that the victim-to-victimizer sequence is mediated by hostility and RCT in the crime context (Walters, 2020f) and by hostility in the bullying context (Walters & Espelage, 2018b), whereas the victimizer-to-victim sequence is a consequence of regular and close contact with delinquent (Walters, 2020i) and bullying (Walters, 2020s) peers, a process known as person proximity.

Animal Cruelty

Like school bullying, animal cruelty is more conducive to the planned, amoral, and instrumental aspects of crime, criminality, and criminal thinking than to the spontaneous, emotional, and expressive aspects. The animal cruelty-antisocial behavior literature has recently been covered in not one, but two reviews. In one paper, Chan and Wong (2019) reviewed 87 studies, the results of which revealed the presence of a strong link between child and adolescent animal cruelty and adult violent and nonviolent criminal behavior. Chan and Wong note that most of the children who engaged in animal cruelty had either witnessed or experienced domestic violence and that animal cruelty was more prominent in younger than in older children and in males than in females. Also, an earlier age of onset appeared to be prognostic of subsequent aggressive and general antisocial behavior. Reviewing this same literature, Longobardi and Badenes-Ribera (2019) identified a retrospective relationship between juvenile animal cruelty and adult interpersonal violence and a concurrent relationship between juvenile animal cruelty, bullying victimization/perpetration, and juvenile delinquency. The vast majority of studies in these two systematic reviews were cross-sectional or retrospective in nature which suggests a need for greater investment in longitudinal research.

Given its role as a developmental antecedent to the proactive features of a criminal lifestyle, animal cruelty should demonstrate nomological patterns similar to those found with school bullying. And for the most part, this is exactly what has been found. Just like school bullying, animal cruelty correlates moderately with fearlessness (Walters, 2017a), callous-unemotional traits (Vaughn et al., 2011), and lack of empathy (McPhedran, 2009). The previously reviewed Walters's (2019a) investigation determined that commensurate with bullying, the animal cruelty-delinquency relationship was mediated by cognitive insensitivity but not cognitive impulsivity. In an earlier study using data from this same sample of participants—that is, delinquents from the multi-wave Pathways to Desistance study—Walters (2014d) discovered that the association between childhood animal cruelty and future aggressive and nonaggressive delinquency was mediated by hostility and callous-unemotional traits. This would seem to suggest that as was noted with regards to school bullying, youth who engage in animal cruelty are confronting issues that lend themselves more to proactive forms of thought and behavior than reactive forms of thought and behavior.

Several theories have been advanced in an effort to account for the connection between child and adolescent animal cruelty and adult criminality. One of the more popular explanations for the animal cruelty-crime nexus is the violence graduation hypothesis. According to this hypothesis, a direct causal link connects animal cruelty to aggressive forms of antisocial behavior. This hypothesis further assumes that animal cruelty precedes violence and that the effect is specific to violent offending. A meta-analysis by Walters (2013), however, failed to support the second assumption in that animal cruelty was just as likely to support nonviolent offending as it was violent offending. Other possible explanations for the animal cruelty-crime relationship include the deviance generalization hypothesis, which maintains that youth who engage in animal cruelty also engage in other forms of deviant behavior such as delinquency and violence (Jesser & Jesser, 1977), and frustration theory, which holds that individuals who experience humiliation strike out in an effort to cope with the mounting frustration (Amsel, 1958). There is currently insufficient evidence to rule out either of these two hypotheses (Chan & Wong, 2019), and these and other theories, such as the overlapping lifestyles model, in which animal cruelty and offending are viewed as overlapping lifestyles with similar cognitive support systems (Walters & Noon, 2015), also deserve attention.

Firesetting

Whereas school bullying and juvenile animal cruelty are believed to interface primarily with proactive criminality, firesetting and other impulse control disorders are more likely to contribute to the reactive side of the criminal lifestyle equation. Firesetting constitutes one-third of Macdonald's (1961) sociopathic triad, which is composed of animal cruelty, bed-wetting, and firesetting and used by some psychiatrists to predict violent and aggressive criminality. Although the Macdonald triad itself has produced mostly equivocal findings when it comes to predicting violence and criminality, animal cruelty and firesetting have generally fared better when considered alone (Langevin, 2003). In a review of the literature on firesetting as a correlate and predictor of aggressive and violent behavior, Dolan et al. (2011) report that firesetting is associated with externalizing problems like conduct disorder, delinquency, aggression, hyperactivity, hostility, and impulsivity and that there are few meaningful differences between firesetters and other types of delinquents except for a greater interest in pyromania and poorer attentional skills in firesetting youth.

A study comparing the temperamental correlates of animal cruelty and firesetting confirmed that while animal cruelty correlated with fearlessness and failed to correlate with disinhibition, firesetting did just the opposite, correlating with disinhibition but not with fearlessness (Walters, 2017a). This is consistent with the supposition that animal cruelty reflects the proactive features of a criminal lifestyle, whereas firesetting reflects the reactive features. When a group of 133 children reported by their parents to have set one or more fires in the past year were compared to 34 children who only engaged in match play and 140 children who engaged in neither match play nor firesetting, several noteworthy differences surfaced. Firesetting youth were rated by their parents as exhibiting more internalizing and externalizing problems and as having more issues with impulsivity, aggression, and hostility than non-firesetting children, and rated themselves as more aggressive and impulsive than non-firesetting youth (Kolko & Kazdin, 1991). Employing a community sample of Australian youth, Martin et al. (2004) determined that self-reported firesetting was associated with elevated levels of conduct disorder, more extreme forms of antisocial behavior, excessive drug use, suicidal actions, and perceived school failure.

There are a variety of other impulse control disorders besides firesetting that may correlate with or predict delinquency, but there are no studies that have explored the proactive and reactive roots of a criminal lifestyle specific to other impulse control disorders. In a study conducted on a large sample of delinquent and non-delinquent adolescents, 99,602 male and female delinquent youth were compared to a matched group of non-delinquent youth (Barrett et al., 2013). Analyses revealed a strong connection between DSM-IV diagnoses of aggressive and impulse control disorders (i.e., antisocial personality, conduct disorder, disruptive behavior disorder, impulse control disorder not otherwise specified, oppositional defiant disorder) and the likelihood of a second arrest, the severity of the delinquency, and the age of delinquency onset. In fact, with a one-year reduction in age of onset there was a 25% increase in the likelihood of delinquency. There was also evidence that a public school classification of learning disability or emotional/behavioral disorder was predictive of delinquent outcomes on par with a DSM-IV diagnosis of an impulse control or aggressive disorder.

ORIGINS OF INDIVIDUAL CRIMINAL THOUGHT PATTERNS

Before concluding this chapter, I think it would be helpful to discuss the developmental origins of the seven criminal thinking styles that serve as building blocks for the proactive and reactive dimensions of criminal thought process. There was some discussion of this in chapter 4 in a section on assessing criminal thought process and content. Given that the PICTS may not be appropriate for use with juveniles and the juvenile version of the PICTS has not been properly validated, Walters (2020b) has advised researchers and clinicians to consider using existing measures of neutralization, moral disengagement, and positive outcome expectancies to assess youthful forms of PCT and measures of thrill/sensation seeking, hostile attribution biases, and temporal discounting to assess youthful forms of RCT. More than just finding ways to accurately assess the proactive and reactive dimensions in youth samples, it is important to understand the source of criminal thinking. The source or origin in this case is inadequate resolution of various developmental tasks that provide a lead-in to delinquency and crime (see table 5.1).

Mollification is the first of the four criminal thinking styles that contribute to proactive criminal thought process. Here, the developmental task is to accept responsibility and be accountable for one's actions (Karabanova et al., 2014). Unsuccessful resolution of this moral task can lead to blaming

Table 5.1 Developmental Tasks and Crime-Promoting Consequences of the Seven Thinking Styles That Form the Proactive and Reactive Dimensions of Criminal Thought Process

Thinking Style	*Dimension*	*Developmental Task*	*Crime-Promoting Consequences*
Mollification	PCT	Personal Accountability	Blaming Attributions and Other Biases
Entitlement	PCT	Theory of Mind and Perspective Taking	Low Empathy
Power Orientation	PCT	Internalization	Externalization
Superoptimism	PCT	Cause and Effect	Magical and Superstitious Thinking
Cutoff	RCT	Effortful Control	Weak Personal and Emotional Control
Cognitive Indolence	RCT	Critical Reasoning	Conspiratorial Thinking
Discontinuity	RCT	Selective and Sustained Attention	Easy Distractibility

Note: Thinking Style = specific criminal thinking style; Dimension = dimension of criminal thinking; PCT = proactive criminal thinking; RCT = reactive criminal thinking, Developmental Task = childhood developmental task that counters the thinking style; Crime-Promoting Consequences = result of not fully resolving the developmental task.
Source: Table created by author.

attributions and biases the individual then uses to evade responsibility for the bad decisions they make in life. The developmental task in the case of entitlement concerns developing a theory of mind (Schurz et al., 2020). Failure to fully appreciate that other people may not perceive the world or a specific event, the same way you do can lead to weak perspective taking and low empathy. The third PCT style is power orientation, with a developmental task of internalizing learning experiences, particularly moral lessons (Holodynski, 2013). Unsuccessful resolution of this task leads to a near exclusive focus on the external environment. Finally, there is superoptimism, a thinking style that develops as a consequence of failed causal learning (Sobel & Legare, 2014) and which can lead to magical and superstitious thinking and a distorted sense of morality.

Whereas morality served as the cardinal feature of the four PCT styles, executive function is the cardinal feature of criminal thinking styles that fall along the reactive dimension. Cutoff is the first of these RCT styles. The developmental task bearing most directly on the cutoff is effortful control (Lin et al., 2019). Deficits in executive function specific to effortful control are ordinarily expressed as weak behavioral and emotional restraint. A second criminal thinking style that falls into the reactive camp, cognitive indolence, touches on a different executive function. The developmental task that is distorted by cognitive indolence is critical reasoning (Di Lieto et al., 2020).

Unsuccessful resolution of the critical reasoning task can lead to uncritical acceptance of conspiracy theories and decisions based more on intuitive and faulty logic than on facts. The third and final thinking style known to contribute to RCT is discontinuity. The developmental task that counters discontinuity is the growth of sustained and selective attention, yet another executive function (Soleimani et al., 2020). Minus a strong reservoir of selective and sustained attention, the individual will be easily distracted and find it difficult to stay on track when pursuing various life goals.

CONCLUSION

Social, cognitive, and developmental factors clearly complement one another in the formation, expansion, and alteration of a criminal lifestyle. Whereas social (as well as biological) factors more often than not serve as initiating or independent variables and contribute primarily to criminality, cognitive factors are well-suited to the mediating role and contribute equally to criminality and crime, and developmental factors are often used as moderating variables and contribute primarily to crime, there is significant overlap in function between these three sets of factors. This is particularly true of cognitive and developmental factors, both of which can serve multiple functions. There are many studies, for instance, where cognition serves as a mediator between a social variable and delinquency, but there are other studies in which cognition is a moderator or is moderated by a social or developmental factor. The same can be said for developmental factors. Although developmental factors are good at establishing context, which makes them ideal as moderator variables, they can also serve as independent and mediating variables. As we move into the next section of chapters, we will see that biological, social, cognitive, and developmental factors contribute to the three main models of criminal lifestyle theory—the moral model of criminality, the control model of criminality, and the decision-making model of crime—starting with the moral model.

Section II

Chapter 6

The Moral Model of Lifestyle Criminality

"Learning Right from Wrong"

This chapter marks the beginning of a new section of the book. In section I, the focus was on trees, or more precisely, related groups or types of trees. The types of trees discussed in section I are biological factors, social and physical environmental factors, cognitive factors, and developmental factors. Each factor is believed to have a significant effect on criminality, crime, or both. Section II attempts to integrate these factors by organizing them into three models, two of which are designed to explain criminality (moral model of lifestyle criminality and control model of lifestyle criminality) and one of which is designed to explain crime (decision-making model of crime). These three models can be viewed as groves or sub-forests, more integrated than the biological, social, cognitive, and developmental factors described in section I but less integrated than the forest as discussed in section III.

As stated in chapter 2, if a criminological theory is to be considered comprehensive, it should be able to explain both crime and criminality. In an effort to do just that, criminal lifestyle theory has been partitioned into three explanatory models. The moral model, one half of a two-dimensional theory of criminality, serves as the centerpiece of the current chapter. Knowing the difference between right and wrong, the core question posed by the moral model is not knowledge that is inherent; instead, it is something that must be learned through interaction with the environment. Internalizing a coherent moral code acquired from family, friends, associates, and the electronic media will, according to lifestyle theory, greatly reduce a person's chances of engaging in future criminality. The current chapter begins by comparing lifestyle theory's views on moral relativism and moral universality. This is then followed by a discussion on conscience development and the moral model of lifestyle criminality. Finally, the chapter concludes with a case history designed to illustrate how the moral model can be used to explain the behavior of an individual offender.

MORAL RELATIVISM AND MORAL UNIVERSALISM

Moral relativism and moral universalism have been debated as least as far back as the ancient Greeks, with Sophists arguing for moral relativism and Stoics taking the side of moral universalism. The debate, in one form or another, has continued throughout history. In the second and third centuries AD, the Greek philosopher Sextus Empiricus developed a version of moral relativism that became popular with a group of philosophers known as the Pyrrhonian skeptics. As Europe entered the Middle Ages, moral relativism grew dormant, and it stayed that way until the seventeenth or eighteenth centuries when Enlightenment scholars like David Hume and Thomas Hobbes reawakened interest in relativism by arguing that morality had no objective standard (although neither advocated for moral relativism per se). Moral universalism, by contrast, remained strong from the Middle Ages through the Enlightenment, as represented first by the thirteenth-century compositions of Saint Thomas Aquinas, and later in the seventeenth and eighteenth centuries with the works of John Locke and Immanuel Kant. By denying the existence of universal truths and rejecting the idea that laws are applicable to all human beings, moral relativists embraced a postmodern view of morality. This contrasts with the natural law emphasis of moral universalism, in which systems of ethical principles are said to apply to all people, regardless of race, creed, color, culture, or sexual orientation.

Legal scholars often partition crimes into those that violate natural law (mala in se) and those that violate laws derived from legislative action (mala prohibita). The Latin term "mala in se" means wrong, bad, or evil in itself. Murder, rape, robbery, and incest are clear-cut examples of offenses that can be classified as mala in se. Throughout history and across cultures these behaviors have been deemed wrong and deserving of punishment. Jaywalking, public drunkenness, indecent exposure, and drug possession, on the other hand, would be classified as crimes based on mala prohibita. They are so classified because they are acts made illegal by legislation rather than being inherently bad or evil in and of themselves. Under the law, an individual can be charged with attempted murder or rape because these are mala in se offenses and mala in se offenses are characterized by harmful intent. You cannot, however, charge someone with attempting to engage in a mala prohibita offense because mala prohibita offenses lack harmful intent. With respect to moral relativism and universality, mala in se offenses are based on moral universality principles, whereas mala prohibita offenses tend to be grounded primarily in moral relativism principles. In reality, many offenses manifest features of both mala in se and mala prohibita. The moral issues raised in the current chapter are consequently centered around those offenses and offense features that are mala in se.

CONSCIENCE IN THREE PARTS

Using the analogy of a play or movie, it is possible to view the conscience as an entity composed of three acts or parts. Like a play, the parts are reasonably independent, yet build on each other to form a meaningful whole. The meaningful whole in this case is what is commonly referred to as conscience. The three acts in this play are empathy, self-conscious emotions, and moral reasoning (Schalkwijk et al., 2016). In his book *Without Conscience*, Robert Hare (1993) postulates that psychopathic individuals lack a serviceable conscience and that this is what drives their negative, antisocial, and criminal actions. I would argue that a failed or weak conscience applies to more than just those who have been diagnosed psychopathic. The psychopathic individual may fall at the high end of the amoral continuum, but there are non-psychopathic offenders who also inhabit the upper reaches of this continuum. In most cases, an offender's lack of conscience falls somewhere in the upper half of the amoral region and plays a significant role in their criminal behavior. Following in the tradition of mala in se offenses and behaviors as markers of a weak conscience, we now consider these three parts, starting with empathy.

Empathy

Empathy can be defined as a person's ability to understand, sense, and experience the thoughts, feelings, and perceptions of another. It also encompasses the ability to vicariously experience other people's emotions and see things from other's point of view. The evolutionary value of empathy is that it assists with the development of social relations and in so doing, enhances the individual's odds of survival. It is currently believed that empathy is composed of two parts or dimensions, referred to as affective empathy and cognitive empathy. Whereas affective empathy involves experiencing the emotions of another, cognitive empathy can be defined as the ability to identify the emotional state or perspective of another (Cuff et al., 2016). Co-experiencing another person's feelings would be an example of affective empathy, while adopting the viewpoint or perspective of another person, commonly referred to as perspective-taking, would be an example of cognitive empathy. Relationships tend to differ depending on whether one is examining the affective or cognitive element or dimension. The results of a recent meta-analysis revealed that affective empathy correlated positively with social anxiety in both clinical and general samples, whereas cognitive empathy correlated negatively with social anxiety, although only in clinical samples (Pittelkow et al., 2021). The results of a second meta-analysis disclosed that while affective empathy corresponded with activation of the posterior dorsomedial prefrontal gyrus and inferior frontal gyrus, cognitive empathy corresponded with activation of the anterior dorsomedial prefrontal gyrus and the supramarginal gyrus, the latter of which is located in the parietal lobe (Kogler et al., 2020). The results of these two meta-analyses indicate that affective and cognitive empathy are activated by different areas of the central nervous system and that they correlate differentially with outside criteria like social anxiety.

According to lifestyle theory, empathy has its foundation in the relationships that form between children and their caregivers. John Bowlby (1969/1982) and Mary Salter Ainsworth (1989), among others, can be credited with bringing attention to the effects of early attachment relationships on the social and emotional development of young children. Children who form secure attachments with a primary caregiver demonstrate empathy-related skills like theory of mind (Szpak & Bialecka-Pikul, 2020) and emotional regulation (Cooke et al., 2019) that are superior to the skills found in young children who form insecure attachments with their primary caregivers. One recent study, in fact, found that empathy mediated the relationship between parental support and subsequent child delinquency (Walters, 2021g). Reviewing the literature on attachment and empathy, Stern and Cassidy (2018) identified a modest association between child-caregiver bonding and child empathy. While none of the studies reported an inverse correlation between attachment and empathy, the relationship was nonsignificant in several of the studies. This implies that the attachment-empathy relationship may be mediated by a third variable. It has not yet been determined what that third variable might be, although shared or joint attention is one possibility. That is because shared or joint attention is believed to be the product of a good attachment relationship and it has also been shown to shape empathy (Stephenson et al., 2021). There is some speculation that it does so through mirror neurons that replicate the facial expressions people use to decipher emotion (Schmidt et al., 2021). Before moving into a discussion of other potential mediators of the attachment-empathy relationship, the first order of business is to evaluate the relationship between empathy and antisocial/aggressive behavior.

Jolliffe and Farrington (2004) conducted a meta-analysis in which the relationship between empathy and offending was explored in 35 studies, 21 of which examined cognitive empathy and 14 of which examined affective empathy. Although an inverse correlation was observed between empathy and offending overall, the relationship was moderated by a host of third variables. First, the relationship was stronger for cognitive empathy than it was for affective empathy. Second, the effect was stronger for violent offenders than it was for sex offenders. Third, the effect was stronger from younger people than it was for older people. Finally, the relationship between low empathy and offending was no longer significant once controls were implemented for child intelligence and family socioeconomic status (SES). In a more recent meta-analysis, Vachon et al. (2014) uncovered a weak association between aggression and both cognitive and affective empathy. Because none of the studies included in the Vachon et al. meta-analysis employed physiological measures of empathy, Gantiva et al. (2021) conducted a study in which empathy was assessed with facial electromyographic activity, pulse, and skin conductance, and aggression was assessed with a self-report measure. The results revealed that aggression correlated with cognitive empathy but not affective empathy. Based on the results of both the Jolliffe and Farrington meta-analysis and Gantiva et al. study, it would seem that cognitive empathy may be more strongly connected to antisocial and aggressive behavior than affective empathy.

Given the weak and inconsistent associations that have been observed between attachment and empathy and between empathy and antisocial/aggressive behavior, it may be advisable to consider the possibility that these relationships are mediated by one or more third variables. In searching for a mediator to help explain the attachment-empathy relationship, one variable that comes to mind is an internal working model of social relationships. From some of the earliest research conducted on attachment theory, Bowlby (1969/1982) posited that internal working models of social relationships mediated the association between early attachment security and later social behavior, to include empathy. These internal working models serve as mental representations of social relationships that then help organize cognitive processing of social information (Bretherton & Munholland, 2016). These internal working models make it possible for a child to understand and relate to another person's thoughts and feelings. There is some indication that the relationship between empathy and antisocial behavior may also be indirect. Walters and Espelage (2018c) performed a study on the connection between low empathy and the antisocial spectrum behavior of bullying. Although low empathy failed to predict bullying directly, it did predict bullying indirectly via proactive criminal thinking (PCT), when PCT was assessed with a pro-bullying attitudes scale similar to the neutralization scales used to assess PCT in studies on delinquency. This suggests that while the relationship between attachment and empathy could be mediated by an internalized working model of social relationships, the relationship between empathy and antisocial behavior may be mediated by a different cognitive factor (i.e., PCT).

Self-Conscious Emotions

Self-conscious emotions are a person's affective response to having achieved or failed to achieve certain social goals or met certain social responsibilities. Their importance is reflected in the fact that they play a central role in motivating and regulating people's thoughts, perceptions, and behaviors. Different self-conscious emotions have been proposed but guilt/remorse, embarrassment, shame, and pride are the most commonly mentioned self-conscious emotions. Our understanding of self-conscious emotions is limited by the fact that they have received far less attention from researchers than the "basic" emotions of joy, fear, sadness, surprise, anger, and disgust. Tracy and Robins (2004) list five ways in which self-conscious emotions differ from basic emotions: (1) self-conscious emotions, unlike basic emotions, require self-awareness and are constructed from self-representations; (2) self-conscious emotions emerge later in childhood (18–24 months) than basic emotions (first 9 months); (3) self-conscious emotions serve social goals, whereas basic emotions serve survival and reproductive goals; (4) self-conscious emotions, unlike basic emotions, are not associated with universally recognized facial expressions; and (5) self-conscious emotions are cognitively complex and dependent, whereas basic emotions are largely independent of cognition. What I hope to illustrate in this section is how a basic emotion (fear) gives rise to a self-conscious emotion (guilt) in the formation of conscience.

Self-conscious emotions appear to play an important role in moral and conscience development, but there is one self-conscious emotion in particular that is of cardinal significance when it comes to morality and conscience development, and that emotion is guilt. Guilt can be defined as an uncomfortable feeling or sense of unease over having violated a rule or standard to which one subscribes. Hence, a boy will only feel guilt about stealing money from his father's wallet if he believes that taking money from his father's wallet without permission is wrong. Like empathy, guilt has strong evolutionary roots in that it discourages behaviors that could lead to an individual's ostracization from the group. Its source, however, is very different from that which is believed to give rise to empathy. Whereas empathy is believed to evolve from early attachment relationships, guilt is a product of classical conditioning. A behavior that violates a group rule or norm (conditioned stimulus) is paired with fear/anxiety in the form of increased arousal of the sympathetic branch of the autonomic nervous system engendered by punishment or scolding (unconditioned stimulus) designed to discourage any such behavior in the future. After a sufficient number of pairings, the conditioned stimulus will elicit a negative sympathetic response even in the absence of the unconditioned stimulus. The conditioned response (autonomic fear) that arises from this pairing should not be confused with existential fear, where dopamine and serotonin levels rather than sympathetic arousal are the source of motivation.

Two factors are believed to determine the effectiveness of conditioning in discouraging a person from engaging in behavior that they have been taught violates a moral value, standard, or code. The first factor is the strength of the autonomic response. Some individuals produce weaker than average autonomic responses to punishment or their responses do not map well onto the onset and offset of punishment, thereby making it difficult for the individual to associate negative autonomic arousal with the behavior being targeted for punishment. Because such individuals are less likely to have a strong conditioned response to punishment, they are at increased risk for engaging in delinquent and antisocial behavior (Raine et al., 1997). The second factor required to create an effective conditioned response is the consistency and clarity of punishment. If the child is sometimes punished and sometimes not punished for the same behavior or if they cannot tell which behavior is being punished, then conditioning will be much less effective than if punishment is clear and consistent. Research, in fact, indicates that weak, inconsistent, and harsh parental discipline places a child at increased risk for future conduct and delinquency problems (Murray & Farrington, 2010). It should also be noted that extreme or excessive punishment can produce shame, which hurts more than it helps because the child comes to attribute misbehavior to the stable and global aspects of the self rather than to the unstable and specific aspects to which guilt is conditioned (Tracy & Robins, 2004).

There are several reasons why an individual may produce a less than adequate conditioned response to punishment, although one of the more common reasons is the person's biological response to threat. In most people, a threat, such as punishment, arouses feelings of fear and anxiety, which through repeated pairings, gives rise to guilt (Bybee, 1998). As previously mentioned, sympathetic arousal of the autonomic nervous system is weaker and less efficient in youth at risk for future delinquency and antisocial behavior. This can lead to problems with fear conditioning. In someone with normal sympathetic arousal, fear conditioning elicits self-conscious emotions like guilt and remorse, which, in turn, promote moral behavior. Research indicates that the amygdala—an almond-shaped limbic structure located deep in the temporal lobe of the cerebrum—is the seat of such conditioning. Its role in fear conditioning is well-established (Kim & Jung, 2006), although the conscious experience of fear is more likely a function of the amygdala-to-prefrontal cortex connection and associated changes in the intrinsic neuronal excitability of these two brain structures (Yousuf et al., 2020). Walters and Kiehl (2015) analyzed magnetic resonance imaging (MRI) data on 191 incarcerated juvenile offenders and discovered that fearlessness, as measured by six items from Factor 1 of the Psychopathy Checklist (superficial charm, pathological lying, conning/manipulative, lack of remorse or guilt, shallow affect, and callousness), correlated negatively with gray matter concentrations in the amygdala. This finding suggests that fearlessness and weak fear conditioning may have their foundation, at least partially, in amygdaloid dysfunction.

Using a large sample of early to mid-adolescent schoolchildren, Walters (2020k) speculated that PCT may interface with guilt just as it interfaces with empathy. As with empathy, PCT was found to mediate the relationship between guilt and antisocial behavior, but unlike empathy, its relationship with antisocial behavior was also mediated by guilt. This suggests the presence of a reciprocal or bidirectional relationship between PCT and guilt in their effect on future antisocial behavior. The data for this investigation came from the Gang Resistance Education and Training (GREAT) study, in which PCT and guilt were cross-lagged at Waves 2 and 3 and then linked to delinquency at Wave 4. Controlling for Wave 1 delinquency, Walters discovered that PCT mediated the guilt-delinquency relationship and guilt mediated the PCT-delinquency relationship. Based on these results, it was concluded that PCT may increase the likelihood of future offending by deactivating the counter-delinquency effects of guilt, whereas guilt may decrease the likelihood of future offending by deactivating the pro-delinquency effects of PCT. From the standpoint of prevention and intervention, programs designed to identify and reduce proactive forms of criminal thought process and programs that promote a moral system in which people experience guilt when they violate social and moral norms and principles should be particularly effective in reducing and eliminating future delinquency.

Moral Reasoning

The third and final component of conscience to be examined in this chapter is moral reasoning. This third component of conscience can be defined as using logic and reason to determine whether a course of action is right or wrong. Jean Piaget (1932), the French developmental psychologist, created one of the first formal theories of moral reasoning. He divided moral reasoning into two phases: heteronomous moral reasoning and autonomous moral reasoning. The first or heteronomous phase of moral reasoning is characterized by a belief in the permanence of rules and the notion that rules come from authority figures. The heteronomous phase is observed primarily in children. The second or autonomous phase of moral reasoning, which is observed primarily in adults, is marked by a shift in emphasis which finds behavior being judged more on the basis of intentions than on the basis of consequences. Building on Piaget's work, Lawrence Kohlberg (1981) developed a system that encompassed three levels of moral reasoning, with each level divided into two stages (see table 6.1). Whereas Piaget created his system by observing

Table 6.1 Kohlberg's Three Levels and Six Stages of Moral Reasoning

Level 1		**Preconventional Reasoning**
Stage 1	Heteronomous Morality	Obey out of fear of punishment
Stage 2	Instrumental Morality	Obey out of desire for reward
Level 2		**Conventional Reasoning**
Stage 3	Mutual Interpersonal Expectations	Emphasize trust, caring, and loyalty
Stage 4	Social Systems Morality	Emphasize social order, justice, and duty
Level 3		**Postconventional Reasoning**
Stage 5	Social Contract	Laws required to protect basic human rights
Stage 6	Universal Ethical Principles	Moral standards based on universal human rights

Source: Table created by author based on data from Kohlberg (1981).

children at play, Kohlberg developed his system by presenting children and adults with various moral dilemmas. Several neo-Kohlbergian scholars made further alterations to the theory after Kohlberg's death in 1987, expanding on the social cognitive bases of the theory by focusing on information processing and the use of moral schemas (Narvaez, 2005; Rest et al., 2000).

Perhaps the best way to examine the development of moral reasoning is to review the progression of stages in Kohlberg's moral reasoning model. The first stage in Level 1 (preconventional reasoning) of Kohlberg's model is the same as Piaget's first stage, heteronomous morality. Someone functioning at this stage obeys rules in order to avoid punishment. The second stage of Level 1, instrumental morality, promotes obedience out of a hedonistic desire for reinforcement and pleasure. At both stages of Level 1 there is no internalization of rules and norms. By contrast, Level 2 of Kohlberg's model (conventional reasoning) is characterized by a moderate degree of internalization. Persons operating at Stage 3 of Level 2 (mutual interpersonal expectations) make decisions based on trust, caring, and loyalty to others, while persons operating at Stage 4 of Level 2 (social systems morality) base their decisions on the obligation to maintain social order, achieve justice, and discharge their rightful duties. The third or postconventional level of moral reasoning is distinguished by a high degree of internalization and like the previous two levels is composed of two stages. Stage 5 (social contract) of Kohlberg's model stresses basic human rights, while Stage 6 (universal ethical principles) follows a pattern of moral reasoning in which decision-making is guided by a set of collective ethical values.

The moral reasoning of the average noncriminal adult usually falls somewhere between Stages 3 and 4 of Kohlberg's model, whereas offenders usually don't progress much beyond Stage 1 or 2 (Palmer, 2003). What this means is that the average offender does not internalize social rules and norms, choosing instead to follow the rules out of a fear of punishment (Stage 1) or a desire for reward (Stage 2). Given the fact that most offenders have trouble mustering a sufficient amount of guilt or fear to curb their antisocial inclinations, it is easy to see how social rule breaking has come to define the criminal lifestyle. In a meta-analysis of 72 studies on moral reasoning and delinquency in 11- to 20-year-old participants, Romeral and colleagues (2018) unearthed impressive support for moral reasoning as a correlate of delinquency. Regardless of whether a one-group or two-group design was employed, a production task or recognition task was used to assess moral reasoning, or a self-report measure or the person's presence in a correctional facility served as the delinquency outcome, moral reasoning correlated consistently with youth delinquency. Modeling and operant conditioning/reinforcement are believed to be the two principal ways by which individuals progress through the stages of moral reasoning. Modeling the behavior of parents, siblings, and friends and being reinforced for certain moral or amoral beliefs and behaviors leads the individual to a specific stage of moral development.

PCT has been found to mediate the relationship between empathy and antisocial behavior (Walters & Espelage, 2018c), the relationship between legitimacy beliefs about law enforcement/judiciary and offending (Walters, 2018-LHBj), and appears to enter into a reciprocal relationship with guilt (Walters, 2020k). It has also been suggested that PCT may moderate the relationship between moral reasoning and delinquency. In a sample of 417 Chinese adolescents, Wang et al. (2016) observed a significant interaction between a facet of PCT (moral disengagement) and moral reasoning in relationship to the antisocial spectrum behavior of cyberbullying. Although they interpreted their results as evidence that moral reasoning moderated the moral disengagement-cyberbullying relationship, it is just as likely that moral disengagement moderated the moral reasoning-cyberbullying relationship given the presence of an interaction between two concurrently measured variables. There is also evidence that neutralization beliefs, another facet of PCT, rather than being used to reduce guilt in largely conventional youth who drift into crime as a consequence of shifting opportunities and incentives, as proposed by neutralization/drift theory (Sykes & Matza, 1957), may actually be an expression of a child's low level of moral development and weak moral integrity (Walters et al., 2021b). Additional research is required, however, to determine whether PCT and moral reasoning are separate constructs and if so, how they interface to promote or impede future delinquency and crime.

Sentimentality as a Pseudo-Conscience

Of the eight thinking styles included in the original criminal lifestyle model (Walters, 1990), only seven were subsequently found to load onto a proactive or reactive criminal thinking (RCT) latent factor (Walters, 2014b; Walters et al., 2011). The one original thinking style that did not load onto one of the two latent criminal lifestyle factors and is not part of the hierarchical dual-dimensional model previously described in chapter 4 is sentimentality. It should be noted that sentimentality can be defined as a belief that it is possible to compensate for or excuse prior involvement in crime by performing good deeds and exhibiting superficial charm. Although this thinking style is no longer considered part of a criminal lifestyle, it still has a role to play as a kind of pseudo-conscience in individuals whose conscience is weak or absent. The fact that it lacks consistency and persistence and tends to come and go depending on the situational context indicates that it is not a particularly effective means of moral guidance, although it may be the only thing standing in the way of a heinous crime. Thus, while sentimentality is no substitute for a robust and healthy conscience, it can serve as a temporary stop-gap measure for individuals whose conscience is lacking in important ways.

MORAL MODEL OF LIFESTYLE CRIMINALITY

The current version of the moral model of lifestyle criminality is depicted in figure 6.1. Reading from left to right, we can see that the model starts with low moral integrity. In earlier versions of the moral model, this left-most position was occupied by callous-unemotional traits. Although callous-unemotional traits may capture some aspects of low moral integrity, they do not represent low moral integrity in its entirety. That is because moral integrity is composed of three parts or components, only two of which are addressed by callous-unemotional traits. The three components that make up moral integrity are poor empathy, weak autonomic conditioning (either in the form of a weak unconditioned stimulus or a weak conditioned response), and Stage 1 or 2 moral reasoning leading to inadequate internalization of moral values. The two aspects of low moral integrity that callous-unemotional traits capture best are poor empathy and weak autonomic arousal and conditioning, although coverage is incomplete. And while callous-unemotional traits may do a less than adequate job of mapping onto the weak internalization of Stage 1 or 2 moral reasoning, they do a better job of assessing the overall construct of low moral integrity than any other measure currently available in the crime and delinquency literature. As such, they will continue to serve as an operationalization of moral integrity until a more comprehensive measure can be found.

Starting at the left-hand side of figure 6.1, we can see that low moral integrity can lead to three possible outcomes: criminal thought content, proactive criminal thought process, and antisocial peers. These three outcomes further impinge on identity transformation, which, in turn, is believed to promote

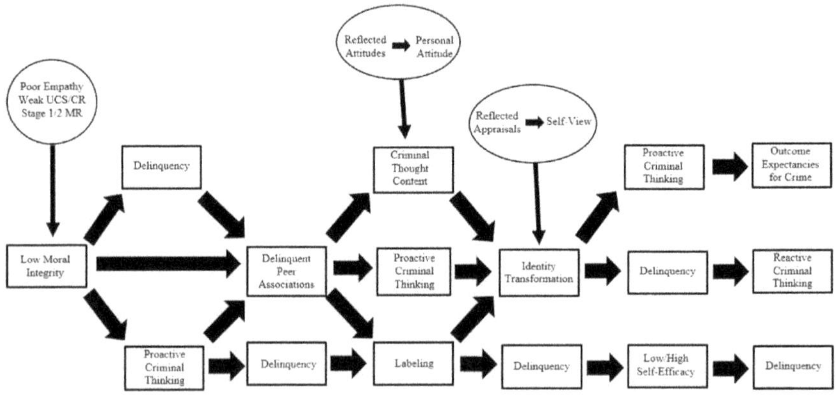

Figure 6.1 Moral Model of Lifestyle Criminality. Note: UCS = Unconditioned Stimulus, CR = Conditioned Response, Stage 1/2 MR = Kohlberg Stage 1 or 2 Moral Reasoning; Circle and Ovals Reveal the Contents of the Box below the Cirlce or Oval. *Source:* Created by author.

PCT and delinquency. Delinquency, in turn, can lead to RCT, the main criminal thinking construct in the control model of lifestyle criminality. A serial pathway at the bottom of figure 6.1 runs from PCT to delinquency to labeling to delinquency to low self-efficacy to delinquency. The importance of PCT to the moral model is highlighted by the fact that it is the only variable, other than delinquency, that is represented more than once in the model. It is actually found in three different places. There are currently 20 paths in the moral model of lifestyle criminality. Each path is identified in table 6.2 and buttressed by a supporting study. The best way to understand the moral model, however, is not to conduct a painstaking review of the 20 individual paths but to take note of the three and four-variable pathways that make up the model. Three of these pathways will be discussed next, along with their supporting mediation mechanisms and occasional moderating contexts.

The Peer Influence Pathway

The standard peer influence effect which runs from peer delinquency to participant delinquency is one of the strongest relationships in criminology (Gifford-Smith et al., 2005; McGloin & Thomas, 2019). Furthermore, despite arguments to the contrary (Young et al., 2013), the peer-participant delinquency association is more than just a projection of a participant's own level of delinquency onto their peers (Walters, 2019f). It is, in fact, the central argument in social learning theories of crime (Akers, 1998; Sutherland, 1947); namely, that individual learns the attitudes and techniques for crime

Table 6.2 The 20 Individual Paths in the Control Model of Lifestyle Criminality along with Studies That Support Each Path

Path	*Supporting Study*
Low Moral Integrity → Delinquency	Frick et al. (2014)
Low Moral Integrity → Proactive Criminal Thinking	Walters and DeLisi (2015)
Low Moral Integrity → Peer Delinquency	Walters (2019c)
Delinquency → Peer Delinquency	Kiesner et al. (2003)
Proactive Criminal Thinking → Peer Delinquency	Ariza et al. (2014)
Proactive Criminal Thinking → Delinquency	Topelli et al. (2014)
Peer Delinquency → Criminal Thought Content	Megens and Weerman (2012)
Peer Delinquency → Proactive Criminal Thinking	Whited et al. (2017)
Peer Delinquency → Labeling	Rocheau and Chavez (2015)
Delinquency → Labeling	De Coster and Lutz (2018)
Criminal Thought Content → Identity	Alexander (2018)
Proactive Criminal Thinking → Identity	Walters (2017f)
Labeling → Identity	Restivo and Lanier (2015)
Labeling → Delinquency	Maruna and Copes (2005)
Identity → Proactive Criminal Thinking	Piotrowski (2019)
Identity → Delinquency	Brownfield and Thompson (2005)
Delinquency → Low Self-Efficacy for Conventional	Bandura et al. (2003)
Delinquency → High Self-Efficacy for Crime	Drozda (2006)
Proactive Criminal Thinking → Outcome Expectancies	Pornari and Wood (2010)
Delinquency → Reactive Criminal Thinking	Walters (2016h)
Low Self-Efficacy for Conventional → Delinquency	Cuevas et al. (2017)
High Self-Efficacy for Crime → Delinquency	Brezina and Topalli (2012)

Source: Table created by author.

by associating with those already involved in crime. Lifestyle theory identifies PCT or one of its facets, either neutralization or moral disengagement, as the variable linking peer and participant delinquency. In a sample of British general population youth, Walters (2015e) discovered that a PCT measure composed of four neutralization items mediated the relationship between peer and participant delinquency. Using a sample of serious delinquents and a 32-item moral disengagement scale to assess PCT, Walters (2016d) uncovered further evidence that PCT mediated the peer delinquency-participant delinquency relationship, whereas RCT did not. Subsequent studies have shown that PCT mediates both the gang affiliation-participant delinquency (Walters, 2019d, 2021c) and co-offender-participant delinquency (Walters, 2020j) relationships. In a further test of this relationship, neighborhood disorder was found to moderate PCT mediation of the peer delinquency-participant delinquency association; thus, while neighborhood disorder appeared to suppress the effect of peer delinquency on PCT, it appeared to enhance the effect of PCT on delinquency (Walters, 2020m), thereby reducing the social effect but increasing the cognitive effect.

The peer influence effect portrayed in figure 6.1 actually has two mediators: PCT and identity transformation. Lifestyle theory assumes that a person's identity or self-appraisal is shaped by reflected appraisals. A reflected appraisal is how a person believes they come across to others. If they perceive that they are viewed by important people in their lives (e.g., parents, siblings, friends) as a law-breaker, then they are more likely to view themselves as a law-breaker. If they perceive that they are viewed by important people in their lives as law-abiding, then they are more likely to view themselves as law-abiding. Although the peer delinquency → PCT → identity transformation → delinquency pathway has yet to be formally evaluated, the reflected appraisal → delinquency path has been studied with cross-sectional (Brownfield & Thompson, 2005), retrospective (Walters, 2016j), and longitudinal (Matsueda, 1992) data and found to be moderate in strength. Recently, Walters (2020d) discovered that having a reflected appraisal as a delinquent interfered with desistance from crime in a sample of mostly white males as they progressed from late adolescence to early adulthood. There is one study that has examined the two-mediator relationship between PCT and identity, but not identity transformation. In that study, Walters (2017f) tested a two-sequential mediator model in which it was predicted that PCT would precede deviant identity but not vice versa in mediating the peer influence effect. Consistent with predictions, the pathway in which the peer delinquency-participant delinquency relationship was mediated by PCT first and deviant identity second achieved significance, whereas the pathway in which the peer delinquency-participant delinquency nexus was mediated by deviant identity first and PCT second failed to achieve significance.

PCT is not the only cognitive variable capable of mediating the peer influence effect. Preliminary studies indicate that criminal thought content correlates better with PCT than with RCT (Walters & Morgan, 2018) and so some of the relationships that have been observed with PCT may also be observed with criminal thought content. The previously mentioned Walters (2017f) investigation revealed that one dimension of criminal thought content—criminal or deviant identity—mediated the peer influence effect, but only when it was positioned as the second mediator behind PCT. Other studies have found that positive attitudes toward deviance and negative attitudes toward authority, two additional dimensions of criminal thought content, may also mediate the peer influence effect. A measure of negative attitudes toward the police was found to mediate the relationship between peer associations and delinquent behavior, as well as the relationship between violent victimization and delinquent behavior (Walters, 2019g). In a study where criminal thought content was assessed with positive attitudes toward deviance, criminal thought content and PCT, both jointly and separately, mediated the peer influence effect (Walters, 2016c). In a study where criminal thought content was assessed with negative attitudes toward the police, the pathway from criminal thought content to criminal thought process mediated the peer influence effect but the pathway from criminal thought process to criminal thought content did not (Walters, 2020h). As shown in figure 6.1, a positive perceived reaction to participant deviance (reflected attitudes) in peers fosters positive attitudes toward deviance in participants (personal attitude) as part of the peer influence effect (Walters, 2021j).

The Primary and Secondary Deviance (Labeling) Pathway

At the third level or rung of the model outlined in figure 6.1 is a three-variable sequence that comes directly from labeling theory. The first path of this three-variable pathway has delinquency leading to being labeled deviant (primary deviance) and the second path has a label of deviance leading to further delinquency (secondary deviance). As one of the first conflict theories in criminology, the labeling perspective maintains that those in power use labels to keep themselves in power and prevent competing groups from usurping their authority (Tannenbaum, 1938). Adults use labels to manage the threat they perceive in juveniles, males use labels to thwart efforts by women to achieve equality, and ethnic majorities use labels to keep ethnic minorities from advancing. Further theorizing by Lemert (1967) led to the realization that labels could be viewed as people's negative reactions to deviance as a personification of the person so labeled. Additional contributions were made by Becker (1963) who argued that the deviant label often becomes the dominant identity, overriding other, less destructive, labels and identities that are also attributed to the individual. Labeling theory is derived from symbolic interactionism (Mead, 1934) and has as its founding premise the belief that while labels can make things more manageable, when applied to people they are restricting, dehumanizing, and subject to becoming self-fulfilling prophesies.

The moral model of lifestyle criminality contends that there are two principal factors that lead to labeling and two principal factors that result from labeling. The two principal factors that lead to labeling are delinquency and deviant peer associations. The delinquency to labeling path is described by De Coster and Lutz (2018). It should also be pointed out that while formal labeling by the criminal justice system is capable of producing a criminogenic effect, informal labeling by family and friends and self-labeling by the person themselves may have an even greater impact on future offending (Adams et al., 2003; Bartusch & Matsueda, 1996). The second factor that leads to labeling is delinquent peer associations. A label can arise from one's own actions, but it can also arise from the actions of those with whom one associates, using the "guilt by association" metaphor (Rocheleau & Chavez, 2015).

Labeling, in turn, gives rise to two factors that link to future offending and thus helps explain secondary deviance. The first factor is identity transformation (Restivo & Lanier (2015), whereby labels lead to reflected appraisals as a delinquent or criminal (Matsueda, 1992) that then increase the likelihood of future offending. This four-variable pathway (delinquency → labeling → identity transformation → delinquency) is depicted in figure 6.1. The other linking factor is a shift from conventional to antisocial peer relations which serves to embed the individual in a deviant social network (Bernburg et al., 2006). Unlike the identity transformation pathway, this four-variable pathway (delinquency → labeling → social rejection → delinquency) is not depicted in figure 6.1.

The High and Low Self-Efficacy Pathway

There is a third pathway that is of significance to the moral model. It too can be found on the third level of figure 6.1, directly behind the labeling pathway. We might call this the self-efficacy pathway (delinquency → high/low self-efficacy → delinquency). Self-efficacy can be defined as a person's estimate of how likely they are to accomplish a task with the skills that they currently possess (Bandura, 1986). It is similar in some ways to self-confidence but where self-confidence involves a general estimate of one's abilities and likelihood of success, self-efficacy refers to one's ability to master a specific task or behavior. The interesting thing about self-efficacy in the moral model is the proposition that high and low self-efficacy can both mediate the relationship between past and future delinquency. Low self-efficacy for conventional behavior, such as working a regular job or following the rules of society, can serve as a link between past and future delinquency. This is another way of saying that delinquency can knife off opportunities for success in conventional activities (Sampson & Laub, 1993), which, in turn, can facilitate further criminality. High self-efficacy for crime, on the other hand, whether it be based on real or imagined success in prior criminal ventures, is quite common in offender populations and research indicates that it correlates with intentions to remain in a criminal lifestyle upon release from prison (Brezina & Topalli, 2012). Those who follow this path may actually entertain the distorted belief that they are successful in crime.

At least three studies have addressed the role of low self-efficacy for a conventional lifestyle in promoting crime continuity. In the first of these studies, Walters (2018f) examined longitudinal data obtained from a large group of criminally involved male and female adolescents. Self-efficacy for a conventional lifestyle and general confidence in one's ability to avoid future legal trouble were assessed six months post-baseline. Delinquency, on the other hand, was assessed at baseline and at a second follow-up 12 months later. Results showed that after controlling for a range of demographic variables and such relevant moral model constructs as callous-unemotional traits and moral disengagement, self-efficacy for a conventional lifestyle mediated the past delinquency-future delinquency relationship. General confidence in one's ability to avoid future legal trouble, however, failed to mediate this same relationship. Using data collected from a general population sample of mid- to late adolescents, Walters (2018g) contrasted self-efficacy for a conventional lifestyle and self-efficacy for deviance as mediators of the two-year prospective relationship between parental monitoring/attachment and child delinquency. This time, self-efficacy for a conventional lifestyle effectively mediated the parental attachment-child delinquency relationship, whereas self-efficacy for deviance did not. In a third study using a third sample, the weak parental support-delinquency relationship was mediated by low academic self-efficacy followed by peer delinquency but not by peer delinquency followed by low academic self-efficacy (Walters, 2019i).

Other Noteworthy Paths

Many of the paths included in the moral model contribute in some way to the three previously mentioned pathways. Even so, there are a number of paths that have yet to be incorporated into pathways. Two such paths are discussed here. The first unattached path is the one between outcome expectancies and PCT. Outcome expectancies are the outcomes a person anticipates receiving upon completing a task or engaging in a behavior. Outcome expectancies, like efficacy expectancies, come from Bandura's (1986) social cognitive theory of personality. And like efficacy expectancies, they play a potentially important role in the moral model of lifestyle criminality. Yet, what that role is, remains a matter of speculation. Research on outcome expectancies and criminal thinking is sparse, though there is evidence that PCT is capable of predicting future positive outcome expectances for crime (Walters, 2007b). It was also observed that positive outcome expectancies for crime dropped significantly in inmates participating in a 10-week criminal lifestyles group, whereas negative outcome expectancies for crime did not change (Walters, 2003b). More research is required to determine the nature of the relationship between criminal thinking and outcome expectancies and how changing outcome expectancies may encourage future desistance.

Another unattached path that requires further study is the one that exists between delinquency and RCT. Being a cardinal feature of the control model of lifestyle criminality (and the focus of discussion in chapter 7), one might be surprised to learn that RCT has a place in the moral model as well. Just as PCT plays a minor role in the control model of lifestyle criminality, RCT plays a minor role in the moral model. Criminal thinking, in fact, is what links the two models. We might go so far as to say that PCT is the glue that holds the moral model together, while RCT is the glue that holds the control model together. Still, there is significant cross-over between models, complements of the overlapping nature of PCT and RCT in their roles as the core criminal thinking dimensions in the moral and control models of criminality, respectively. The relationship between delinquency and RCT will not be discussed here because it will be the major topic of discussion in chapter 7. Suffice it to say that RCT has a place in the moral model for the same reason PCT has a place in the control model, as the intersection between the two criminality models.

CARL PANZRAM: A CASE STUDY

The Life of Carl Panzram

The subject of this case study, Carl Panzram, if he can be believed, is one of the meanest men to ever walk the face of the earth. This habitual criminal, who violated natural law on a daily basis, claimed to have killed over 20 people, though only five of those murders were ever verified. Still, he had the size, strength, and mind-set to commit dozens of murders. Even a cursory review of his central file and criminal record indicates that Panzram satisfied all four criteria of a criminal lifestyle (irresponsibility, self-indulgence, interpersonal intrusiveness, and social rule breaking). Using the Lifestyle Criminality Screening Form (LCSF) as a guide, irresponsibility is present in the form of poor job stability, being fired from several jobs, and dropping out of school at an early age. Self-indulgence is well-represented in the official record which indicates that Panzram began using alcohol in childhood and suffered from a serious drinking problem from adolescence until his death at age 39. He also sported tattoos on his chest and arms and made use of several aliases, providing further verification of his self-indulgent and antisocial tendencies. Interpersonal intrusiveness is particularly prominent in Panzram's background as characterized by a history of violent criminality and mala in se offenses. In addition, he often used a firearm or other weapon when robbing, raping, and murdering people. Finally, social rule breaking is indicated by the presence of over a dozen arrests, almost as many incarcerations, and being sent to a state reformatory for stealing at the age of 12.

Panzram was born on June 28, 1891, and raised by his Prussian immigrant parents in a farming community outside East Grand Forks, Minnesota. His father abandoned the family when Panzram was 7 or 8 years old, which is also around the time Panzram began engaging in delinquent behavior. He was in regular contact with legal authorities and experienced his first incarceration at age 12 when he was sent to the Minnesota State Training School at Red Wing for stealing food and a revolver from a neighbor's house. Like many of the other boys at the school, he was mentally, physically, and sexually abused by staff. This created within him, an intense hatred for humanity. He spent about two years at the training school and near the end of his stay surreptitiously burned down one of the school buildings. He returned home after being released from the training school but ran away shortly thereafter and began traveling across the country. He would frequently hop trains to get from one place to another and reported that during one of these trips he was raped by a gang of hobos. Panzram enlisted in the Army at age 16 but this did not work out for him either. Several months into his enlistment he was convicted of larceny, court martialed, and sentenced to hard labor at the U.S. Disciplinary Barracks at Fort Leavenworth, Kansas. This only served to harden his criminal mentality and inflame his hatred for humanity.

Following his release from the U.S. Disciplinary Barracks, Panzram traveled the country, committing a variety of crimes, and creating havoc wherever he went. During this period in his life he was in and out of prison and jail on a regular basis and earned a reputation as a difficult inmate who would attack guards and other prisoners with minimal provocation. His attitude was such that he would routinely refuse orders. During this period, Panzram reports being involved in multiple escape attempts, several of which were successful. Like most chronic offenders, Panzram was criminally versatile, having engaged in robbery, theft, burglary, arson, rape, and murder, although he was partial to rape and robbery. In fact, he wrote in his autobiography that he would frequently rape the men he robbed. One of his most audacious crimes was burglarizing the home of former president and current chief justice of the U.S. Supreme Court William Howard Taft in New Haven, Connecticut. Panzram blamed Taft, who, as secretary of war, had signed off on Panzram's military confinement, for his incarceration at the U.S. Disciplinary Barracks and ruining his life. He stole money, jewelry, bonds, and a 45-caliber pistol from the residence and bought a yacht, the *Akista*, with his ill-gotten gains. Panzram reports that he would lure sailors from New York City to the yacht, where he would get them drunk, rape them, shoot them, and then dump their bodies into the Atlantic Ocean. These activities came to a halt after the *Akista* ran ashore and sank near Atlantic City, New Jersey.

After losing the *Akista*, Panzram decided it was time to see the world and so he stowed away on a ship bound for Africa, ending up in Luanda, the capital city of what was then Portuguese Angola. He would later acknowledge committing several murders in West Africa, the first of which involved a young African boy who appeared to be about 11 years of age. Panzram recollected that he beat the boy so badly that "his brains were coming out of his ears." He also reported hiring six guides to take him on a crocodile hunting expedition. Instead of hunting crocodiles, he killed the six men and fed their bodies to the waiting reptiles. For a brief period, Panzram worked as a foreman on an oil rig off the coast of West Africa. That was, until he burned the rig down in a fit of anger and rage. After spending a year in West Africa and growing bored, Panzram decided to see what Portugal had to offer. He didn't stay long, though, because the authorities were looking to question him about several murders in West Africa. Panzram took the first ship he could find headed back to the United States. The change in scenery did nothing to improve his outlook on life. Shortly after returning to the United States he raped and murdered three boys. He sodomized a 12-year-old boy from Salem, Massachusetts, and then killed him by striking him in the head with a rock. Several days later, he raped and strangled a preteen male in Connecticut, after which he raped and murdered a 14-year-old paperboy in Philadelphia.

Panzram was arrested in Baltimore in 1928 for a burglary he committed in Washington, DC. It was while being interrogated for this offense that he confessed to killing the three boys from Salem, Connecticut, and Philadelphia. Based on his extensive criminal record he was sentenced to 25-years-to-life, to be served at the United States Penitentiary at Leavenworth, Kansas. Upon arriving at the prison, he advised the warden that he would kill the first man that bothered him. He made good on his threat less than a year later when he murdered his work supervisor, laundry foreman Robert Warnke, who had refused to give him a job change. It is difficult to separate fact from fiction when it comes to Panzram. He had a rich and perverse fantasy life that often colored his perceptions and shaped his reality. No one knows for sure how many people he actually killed because he was rather grandiose in his confessions. At various times he fantasized about poisoning the water supply of a small town in upstate New York, blowing up a popular train trestle, and sinking a British battleship in New York harbor in an effort to start a war between Great Britain and the United States. In addition, he appears to have wanted to die, or at least didn't seem to care if he lived. Perhaps he was hoping that the state would put him out of his misery. Others have speculated that when he learned he was going to Leavenworth, he felt the need to pad his criminal resume with serious crimes given Leavenworth's reputation as one of the toughest prisons in American. There was no doubt, however, that he killed Warnke on June 20, 1929, because he did so in front of inmate and staff witnesses

Panzram was executed for the murder of Robert Warnke on September 5, 1930, using gallows temporarily constructed in the courtyard of the solitary confinement building where he had been held following the murder. In a letter written to one of the only friends he ever had, Washington DC, correctional officer, Henry Lesser, Carl Panzram summed up his life and philosophy of life in a six-sentence diatribe:

> In my lifetime I have murdered 21 human beings. I have committed thousands of burglaries, robberies, larcenys [*sic*], arsons and last but not least I have committed sodomy on more than 1,000 male human beings. For all of these things I am not the least bit sorry. I have no conscience so that does not worry me. I don't believe in Man, God, nor devil. I hate the whole damned human race including myself. (Panzram, 1928, p. 2)

Panzram and the Moral Model

In the quote that precedes this section, Panzram maintained that he was without conscience. Based on his history, I think we can take him at his word. He was cruel to animals as a child and cruel to humans as an adult; both indicate a serious lack of empathy. The roots of Panzram's empathy troubles can be traced to a poor attachment relationship with both parents, neither of whom he liked nor felt particularly close to:

> You asked me about my parents and my early upbringing. I had little of either. My father was no good and mother was very little better. Father pulled his freight when I was 7 or 8 years old so you see I know little about him and none of that good. Mother was too dumb to know anything good to teach me. There was little love lost. I first liked her and respected her. My feelings gradually turned from that to distrust, dislike, disgust and from there it was very simple for my feelings to turn into positive hatred towards her. (Borowski, 2020, p. 170)

The complete or near-complete absence of moral integrity can be further attributed to a weak autonomic response that made it difficult for Panzram to experience guilt and remorse for his antisocial actions ("I am not sorry. My conscience does not trouble me. I sleep sound and have sweet dreams": Borowski, 2020, p. 54). Also, Panzram's moral reasoning appears to have fixated at the first or second stage of Kohlberg's model, focused as it was on avoiding punishment and seeking reward. Unfortunately for his victims, there is no evidence that he compensated for his lack of conscience with sentimentality.

PCT, the driving force behind the moral model, was a central feature of Panzram's cognitive process. In his letters to Henry Lesser he gave clear evidence of mollification whereby he abrogated responsibility for his past criminal actions ("Men made me what I am today, and if men don't like what they have made of me, they must put the blame where it belongs": Panzram, 1928, p. 12) and giving himself permission to break the law through a mammoth sense of entitlement ("I have no desire whatsoever to reform myself. My only desire is to reform people who try to reform me. And I believe that the only way to reform people is to kill 'em. My motto is: 'Rob 'em all, rape 'em all and kill 'em all": Borowski, p. 218). Power orientation, however, was the most prominent feature of Panzram's proactive thought pattern. In an undated letter to Henry Lesser, Panzram expounds on his philosophy of ultimate power and interpersonal domination:

> Force and might makes right. Perhaps things shouldn't be that way but that's the way they are. I learned to look with suspicion and hatred on everybody. As the years went on that idea persisted in my mind above all others. I figured that if I was strong enough and clever enough to impose my will on others, I was right. I still believe that to this day. (Panzram, 1928, p. 12)

There is little evidence that Panzram made much use of superoptimism in that he never appeared to believe that he would get away with the majority of his crimes.

Peer and other interpersonal associations are vital in shaping a person's moral belief system. As outlined by Akers (1998), Sutherland (1947), and other social learning theorists, people learn the attitudes and techniques for crime by associating with those already involved in crime. Hence, delinquent peers are often a principal means by which crime is learned. It is well-documented, for instance, that co-offending is significantly more common in juveniles than it is in adults and that solo offending is significantly more common in adults than it is in juveniles (Reiss & Farrington, 1991). Panzram, however, was a loner who committed the majority of his crimes alone, even as a juvenile. He learned to commit crime nonetheless, and he learned by modeling the behavior of those with whom he came into contact. On a few occasions he learned techniques and attitudes for crime from crime partners. More often than not, however, he learned about crime and violence by being the victim of crime and violence himself. Whether it was being painted black and blue in the "paint shop" at Red Wing training school, gang raped by hobos on a train, or undergoing various tortures and beatings in jail and prison, Panzram learned that violence was power and that he wanted as much power as possible in order to exact his revenge on humanity. And this is where the abused became the abuser. From this point forward, his life goal was to instill as much fear in others as he perceived was instilled in him, preying on the weak and attacking the strong when they were most vulnerable, whether because they were asleep, intoxicated, or just not looking.

A criminal identity, along with weak moral integrity, PCT, and delinquent peer associations are the four corners of the moral model of lifestyle criminality. Panzram's criminal identity was formed at an early age and demonstrates the power of self-labeling:

> All of my family are as the average human beings are. They are honest and hard working people. All except myself. I have been a human animal ever since I was

> born. When I was very young at five or six years of age, I was a thief and a liar, and a mean, despicable one at that. The older I got the meaner I got. (Panzram, 1928, p. 1)

There are several factors that contribute to a criminal identity but two of the most important are labeling and reflected appraisals. It could be argued that being a loner, Panzram was immune to the reflected appraisals of others because he really didn't care what other people thought of him. I take a different view, however. Panzram was very much concerned with how he was perceived by others because this constituted his impact on the world, perhaps the only thing that he really did care about. Why would he spend so much time writing letters to Henry Lesser explaining his actions, perceptions, and general life philosophy, if he did not care what others thought of him? I believe that he was very concerned with how people viewed him, and that this was why he often used exaggeration and hyperbole to create the persona of "meanest man on earth." When he was being led to the gallows, he let out a playful "boo" to see what reaction he would get from the execution party, just another example of his desire to have an impact on the world. This also brings a portion of Panzram's efficacy expectancies into play. Even though he was not a particularly effective thief, he was good at instilling fear in others and in so doing was able to make his mark on the world.

CONCLUSION

Although I do not prescribe to the "blank slate" view of humanity proposed by utilitarian philosophers and behavioral psychologists, I do think this view is applicable to the moral model. Humans are born neither moral nor immoral. Instead, they are born amoral or neutral with respect to their morality. Some people learn a moral code (high moral integrity) through empathy, conditioning of self-conscious emotion, and progressing to conventional and postconventional forms moral reasoning. Other people fail to internalize a coherent moral code (low moral integrity) due to lack of empathy, poor conditioning of self-conscious emotion, and stagnating at a preconventional level of moral reasoning. As implied in the case study of Carl Panzram, people are motivated to make an impact on the world. As will be described in a later chapter, this is how some people attempt to overcome their feelings of existential fear. The impact the person has on the world may be small and circumscribed or large and all-encompassing. Panzram's desired impact was rather grandiose, being the meanest man on earth, and illustrates how he attempted to deal with his own existential fear.

Chapter 7

The Control Model of Lifestyle Criminality

"Seeking Pleasure and Avoiding Pain"

Like the moral model of lifestyle criminality, the control model is designed to explain why people differ in their propensity to commit crime, but where the goal of the moral model is to distinguish between right and wrong, the principal objective of the control model of lifestyle criminality is to maximize pleasure and minimize pain. This reintroduces the utilitarian philosophy of Jeremy Bentham who argued that actions which bring us happiness are utilitarianly right, whereas actions that bring us pain are utilitarianly wrong. According to Bentham, there is no need for complicated algorithms when evaluating the moral intentions of a person, so long as these actions result in maximum happiness or pleasure and minimum unhappiness or pain for the greatest number of people. It should be noted that Bentham's utilitarianism is often considered a precursor to modern-day behavioristic and social learning theories. And while I accept the behavioral "blank slate" view of human nature within the context of the moral model (i.e., people learn both morality and immorality), I do not accept it when it comes to the control model.

I base my rejection of a "blank slate" interpretation of human control on a simple fact. Children are not born neutral in self-control; instead, they are born with no self-control and so must learn to exercise self-control by internalizing lessons from parents and others. Having crime learned in one model and noncrime learned in the other model would seem contradictory. This was a point Hirschi (1979) made with regards to efforts to integrate social learning and social control theories of crime. I disagree with Hirschi on this point, however. It is still feasible to use learning as the overarching paradigm for all three criminal lifestyle models (i.e., moral, control, and decision-making), despite differences in how the learning takes place. In other words, crime is a function of what people learn as well as what they don't learn. Whereas the focus of chapter 6 was on what people learn (i.e., immorality) in furtherance of a criminal lifestyle, the focus of the current chapter is on what people don't learn (i.e., self-control) in furtherance of a criminal lifestyle. Still, the two chapters are similar in their efforts to enlist biological, social, cognitive, and developmental factors in the service of understanding individual differences in the propensity to commit crime.

THE FOUR CORNERS OF THE CONTROL MODEL OF LIFESTYLE CRIMINALITY

Just as there are four corners to the moral model, so too are there four corners to the control model. As a review, the four corners of the moral model are low moral integrity, proactive criminal thinking (PCT), peer delinquency, and criminal identity (see figure 7.1). The four corners of the control model, on the other hand, are low self-control, reactive criminal thinking (RCT), strain, and hostility (see figure 7.2). Although the four corners are not the only areas of interest in each model, they constitute the principal or core elements of each model. The reason for the double-headed arrows between each element in figures 7.1 and 7.2 is to illustrate the possibility of a reciprocal or bidirectional relationship between each of the four corners. There is also the possibility of a reciprocal or bidirectional relationship between each corner and crime/delinquency. Reciprocity is the central theme of Thornberry's (1987) interactional theory of crime. In the moral and control models of criminal lifestyle theory, however, reciprocity

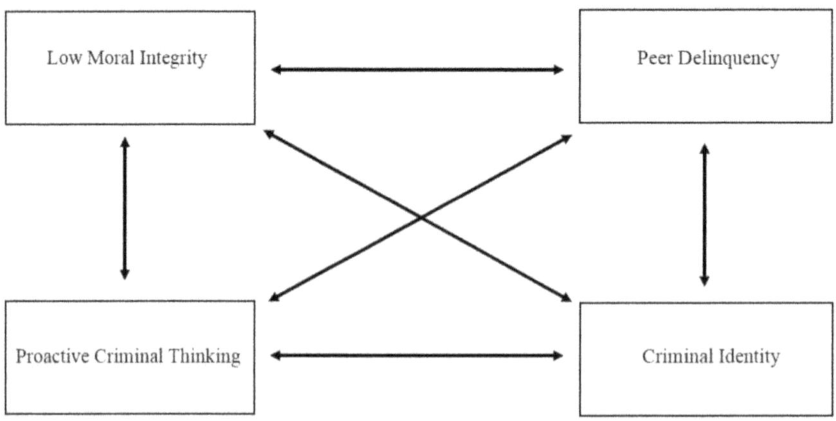

Figure 7.1 The Four Corners of the Moral Model of Lifestyle Criminality. *Source:* Created by author.

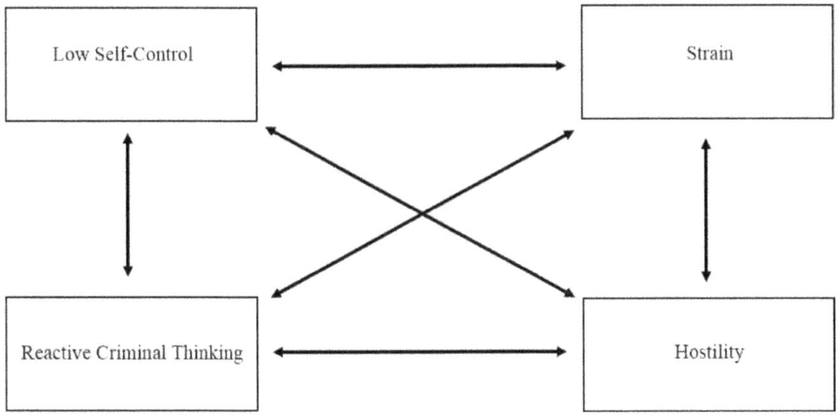

Figure 7.2 The Four Corners of the Control Model of Lifestyle Criminality. *Source:* Created by author.

is an empirical question rather than an assumption. Several studies have shown, for instance, that while RCT forms a bidirectional relationship with delinquency, the relationship between PCT and delinquency is unidirectional, running from PCT to delinquency but not from delinquency to PCT (Walters, 2016h, 2019h). We begin this discussion of the four corners of the control model by taking a look at what is perhaps its most fundamental element, low self-control.

Low Self-Control

The terms low self-control and behavioral impulsivity are used interchangeably in lifestyle theory to describe the core feature of the control model. The role it plays in the control model is similar to the role moral integrity plays in the moral model. A major difference between the two constructs, however, is that while high and low moral integrity are learned as part of a person's interactions with the environment, low self-control is an extension of the human organism's natural state. Unlike high and low moral integrity, which are acquired, low self-control is an inherent feature of the human condition. As such, it is high self-control rather than low self-control that is learned. Whereas Gottfredson and Hirschi (1990) used a rational approach to derive the main elements of low self-control (i.e., impulsivity, preference for simple tasks, risk-seeking, physicality, self-centeredness, and a bad temper), an empirical approach was taken in constructing components of low self-control/behavioral impulsivity for lifestyle theory. Based on the results of a meta-analytic principal components analysis of self-report and behavioral measures of impulsivity, low self-control is partitioned into three principal factors or dimensions: disinhibition, sensation seeking, and negative emotionality (Sharma et al., 2014).

Disinhibition

Disinhibition or lack of personal constraint is one dimension of impulsivity identified in the Sharma et al. meta-analysis. Although there has only been a modicum of research conducted on the relationship between disinhibition and delinquency, that which has been conducted suggests that there is a fairly robust and consistent connection between a disinhibited temperament and delinquency. An early study in this area used growth mixture modeling and a longitudinal design to assess offending in a large group of individuals between the ages of 12 and 31 (White et al., 2001). Of the four trajectories identified in this study, one represented a life-course-persistent pattern, and a second suggested an adolescent limited pattern. This tends to support Moffitt's (1993) taxonomic theory of delinquent development. The only variable that differentiated between the two groups, however, was a higher score on a disinhibition scale administered during adolescence in participants from the life-course-persistent group. In a study where 260 youth were administered the adolescent version of the Minnesota Multiphasic Personality Inventory, a scale designed to measure behavioral disinhibition correlated with nonviolent delinquency, whereas a scale designed to measure instrumental aggression and interpersonal dominance correlated with violent delinquency (Veltri et al., 2014). In a recent study on low self-control and disinhibition, Venables et al. (2018) witnessed a strong correlation between self-control and trait disinhibition in a manner that supported a biobehavioral conceptualization of disinhibition.

Although disinhibition, like all three facets of low self-control, is an inherent characteristic of the human organism, it is not evenly distributed across the population. In other words, there are clear individual differences in disinhibition. Some of these individual differences are biologically based and others are environmentally based. As previously stated, the Venables et al. (2018) study revealed that individual differences in low self-control and disinhibition could be traced to biological factors. This possibility was further explored in a study by Walters and Kiehl (2015). As mentioned in chapter 6, Walters and Kiehl observed a correlation between callous-unemotional traits, as measured by several Factor 1 items from the Psychopathy Checklist: Youth Version (PCL: YV), and lower-than-normal amygdaloid gray matter in a group of juvenile offenders. They also discovered that weak personal constraint, as measured by a different set of PCL: YV items, correlated with gray matter depletions in the hippocampus. The hippocampus is a seahorse-shaped structure located below the outer core of the brain in an area known as the allocortex. Like the amygdala, it is part of the limbic system and forms a neural circuit with the frontal cortex. Unlike the amygdala, it is heavily involved in promoting behavioral control. The Walters and Kiehl investigation revealed that low gray matter volumes in the hippocampus aligned with behavioral disinhibition, as measured by four items from Factor 2 of the PCL: YV (need for stimulation, lack of realistic long-term goals, impulsivity, and irresponsibility). Heightened reward sensitivity in the amygdala and anterior cingulate cortex (ACC) may also explain individual differences in disinhibition (Kerr et al., 2015).

In contrast to the relatively static risk presented by a below-average number of cell bodies (gray matter) in the hippocampus or the heightened sensitivity to reward that appears to accompany abnormalities in the amygdala and ACC, stable and acute dynamic risk factors, while clearly capable of altering disinhibition levels, are more subject to change over time and across situations. Gottfredson and Hirschi (1990) postulate that parental control in the form of consistent discipline and firm rule-setting is the sole means by which a child learns self-control. Parental support, another stable dynamic promotive factor, however, may exert an even stronger effect on a child's self-control. In a recent study by Feldman and Olson (2021), it was determined that supportive caregiving by either parent when the child was 34–39 months of age predicted increased levels of effortful control and personal constraint by the time the child was 60–81 months old. Research has long supported the conclusion that disinhibition encourages future substance misuse (Rioux et al., 2016; Tarter et al., 2004), but a study by Wilson et al. (2021) took this one step further. Not only did disinhibition predict future substance use, but substance use, in turn, predicted significant increments in disinhibition. Substance use and disinhibition, at least in the Wilson et al. study, formed a bidirectional relationship in which a rise in one, led to a rise in the other.

Sensation Seeking

Positive emotionality in the form of sensation seeking is a second dimension of behavioral impulsivity identified in the Sharma et al. (2018) meta-analysis. Sensation seeking refers to the tendency to pursue novel and stimulating activities and experiences. Other terms used to describe this phenomenon include thrill seeking, novelty seeking, and excitement seeking. This is the indulgent aspect of low self-control and it differs from the other two aspects in that it grows during adolescence (Zuckerman, 2007) in concert with a rise in dopaminergic activity (Wahlstrom et al., 2010). Although sensation seeking has traditionally been viewed as a personality trait, there is evidence that it is can change rapidly over a relatively short period of time (Lynne-Landsman et al., 2011). As such, researchers need to be cautious in labeling juveniles as high or low sensation seekers and focus instead on how sensation seeking changes, particularly in relationship to other variables. That said, a fairly robust relationship has been documented between sensation seeking and delinquency in both individual studies and a recent meta-analysis (Ljubin-Golub et al., 2017; Mann et al., 2016; Walters, 2020b). The causal nature of this association was explored in a study by Harden et al. (2012) using latent growth curve analysis. The results revealed that a genetically driven change in sensation seeking over the course of adolescence preceded a rise in delinquent behavior.

Holmes et al. (2016) examined magnetic resonance imaging (MRI) data on 1,234 general population adults and identified areas of reduced cortical thickness (gray matter) in the ACC and middle frontal gyrus that corresponded with motor impulsivity, sensation seeking, and substance use. These biologically based static correlates of sensation seeking and impulsivity are complemented by several environmentally based dynamic correlates of sensation seeking and impulsivity. The stable dynamic promotive factors of parental monitoring and warmth, for instance, have been found to moderate the relationship between sensation seeking and delinquency, such that youth whose parents monitored their behavior and interacted with them in a warm and loving manner reported fewer legal problems than youth whose parents did not closely monitor their behavior and did not interact with them in a warm and loving manner. These relationships persisted even when sensation seeking was high (Okuda et al., 2019). Substance use once again provides an example of an acute dynamic risk factor that can serve as both a cause (Kaiser et al., 2018; Malmberg et al., 2013) and consequence (Afzali et al., 2020; LaSpada et al., 2020) of sensation seeking. Individual differences in demographics have also been reported for sensation seeking, with males and younger individuals achieving higher scores on a sensation-seeking scale than females and older individuals (Butković & Bratko, 2003).

Negative Emotionality

One of the principal points of differentiation between the moral and control models of lifestyle criminality is the role of emotion in each model. Whereas the moral model centers around efforts to suppress or dampen emotion, the control model is directed at amplifying emotion. The role of positive emotionality in low self-control was discussed in the previous section on sensation seeking. Negative emotionality also appears to be part of the low self-control dynamic and is the third and final component of behavioral impulsivity identified in the Sharma et al. (2018) meta-analysis. A variety of emotions fall under the umbrella of negative emotionality, although anger, anxiety, depression, irritability, and fear are among the most commonly mentioned expressions of negative affect in research on antisocial behavior. The role of negative emotionality in impulse control was recently explored in a longitudinal study of 561 adoptees followed from age 9–27 months to age 7 years. The results of this study showed that higher negative emotionality at age 9–27 months and at age 4.5–7 years was associated with lower child executive function and effortful control at ages 27 months and 7 years, respectively (Cioffi et al., 2021). Thus, negative emotionality may be just as vital to the development of low self-control as disinhibition and sensation seeking.

Lahey and colleagues (2021) discerned that higher volumes of gray matter in the amygdala at age 10–17 predicted higher levels of negative emotionality in adulthood. This is interesting because in the previous chapter we learned that lower levels of gray matter in the amygdala correlated with higher levels of fearlessness and weaker fear conditioning. There is also evidence that negative affect is connected to certain adverse childhood experiences (ACEs) in those who embrace a delinquent lifestyle. This suggests that environmental stress plays a central role in the negative emotionality that oversees low self-control. Multiple assessments conducted annually over a period of seven years were subjected to multi-trajectory, group-based analysis, resulting in four trajectories, the most severe of which was a multidomain (alcohol use, delinquency, and interpersonal aggression) high-risk group (Reyes et al., 2020). Membership in this group was associated with high levels of ACE family violence, low self-control, and negative emotionality. Wolff and Baglivio (2017) used structural equation modeling to evaluate the effect of ACEs (e.g., physical and emotional abuse/neglect, family violence, household substance abuse) on future delinquency. The results of this study revealed that ACEs have both a direct and indirect effect, via negative emotionality, on future delinquency.

Learning Self-Control

Before moving onto the next corner of the control model of lifestyle criminality, I think it important that we discuss how children learn to overcome their natural tendency to be impulsive, self-indulgent, and negatively disposed to stress. In other words, we need to know how children learn self-control. Gottfredson and Hirschi (1990) believe that low self-control is the exclusive province of poor parenting and that nothing can be done to alter a person's relative degree of self-control once they reach the age of 8 years. I disagree with both premises. First, there is research to suggest that while parental discipline is critical to the development of self-control, other factors are also important. A partial list of these factors includes parental support (Kurtz & Zavala, 2017), genetics (Beaver et al., 2008), serotonin levels (Boisvert et al.,

2018), peer pressure (Meldrum, 2008), and neighborhood context (Pratt et al., 2004). Second, while Gottfredson and Hirschi (1990) allow for age-related improvements in absolute self-control, they are adamant that relative self-control is highly stable after age 8. Gottfredson and Hirschi's rationale for the age 8 cutoff is never fully articulated, although it could reflect their belief that there is a critical period during which self-control is learned in humans.

Critical periods have been proposed for language acquisition and human mother-child attachment (Knudsen, 2004), but unlike imprinting in birds, language acquisition and mother-child attachment occur over a period of years and have more variable outcomes than a duck following the first large moving object it encounters after birth. Today, developmental psychologists are more apt to use the term "sensitive periods" to describe the brain plasticity that leads to human preparedness for certain types of learning. Self-control may very well fit this pattern. Attachment to a parent, coach, or older sibling will make the parent, coach, or older sibling a source of reward and guidance for the child. A sensitive period is not only longer than a critical period, it also tends to vary in strength over time (Goldberg, 2000). Thus, it may be less a matter of missing an opportunity for learning than it is a matter of missing the optimal period for learning. These sensitive periods vary depending on the skill in question. It may be that when it comes to learning something like self-control, there are several different sensitive periods with different ages of optimal learning. Hence, mother-child attachment, effortful control, and self-monitoring may all set the stage for self-control development, but their sensitive periods may vary from one skill to the next.

The key to learning self-control is similar to the key to learning morality—namely, internalization. The ability to internalize rules, ideas, and values, as described in chapter 6 of this book, is vital to the development of the empathy, guilt, and higher moral reasoning that contribute to a healthy moral system. The same goes for self-control. An individual must internalize the parental discipline and support, observational learning opportunities, and wider social lessons that give rise to an effective system of behavioral control. It should be noted that as with moral integrity, very few people achieve total or complete behavioral control. There are limits to our behavioral control just as there are blind spots in our conscience. We just hope that the limits are not too deep and that the blind spots are neither large nor extensive. By the same token, someone with low self-control will not always act impulsively, there will still be pockets of self-restraint that allow the individual to pull back from situations where they perceive that the costs outweigh the benefits. We should remind ourselves that the human animal, despite its complexity, is still an animal and will react to situations based on its assessment of the anticipated pains and pleasures of a calculated course of action. Therefore, even the most hardened criminal will exhibit self-control some of the time just as the most pious person will commit the occasional peccadillo. In short, to be human is to be inconsistent.

Reactive Criminal Thinking

As one of the four corners of the control model, RCT is something that needs to be explored whenever the control model of lifestyle criminality is being discussed. As defined in chapter 4, RCT is one of the two dimensions of criminal thought process in lifestyle theory, the other being PCT. Whereas PCT is planned, calculated, and devoid of emotion, RCT is impulsive, irresponsible, and saturated in emotion. RCT is the cognitive counterpart to low self-control/behavioral impulsivity. Hence, RCT is sometimes referred to as cognitive impulsivity. Unlike behavioral impulsivity or low self-control, which is an innate quality of the human organism, cognitive impulsivity evolves, in part, from behavioral impulsivity. One of Piaget's (1954) most lasting contributions to the field of developmental psychology was demonstrating how infants and toddlers use their reflexes, senses, and interactions with the environment—processes he referred to as primary, secondary, and tertiary circular reactions—to begin symbolizing their experience and developing cognitive skills. By the end of the sensorimotor stage of cognitive development (age 18–24 months), a child has developed the capacity for representative thought and has started internalizing their environmental experience with schemas. Some of these thoughts will be asocial, others prosocial, and still others, antisocial. Some of the preliminary antisocial thoughts will serve as the groundwork for future cognitive impulsivity or RCT.

One major unresolved issue with low self-control is determining how it should be measured. Gottfredson and Hirschi (1990) assert that self-control estimates should be based entirely on behavior and be independent of attitude. They also maintain that the best way to assess this construct is by having parents and teachers rate a child's ongoing behavior. Even if a self-report measure is used, as parental or teacher ratings are not always available, the focus should be on specific behaviors rather than on the individual's attitude toward these behaviors. The irony is that the Grasmick et al. (1993) scale is the measure of low self-control most commonly used to test Gottfredson and Hirschi's General Theory of Crime. Not only is the Grasmick scale a self-report measure, but it is based on a respondent's attitude rather than on their behavior. Constructing and then comparing behavioral and attitudinal measures of "low self-control" from the National Longitudinal Survey of Youth (NLSY)-Child database, Walters (2017d) determined that the behavioral rating scale completed by the child's mother and the attitudinal self-report scale completed by the child produced results indicating that the two measures were assessing separate but related constructs. This illustrates the importance of differentiating between low self-control and RCT when creating measures and drawing conclusions about criminal behavior and criminal thinking.

RCT can be traced to two principal sources. One source is low self-control, the other is delinquency. Walters (2017g) examined both sources in a sample of 5,427 youth from the longitudinal Add Health study organized into three waves of data. Regardless of whether offending preceded low self-control or low self-control preceded offending, the sequence predicted Wave 3 RCT. Hence, low self-control and delinquency each predicted RCT when positioned as a mediating variable in a three-variable-mediated pathway. Additional research indicates that the past delinquency-future delinquency relationship is mediated by RCT but not by PCT (Walters, 2016h, 2019h). When an antisocial spectrum antecedent to delinquency, bullying perpetration, replaced delinquency as the independent/dependent variable in a three-variable pathway, RCT but not PCT mediated the past bullying-future bullying relationship (Walters & Espelage, 2018a). In each of the three studies, the *a* path of the indirect effect (delinquency/bullying → RCT/PCT) was significant in the RCT-mediated pathway but not in the PCT-mediated pathway. In a fourth study, PCT, as measured by neutralization techniques, predicted delinquency but delinquency did not predict PCT (Morris & Copes, 2012). It would appear then that engaging in delinquent and para-delinquent (i.e., school bullying) behavior, probably because of their disorganized and chaotic nature, gives rise to disorganized thinking, the essence of RCT. Substance use is a third variable that appears to increase RCT (Walters, 2012, 2022b).

Strain

Whenever someone is blocked in achieving a major societal goal, fails to achieve a positively valued personal goal, experiences the loss of a positive stimulus, or is exposed to a negative stimulus, they are said to be experiencing strain. Unlike low self-control and RCT, the source of strain is located in the external environment rather than within the person. At the aggregate or macro-level, the source of strain is failure to achieve a major societal goal as outlined in Merton's (1957) classic strain theory and Messner and Rosenfeld's (1994) institutional anomie theory (IAT). At the individual or micro-level, strain comes from more personal sources like being exposed to a noxious stimulus or losing something of value as described in Agnew's (1992) general strain theory. Whether strain comes from a macro- or micro-level source, however, it is always experienced at the individual level. Members of certain groups may be at greater risk for experiencing macro-level strain, but it is not the group that is strained but the individual within the group. Not everyone from the lower social classes experiences macro-level strain, although such individuals are at greater risk for experiencing macro-level strain relative to those in the middle and upper social classes.

Four of the most important macro-level strains are (1) the belief that personal success is measured in terms of material wealth; (2) structural arrangements that do not allow adequate access to the goal of material wealth for a large portion of the population (i.e., the lower social classes); (3) an emphasis on the goal of material wealth to the detriment of the means by which the wealth is obtained; and (4) domination and subjugation of noneconomic institutions like the family, school, and polity by the economic system (Merton, 1957; Messner & Rosenfeld, 1994). Walters (2021i) studied 65,923 youth from 28 different countries in an effort to test the interaction between a macro-level concept from classic strain and institutional anomie theories, a free market cultural ethos, and a micro-level construct from criminal lifestyle theory, general criminal thinking (GCT)/PCT/RCT. Outcome was measured with an offense variety score. Subjecting the data to multilevel analysis revealed a significant interaction between the macro- and micro-level variables for all three criminal thinking scales: GCT, PCT, and RCT. The results suggest that the criminal thinking-offense variety relationship is significantly stronger in youth from countries holding to a stronger free market cultural ethos.

Micro-level or individual-level strain derives from several sources. One source is failure to achieve a desired goal, such as not making the cut for the freshman baseball team. A second source of micro-level strain is loss of a positive stimulus. A relationship breakup is an example of this type of micro-level strain. A third source of micro-level strain is exposure to an aversive or noxious stimulus. Living in an abusive home with ongoing conflict would be an example of this type of micro-level strain. Whether the strain has a micro- or macro-level source, the road to crime will nearly always travel through an intervening cognitive or emotional variable. Agnew and Broidy (Agnew, 1992; Broidy, 2001; Broidy & Agnew, 1997) designate anger as the key mediator between strain and antisocial behavior, although other negative emotions, such as depression and anxiety, could also play a mediating role in such relationships. Anger may be too short-lived an emotion, however, to be of much use in mediating relationships over several months as is required in a criminality analysis. In studies that have compared anger to the cognitive-affective variable hostility (Walters & Espelage, 2018b) and the cognitive variable RCT (Walters & Espelage, 2017), hostility and RCT have been found to mediate the long-term relationship between strain and antisocial behavior, but anger has not. All is not lost, however; anger may still be useful in predicting individual criminal events, as we shall see in chapter 8.

Hostility

In the previous section, we learned that anger is not a particularly effective mediator of variable relationships when the variables are separated by several months to several years as they are when criminality is assessed. Hostility, perhaps because it is more stable than anger, may be a useful addition to a model designed to explain individual differences in the propensity to commit crime. In research on crime and delinquency, hostility is frequently studied as a function of hostile attribution biases. Hostile attribution biases are emotionally toned misinterpretations of hostile intent attributed to others (Dodge, 2006). If you were to bump into someone with strong hostile attribution biases, they are liable to view the bump as hostile, intentional, and challenging, even if you said, "excuse me." Hostile attribution biases have been studied primarily in youth and have been observed in children as young as 3 years of age (van Dijk et al., 2018), although they have also been found to exist in incarcerated adult offenders with a history of violence (Wegrzyn et al., 2017). Like RCT, hostile attribution biases mediate variable relationships, although they are more likely to lead to a violent response than RCT, particularly in persons who believe they have been wronged, disrespected, or mistreated in some way.

In a systematic review of the literature on hostile attribution biases in children and adolescents, Martinelli et al. (2018) concluded that hostile attributions were more closely tied to reactive than proactive aggression and were equally distributed among boys and girls. They also discovered that relational aggression was specifically associated with relational hostile attribution biases and physical aggression with physical hostile attribution biases. A review of studies on hostile attribution bias and aggression in adults also uncovered evidence of a connection between the two variables but was less definitive because of the relatively small number of studies available for review (Klein Tuente et al., 2019). In a study that was not included in this review, it was determined that hostile attribution biases were more closely aligned with RCT than PCT in a group of medium security prison inmates (Walters, 2007b). The most common response in those who display hostile attribution bias is hostility and aggression (Wang & Xia, 2019). Because hostility rather than hostile attributions is more often included in the databases that have been used to test the moral and control models of lifestyle criminality, "hostility" is the term used to describe the fourth corner of the control model of lifestyle criminality.

CONTROL MODEL OF LIFESTYLE CRIMINALITY

The current version of the control model of lifestyle criminality is depicted in figure 7.3. Commencing with the left-most construct and reading from

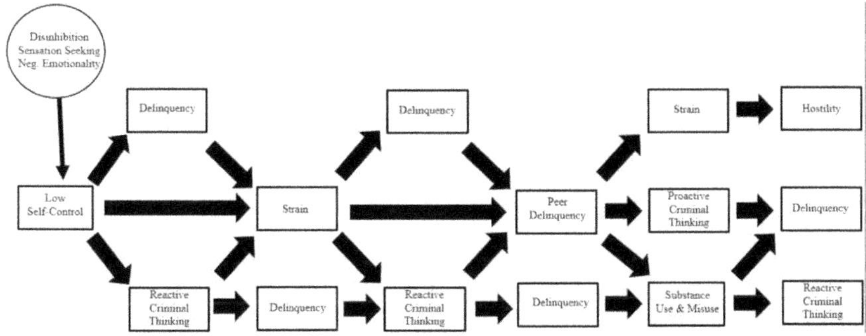

Figure 7.3 Control Model of Lifestyle Criminality. Note: Neg. Emotionality = Negative Emotionality. *Source:* Created by author.

left to right, we see that low self-control is the starting point for the control model just as low moral integrity is the starting point for the moral model. The three principal elements that make up low self-control are positioned in a circle above low self-control and include disinhibition, sensation seeking, and negative emotionality. The relevance of these variables to low self-control is signified by an arrow that connects the circle containing the three elements to the rectangle denoting low self-control. Low self-control, in turn, leads to delinquency, strain, and RCT. Delinquency and RCT also lead to strain. From strain, the model moves to participant delinquency, peer delinquency, and RCT. Peer delinquency, in turn, leads to strain, PCT, and substance use/misuse. On the right side of figure 7.3, strain leads to hostility, and PCT and substance use/misuse both lead to delinquency. On the bottom rung of figure 7.3, RCT is shown leading to delinquency, which, in turn, leads to RCT, which then leads to a second delinquency. The second delinquency goes on to predict substance use/misuse which then leads to a third delinquency and RCT.

The 21 paths that form the control model of lifestyle criminality are enumerated in table 7.1. A supporting study is also provided for each of the 20 unique paths (the RCT → delinquency path is repeated). Attempts were made, as was the case with studies supporting paths in the moral model, to feature longitudinal investigations, although in a few cases only cross-sectional studies were available. For the majority of paths listed in table 7.1, there are not yet a sufficient number of studies to perform a literature review or meta-analysis, although both will be required at some point in the future as the literature on each path grows. Parenthetically, literature reviews and meta-analyses could go a long way toward shedding light on the control and moral models of lifestyle criminality. The moral model with its 20 unique paths was described in chapter 6, although it shares three of these paths (delinquency → RCT; peer delinquency → PCT; PCT → delinquency) with

Table 7.1 The 21 Individual Paths in the Control Model of Lifestyle Criminality, 20 of which Are Unique, along with Studies That Support Each Path

Path	*Supporting Study*
Low Self-Control → Delinquency	Courey and Pare (2016)
Low Self-Control → Strain	Walters (2016e)
Low Self-Control → Reactive Criminal Thinking	Walters (2017g)
Delinquency → Strain	Agnew (1989)
Reactive Criminal Thinking → Strain	Connolly et al. (2020)
Reactive Criminal Thinking → Delinquency	Joo and Lee (2020)
Strain → Delinquency	Bunch et al. (2018)
Strain → Peer Delinquency	Gao and Wong (2018)
Strain → Reactive Criminal Thinking	Agnew et al. (2011)
Delinquency → Reactive Criminal Thinking	Walters (2016h)
Delinquency → Peer Delinquency	Vásquez and Zimmerman (2014)
Reactive Criminal Thinking → Peer Delinquency	De Buck and Pauwels (2019)
Reactive Criminal Thinking → Delinquency (2)	Joo and Lee (2020)
Peer Delinquency → Strain	Barbieri et al. (2019)
Peer Delinquency → Proactive Criminal Thinking	Whited et al. (2017)
Peer Delinquency → Substance Use/Misuse	Barnes et al. (2006)
Delinquency → Substance Use/Misuse	Zhang et al. (2011)
Strain → Hostility	Chambers et al. (2015)
Proactive Criminal Thinking → Delinquency	Topelli et al. (2014)
Substance Use/Misuse → Delinquency	Brook et al. (2011)
Substance Use/Misuse → Reactive Criminal Thinking	Walters (2012)

Source: Table created by author.

the control model. The 20 paths in table 7.1 can be combined to form three and four-variable pathways. Three of these pathways are reviewed next: the peer selection pathway, the strain pathway, and the crime continuity pathway.

The Peer Selection Pathway

There are several variables that appear in both the moral and control models of lifestyle criminality. Peer delinquency is one of them. In the moral model, peer delinquency precedes participant delinquency to form what is known as the peer influence effect. In the control model, peer delinquency follows from participant delinquency to form the peer selection effect. Peer selection refers to the fact that youth, in addition to or instead of being influenced by their peers, create their own peer group by selecting only those individuals as companions with whom they share the most in common or feel the strongest affiliation. What the delinquency → peer delinquency path signifies is that people with a propensity for delinquency will select other people with a propensity for delinquency as friends and associates. The aphorism "birds of a feather stick together" is sometimes used to describe this effect. The peer selection effect is represented in two places on figure 7.3. The simple peer selection effect (delinquency → peer delinquency) starts in the top row of the fourth column of figure 7.3 and ends in the middle row of the fifth column. The mediated peer selection effect (delinquency → RCT → peer delinquency), begins at the bottom row of the third column of figure 7.3, runs through the bottom row of the fourth column, and ends in the middle row of the fifth column.

There are at least three published studies comparing RCT and PCT as mediators of the peer influence effect. In one of these studies, PCT mediated the peer influence effect for friends but RCT did not (Walters, 2015e, 2016d). In the other two studies, gang peer influence (Walters, 2019d) and co-offender peer influence (Walters, 2020j) were found to predict future delinquency indirectly by way of PCT. RCT, on the other hand, failed to mediate the peer influence effect in either study. One of these studies (Walters, 2016d), in addition to examining the peer influence effect, also probed the peer selection effect. The results of this study showed that RCT but not PCT mediated the peer selection effect (delinquency → peer pelinquency). As previously stated, RCT is stimulated by a person's involvement in delinquent activities. The reckless, impulsive, and irresponsible nature of the person's thinking serves as a beacon that attracts the attention of other crime-prone individuals in close proximity to the individual. Once interest is aroused, it is only a matter of time before others begin picking up on the fact that you are just like them in thought if not action. It is at this point that acceptance into a group of like-minded and antisocial peers becomes a distinct possibility and one's likelihood of engaging in criminality expands proportionately.

The Strain Pathway

There is no single strain pathway. Instead, there are multiple strain pathways. Some of these pathways rely on micro-level strain variables, others rely on macro-level strain variables. Examples of both are reviewed in this section. The inaugural attempt to test a strain pathway as part of the control model of lifestyle criminality was a two-study investigation by Walters (2016e) in which peer rejection served as a micro-level strain variable. The first study was conducted with data from the 411-member Cambridge Study in Delinquent Development and explored the path from low self-control to strain. Cross-lagged correlations between low self-control and peer rejection produced results consistent with the control model. What I mean by consistent with the control model is that the correlation between Wave 1 low self-control and Wave 2 peer rejection was significant, whereas the correlation between Wave 1 peer rejection and Wave 2 low self-control was not. The second study reported in Walters (2016e) was conducted using data from the NLSY. Findings from this study also supported predictions from the control model of lifestyle criminality. The two three-variable pathways running from strain to peer delinquency (peer rejection → delinquency → peer delinquency; peer rejection → RCT → peer delinquency) in figure 7.3 were significant, whereas a control pathway (peer rejection → depression → peer delinquency) was not.

Macro-level strain variables have also been found to conform to some of the paths, patterns, and pathways outlined in figure 7.3. Walters (2021i), for instance, tested the moderating effect of a macro-level strain variable (free market cultural ethos) on the micro-level relationship between criminal thinking and offense variety using a large group of youthful participants (ages 10–20) from the Second International Self-Reported Delinquency Study (ISRD-2). The results revealed that the association between criminal thinking, whether measured with GCT, PCT, or RCT, and offense variety was significantly stronger in youth from countries that were rated by the Heritage Foundation as exhibiting a robust free market cultural ethos than in youth from countries displaying a weak free market cultural ethos. Walters (2021a) also used the ISRD-2 to explore the moderating effect of ambient temperature on the RCT-violence relationship. Using middle-school students from 24 European countries that participated in the ISRD-2, he discovered that the RCT was not only more elevated in countries with a higher average annual ambient temperature, but that it also correlated better with violent offending, after PCT and property offending were controlled. Hence, macro-level strain may be just as important as micro-level strain in promoting attitudes conducive to crime. It should be noted, however, that proper temporal order between the predictor (criminal thinking) and outcome (offending) in these studies could not be established because the ISRD-2 used a cross-sectional design.

One of the more robust reciprocal relationships in criminology is the one between crime perpetration and victimization, better known as the victim-offender overlap (Jennings et al., 2012). An early (furthest to the left on figure 7.3) path in the control model (low self-control → strain) received support in a study by Walters (2018c) in which childhood victimization served as a micro-level indicator of strain. In this study, Wave 1 (mean age = 10.7 years) low self-control from the control model and callous-unemotional traits from the moral model were regressed onto Wave 2 childhood maltreatment (victimization). Only low self-control predicted victimization and it did so significantly better than callous-unemotional traits. The pathway in figure 7.3 that represents the offending to victimization portion of the victim-offender overlap can be found in the top two rows of the middle columns in figure 7.3 (delinquency → peer delinquency → strain). This pathway was tested, verified, and attributed to person proximity (Walters, 2020i). In other words, those who offend (delinquency) come into direct and close contact with others who offend (peer delinquency), thus increasing the person's likelihood of becoming a victim of their own peer group (strain). The victimization to offending portion of the victim-offender overlap is represented at the top of the last two columns of figure 7.3. Victimization (strain) leads to hostility, which then leads directly to offending or indirectly to offending via a second mediator (RCT). The latter two constructs were left out of figure 7.3 for space-saving reasons, but the pathway was verified by Walters (2020f).

The Crime Continuity Pathway

Crime continuity reflects the fact that there is a significant amount of continuity in crime and other antisocial behaviors (Nagin & Paternoster, 2000). This was previously discussed in chapter 5 under the heading "Stability in Crime: Crime Continuity and Psychological Inertia." Psychological inertia, as depicted in the bottom row of figure 7.3 (delinquency → RCT → delinquency), is a principal pathway in the control model of lifestyle criminality. There are at least three studies that have directly evaluated the psychological inertia crime continuity pathway. Performing a path analysis of self-report data provided by 673 mid- to late-adolescent British youth from the Offending, Crime, and Justice Survey, Walters (2016h) determined that RCT mediated the past offending-future offending relationship, whereas PCT did not. These findings were replicated in a sample of 1,354 adjudicated delinquents from the Pathways to Desistance study, in which RCT but not PCT mediated the past offending-future offending relationship (Walters, 2019h). A third study was conducted on the antisocial spectrum behavior of bullying perpetration in a group of 1,161 early adolescents from the Illinois Study of Bullying and Sexual Violence. Results showed that cognitive impulsivity (RCT) but not cognitive insensitivity (PCT) mediated the past bullying-future bullying relationship (Walters & Espelage, 2018a). In all three studies, the reason why PCT failed to mediate crime/bullying continuity was that while prior delinquency or bullying consistently predicted RCT, they consistently failed to predict PCT.

Another variable capable of explaining crime continuity is substance use and misuse. Whereas RCT mediates the relationship between past crime and future crime by way of psychological inertia, substance use and misuse may also give rise to crime continuity by way of the drug-crime connection. What, however, is responsible for drug-crime connectivity? One possibility is that drugs and crime are reciprocally related. A bidirectional association has been proposed and found to exist between drugs and crime across the lifespan, from early adolescence through middle adulthood (D'Amico et al., 2008; Felson et al., 2019;

Green et al., 2019). Further evidence of reciprocity can be found in studies demonstrating that continued drug usage tends to impede the natural maturing out of crime process that leads to desistance and that continued involvement in crime tends to inhibit the natural maturing out of drug use process that leads to recovery (Prins, 2008; Walters, 2018e; Welte et al., 2005). The lower right portion of figure 7.3 displays the reciprocal relationship between substance use/misuse and delinquency. It also suggests that peer delinquency may contribute to participant substance use/misuse and that substance use/misuse may increase RCT. As indicated in table 7.1, both paths have received preliminary support (Barnes et al., 2006; Walters, 2012). There is also evidence that substance use/misuse may function as a form of strain as indicated by a four-variable chain recently verified by Walters (2021e). In that chain, drug use (strain) led to negative peer associations, which then led to either PCT or victimization (strain), with PCT and victimization both leading to delinquency.

Other Noteworthy Paths

Hostility, in particular, requires further study and development before its role in the control model of lifestyle criminality can be fully appreciated. It is considered one of the four corners of the control model of lifestyle criminality yet is only involved in one of the 21 paths depicted in figure 7.3. This is partly because certain subsequent constructs that likely flow from hostility, like delinquency and RCT, could not be placed to the right of hostility because of space restrictions. In the previously reviewed Walters (2020f) investigation, hostility served as the first of two mediators, preceding RCT, in a serial mediator model that linked violent victimization to violent offending measured 18 months apart. Results such as these and the fact that hostility but not anger has been found to mediate the victimization-bullying (Walters & Espelage, 2018b) and sibling aggression-school aggression (Walters & Espelage, 2020a) relationships suggest the need for more information on hostility, its relationship to hostile attribution biases, and its role in the control model of lifestyle criminality. It should also be noted that while RCT is the main thinking pattern in the control model, PCT was also present, just as RCT was present in the moral model. This illustrates how PCT and RCT provide a doorway between the two models.

THE DRUG-CRIME CONNECTION AND THE WORST OF BOTH WORLDS HYPOTHESIS

Even though substance use/misuse is not one of the four corners of the control model of lifestyle criminality, it nonetheless contributes significantly to the functioning of the control model. First, we saw how substance use can affect low self-control by augmenting or distorting disinhibition, sensation seeking, and negative affect. Next, we observed how substance use contributes to RCT and delinquency development. Finally, we learned that substance use can serve as a source of strain. Its most valuable contribution, however, may be its ability to serve as an alternate lifestyle that partially overlaps with the criminal lifestyle (there is also evidence that early drug use falls on the antisocial spectrum and serves as a developmental antecedent to delinquency and crime via cognitive impulsivity: Walters, 2022). It has been proposed that substance misuse can be classified as a lifestyle and that this lifestyle shares features in common with the criminal lifestyle. For example, the behavioral patterns that define the two lifestyles are similar. As previously stated, the four behavioral styles of a criminal lifestyle are irresponsibility, self-indulgence, interpersonal intrusiveness, and social rule breaking. The four behavioral styles of a drug lifestyle are irresponsibility/pseudoresponsibility, stress-coping imbalance, interpersonal triviality, and social rule breaking/bending (Walters, 1992a). The overlapping lifestyles interpretation of the drug-crime relationship has given rise to what has come to be known as the Worst of Both Worlds (WBW) hypothesis.

The WBW derives from the overlapping lifestyles interpretation of the drug-crime connection. The founding premise of the WBW is that comorbid crime and substance misuse are associated with more negative outcomes than either condition (crime or substance misuse) alone. In the original study on the WBW, Walters (2014a) ascertained that youth with both a criminal and substance misuse background achieved significantly poorer outcomes in terms of future crime and drug involvement than youth with just a criminal background or just a drug background. Using data provided by 6,502 members of the Study of Adolescent Health (Add Health), Walters (2015b) determined that a GCT score assessed at age 18–26 mediated the relationship between age 13–20 criminal and substance comorbidity and age 24–32 criminal and substance involvement. Subsequent research on the WBW has shown that the effect works as well with age of drug/crime onset as it does with presence/absence of drug/crime involvement (Walters, 2016a) and is as strong when measured with antecedent conditions like bullying and alcohol experimentation as when measured with delinquency and substance misuse (Walters, 2021f). It also appears to operate along the lines of the risk principle in which individuals with greater drug-crime comorbidity receive greater benefit from intensive treatment than individuals with lesser drug-crime comorbidity (Walters, 2016b). The feasibility of using drug-crime comorbidity as a risk factor has given rise to a concept known as reciprocal risk in which crime and substance misuse serve as risk factors for each other.

PANZRAM AND THE CONTROL MODEL

From the previous chapter, one might surmise that the moral model was specifically designed with Carl Panzram in mind. As will be shown in the present chapter, the control model is no less descriptive of Panzram's thoughts, actions, and ongoing troubles with the law. There is clear evidence of all three elements of low self-control in his letters to Henry Lesser and other autobiographical writings. Disinhibition and low moral integrity are displayed in a single sentence of a letter he wrote to Lesser: "surely you know that I am very impulsive, very vindictive and absolutely unscrupulous" (Borowski, 2020, p. 166). Panzram's sensation-seeking tendencies are encapsulated in an anecdote from his autobiography where he talks about lighting fires and watching them burn: "I burned old barns, sheds, fences, snowsheds, or anything I could and when I couldn't burn anything else I would set fire to the grass on the praries [*sic*], or the woods, anything and everything" (Panzram, 1928, p. 21). Low frustration tolerance and strong negative affect in response to stress are expressed in a letter Panzram wrote to Lesser a little more than a month after Lesser sent him a copy of Kant's *Critique of Pure Reason*:

> The book which you sent me Kants Critique, I read for about a month but it is too deep for me to understand. . . . Finally I got so disgusted and discouraged that I went into a tantrum and in a mad rage, I tore it up into 10,000 pieces and fired it out of my door. (Borowski, 2020, p. 197)

We know that low self-control is the natural state of the human organism, but Panzram's natural state was very likely aggravated and inflated by a range of genetic and early environmental anomalies. Panzram reports that his parents divorced when he was 7 or 8 years old and that he never got along with either one. He also notes that he grew up in a family of five brothers and one sister and that he was the only one to ever get in trouble with the law. Age of onset was right around the time his father left the family, at which point he started breaking into neighbors' homes and stealing things, a pattern that conforms to Moffitt's (1993) life-course-persistent trajectory. While early attachment to one or more parenting figures and parental discipline is vital in teaching children self-control, a criminal is not normally created by parenting alone. More often than not, it is the parent × child interaction that is of principal concern in creating risk for future offending. The biological and early environmental aberrations that set young Panzram apart from his siblings may help explain why he was the only one with a criminal record. During the latter stages of the sensitive period when Panzram should have been learning to control himself, he was learning the power of violence at Red Wing, running away from home, hopping trains, and setting fire to structures he associated with his tormentors, from the Red Wing "paint shop" to any church he came across.

Panzram suffered from weak internalization with regards to both morality and self-control, but as I mentioned earlier, internalization is not usually an all-or-nothing phenomenon. Panzram, in fact, was very adept at internalizing certain life lessons, even though he never had an internalized moral system or set of beliefs about self-control. He is alleged to have told another inmate "the way to get any man (is) to get him while he is not looking" (Borowski, 2020, p. 103). In his autobiography, Panzram writes about an inmate who was giving him trouble. From the sound of it, this inmate was of equal or greater size and status and so could not be easily intimidated or bullied. Panzram therefore decided to do the following:

> I sneaked up behind him as he was sitting in a chair and I hit him on the back of the head with a 10 pound club. It didn't kill him but he was good and sick, and he left me alone after that. (Panzram, 1928, p. 35)

This illustrates how Panzram dealt with a threat in prison, a situation with which he was likely familiar and for which he had an internalized script as to how it could best be handled. Confronting the other inmate directly brought with it a risk of injury or death, while ignoring the threat could lead to a loss of status among other prisoners, and so he did what he thought would provide him with the best outcome. His actions, while they could have proven costly, from indictment if the other inmate were to die or retaliation if the inmate were to survive, demonstrate forethought and reason rather than pure instinct and impulse.

Panzram displays above-average intelligence despite having no more than a fifth- or sixth-grade education. Yet, he is not particularly psychologically minded, and he tends to think in overly concrete terms. His autobiography is little more than a chronology of life events, victimization experiences, and crimes. Unfortunately, the thinking that drives Panzram's participation in these events, experiences, and crimes is unavailable to the reader because it was largely unavailable to him. Even so, he displays clear signs of at least one reactive dimension thinking style, that of cutoff. One example is when he ripped the Kant book into thousands of pieces because he was frustrated at not being able to understand much of what was written in the book. Another example was his response to organizations wanting to help him avoid the death penalty for killing his work supervisor at USP Leavenworth:

> If I had the power and the opportunities, then I would soon show you what real meanness was. You overlook the fact that the law and a great many people have been trying their damnedest for 25 years to reform me. I am tired of having

> people try to reform me. What I want to do is reform them and I think the best way to reform 'em is to put 'em out of their misery. (Borowski, 2020, p. 178)

The RCT styles of cognitive indolence and discontinuity are less evident than cutoff in Panzram's letters and autobiography, but when we consider the general absence of conventional success that Panzram has experienced in life it is difficult to imagine that impulsive decision-making (cognitive indolence) and volatility (discontinuity) did not somehow play a role in his life failures.

While one must dig deep into Panzram's writings to find evidence of non-cutoff RCT, there is no lack of strain in these accounts. In narrating his life story, Panzram repeatedly returns to the real and perceived mistreatment he received from parents, teachers, supervisors, police, and correctional officers and the felt need to retaliate, not only against his aggressors but against society at large. Physical and sexual abuse at Red Wing, gangraped by four hobos, ongoing brutalization in jail and prison, and a wide variety of other victimizations, took their toll on Panzram. In his autobiography he recounts a long list of tortures he has allegedly endured in the jails and prisons where he spent the majority of his adulthood:

> During my twenty years in all the various prisons and jails I have been in, I have undergone every kind of abuse and punishment that the ingenious minds of many men could devise and, believe me, men can surely figure out some horrible tortures to impose on other men . . . I have been in solitary confinement for years at a time where I could have no privileges or pleasures of any kind. Every single thing in life that men hold worthwhile and that go to make life worth living for, I have been denied and deprived of. (Panzram, 1928, p. 3)

His response to the strain of these tortures was to turn the tables on his torturers and go from being a victim to becoming a victimizer.

In a case like Panzram's, strain leads to hostility and hostility leads to violence. This is consistent with what has been observed in research on delinquency (Walters, 2020f) and bullying (Walters & Espelage, 2018b) in which hostility has been found to mediate the relationship between strain and antisocial behavior. There is little doubt that Panzram exuded a great deal of hostility and that his hostility emanated from a long list of violent victimizations, some of which may have been fabricated or exaggerated. In someone like Panzram, hostility is not only a reaction to losing a valued object or relationship, exposure to a noxious stimulus, or failure to achieve a positively valued goal, it is also a way of manipulating others and keeping them at a distance: "I am getting along all right but I am pretty hostile and I might blow up any time" (Borowski, 2020, p. 69). Although substance misuse is not one of the four corners of the control model, it can play a significant role in a person's relationship with the law. In his autobiography and letters to Henry Lesser, Panzram denied that he had a problem with alcohol or drugs, yet it appears that alcohol was involved in a number of his crimes and in some of his victimizations. There is not enough information to determine exactly what role alcohol played in Panzram's criminal lifestyle, but it could have been substantial.

CONCLUSION

The goal of this chapter was to describe the second of three models included under the umbrella of criminal lifestyle theory. Unlike the moral model, where the individual enters the world without any preconceived patterns of moral behavior, children are born into the world with low self-control. In the moral model, a person learns to be either moral or immoral, or in most cases, a mixture of the two. In the control model, a person enters the world with low self-control and must learn to exercise self-restraint by internalizing their interactions with parents, siblings, teachers, coaches, and others. Hirschi (1979) has argued that these two views of human nature—representing the social learning and social control theories of crime, respectively—are incompatible. Lifestyle theory, however, provides an overarching perspective under which both models, along with a third, the decision-making model of crime, not only coexist, but actually complement one another. This overarching perspective holds that crime is a function of learning or lack thereof. We continue this discussion in the next chapter with a decision-making model that is designed to explain the processes that give rise to specific criminal events.

Chapter 8

The Decision-Making Model of Crime

"Specific Criminal Events Come Down to a Choice"

Lifestyle theory is made up of three models. The first two models, the moral model of lifestyle criminality and the control model of lifestyle criminality, were reviewed in chapters 6 and 7 of this book, respectively. The third model, the decision-making model of crime, is examined in the current chapter. What separates the first two models from the third is that while the moral and control models are designed to explain criminality or a person's propensity for crime, the decision-making model is designed to explain crime or a person's involvement in a specific criminal act. All three models fall under the same umbrella, however, that umbrella being that crime is learned. Just as people learn or fail to learn the skills and attitudes that place them at risk for or protect them against future criminality, so too do they learn or fail to learn the skills and attitudes that lead to specific criminal acts. It is the criminal event, then, that is of principal concern in the current chapter. Like the moral and control models of criminality described in the previous two chapters, the decision-making model is made up of multiple biological, social, cognitive, and developmental elements. Before addressing these elements, however, it is imperative that we examine the philosophical roots and underpinnings of the model itself.

PHILOSOPHICAL ROOTS OF THE DECISION-MAKING MODEL

The philosophical roots of lifestyle theory's decision-making model of crime can be traced back to existentialism and a belief in human agency. These two philosophical perspectives, along with the three C's of lifestyle theory (conditions, choice, and cognition), are discussed in this section.

Existentialism

There are two schools of philosophical thought that emphasize free will. One is humanism, and the other is existentialism. Humanism is a rational approach to solving the problems of humanity in which reason and science replace religion and the supernatural as explanatory tools. Choice and human agency are also stressed by philosophers and psychologists associated with the humanistic approach. These themes run through the works of humanistic philosophers like John Dewey (1859–1952) and Julian Huxley (1887–1975) and such humanistic psychologists as Carl Rogers (1902–1987) and Abraham Maslow (1908–1970). Existentialists also emphasize freedom but contend that it must be accompanied by responsibility to be realized. According to existential philosophers like Søren Kierkegaard (1813–1855), Jean-Paul Sartre (1905–1980), and Martin Heidegger (1889–1976), we are thrown into a world not of our choosing. To achieve freedom, we must come to terms with the thrownness of our lives and rise above the historical and contextual conditions in which we find ourselves. This is another way of saying that many of the conditions in a person's life are beyond their control and it is their responsibility to make the best of their circumstances by living as genuine a life as possible. Too often, people respond to the conditions of their lives by becoming angry, wallowing in self-pity, or thinking irrationally. The truly free individual rises above the conditions or thrownness of their existence, much as Viktor Frankl (1905–1997) did when he found himself incarcerated in a Nazi concentration camp because of his Jewish heritage.

Human Agency

Human agency is the belief that people make choices and that they implement these choices by acting on their environment. In this way, human agency is often viewed as the polar opposite of hard determinism where the external environment or a person's biology is said to act on the individual. Although not normally classified as a humanistic psychologist, Albert Bandura (1925–2021) was a leading advocate of human agency during his lifetime. He believed that self-regulatory processes and a person's ability to observe and reflect on their thinking, a process known as metacognition, explain how self-efficacy, a person's appraisal of their likelihood of succeeding at a particular task, is realized. In his 1989 article on human agency and social cognitive theory, Bandura discussed how a strong sense of self-efficacy has allowed scientists, artists, and musicians to pursue ideas and projects that were often disparaged by their contemporaries and effectively cope with the disappointment and stress of having their manuscripts, paintings, and music rejected. An aspect of human agency emphasized by Bandura which is particularly relevant to criminal decision-making is the notion of forethought. Human agency allows an individual to evaluate an option based on a review of the anticipated consequences and likelihood of future success. Because decisions about crime often include consideration of the likelihood of future success and the anticipated costs and benefits of a particular course of action, human agency is vital to any such theory.

The Three C's

Bandura's triarchic model of reciprocal determinism is another way social cognitive theory has contributed to our understanding of the criminal lifestyle. In a 1978 article entitled "the self system in reciprocal determinism," Bandura wrote that cognitive functions, the external environment, and a person's behavior form a system of bidirectional influences. Lifestyle theory, it should be noted, proposes a similar conceptualization known as the three C's. The three C's—conditions, choice, and cognition—are said to enter into a reciprocal relationship with one another, similar to how the four corners of the moral and control models of criminality enter into reciprocal relationships with each other. Hence, conditions from the social environment, the physical environment, and a person's biological makeup shape choice and cognition, but are, in turn, shaped by these same choices and cognitions. Choice does the same with conditions and cognition, and cognition with conditions and choice (see figure 8.1). According to this conceptual model, conditions limit a person's options, but do not determine a person's choices. Even when faced with a severely restricted range of options (e.g., a demand from an armed bank robber to "hand over the money or die"), the person still has a choice. Choice is such a vital feature of our system of jurisprudence that we do not hold those who are deemed insane at the time they commit a criminal act legally culpable because it is believed that they lacked "mens rea" (a guilty mind or ability to choose) at the time of the offense.

DETERRENCE AND RATIONAL CHOICE THEORIES

Any serious discussion of criminal decision-making should include a review of deterrence and rational choice theories. In fact, Cesare Beccaria's (1764/1995) philosophy of deterrence is often considered one of the first theories of crime. He and Jeremy Bentham (1748–1832) laid the groundwork for what has become known as the classical school of criminology and deterrence theory whereby offenders are viewed as rational decision-makers who

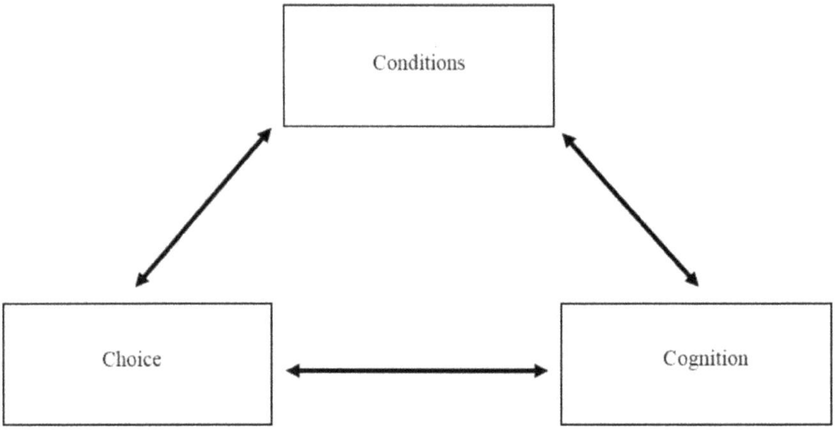

Figure 8.1 Reciprocal Relationships Proposed to Exist between Conditions, Choice, and Cognition by Lifestyle Theory. *Source:* Created by author.

factor in the celerity, severity, and certainty of punishment when deciding whether to commit a criminal act. Rational choice theory takes this a step further by calculating and comparing the anticipated rewards (benefits) and punishments (costs) of engaging in criminal activity. Both are theories of crime. Major modern-day deterrence and rational choice theorists include Gary Becker, Derek Cornish, Ronald Clarke, Daniel Nagin, and Raymond Paternoster. With an eye toward rational decision-making and cost-benefit analysis, rational choice theory is frequently classified as an economic theory of crime and some of its principal proponents have, in fact, been economists (Becker) or academics housed in departments or schools of economics (Cornish). In this section, we examine the deterrence doctrine upon which deterrence theory is based, cost-benefit analysis upon which rational choice theory is based, the principal limitations of deterrence theory and cost-benefit analysis, the developmental and situational context within which decisions are made, and the role of nonrational factors in human decision-making.

The Deterrence Doctrine

When Beccaria first published "on crimes and punishments," he did so anonymously for fear of retaliation from the Italian government. To his surprise, the book was well-received, not only in Italy, but throughout Europe and across the Atlantic in America. Catherine the Great of Russia praised the book extensively. And it led directly to abolition of the death penalty in the Grand Duchy of Tuscany. In America, it became a template for the U.S. Constitution and Bill of Rights. The book called for sweeping reforms in how crimes were coded, defendants represented, cases adjudicated, convicts sentenced, and victims treated. Its greatest contribution to the present chapter, however, is the deterrence doctrine. According to the deterrence doctrine, punishments that are swift, certain, and severe have the greatest likelihood of deterring future crime. Thus, crime opportunities perceived by an individual as having a high likelihood of leading to apprehension and punishments that are swift and severe are much less likely to be acted upon than crime opportunities perceived to have a low likelihood of apprehension and punishments that are delayed or mild. These perceptions are learned from personal experience as well as vicariously, through observing others (Stafford & Warr, 1993).

Celerity or swiftness is the least studied aspect of deterrence theory. For both practical and due process reasons, the celerity prong of the deterrence doctrine is difficult to study and for ethical reasons, it is virtually impossible to examine experimentally. Most of the aggregate, perceptual, and correctional intervention studies that have been performed on celerity have produced either inconclusive or non-supportive results (Pratt & Turanovic, 2018). Although more research is available on the severity prong of the deterrence doctrine than on the celerity prong, the results are no more encouraging. Whether using perceptual measures of severity or more objective indices like sentence length and the death penalty, severity appears to have little deterrent value and the few effects that have been observed are small and depend on a high level of certainty (Grasmick & Bryjak, 1980). Of the three prongs of the deterrence doctrine, certainty of punishment is the one most likely to lead to deterrence. Studies show that both the perceived certainty of getting caught and objective indicators like "hot spot" policing serve as deterrents to future crime (Nagin, 2013). Based on this research, lifestyle theory incorporates the perceived certainty of apprehension and punishment as a deterrent to crime into several of its tenets.

Cost-Benefit Analysis

Proponents of rational choice theory maintain that a person weighs the anticipated costs against the anticipated benefits of engaging in crime or the anticipated costs and benefits of crime versus noncrime when deciding whether or not to take advantage of a criminal opportunity. In situations where the perceived benefits of crime outweigh the perceived costs, the individual is more liable to act on a criminal opportunity than when the perceived costs of crime outweigh the perceived benefits. The cost-benefit analysis could be formal, with individual weights assigned to each cost and each benefit and a total score derived, or it could be informal, by estimating in a general sense whether the costs seem to outweigh the benefits or the benefits seem to outweigh the costs. Rational choice theory and the cost-benefit analysis are usually more complex than the deterrence doctrine because they require multiple decisions (whether to participate in the crime, when to participate in the crime, whether to include a crime-partner, etc.), whereas the deterrence doctrine centers around the question of whether or not the person is deterred from criminal action (Paternoster, 1989). There are idiosyncrasies to the cost-benefit analysis, however, that can bias the results. For instance, the benefits of crime tend to be short-term, whereas the costs are more often long-term. Many offenders have what Wilson and Herrnstein (1985) refer to as a short time horizon whereby they pursue short-term outcomes to the exclusion of long-term outcomes. This not only contributes to their impulsivity but also explains why they prefer criminal options to noncriminal ones.

According to rational choice theory, the best way to reduce crime is to raise its cost or reduce its benefit (Clarke, 2004). Situational crime control and prevention techniques were specifically designed to do just that. Altering the external environment, it was reasoned, can make a criminal opportunity seem more risky and less rewarding than a noncriminal opportunity. Some critics have argued that crime will simply be displaced to an area that does not use situational crime control (Reppetto, 1976), whereas supporters contend that this is more than compensated for by a positive diffusion effect to neighboring districts (Weisburd et al., 2006). Situational crime prevention techniques, which are discussed in some detail in chapter 11 of this book, are designed to either increase the cost of crime or decrease its benefit. There is ample evidence that both are achieved, along with roughly equal amounts of displacement and diffusion (Guerette & Bowers, 2009). A related model, routine activity theory, holds that crime is a function of three factors: a motivated offender, a suitable target, and the absence of capable guardians against crime (Cohen & Felson, 1979). Similar to the rational choice model, routine activity theory asserts that reducing suitable targets for crime and increasing capable guardians against crime should prevent a certain proportion of crime, a proposition for which there is some empirical support (Hollis-Peel et al., 2011).

Limitations of Deterrence and Rational Choice Theories

The principal limitation of deterrence theory is that deterrence effects are often small, offense-specific (with illegal parking, speeding, and littering achieving more consistent results than serious crimes), and centered on police presence rather than on interpretation of the law (Tonry, 2008). In fact, most people do not have enough knowledge of the law and the specific penalties associated with violating the law for it to have much of an impact on their behavior (Wright, 2010). The early successes of policies establishing mandatory arrests for misdemeanor domestic violence (Sherman & Berk, 1984), "shall-issue" laws mandating issuance of concealed carry permits to most adults (Lott, 1998), and the death penalty (Dezhaksh et al., 2003) were eventually found to either be incorrect or ungeneralizable (Tonry, 2008). Get-tough-on-crime mandatory minimum sentencing initiatives like three-strike and truth-in-sentencing laws never showed an initial positive effect, even though they remain popular to this day (Kovandzic et al., 2004). Furthermore, as previously noted, emphasizing the swiftness of punishment is often impractical and the severity of punishment is usually an ineffective deterrent. This leaves certainty, which research indicates is moderately successful in deterring a range of crimes using the micro-level perceptual deterrence/experimental approach or the macro-level aggregate approach (Nagin, 2013). What the reader needs to understand, however, is that perceptual deterrence research and experimental studies often make use of college student samples who are at very low risk of committing the types of crimes that are used to conduct most scenario studies (Wikström et al., 2012).

Rational choice theory does a much better job of explaining economic or acquisitive crime than it does violent or expressive crime (Hayward, 2007). This is because emotions are often involved in violent or expressive crime and the basic utilitarian (cost-benefit) approach to decision-making fails to account for nonrational factors in human decision-making (Damasio, 1994). All the more troubling, it has been estimated that one-third to one-half of all economic decisions are based on emotional or nonrational processes (Zafirovski, 2012). It has also been found that multiple emotions may be involved in a single criminal act. In interviews conducted with 76 robbers, Lindegaard et al. (2014) discovered that fear was the predominant emotion prior to the offense, but that happiness rose to prominence at the conclusion of a successful robbery. Simon (1982) characterized these nonrational processes as elements of bounded rationality and maintained that decision-making was limited by the decision itself, the time available to make the decision, and the cognitive capacity of the brain. The decision-making model of crime described in this chapter focuses on three aspects of boundedness. First, decisions are made in a developmental context in that a person's developmental stage will affect how well they conduct the rational cost-benefit analysis. Second, there is a situational context in which situational factors such as the amount of time available to make a decision and the nature of the decision itself influence the outcome. Finally, emotions and other nonrational elements like criminal thinking help shape the decision to commit crime. These three factors are discussed next.

Developmental Context

As the human brain develops, so too does a person's ability to choose and make decisions. We would not expect a 5-year-old child to have the same capacity for decision-making as a 15-year-old adolescent and we would not expect the 15-year-old adolescent to be as adept at decision-making as a 25-year-old adult. This is why we do not hold a child to the same standards of conduct as we do an adolescent and an adolescent to the same standards of conduct as we do an adult. The difference comes down to brain development and experience. Brain development adds significantly to decision-making capacity and competence. Limbic structures of prime importance in achieving optimal decision-making, it should be noted, undergo myelination and pruning in the transition from childhood to early adolescence, whereas the prefrontal and striatal cortexes that support self-control and effective decision-making undergo accelerated myelination and pruning in the late teens and early adult years (Hartley & Somerville, 2015). Experience is just as important as neural-biological development in the evolution of adolescent and early adult decision-making. The idea that self-control and decision-making follow a smooth path from adolescence to early adulthood is viewed by Romer et al. (2017) as an oversimplified perspective. Adolescents, they argue, display a mixed pattern of decision-making competence, with some of their skills on par with adults and other skills clearly inferior to that found in the typical adult.

A variety of experiences help shape adolescent decision-making for the better, although there are also experiences that help shape adolescent decision-making for the worst. Blakemore and Robbins (2012) report that adolescents were more likely to engage in risky decision-making when they performed a task in front of peers, particularly when their self-esteem was threatened and their emotions stimulated. These "hot" situations appear to interfere with an adolescent's ability to conduct a proper cost-benefit analysis. This then increases the likelihood of a youth making an impulsive or risky decision. It should also be pointed out that the developmental context for decision-making is not restricted to the formation of self-control as a counter to cognitive and behavioral impulsivity. That is because moral issues also play an important role in the development of decision-making competence as children grow into adolescents. Research indicates, for instance, that while young children frequently experience a positive emotion like happiness upon committing a moral transgression (Arsenio et al., 2009), adolescents are more apt to experience a positive emotion like pride when they make a positive moral choice (Malti et al., 2012). There is also evidence that adolescent improvements in decision-making relate to moral reasoning and advancements in theory of mind (Sommer et al., 2014).

Situational Context

A number of situational factors can also have a bearing on criminal decision-making. Some of these factors operate along the lines of bounded rationality.

As was previously mentioned, bounded rationality hampers the overall effectiveness of a cost-benefit analysis by limiting the precision with which the cost-benefit analysis can be carried out. Chief among these bounded rationality factors are the actual decision the individual must make and the time available to make it. Another group of situational factors influence the decision-making process by providing a context for the decision. These contextual situational factors, like the contextual developmental factors described in the previous section, can exert either an aggravating (making crime more likely) or mitigating (making crime less likely) impact on a criminal decision. Peers may be particularly important in this regard. Hoeben and Thomas (2019) recently discussed how peers may provide a social context for a criminal decision by exerting either an active or passive influence. Active peer influence might include peers as instigators of an actor's interest in offending, as conversational partners who encourage or incite the actor's involvement in criminal behavior, or as co-offenders in one or more crimes. Passive peer influence might include the fact that by their mere presence, peers alter the actor's perception, appraisal, and calculation of the costs and benefits of a particular criminal opportunity.

Situational context has been studied with some crimes more than others. One of the more extensively studied crimes with respect to situational context is sex offending. Beauregard and Leclerc (2007) took note of the fact that while criminal decision-making has been a topic of research for quite some time, the focus of attention in nearly all of the studies up to that point had been on the inner workings of the offender's mind, with little apparent concern for how these psychological factors interfaced with situational and environmental factors. Using data gathered from semi-structured interviews conducted with 69 serial sexual offenders who had committed sex crimes against strangers, Beauregard and Leclerc were able to establish a connection between the amount of force and violence displayed during the sexual assault and the degree of victim resistance. The results implied that as the victim resisted, the perpetrator used increased levels of force and violence to gain compliance, although results from an earlier study suggested that it was perpetrator force and violence that led to increased victim resistance (Ullman & Knight, 1992). Selecting both a target for predation and an environment in which to prey are part of the sex offender's decision-making process. Rebocho and Silva (2014), in fact, discovered that routine activities were particularly important when selecting a suitable target for victimization and an environment conducive to predation where capable guardianship was weak.

Nonrational Elements

The two most important nonrational elements in the decision-making model of crime are emotion and criminal thinking. Emotion has the ability to both impede and facilitate decision-making. Paulus and Yu (2012) report that poorly calibrated affect resulting from clinical anxiety and depression can disrupt the objective cost-benefit analytic process by misrepresenting the odds and potential outcomes of various options. Even if emotion could be divorced from the decision-making process, which I don't believe it can, it would be unwise to base a decision solely on a rational assessment. People with lesions in the ventromedial prefrontal cortex—a condition known to interfere with the normal processing of emotion, but which leaves most of the cognitive functions intact—normally display poor decision-making competence (Bechara, 2004). What this means is that while emotion is an essential part of the decision-making process, it should be modulated by cognition. Martin and Delgado (2011), as a case in point, discovered that cognitive modulation of emotion led to decisions that were less impulsive and less risky than when participants were instructed not to try and cognitively regulate their emotions. Of course, cognition also has the ability to interfere with decision-making by stimulating emotions that impede the problem-solving sequence. This topic is covered next.

The other nonrational element of central significance to criminal decision-making is antisocial or criminal thinking. PCT and RCT are classified as nonrational because they are irrational forms of cognition or thought that support a criminal lifestyle and give rise to criminal decisions. By interfacing with the situational/developmental context, interacting with certainty, obstructing moral emotion, and exacerbating hedonistic emotion, they make it more likely that a person will select a criminal option. PCT and RCT don't just put a person at risk for future criminality, they are also instrumental in encouraging participation in isolated criminal events. As we saw in chapters 6 and 7, PCT is most relevant to moral issues and the moral model of lifestyle criminality, whereas RCT is most relevant to control issues and the control model of lifestyle criminality. In the decision-making model of crime described next, PCT has ties to the moral belief system and RCT has ties to the hedonistic belief system. At the outset, we would be well advised to remember that criminal decision-making is composed of both rational and nonrational elements and that trying to understand criminal decision-making while ignoring the nonrational elements is as shortsighted as trying to understand criminal decision-making without the rational elements.

THE DECISION-MAKING MODEL OF CRIME

The decision-making model of crime was originally proposed by Walters (2015c) as a means of explaining how criminal decisions are made. It has been expanded to eight principles, each of which is listed and defined in table 8.1. Starting with the rationality principle, the model maintains that humans are rational organisms capable of making reasoned decisions. The utility principle asserts that means/ends calculations constitute the rational elements of the decision. According to the hedonism principle, the ultimate goal of means/ends thinking is to maximize pleasure and minimize pain. The moral principle maintains that interpretations of right and wrong also enter into the decisional matrix. Decisions are based on anticipation of pain versus pleasure and guilt versus pride as outlined in the expectations principle. Social exchange, on the other hand, refers to the fact that a decision is based on the results of a cost-benefit analysis of the different advantages and disadvantages of each course of action factoring in both hedonistic and moral considerations. Bounded rationality, the seventh principle, holds that an actor evaluates alternatives within the limits of their knowledge, abilities, emotions, and nonrational thoughts. The final principle, punishment, holds that legal or extralegal sanctions are most effective when certainty of apprehension and punishment is high.

Whereas transitions taking place in the moral and control models of lifestyle criminality (i.e., two-variable paths in figures 7.3 and 8.1, respectively) ordinarily occur over a period of weeks, months, or even years, transitions taking place in the decision-making model of crime (see figure 8.2) are much quicker, the entire process usually taking no longer than a few seconds to complete. Although the decisional process begins with a perceived opportunity for crime, everything that follows occurs almost simultaneously. Lifestyle theory contends that once a criminal opportunity presents itself the individual will do one of three things: (1) process the opportunity further by exploring incentives and deterrents to participation in the crime; (2) halt the sequence by refusing to further explore incentives and deterrents to participation in the crime; and (3) delay the decision pending further review or clarification. An example of the latter would be an individual who plans to

Table 8.1 Eight Principles of the Decision-Making Model of Crime

Rationality	*Humans Are Rational Actors*
Utility	Means/ends calculations are part of the decision-making process.
Hedonism	Goal of means/ends is to maximize pleasure and minimize pain.
Moral	Judgments of right and wrong also weigh on the decision.
Expectations	Anticipation of pain versus pleasure and guilt versus pride shape decisions.
Social Exchange	Decisions are based on ongoing cost-benefit analyses.
Bounded Rationality	Evaluate alternatives taking into account nonrational elements.
Punishment	Sanction effectiveness depends on perceived certainty of punishment.

Source: Table created by author using data from Walters (2015c).

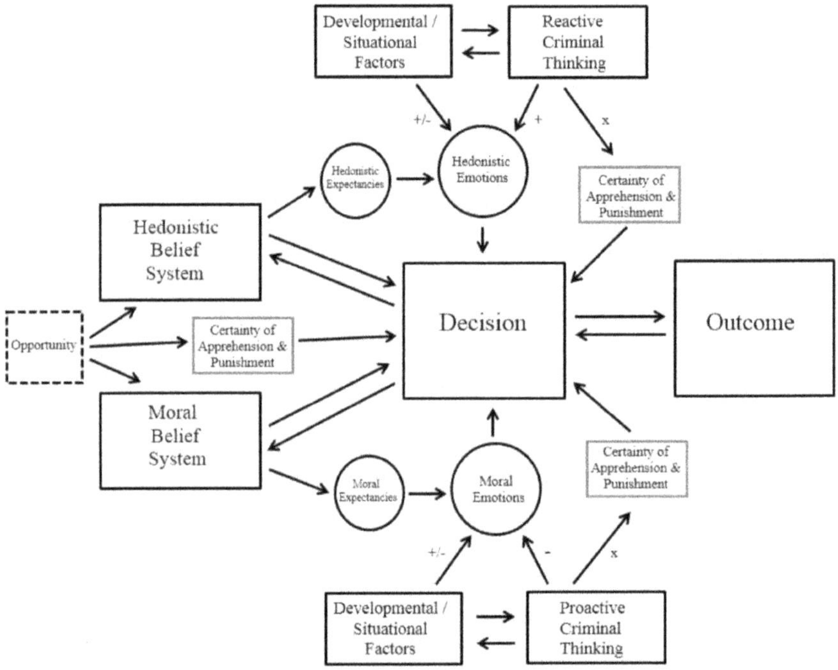

Figure 8.2 The Decision-Making Model of Crime. Note: + = excitatory influence, – = inhibitory influence, x = interactive effect. *Source:* Created by author.

rob a bank but believes they can only do so if they have a crime-partner and so delays the decision until they can find someone willing to assist them with the bank robbery. According to lifestyle theory, the criminal decision-making process can be broken down into three steps or stages. These three steps will be examined in the following sequence: opportunity, incentive/deterrence, and aggravating and mitigating conditions. Before proceeding, special note should be taken of the bidirectional relationships proposed to exist between the decision and several of the other variables in the decision-making model, including the outcome.

Opportunity

The decision-making model of crime, as conceptualized by lifestyle theory, maintains that opportunity is a necessary but not sufficient condition for crime. This is another way of saying that crime cannot occur in the absence of opportunity, but opportunity alone does not automatically lead to crime. Given the significance of opportunity in promoting individual criminal events, it is imperative that the reader understand how lifestyle theory conceives of opportunity. First, because there is no crime without opportunity, reducing opportunities for crime would seem to be an effective crime control strategy; yet, opportunities for crime are so abundant that limiting opportunities will have only a small effect on the overall crime rate. Second, people are not equally sensitive to criminal opportunities. Most people, as they walk through a crowded parking lot, are not looking for unlocked doors and unsecured items, but there are some individuals who are. These are your habitual thieves and criminals. Likewise, most people do not size up everyone they meet as a potential victim of an assault or con job, but some do. These again are your habitual criminals. One of the factors that separates people high and low in criminality is that those who are high in criminality tend to be more sensitive to opportunities for crime than those who are low in criminality. Using a sports analogy, high-risk individuals create their own opportunities for crime. Third, opportunity is a perception and as such, it can be rather ephemeral and fluid.

Opportunity is highlighted in the general theory of crime (Gottfredson & Hirschi, 1990), differential opportunity theory (Cloward & Ohlin, 1960), and rational choice theory (Clarke & Cornish, 1985), although in most theories of crime, opportunity is simply assumed. Even in theories that emphasize the importance of opportunities for crime, the definition of opportunity as applied to the theory is not always clear. I attribute this to two factors. First, the notion of opportunity as a precondition for crime is so self-evident that many criminologists accept it as a given. Second, crime opportunities and incentives/deterrents are so intertwined and can happen so quickly that they are often treated as one and the same. Drawing on the results of 110 semi-structured interviews with male street thieves, Hochstetler (2002) concluded that criminal decision-making can occur in an instant and that the opportunity to commit crime and the decision to take advantage of the opportunity to commit crime occur almost simultaneously. Furthermore, in an earlier study conducted with 50 male robbers and burglars, Hochstetler (2001) determined that peers play an important role in defining criminal opportunities and setting the criteria for a criminal decision. The difficulties associated with treating opportunity and incentives/deterrents as separate but interrelated processes notwithstanding, it may still be helpful to distinguish between them.

Experienced criminals perceive many more opportunities for crime than the average citizen because of differential sensitivity and conditioning. I have spoken to former offenders who years after their last offense are still hounded by thoughts of taking that which does not belong to them upon entering a store or visiting another person's residence, even if they have no intention of acting on these unwanted criminal opportunities. I doubt very much whether the average person is bothered by such thoughts every time they walk into a department store or attend a party at a friend's house. The conditioning or sensitivity to criminal opportunities that seasoned criminals go through makes it more likely that they will act on a criminal opportunity than the average person. Most people, if a woman in front of them in line were to leave her purse unattended at the counter as she chased down her young daughter two aisles away, would not take advantage of this open opportunity for crime, whether it be on moral or practical grounds. An experienced offender, on the other hand, particularly if the cashier is not paying attention, would have the purse stuffed down their pants and be halfway out the door before anyone was the wiser. In the case of many habitual offenders, opportunity leads almost instantaneously to an incentive/deterrent that automatically seeks to capitalize on the criminal opportunity or ignore it entirely.

Incentives and Deterrents

As outlined in figure 8.2, the criminal decision-making process begins as soon as a criminal opportunity is perceived. Once perceived, the opportunity stimulates the three branches of incentive/deterrence. These three branches are (1) the hedonistic belief system, (2) the moral belief system, and (3) the certainty of getting caught and punished (see figure 8.2). Opportunity and incentive/deterrence occur almost simultaneously in someone who participates regularly in crime. Based on mechanisms from all three major theories of learning—classical conditioning, operant conditioning, and observational/social learning—the link between opportunity and incentive/deterrence becomes increasingly more automatic as the person begins committing or avoiding crime on a regular basis. Eventually, a perceived criminal opportunity will lead almost reflexively to the stage of criminal incentives and deterrents. Although opportunity and incentive/deterrence may appear to be part of the same process, they are actually distinct mechanisms that warrant separate treatment. In fact, as will be discussed in chapter 11, one way to reduce the future likelihood of a crime being committed is to extend the time period between opportunity and incentive so that the actor has more time to think about the criminal opportunity instead of simply responding to it in lock-step. The three branches of incentive/deterrence (hedonistic belief system, moral belief system, and certainty) are discussed next.

Hedonistic Belief System

With ties to the control model of lifestyle criminality, the hedonistic belief system is a repository of reward and punishment experiences and associations. These stored and coded memories guide the individual in making decisions based on a Benthamian assessment of the pains and pleasures associated and anticipated with a particular criminal opportunity. The double arrows in figure 8.2 signify that that the hedonistic belief system influences a person's decisions and is, in turn, influenced by these same decisions. The system is said to be driven by the excitatory neurotransmitter, dopamine, and involves communication between such dopamine-rich structures as the hippocampus, striatum, and ventral tegmental area. The hedonistic belief system generates hedonistic emotions (anger, frustration, urgency, excitement, pleasure) that demand immediate gratification. Anticipation of these emotions is achieved through the intervening or mediating effect of hedonistic expectancies. When the hedonistic belief system and hedonistic emotions are properly modulated by serotonin and effective cognitive controls, decision-making is optimal. When the system or emotions are not properly modulated, risky decision-making dominates the person's thinking and criminal decisions are more likely. In a meta-analysis of research on emotions and decision-making, Angie et al. (2011) determined that unmodulated anger interfered with effective problem-solving.

Moral Belief System

Whereas the hedonistic belief system is a repository of stored experiences coded for pain and pleasure, the moral belief system is a repository of stored experiences coded for right and wrong; and whereas the hedonistic belief system has ties to the control model and dopamine, the moral belief system has ties to the moral model and serotonin (Siegel & Crockett, 2013). The moral belief system is composed of standards, norms, values, and other morally relevant sources of information that if used properly can guide an individual's decision-making, and like the hedonistic belief system, expectancies are created that allow the individual to anticipate the types of emotions they are likely to encounter if they pursue a particular course of action. Moral emotions signal either approval (pride, dignity, satisfaction) or disapproval (guilt, remorse, shame) of one's plans and actions. In direct contrast to the hedonistic belief system, where unmodulated hedonistic emotion is said to interfere with effective decision-making, it is the absence of moral emotions like guilt and remorse that gives rise to a criminal decision in the moral belief system. Guided by Wikström's (2006) situational action theory (SAT), Trivedi-Bateman (2019) discovered that moral emotion interacted with moral reasoning to lower guilt/shame and impair empathy, which, in turn, led to increased aggressive and total offending.

Certainty

As previously noted, the deterrence doctrine is composed of three prongs (certainty, celerity, and severity of punishment), only one of which (certainty) has been found to be effective in deterring crime. A reading of the literature indicates that certainty achieves a modest to moderate but consistent deterrent effect (Nagin, 2013; Paternoster, 2010). Severity and celerity produce much weaker and less consistent results and for either to have any deterrent value at all, certainty must be high (Grasmick & Bryjak, 1980; Pratt & Turanovic, 2018). Therefore, in lifestyle theory's decision-making model of crime, certainty is emphasized over severity and celerity. The reason why it is classified as a deterrent is that the more certain the individual is of getting caught and punished for a specific criminal act, the less motivated they will be to act on the opportunity to participate in the crime. Hirtenlehner (2020) contrasted Gottfredson and Hirschi's (1990) general theory of crime with Wikström's (2007) SAT in explaining the relationship between certainty and low self-control and found results consistent with SAT and criminal lifestyle theory but inconsistent with the general theory of crime: that is, while youth with lower self-control reported lower sanction certainty perceptions, these certainty perceptions had a greater impact on youth with low self-control than they did on youth with high self-control.

Aggravating and Mitigating Effects

Two general categories of aggravating and mitigating effects are included in the decision-making model of crime: developmental/situational factors and criminal thinking. Each is discussed in this section.

Developmental/Situational Factors

Developmental and situational factors play a role in criminal decision-making by creating aggravating and mitigating conditions and effects. Youthfulness is an example of an aggravating condition for crime. For such varied reasons as incomplete myelination of the prefrontal cortex (Hartley & Somerville, 2015), a rise in sensation-seeking tendencies during adolescence (Zuckerman, 2007), and a general lack of experience (Dow-Edwards et al., 2019), juveniles make less reasoned and more risky decisions, although there are areas of judgment in which adolescents perform on par with or even better than adults (Romer et al., 2017). Adolescence may also be a period during which youth are particularly vulnerable to the effects of adverse physical conditions, negative emotional states, and stressful life and social circumstances. Timmer et al. (2020) analyzed data from the Add Health study and discovered that a number of "hot trigger" issues (depression, sleep problems, general strain) interfered with a youth's ability to reason in a calm, collected, and rational manner and make decisions that were thoughtful and reflective.

Situational factors can also affect the decision-making process. Family dysfunction, peer pressure, and neighborhood disorder are social factors capable of interfering with youthful decision-making, whereas family communication, prosocial peers, and community support can have a fortifying effect on a child's decision-making capabilities. Other social situational factors have been found to aggravate and mitigate real-time physical confrontations depending on whether bystanders acted as agitators or mediators (Felson et al., 1984). Physical environmental factors can also exert an aggravating or mitigating effect on youth decision-making. Ambient temperature has been found to correspond with violence (Anderson & Anderson, 1984), in part, because it interferes with effective problem-solving. Cool temperatures, on the other hand, are more likely to have a calming effect (Heilmann et al., 2021). Although tested at the aggregate (country) level, the previously reviewed Walters (2021a) investigation determined that high ambient temperatures were associated with elevated levels of both RCT and violent offending.

Criminal Thinking

RCT and PCT are of equal importance in the decision-making model of crime, where they both play dual roles. One role assumed by RCT is to facilitate crime by stimulating irrelevant or hedonistic emotion (e.g., short-term hostility: Walters, 2020g). This emotion is considered irrelevant because it impedes rather than supports effective problem-solving. The exacerbating nature of this emotion is denoted by the "+" sign along the path connecting RCT to hedonistic emotion. RCT can also facilitate crime by interacting with certainty of apprehension and punishment. The arrow connecting RCT to certainty is marked with an "x" to designate the interactive effect believed to exist between the two variables. PCT facilitates crime, not by stimulating irrelevant emotion, but by blocking relevant or moral emotion (Walters, 2020g). The emotion in this case is considered relevant because it facilitates rather than impedes effective problem-solving. Marking the path from PCT to moral emotion with a "-" denotes that the effect of PCT on moral emotion is inhibitory. Just like RCT, PCT facilitates crime by interacting with certainty. One difference in how PCT and RCT interface with certainty is that one of the PCT thinking styles—superoptimism—may have a more direct effect on certainty. Superoptimism, it would seem, may be capable of reducing certainty and a person's estimate of their odds of getting caught and punished for a crime. It could do so by giving the individual the false impression that they can indefinitely avoid or postpone the negative consequences of a criminal lifestyle. In the moral and control models, RCT and PCT achieve their effect by mediating variable relationships. In the decision-making model, RCT and PCT achieve their effect by stimulating or inhibiting emotion and moderating the certainty-offending relationship.

Several scenario studies have been conducted on criminal thinking, certainty, and one's stated likelihood of engaging in antisocial behavior. Studying a convenience sample of 315 college students, Walters and Morgan (2019) observed that students with elevated PCT and RCT scores perceived that they were less likely to get caught cheating on a test regardless of whether certainty of apprehension was estimated to be 10% or 50%. Criminal thinking and certainty also interacted to where students with moderate PCT scores or moderate-to-high RCT scores were significantly less likely to be deterred from cheating when the odds of getting caught were low (i.e., 10%). Similar results were obtained in a follow-up study performed on a different group of college students in which the likelihood of getting caught was expanded to include a very low likelihood (1%) and scores were averaged across three scenarios (cheating on a test, stealing $50, selling marijuana). As in the previous study, the gap between lower and higher criminal thinking students grew as the probability of getting caught dropped (Walters et al., 2019). In the most recent study on this issue, Walters and colleagues (2021) used three scenarios (cheating on a test, minor property damage, driving drunk) to assess the moderating effect of criminal thinking on the certainty-offending nexus. Participants were 67 probationers attending a day treatment program and results indicated that respondents with higher PCT and RCT scores saw themselves as significantly less likely to get caught for these antisocial acts as respondents with lower PCT and RCT scores. This occurred at all three levels of certainty (1%, 10%, 50%). In addition, respondents with high PCT, but not high RCT, were significantly more likely to say they would engage in one of the antisocial acts as the certainty of getting caught went down.

PANZRAM AND THE MURDER OF LAUNDRY FOREMAN WARNKE

In a memo to the Superintendent of Prisons in Washington, DC, dated June 20, 1929, Thomas B. White, Warden at the United States Penitentiary (USP) at Leavenworth, Kansas, reported that Laundry foreman Robert E. Warnke had been fatally injured by inmate Carl Panzram (Reg. No. 31614). This was followed by a period of intense investigation and legal proceedings that would eventually result in inmate Panzram's execution in the courtyard at USP Leavenworth a little over a year later.

Background

In the lead up to the murder, it should be noted that Panzram was continually making generalized threats against staff and inmates, and that he made specific threats against two individuals. Those two individuals were Dave Watkins, a prison guard, and Robert Warnke, a civilian Laundry foreman. According to inmate Jack Shapiro (Reg. No. 24298), Panzram was upset with Watkins because Watkins had told him to "button up his shirt collar" and he was angry with Warnke because he "had asked Mr. Warnke to make a change in his, Panzram's work, and Mr. Warnke had refused to do so" (Borowski, 2020, p. 108). A second inmate, Louis Kelly (Reg. No. 29150), observed that two months prior to the murder:

> Panzram and Mr. Warnke had a few words over three handerchiefs [*sic*] which Panzram had and was washing in a bleacher in the Laundry . . . Panzram argued, saying that he was only trying to bleach three handerkerchiefs [*sic*], but Mr. Warnke said he could not have his rules run over and repeated that Panzram was no better than the rest of the prisoners employed in the Laundry. He, Panzram, remarked that if Warnke did not "lay off of him" he would "get" Warnke. (Borowski, 2020, p. 103)

A third inmate who also worked with Panzram in the Laundry, Raymond Thomas (Reg. No. 31996), heard these same threats and reported them to Mr. Warnke the morning Warnke was murdered.

There is no doubt that Panzram was an angry, sullen, ill-tempered man who held unreasonable grudges and believed that he was justified in treating the world as badly as he believed he had been treated by the world. Panzram, like most of us, was inconsistent, which in a way made him an enigma. He was habitually impulsive but could be patient if need be. He once told inmate Louis Kelly that "if anybody does me dirty, I don't forget it" (Borowski, 2020, p. 103). Panzram was always talking about retaliation and getting even, but he was more than willing to wait for an opportune time to exact his revenge and even the score. A recollection of an assault Panzram perpetrated on an inmate he viewed as a problem or threat was previously described in chapter 7. That incident illustrates how Panzram was willing to delay gratification and bide his time before attacking an inmate with whom he had a conflict. Panzram appeared to adopt a similar strategy with Robert Warnke as he weighed the alternatives available to him as to how best to handle his deteriorating relationship with his work supervisor.

The Murder

At approximately 7:50 AM on Thursday, June 20, 1929, inmate Carl Panzram murdered laundry foreman Robert G. Warnke. According to eye-witness testimony, Panzram snuck up behind Warnke, who was bending over a washing machine at the time, and struck him in the back of the head with an iron bar that was approximately 3 feet long and nearly 2 inches in diameter. After Warnke fell to the floor, Panzram hit him once more. After briefly chasing several of the inmates who had witnessed the murder around the laundry and threatening them with the iron bar, Panzram hit Warnke one last time, exclaiming "here's another one for you, you Son of a Bitch!" (Borowski, 2020, p. 109). Warnke was then taken to the institution hospital on a makeshift stretcher. The hospital physician counted at least 6 lacerations of the scalp, ear, nose, and mouth that measured 1–9.5 inches in length. There was profuse bleeding of the head and face, hematomas in both eyes, a fractured lower jaw, and brain matter hanging from at least two of the lacerations where the skull had been crushed. Panzram was described by several witnesses as "running amuck" following the murder, chasing inmates and staff around the prison compound, while waving the iron bar above his head. He had enough wherewithal, however, to avoid being drawn into the open where he could have been a target for one of the armed guards in the towers that surround the prison.

In analyzing the Warnke murder from the standpoint of lifestyle theory's decision-making model, we should start with opportunity. As someone who seemed as if they were in a perpetual state of hostile rage and angry agitation, Panzram's daily life was filled with criminal opportunities, particularly violent ones. He found a suitable target for his rage in Warnke who was both available and vulnerable. We can only imagine the hateful joy that poured through the hedonistic belief system as Panzram brought the iron bar down on Warnke's head and the corresponding hedonistic expectation of righting the wrongs he believed he had suffered at the hands of Warnke and others. Panzram's moral belief system was too weak to even get him to think twice about what he planned to do based on a criminal opportunity that promised the kind of retribution to which he believed he was entitled. Certainty of punishment never held much sway with Panzram and was clearly not a deterrent to murder in this case given that the crime was committed in full view of witnesses. Even the superoptimistic belief that he would somehow get away with murdering a staff member cannot explain his utter disregard for the consequences of his actions. Getting away with murder was clearly not part of the plan. Criminal thinking in the form of RCT and PCT probably fueled his anger, rage, and desire for revenge and situational factors played a role to the extent that Panzram came across Warnke in a vulnerable position and there were no other staff members close enough to intervene.

Aftermath

Panzram went on trial in Topeka, Kansas, for the murder of Robert Warnke on April 14, 1930. From the very start, the defendant refused counsel and asserted that he wished to plead guilty to first-degree murder. The federal judge refused to accept the guilty plea and appointed an attorney to represent Panzram. After a two-day trial, it took the jury just 45 minutes to convict him of first-degree murder, after which the judge sentenced him to death by hanging. Following the verdict, Panzram said that he was fully satisfied with the sentence, was not at all interested in appealing his conviction, and wanted no help from human rights activists who were following the case. Panzram went to the gallows, which were constructed behind the institution's segregation unit, on the morning of September 5, 1930. Up to the end, he showed no remorse for his actions. His alleged last words are especially revealing: "They tell me when I drop down there and hit the end of the rope I'll crap in my pants. I just wish I could take them off so I could crap all over you dirty bastards" (Borowski, 2020, p. 245).

OVERLAP BETWEEN THE THREE MODELS

Lifestyle theory consists of three models: the moral model of lifestyle criminality, the control model of lifestyle criminality, and the decision-making model of crime. In the previous chapter, the overlap between the moral and control models was discussed. That overlap, as mentioned briefly in one of the final sections of chapter 7, is primarily a function of criminal thinking. Although PCT is the principal criminal thought process in the moral model and RCT is the principal criminal thought process in the control model, RCT plays a small role in the moral model and PCT does likewise in the control model. These two criminal thought processes serve as doorways between two dimensions, one dimension being the moral model and the other dimension being the control model. Hence, we can step from the moral model to the control model through the doorway provided by RCT and from the control model to the moral model through the doorway provided by PCT. This underscores the point that the three models of lifestyle theory—moral, control, and decision-making—are interdependent and attached rather than independent and detached. Furthermore, we should be able to move effortlessly from one model to the next and apply what we've learned from one model to expand our knowledge of the other two models.

The two criminality models might seem more amenable to linkage than either one is to the crime model. Nothing, however, could be further from the truth. The crime model shares PCT in common with the moral model and RCT in common with the control model, just as PCT and RCT serve as doorways between the two criminality dimensions. And there is more binding the decision-making model of crime to the two criminality models than just criminal thinking. The decision-making model incorporates the moral belief system, moral expectancies, and moral emotion, all of which could be considered features of the moral model, although they were not necessarily described that way in chapter 6. The decision-making model also incorporates the hedonistic belief system, hedonistic expectancies, and hedonistic emotion, all of which could be considered aspects of the control model, even though they were not described as such in chapter 7. Thus, there is as much, if not more, overlap between the two criminality models and the crime model as there is between the two criminality models, and so moving from the moral or control models to the decision-making model may be as smooth and seamless as moving from the moral model to the control model.

CONCLUSION

This chapter marks a shift in emphasis from the criminality models of chapters 6 and 7 to the crime model described in the current chapter. All three models fall within the purview of criminological science, but the field itself has been defined in various and sundry ways. The definition adopted by lifestyle theory is that criminology is the study of criminality and crime. Most traditional criminological theories have focused either on criminality (e.g., social learning theory, self-control theory, general strain theory) or crime (e.g., rational choice theory, routine activity theory, SAT), but not both. As the preceding section demonstrates, however, theories of crime and criminality are not incompatible; in fact, with proper integration they can be complementary. In fact, for a theory to be useful it should address both the propensity to commit crime (criminality) and the individual criminal event (crime). Lifestyle theory is the overarching perspective under which the moral, control, and decision-making models are linked and organized using a general learning framework, whether the faulty learning is one of commission (moral), omission (control), or both (decision-making).

Section III

Chapter 9

Managing Criminality

Part I. Reducing Risk by Building Competencies

"Skill Development Is an Effective Means of Reducing Criminality Risk"

The focus of this third and final section of the book will be on application and further integration. In section II, the emphasis was on organizing groups of trees into groves. The goal of section III is to illustrate how these groves can be organized into larger entities like forests and the practical benefits of doing so. This chapter and chapter 10 consider how criminality or the propensity to commit crime comes down to managing or reducing risk. The central argument in this and the next chapter is that risk is reduced and its negative consequences mitigated by building competences and changing environments using information found in the moral and control models of lifestyle criminality. Chapter 11, on the other hand, will consider how individual crimes can be prevented by limiting opportunities for antisocial behavior, altering incentives for crime, and addressing crime-promoting aggravating and mitigating conditions. Section III will then close with chapter 12 where the focus is on integrating information from the previous 11 chapters to both understand and change a criminal lifestyle.

Criminality and crime not only differ on a conceptual level, they also differ on a practical level. What I mean by this is that the manner in which criminality and crime are managed differs markedly. Previously, it was noted that criminality represents a person's propensity to commit crime, whereas crime represents a person's involvement in a specific criminal act or event. Criminology, according to the perspective adopted in this book, is defined as the study of both criminality and crime. This chapter has several goals, but the overarching goal is to demonstrate how a person's propensity for crime can be mitigated and reduced by building competencies in the client.

In the chapter that follows this one, the goal will be to show how a person's propensity for crime can be alleviated by changing internal, external, and institutional environments. We begin, however, by examining ways by which criminality can be reduced by building competencies, and because criminality is measured in units of risk, the chapter begins with a brief discussion on risk assessment.

RISK ASSESSMENT

Risk assessment is a systematic process by which risks, hazards, and dangers are identified, analyzed, and controlled in an attempt to reduce their impact on human behavior. There are a number of fields that make use of risk assessment, such as medicine, engineering, information technology, social work, and the food industry. For the purposes of this chapter, we consider risk as it pertains to crime, violence, and recidivism. Biological risk factors were discussed in chapter 2 as a way of demonstrating how biology may be involved in the etiology of delinquency and crime without necessarily determining delinquent and criminal behavior. It should be noted that risk assessment is a rather broad term that is often broken down into two more specific concepts: risk prediction and risk management (Heilbrun, 2003). Risk prediction refers to efforts to identify, document, and categorize a person's degree or level of risk. This is usually accomplished by summing across a number of relevant risk dimensions. Risk management is a more complex process in which attempts are made to lower the odds that someone rated as being at high risk for an outcome like violence or recidivism will actually engage in violence or recidivism.

Risk Prediction

Compared to risk management, risk prediction is a fairly simple and straightforward procedure. When conducting a risk assessment, the evaluator measures and then sums the requisite risk factors to estimate a person's risk of future problem behavior. The key to effective risk prediction is selecting risk factors that are reliable, accurate, and have documented predictive validity. Risk factors, it should be noted, can be classified as either static (unchangeable) or dynamic (changeable). It has traditionally been assumed that static risk factors like age, gender, and criminal history are superior to dynamic risk factors like peer associations, current substance use problems, and antisocial attitudes in predicting recidivism. Several meta-analyses of criminal-justice involved persons released from prison or under community supervision, however, indicate that dynamic risk factors are just as effective, if not more effective, than static risk factors in predicting a person's likelihood of future violence and criminal involvement regardless of whether the analysis targets offenders in general or more specific groups like sex offenders (Eisenberg et al., 2019; Gendreau et al., 1996; Hanson & Bussiére, 1998; Hanson & Morton-Bourgon, 2005). Therefore, while it is important to include easily obtainable static risk factors like age and criminal history in a risk-prediction paradigm, dynamic risk factors should be included as well.

Risk Management

Whereas static and dynamic risk factors are roughly equivalent in predicting risk, dynamic risk factors are significantly more useful than static risk factors in managing risk. This does not mean that static risk factors have no role to play in risk management. That is because static risk factors can be of assistance in determining specific responsivity, whereby certain categories of static risk are more responsive to one type of intervention than another. Gender is one potentially important specific responsivity factor for offending. Bonta and Andrews (2017) provide guidance to those working with incarcerated female offenders in recommending women-only groups run by female therapists, creation of a community with a sense of connection, an emphasis on safety, a focus on strengths, and fostering an environment where issues are raised and explored. These recommendations may also be relevant to men, but they are viewed by Bonta and Andrews as especially germane to incarcerated women. Dynamic risk factors, which are often referred to as needs, can also assist with specific responsivity, but have the added benefit of showing progress over time given the fact that they are subject to change. Hence, monitoring changes in criminal thinking or antisocial associates over time can provide valuable clues as to how the individual is progressing in treatment.

The goal of risk management is to reduce risk and there are at least three ways in which this goal can be accomplished. One way is to remove or eliminate the risk factor. In the case of a child who lives in a high crime neighborhood or is bullied at school, the family might consider moving to another neighborhood or requesting that the child be transferred to a new classroom. This is not always possible or even advisable, however. The family may not have the resources to move to a more affluent neighborhood and transferring a child out of a classroom where they are bullied may send the wrong message (i.e., that the child is unable to handle their own problems). A second way to reduce risk is to develop skills that run counter to the risk factor. These skills are referred to as promotive factors (Farrington et al., 2016). If a child is at risk for delinquency by virtue of weak parental discipline, instructing the parents on how to become more effective disciplinarians should reduce the risk by creating a promotive factor. A third way to reduce risk is to find a protective factor that nullifies the effects of a risk factor. Protective factors interact with risk factors to lessen their impact on the individual (Farrington et al., 2016). The risk presented by prior bullying behavior has been shown to respond to increased parental support, such that parents who provide their bullying children with support have children who are less likely to engage in future delinquency (Walters et al., 2020).

PRECONDITIONS FOR CHANGE

Change can either be assisted or unassisted. Assisted change occurs with the help of a professional therapist or formal treatment program. Unassisted change occurs without assistance from a professional therapist or formal treatment program, although as McMurran (1994) points out, it can and often does include support from significant others in a person's life. Social support and interpersonal relationships, in fact, are central to the change process, whether the change is assisted or unassisted (McMurran & Delight, 2017). Studies indicate that when it comes to criminal behavior and substance misuse, unassisted change is several times more common than assisted change, but otherwise the two groups are largely indistinguishable (Adler, 1993; Walters, 2000). The four preconditions for change described in this section (motivation for change, expectancies for change, cognitive-behavioral inconsistency, and planning for change) apply equally to individuals undergoing assisted or unassisted change because the change process is the same regardless of whether it occurs in one-on-one therapy, group counseling, or in one's interactions with family and friends.

Motivation for Change

Just as there can be no crime without opportunity, so too can there be no change without motivation. A person must overcome several obstacles—most notably, fear of change and psychological inertia—to alter the thoughts and behaviors that have become ingrained through years of repetition and reinforcement. Given how difficult change can be, it is usually easier to follow the path of least resistance, which in this case would mean letting things stand as they are and telling yourself that change is too difficult, not worth the effort, or altogether impossible. Leaving a criminal lifestyle means abandoning a way of thinking, feeling, and behaving to which the person has grown accustomed and leaving a way of life that affords them meaning, continuity, predictability, and pleasure. This way of life can also become a source of discomfort for the individual and this is where unassisted change or natural recovery comes into play. Chronological age (Sparks & Day, 2016), psychological/emotional maturity (Coyle, 2019), and the accumulated negative consequences of a criminal lifestyle (Paternoster & Bushway, 2009) spur many individuals to abandon the lifestyle by the fourth or fifth decade of life. The question this section seeks to answer is what can be done for those who do not respond to these natural oases of desistance and for those who are too young to be at a stage of burnout and maturity, as described in chapter 5. The answer can be found in the development of a therapeutic alliance and the use of motivation-enhancing techniques like motivational interviewing (MI). These will be discussed, but first we need to consider two common obstacles to motivation for change.

Obstacles to Motivation for Change

The two factors that serve as obstacles or impediments to motivation for change are fear of change and psychological inertia. Fear of change is a direct expression of existential fear. As touched upon in chapters 2, 5, and 6, existential fear is an innate fear of nonexistence and insignificance that people learn to cope with by finding ways to impact on the world. Existential fear is initially experienced as trepidation over nonexistence or death. This trepidation is coded in the dopamine and serotonin pathways of the brain that have evolved in support of physical survival. With time, the innate fear of physical nonexistence becomes conditioned to situations and relationships in the environment. One way this is expressed is in one's desire to make an impact on the world. This impact could be relatively small and conventional (e.g., wanting to raise loving, responsible children) or it could be grandiose and unconventional (e.g., Carl Panzram's desire to be seen as the "meanest man in the world"), but the goal in both cases is to ease existential fear. Lifestyles of patterned behavior are one way people learn to cope with existential fear. The irony is that something like a criminal lifestyle, initially motivated by a fear of nonexistence, actually puts a person's physical survival in jeopardy. Interventions designed to make the individual aware of this can sometimes help motivate them for change.

Psychological inertia is another obstacle to desistance from crime. Previously described in chapter 5, psychological inertia was originally designed to explain crime continuity or why past criminal involvements predict future criminal actions. According to lifestyle theory, prior criminal involvements stimulate cognitive processes like RCT which then encourage future criminal activity. The crime → RCT → crime pathway can therefore be used to explain crime continuity. The specific reactive criminal thinking style believed to be most heavily involved in psychological inertia is cognitive indolence, although cutoff and discontinuity also play a role in the formation of psychological inertia. The lack of critical reasoning and pan-impulsivity that characterize cognitive indolence help block counter-criminal influences and sources of desistance, protecting the criminal lifestyle in a manner similar to fear of change. The statement "it is what it is," which can be found in virtually every mob movie since "Goodfellas," not only reflects a dismissive attitude toward the misery of others but also exemplifies the cognitive indolence that drives psychological inertia. In each of the four preconditions for change, there is a counter-change mechanism that forms a dynamic opposing tension with the change agent. In the case of motivation for change, the counter-change mechanisms are fear of change and psychological inertia.

Therapeutic Alliance

The therapeutic alliance is the working relationship or bond that develops between a therapist/counselor/helper and client. It is an alliance based on trust. The alliance assists the client in overcoming the obstacles presented by such counter-change mechanisms as fear of change, psychological inertia, and lack of social support, the latter being the antithesis of a therapeutic alliance. Longitudinal studies indicate that when the alliance is strong, criminal justice clients are more engaged in treatment and are less likely to be involved in future drug use and crime (Joe et al., 2001; Polaschek & Ross, 2010). In a study using data from the Step'n Out program, Walters (2016k) determined that substance-abusing parolees who reported having a strong working alliance with their counselors and parole officers reported lower levels of future drug use, experienced fewer subsequent arrests, and spent less days in jail than parolees who reported a weak working alliance with their counselors and parole officers. Further analysis revealed that the working alliance served as a mediating mechanism linking treatment condition (collaborative behavioral management versus standard parole) to drug use, arrests, and jail days. A strong client-helper relationship is just as vital to the success of an assisted change program as supportive interpersonal relationships are for unassisted change. Yet, there are questions as to how such an alliance can be created and sustained in the adversarial environment under which the criminal justice system in the United States currently operates.

Motivational Interviewing

In looking for a procedure capable of enhancing motivation for change, motivational interviewing (MI) would be a good place to start. Based on the notion that motivation for change is a consequence of the helper-client relationship and not a stable character trait possessed by the client, clinicians attempt to overcome the ambivalence most people feel about change by adopting certain attitudes and actions. These attitudes and actions include expressing empathy and acceptance, supporting self-efficacy, highlighting discrepancies between goals and current behavior, avoiding arguments and direct confrontations, and rolling with the resistance (Miller & Rollnick, 1991). Although MI was originally designed for substance-abusing populations, it has applicability to a wide range of client groups, including criminal offenders. Research conducted on both juvenile (Clair-Michaud et al., 2016; Stein et al., 2020) and adult (Anstiss et al., 2011; McMurran, 2009) offenders reveals that MI can enhance treatment retention and motivation for change. The procedure, which is often used as an adjunct to cognitive-behavior therapy, has been found to be particularly effective when paired with Prochaska and DiClemente's (2005) transtheoretical or stages of change model. The transtheoretical model reminds the therapist that different techniques and strategies are required at different stages of change, particularly when moving from precontemplation/contemplation, where the client is either not thinking about change or is ambivalent about it, to the preparation and action stages where the client is actively engaged in change.

Expectancies for Change

A second precondition for change is strong expectancies for change. What this means is that the individual believes that change is necessary, possible (in a theoretical sense), and attainable (in a practical sense). This is sometimes referred to as the attribution triad: a belief in the necessity of change, a belief in the possibility of change, and a belief in one's ability to effect change (Walters, 2001b). The third belief, belief in one's ability to effect change, refers to a construct discussed in some detail in chapter 6 on the moral model of lifestyle criminality; namely, self-efficacy. As the reader may recall, self-efficacy is a person's assessment of their likelihood of accomplishing a task or achieving a particular behavioral outcome with the skills they currently possess (Bandura, 1986). In chapter 6, we learned that the contrast between self-efficacy for living a conventional lifestyle and self-efficacy for living a criminal lifestyle has important implications for desistance. In the current context, we consider self-efficacy for changing thoughts and behaviors supportive of a criminal lifestyle versus lack of self-efficacy for changing thoughts and behaviors supportive of a criminal lifestyle. Having confidence that one either possesses the skills or can acquire the skills necessary to bring about a change is what the expectancies for change precondition are all about.

As previously mentioned, the preconditions for change are each balanced against a counter-change attitude or opposing tension, which in the case of self-efficacy is a person's lack of self-efficacy for change. In order to be successful, the client must not only achieve high self-efficacy for change but also effectively combat and defeat thoughts of low self-efficacy for change that may have been nurtured and exacerbated by prior unsuccessful attempts at change. Self-efficacy for change is said to reflect a person's readiness for change (Salcido et al., 2019) and engagement in the treatment process (Belenko et al., 2017) and, as such, has been found to predict treatment retention of clients court-mandated for community-based cognitive skills training (Hatcher & Roberts, 2019). The first two parts of the attribution triad (i.e., belief in the necessity of change and belief in the possibility of change) should be firmly in place once the pre-intervention is over and before the cognitive-behavioral intervention begins. The third part of the attribution triad (i.e., belief in one's ability to effect change) takes longer to materialize because it requires confidence in one's current skill level which will only occur as the client practices and internalizes skills learned in cognitive-behavior therapy. This assumption is backed up by research showing that self-efficacy builds over the course of treatment (McCulloch & McMurran, 2008).

Cognitive-Behavioral Inconsistency

When discussing Panzram's lack of internalization in chapter 8, I made a point of emphasizing that he displayed weak internalization in many areas of functioning but possessed a few pockets of internalization, particularly when it came to getting away with interpersonal violence. Given how consistent Panzram was in so many other ways, this suggests that inconsistency is not only part of being human, it may also leave room for change. It was further speculated that inconsistency or uncertainty in thought and action may facilitate change by stimulating curiosity and personal investigation. If people were 100% consistent, as say, a computer is, there would be no room or need for change. The fact that they are not, leaves the door open to new experience, although the degree of change differs from one person to the next. Inconsistency between behavior and cognition is central to Festinger's (1957) theory of cognitive dissonance. Research, in fact, demonstrates that cognitive dissonance is capable of explaining late childhood-to-early adolescent antisocial behavior (Ridenour et al., 2011), mid-to-late-adolescent delinquent behavior (Cassel et al., 2001), and adult-level intimate partner violence (Maglinte et al., 2016).

Whereas cognitive dissonance can serve as an excuse or defense mechanism designed to rationalize or excuse antisocial, delinquent, or violent behavior, it can also be used to disrupt the patterns of a criminal or drug lifestyle and redirect the individual toward a more positive life trajectory. In a systematic review of the literature on cognitive dissonance and health behavior, Freijy and Kothe (2013) discovered that dissonance-based interventions were capable of changing health practices in a positive direction. Other studies have found that cognitive dissonance is an important part of the change process in MI for underage drinkers (Magill et al., 2017) and justice-involved heroin users (Ayers et al., 2014). It should also be noted that the inconsistency or conflict created by cognitive dissonance need not be between behavior and cognition, it could just as easily be between two behaviors or two cognitions. Inconsistency, as the reader may recall, facilitates change in MI every time the helper highlights discrepancies between a client's goals and current behavior. It can also facilitate change through bifurcation, a concept borrowed from nonlinear dynamical systems theory (Walters, 2017e) and which is described, along with other aspects of chaos theory, in chapter 12.

The counter-change or opposing tension to cognitive-behavioral inconsistency is the social-psychological concept of confirmation bias. Although the term "confirmation bias" was originally coined in the early 1960s (Wason, 1960), the last decade has seen an explosion of research on this topic across a wide variety of fields. Confirmation bias involves interpreting, favoring, and recalling information consistent with one's prior beliefs and disregarding, rejecting, and distorting information inconsistent with these prior beliefs. In this way, the individual selectively processes information to make it consistent with their preexisting belief systems. The bias, in turn, eliminates inconsistencies and obviates the need for change. Confirmation bias displays a serious lack of critical reasoning, something it shares in common with cognitive indolence. In fact, cognitive indolence appears to be involved in another counter-change variable described earlier in this chapter; namely, psychological inertia. This would seem to suggest that cognitive indolence should be addressed during the early stages of an intervention. Two ways in which confirmation bias can be reduced is by exposing the person to computer-generated preference-inconsistent information that runs counter to the person's belief systems and is capable of stimulating divergent thinking (Schwind et al., 2012) and participation in debiasing training designed to reduce a person's reliance on prior beliefs and faulty information (Sellier et al., 2019).

Planning for Change

A fourth precondition for change entails making a plan capable of guiding the change process. Too often, there is no plan, or the plan is deficient in some way. Weak or absent plans are the change-inhibiting counter to a change plan that serves as the cumulation of all four preconditions for change (see table 9.1). Without a well-defined plan, the change process quickly loses momentum, meaning, and direction. When this occurs, the individual is subject to relapse, recidivism, or some other type of negative outcome. Clinicians often construct treatment plans when working with clients. Walters (1998b) argues that a more generic term like change plan does a better job of reflecting the fact that change can occur outside of treatment and that whether change is assisted or unassisted, it follows the same general path. Walters's original

Table 9.1 The Change-Promoting and Change-Inhibiting Trends in the Four Preconditions for Change

Precondition for Change	*Change-Promoting Trend*	*Change-Inhibiting Trend*
Motivation for Change	Strongly motivated for change	Fear of change and psychological inertia
Expectancies for Change	High self-efficacy for change	Low self-efficacy for change
Inconsistency	Cognitive and behavioral dissonance	Confirmatory bias
Planning for Change	Effective change plan	Ineffective or absent change plan

Source: Table created by author.

change plan was based on themes running through the reports of individuals who had abandoned a drug or criminal lifestyle without formal assistance. The three elements highlighted in the original plan (involvements, commitments, and identifications) have been expanded to four by adding beliefs and the right side of the plan now considers three categories of competency (i.e., opposite pole promotive factors, preventive factors, and stand-alone promotive factors) designed to manage risk factors spread across the four element domains.

The risk factors for the change plan come from the criminological literature, with particular emphasis on desistance, whereas the competencies can be traced back to the work of Bandura and Schunk (1981) as well as Farrington et al. (2016). Bandura and Schunk note that competencies are most likely to be achieved when proximal rather than distal goals are pursued. In their study, children who were encouraged to complete six pages of instructional items per session learned the material significantly better and exhibited higher levels of self-efficacy and intrinsic interest than children instructed to complete the entire 42 pages of instructional items by the end of the seventh session or children who completed the task without reference to goals. Farrington and colleagues (2016) provide further insight into competencies by proposing that risk factors can be managed by creating promotive factors (which fall at the opposite pole of a risk factor or are related to the risk factor in some other way) and protective factors (which interact with the risk factor to reduce its impact). The four elements of the change plan (involvements, commitments, identifications, and beliefs) can be crossed with the three competencies (opposite pole promotive factors, protective factors, and stand-alone promotive factors) to create a 4 × 3 matrix. This matrix will be discussed, along with an example, but first, it is necessary to review how traditional theories of desistance stack up against these elements and competencies.

TRADITIONAL THEORIES OF DESISTANCE

Desistance means ceasing to engage in a behavior and desistance from crime means ceasing to engage in criminal behavior. Two of the more popular theories of desistance are Sampson and Laub's (2016) turning points model and Paternoster and Bushway's (2009) identity theory of desistance (ITD). Both have contributed to our understanding of desistance by pointing out that desistance is a process rather than an event. Yet, these two theories are far from complete when compared to the four elements and three competencies that make up a change plan. The exact limitations differ from one theory to the next but help clarify some of the advantages to taking a change plan approach to intervention. These limitations are examined next.

Turning Points

Turning points are a core constituent of Sampson and Laub's (1993) age-graded theory of crime. According to Sampson and Laub (2016), there are turning points in a person's life capable of steering them away from crime and toward a conventional lifestyle. The turning points that Sampson and Laub emphasize are marriage, employment, and military service, but other life-defining events, such as graduating from college (Walters, 2018d), becoming a parent (Wocjciechowski, 2021), and being incarcerated (McCuish et al., 2018), can also serve as turning points for change. Most criminologists do not believe that getting married or holding down a job directly leads to desistance from crime. Rather, it is more likely that getting married and holding down a job reflect a change in interests and priorities that is more in line with a conventional lifestyle than it is with a criminal lifestyle. This may be why research has only partially confirmed the role of turning points in criminal desistance (McGloin et al., 2011; Skardhamar & Savolainen, 2014) and why some scholars have argued that it may not be the turning points that cause desistance but desistance that causes the turning points (Skardhamar et al., 2014).

In addition to the mixed empirical support the turning point hypothesis has received, there are questions as to the mechanism responsible for the alleged effect. Mechanisms covering all four elements of the change plan are possible, and in some cases, have been proposed. For instance, it could be argued that turning points like marriage and a regular job lead to changes in involvements whereby the individual spends more time with family and coworkers than they do with criminally involved peers. It is also possible that turning points reflect a change in values and priorities, particularly as one gets older, and that these changes in values and priorities are the cause of both turning points and desistance. Turning points and desistance could also be the product of a change in identity or identifications (Bachman et al., 2016). Finally, a reduction in criminal thinking, often observed in youthful offenders as they move from adolescence to early adulthood (Walters, 2022a), could lead to both turning point events like marriage and military service, as well as desistance. The usefulness of the turning point hypothesis to manage criminality is limited by uncertainty on the causal nature of the relationship and a lack of specificity as to the exact mechanism of change.

Identity Theory of Desistance

It has also been suggested that desistance is motivated by a change in identity. In their identity theory of desistance (ITD), Paternoster and Bushway (2009) contend that desistance occurs once offenders begin linking current failures (e.g., arrest, loss of family) to future failures. This propagates a prosocial identity designed to replace the criminal identity responsible for these failures and which has now become a feared self for the individual. A change in identity has, in fact, been found to precede a change in criminal behavior, a finding consistent with ITD and the previous theorizing of Giordano and Maruna (Giordano et al., 2003; Maruna, 2004). Based on interviews conducted 20 years apart, Bachman et al. (2016) determined that the vast majority of male and female drug-involved offenders who had desisted from crime and drug use had transformed their offender identity into a non-offender identity. In a study using growth curve modeling to assess change over time, Rocque et al. (2016) discovered that prosocial identity increased from adolescence to early adulthood and that an increase in prosocial identity predicted a lower level of future offending. Analyzing quantitative data from the previously reviewed Bachman et al. study, Liu and Bachman (2021) discovered that offenders with more prior sanctions for antisocial behavior were more likely to have desisted from crime and had apparently done so via a transformational prosocial identity.

Whereas the turning points hypothesis suffers from a lack of specificity in and an overabundance of possible mechanisms for desistance, ITD suffers from the opposite problem, a poverty of mechanisms designed to explain desistance. Unlike the turning point hypothesis, ITD is focused mainly on a single element of the change plan—namely, identifications—although it may rely too heavily on the rational choice assumption that offenders are primarily rational decision-makers. As previously mentioned, higher levels of criminal thinking distort even the certainty prong of the deterrence doctrine (Walters & Morgan, 2019; Walters et al., 2019, 2021a), thereby making the decision less than fully rational. Also, important mechanisms appear to be missing. ITD assumes that past failures in a criminal lifestyle lead the individual to anticipate future failure in that same lifestyle, but if this were true then desistance should occur sooner and more reliably than it does. There must be some mechanism or mediator that links perceptions of past failures and anticipation of future failures that is not articulated in the theory. Likewise, why should a feared self as a failed criminal necessarily, at least from what is written in Paternoster and Bushway (2009), lead to a prosocial identity? Could not another antisocial identity take its place?

FROM RISK TO COMPETENCY

Using risk factors selected for each of the four elements in a change plan, I will illustrate how different competencies can be assigned as a way of addressing each of the identified risks. The emphasis of this and the next two chapters is on practical matters and so comprehensive reviews of the literature will not be conducted. In fact, much of that information for such a review can be found in chapters 3–8.

Changing Involvements

The involvements element of the change plan covers the activities the individual engages in and the relationships they pursue (i.e., what you do and who you do it with). A shift in a person's activities and associations can have a major impact on their propensity to commit crime by changing risk factor patterns and alignments. The risk factor to be discussed in this, the involvements section, is delinquent peer associations. There is a large body of research confirming the supposition that socializing with those who are already involved in delinquency greatly enhances one's own chances of engaging in delinquency (see chapter 3 for a review). Debates over whether peer influence or peer selection is the principal cause of the robust relationship observed to exist between peer and participant delinquency and whether informants project their own level of delinquency onto their friends are ongoing. Yet, there is little doubt that a significant portion of the variance in the peer-participant delinquency relationship is a consequence of a peer influence or socialization effect. As such, peer delinquency serves as a major risk factor for criminality, which if not addressed can lead to individual criminal events. The opposite pole of the risk factor, few to no delinquent peer associations, serves as a promotive factor and has been found to predict a low level of subsequent delinquency (Bernat et al., 2012).

A protective effect, according to Farrington et al. (2016), occurs when a putative protective factor interacts with a risk factor, thereby reducing or eliminating the risk effect. In a study by Walters (2018k), however, the interactive effect registered at the low end, or promotive pole, of the risk factor. Youth from the Pathways to Desistance Study had been assessed on their ability to resist negative peer pressure. Peer delinquency and peer resistance had been found to exert indirect effects on subsequent offending by enhancing or inhibiting the mediating effect of moral disengagement, a facet of proactive criminal thinking (PCT), on future offending behavior. Peer delinquency registered a positive association with moral disengagement, whereas peer resistance skills recorded a negative association. The peer delinquency x peer resistance interaction was also significant and implied that youth with fewer delinquent peer associations were disproportionately less likely to score high in moral disengagement if they were high in resistance to negative peer influence. In effect, high peer resistance skills aided youth with fewer delinquent peer associations—making it a promotive rather than protective effect—and discouraged them from engaging in PCT, which was found to be a potent predictor of subsequent offending in this study. Although these skills were not something participants necessarily learned as part of a formal intervention, they can just as easily be taught as part of an assisted change program as they can be acquired naturally.

An additional competency that may be useful in managing the risk factor of delinquent peer associations is prosocial peer associations. Instead of associating with peers who get in trouble at school, in the home, or with the law, the youth associates with peers who do well in school, respect the law, and engage in conventional activities. Walters (2020p) examined the relationship between delinquent peer associations, prosocial peer associations, and subsequent delinquency/drug use in a group of early to mid-adolescents from the Gang Resistance Education and Training (GREAT) study. Results revealed that prosocial peer associations did not interact with delinquent peer associations but did have a direct suppressant effect on future delinquency. Based on these results, prosocial peers did not produce a protective effect, although they were a competency that seemed to reduce the criminogenic effect of delinquent peer associations. Thus, developing, fostering, and nurturing positive peer associations could be beneficial to youth who are at risk for future delinquency by virtue of a relationship network composed of many delinquent friends. Whether acquiring peer resistance skills or developing new prosocial peer relationships, learning is most effective when it is broken down into smaller units or proximal steps (Bandura & Schunk, 1981).

Changing Commitments

According to Wilson and Herrnstein (1985), most offenders have a short time horizon and are much more focused on the present than they are on the future. And because the short-term effects of crime appear to provide more pleasure than pain, the criminal option is often viewed more favorably than the conventional option (where the long-term benefits offer more pleasure than pain) by those with a short time horizon. One approach to working with someone who is committed to short-term gratification, with the incumbent disregard for the negative long-term consequences of their actions, is helping them extend their time horizon. This can be accomplished by developing competencies in such areas as means-ends thinking, consideration of future consequences, and delay of gratification. General social skills training has been applied to offenders, but the results are often weak and inconsistent (van der Stouwe et al., 2016). It makes more sense to target specific skill deficits rather than perform a general intervention (Pardini, 2016), although broad-based cognitive-behavioral interventions have been found effective in countering the present-orientation and impulsivity of those with a short time horizon (Ly et al., 2019; Wong et al., 2018).

Another way to reduce the risk presented by a short time horizon is to look for protective factors. Recently, Brumback and colleagues (2021) alleged having identified a protective factor for impulsivity in a study on alcohol and marijuana use in adolescents and emerging adults, ages 13–25. Emotional regulation seemed to "protect" this group of individuals against early alcohol and marijuana use. The problem with this study is the problem with many studies on protective factors—namely, it uses an overly broad definition of protection and fails to differentiate between a protective effect and a promotive effect. Some variables are risk factors, others are promotive factors, and still others are both risk and promotive factors. In the Brumback et al. (2021) study, emotional regulation served as a promotive factor just as peer resistance skills served as a promotive factor in Walters (2018k). Neither, however, was a verified protective factor in the sense that it reduced the impact of a risk factor on an outcome like delinquency by interacting with it. This does not mean that emotional regulation and peer resistance have no role in managing a short time horizon or peer delinquency; it just means that they exert their effect through promotive rather than protective channels. It also serves as a call for more research on genuine protective relationships.

Another competency capable of expanding a person's time horizon and serving as a catalyst for desistance is a growing future orientation. Several studies have examined the relationship between future orientation and desistance from crime and all have identified a meaningful relationship between the two variables (Clinkinbeard, 2014; Monahan et al., 2009; Petrich et al., 2020; Walters, 2019e). It should be noted, however, that three of the studies (Monahan et al., 2009; Petrich et al., 2020; Walters, 2019e) employed the same sample (Pathways to Desistance) and the fourth (Clinkinbeard, 2014) utilized a cross-sectional design. Therefore, while future orientation would appear to be of potential utility in promoting desistance, more research using longitudinal data other than the Pathways study is required to determine just how meaningful a predictor of desistance future orientation really is. By becoming more future-oriented, the individual gains independence from the tyranny of a criminal lifestyle with its promises of immediate gratification and dismissal of future considerations. Other competencies like stronger means-ends thinking, greater delay of gratification, and better emotional regulation should also help extend the person's time horizon.

Changing Identifications

It has been proposed that identifications change over the course of the desistance process. This, in fact, is the premise upon which ITD is based. The criminal identity becomes a feared self that then encourages the individual to adopt a noncriminal or conventional identity (Paternoster & Bushway, 2009). As previously stated, however, there is no indication from the framers of ITD as to how present failures lead to anticipation of future failures and how this knowledge converts a criminal identity into a feared self. In my 29-plus years working with incarcerated offenders, I ran across many inmates who believed it was someone else's fault that they were behind bars. Other researchers have also found that a good portion of offenders view themselves as successful, even those sitting in prison (Brezina & Topalli, 2012). They rationalize that the only reason they are locked up is because the police "lied" or someone "snitched" on them. Although there is not a great deal of research on this issue, it stands to reason that an identity as a successful criminal might serve as a risk factor for future criminality whereas viewing oneself as unsuccessful in crime might serve as a promotive factor capable of encouraging desistance. This, however, does not answer the larger question of what differentiates a successful criminal from an unsuccessful one, if many incarcerated offenders do, in fact, view themselves as successful.

According to Brezina and Topalli (2012), the offender who fancies themselves a successful criminal has high self-efficacy for crime but low self-efficacy for conventional behavior. It should therefore follow that the offender who self-identifies as unsuccessful will have lower self-efficacy expectancies for crime and be more likely to desist than the offender who considers themselves a successful criminal (Maruna, 2001). The self-labeled unsuccessful criminal may also have higher self-efficacy for conventional behavior than the successful criminal, although this will not always be the case. The nice thing about self-efficacy is that it can be changed—increased in the case of self-efficacy for conventional behavior and decreased in the case of self-efficacy for crime—using the proper cognitive-behavioral techniques. For the sake of argument, let's assume that low self-efficacy for crime and/or high self-efficacy for conventional behavior is capable of serving as a protective factor in someone who self-identifies as a successful criminal. As we saw with peer delinquency and a short time horizon, there is currently a lack of data with which to test this hypothesis. The closest I came to finding a protective factor were two studies by Walters in which self-efficacy for a conventional lifestyle was tested as a mediator of the parenting-delinquency and past delinquency-future delinquency relationships.

In the first of these studies, Walters (2018g) utilized longitudinal data collected at three points in time from a large sample of high school students, grades 10–12. Students were asked to estimate their level of self-efficacy for deviance and their level of self-efficacy for a conventional lifestyle at Time 2, in an effort to determine whether self-efficacy mediated the relationship between parental support/control at Time 1 and delinquency at Time 3, after controlling for delinquency at Time 1. The results revealed that high self-efficacy for a conventional lifestyle led to a reduction in delinquency from Time 1 to Time 3, but that high self-efficacy for deviance had no mediating effect. In the second study, Walters (2018f), using data from the Pathways to Desistance Study, determined that self-efficacy for a conventional lifestyle, but not general confidence, deterred future offending. Although the results of these two studies are in no way definitive, they do suggest that high self-efficacy for a conventional lifestyle potentially facilitates desistance. As such, there is a need for additional research to determine whether the interaction between identifying as a successful criminal and having self-efficacy for a conventional lifestyle predicts future delinquency.

Changing Beliefs

It is a well-known fact that desistance increases as an individual moves from adolescence to middle adulthood (Doherty & Bersani, 2018). The assertion that criminal thinking decreases with age is also implied but requires further study (Walters, 2017e). The logical assumption, then, is that reduced criminal thinking predicts desistance. Studies have detected a modest to moderate but highly consistent relationship between criminal thinking and criminal behavior, with arrests, violations, and recidivism elevated when criminal thinking is high and depressed when criminal thinking is low (Healy, 2010; Taxman et al., 2011; Walters & Lowenkamp, 2016; Warner et al., 2018). Perhaps the most important competency for someone with a high level of criminal thinking to possess, whether the criminal thinking is proactive or reactive, is a systematic method for identifying and challenging criminal thinking. The method, which is described in greater detail in chapter 11, consists of three steps: (1) identifying the most salient criminal thinking styles; (2) Challenging the logic and rationality of these thinking styles; and (3) working to develop a more rationale alternate way of thinking. A hypothesis-testing approach similar to this three-step model has been proposed by Gannon (2016).

Low coldheartedness or its complement, high tenderheartedness, is a possible protective factor against the risk of PCT. Someone who is tenderhearted is warm, compassionate, and empathetic. Walters (2016i) explored the relationship between PCT and coldheartedness in a sample 4,638 male and female correctional clients undergoing substance abuse treatment. The interaction between PCT and coldheartedness was found to be significant in predicting client-rated counselor rapport. This suggests that participants exhibiting low coldheartedness (or high tenderheartedness) in combination with low PCT reported a disproportionately higher level of rapport with their counselors. As with the peer delinquency × peer resistance interaction, however, the interaction between PCT and coldheartedness does not identify a protective effect but rather a promotive effect in which the impact of tenderheartedness accelerates the promotive effect of low PCT on counselor rapport. The therapeutic alliance was discussed earlier in this chapter as a way of increasing a client's motivation for change. Counselor rapport is a reflection of this alliance. Without rapport there can be no alliance, and without an alliance there is very little likelihood of change. The inability to identify a true protective effect for any of the four examples included in this chapter illustrates the gap that exists in research on protective factors and crime.

Outcome expectancies are another competency that could be of assistance in managing the risk presented by high PCT. In one study, Walters (2003b) observed a significant prospective relationship, moderate in magnitude, running from positive outcome expectancies for crime to general criminal thinking (GCT) in inmates participating in a 10-week criminal thinking intervention. The alternate cross-lag, which ran from criminal thinking to positive outcome expectancies for crime, was nonsignificant. Although there was no relationship between criminal thinking and negative outcome expectancies for crime in this study, negative outcome expectancies for crime did demonstrate a significant reduction in a different sample of inmates participating in the same 10-week criminal thinking intervention (Walters, 2004). The results of this second study revealed that an intervention with documented efficacy in reducing criminal thinking and behavior (Walters, 2017c) may work, in part, by increasing negative outcome expectancies for crime (loss of family, freedom, and self-respect). Based on the results of a study denoting that outcome expectancies for crime correspond with PCT but not RCT (Walters, 2007b), it could be argued that outcome expectancies for crime are a competency that may be particularly relevant in promoting desistance in persons with elevated PCT scores. Examples of risk, promotive, and protective factors for each element of the change plan are listed in figure 9.1.

Figure 9.1 Examples of Risk, Promotive, and Protective Factors for Each Element of the Change Plan. Note: Promotive Factor-1 = promotive factor at opposite pole of a risk factor; Promotive Factor-2 = stand-alone promotive factor; light font = does not fulfill role as a protective or promotive factor. *Source:* Created by author.

A Word about Labeling

A label like delinquent or criminal can serve as a major impediment to change, particularly when applied to a young person in the early stages of a delinquent lifestyle, where it can become a self-fulfilling prophesy and a barrier to conventional relationships and social support (Adams et al., 2003). In an adult like Carl Panzram, who presents with an extensive history of criminal behavior, however, the situation can be viewed differently. Many such individuals will attempt to minimize and mollify their past criminal conduct by euphemistically referring to themselves as hustlers, businessmen, or in the case of one long-time drug dealer, a "street pharmacist." In these situations, I believe it is appropriate for the therapist to respond with something along the lines of "you were not a hustler, you were a criminal," provided the person making this statement understands and believes that "criminal" is a state of mind that can be changed once the individual stops thinking like a criminal and that this understanding is conveyed to the client.

CARL PANZRAM AT AGE 16

I am firmly of the opinion that everyone is capable of change and that change is possible at any age. That said, some people are more amenable to change than others, and change is more likely to occur in childhood and adolescence than it is in middle adulthood. When Carl Panzram arrived at USP Leavenworth at the age of 37, change was possible but highly unlikely given his mindset. We will therefore return to an age and time when Panzram may have been more receptive to change. My objective is to illustrate how it may be possible to manage criminal propensity by building competencies, even in someone as hardened, recalcitrant, and unrepentant as Panzram at age 16. The age selected for this analysis coincides with Panzram's arrival at the United States Disciplinary Barracks (USDB) at Fort Leavenworth, Kansas, a military prison, not to be confused with United States Penitentiary (USP), Leavenworth, in April 1908. It was here that he would spend the next two-and-one-half years serving a three-year sentence for theft.

Preconditions for Change in Panzram

Motivation for Change

The first precondition for change is finding the motivation to change. Most people change on their own in a process known as unassisted change. In such cases, the person normally finds their motivation in their interactions with family and friends. For those who do not change on their own, assisted change is a possibility, although the person must find motivation and overcome the natural fear of change and psychological inertia by developing a therapeutic alliance with their therapist or counselor. Though records are sketchy for this period in Panzram's life, it is probably safe to assume that he feared change. If he did not fear change, he certainly gave every indication that it was not something he was interested in or believed he could attain. Panzram engaged in a daily ritual of property offending and serious interpersonal intrusion that began right after he left Red Wing reformatory, implying that psychological inertia was as much a part of the picture as fear of change. To overcome his ever-expanding fear of change and growing psychological inertia, MI should probably be utilized. Presenting Panzram with open-ended questions, reflecting back emotions, pointing out discrepancies between goals and current behavior, and rolling with the resistance should put one in a position to form a preliminary therapeutic alliance with the 16-year-old Panzram.

Expectancies for Change

The advantage of performing MI early in an intervention is that it provides the counselor or therapist with a head start on the next precondition for change—expectancies for change. Expectancies for change are encompassed by the three branches of the attribution triad. Therefore, developing expectancies for change means holding to change-facilitating beliefs in the necessity, possibility, and ability to effect change. Panzram, even at age 16, will need a great deal of assistance internalizing beliefs about the necessity and theoretical possibility of change. This could be accomplished through MI, although the procedure may need to be expanded beyond the usual five or six sessions to achieve the desired effect. In addition, the third branch of the attribution triad (belief in one's ability to effect change) will require role plays and homework assignments designed to furnish young Panrzam with the necessary prosocial skills and opportunities for using and practicing these skills in his daily interactions with others. It is the successful completion of these role plays and homework assignments that gives rise to a strong sense of self-efficacy for change. Believing not only that change is necessary and theoretically possible but also that they, as a client, possess the skills and competencies required to effect change in their lives can lay the groundwork for more substantial changes in later stages of the treatment process.

Cognitive-Behavioral Inconsistency

The third precondition for change is inconsistency or cognitive and behavioral dissonance. As was mentioned in previous discussions on Panzram, there are several cognitive and behavioral inconsistencies even though he is trying to project an image of himself as an inhuman monster ("All of my family are . . . honest and hard working people. All except myself. I have been a human animal ever since I was born. When I was very young at five or six years of age, I was a thief and a liar, and a mean despicable one at that": Panzram, 1928, p. 1). The fact that he exhibits internalization and self-control when dealing with problems involving other inmates can be interpreted as inconsistencies capable of persuading him to strive for even higher levels of internalization and self-control. Inconsistencies, if properly developed, can lead to change because they identify areas of uncertainty and uncertainty is something that can open the door to new learning opportunities and new behaviors. Of equal importance in working with someone like Panzram is challenging the counter-change mechanism of confirmation bias. When interacting with Panzram, at 16 or 37, it is vital that the therapist or counselor identify and challenge instances of confirmation bias and encourage Panzram to do the same.

Planning for Change

The fourth precondition for change is construction of a change plan. This is a dual responsibility shared by both the client and counselor. Elements of the change plan and competencies designed to alter the risk factors for each element are reviewed next in Panzram's Change Plan at 16. This should be looked upon as an abbreviated change plan designed to illustrate the model. As the reader will notice, there is only one risk factor identified for each element. If this were an actual change plan, then you would want to identify multiple risk factors and competencies at each element level.

Panzram's Change Plan

Changing Involvements

The risk factor selected for the involvements element of Panzram's change plan is an early history of severe conduct disorder. From what we know of Panzram, he started offending at an early age, with an age of onset for stealing and breaking and entering starting around age 5 or 6, according to his own report. The lower (less pathological) end of the risk factor continuum (absence of early conduct disorder) is not particularly helpful as a promotive factor given its static (historical) nature. A protective factor, however, can be identified for early conduct disorder in the form of nonverbal problem-solving. Walters (20211) explored the interaction between early conduct disorder and the WISC-IV matrix reasoning scale as a predictor of subsequent delinquency and identified a protective effect in which delinquency was disproportionately lower in conduct disordered youth who scored high on matrix reasoning. This suggests that possessing nonverbal problem-solving skills may help protect against future delinquency in youth with a prior history of conduct disorder. A promotive factor that may have been effective with Panzram at age 16 but which was not invented until 60 years after his death is an intensive intervention for seriously conducted disordered youth known as multisystemic therapy (MST: Henggeler et al., 1998). MST has proven effective in randomized controlled trials in Europe and the United States (Tan & Fajardo, 2017).

Changing Commitments

The risk factor for the commitments element of Panzram's change plan is a lack of care and concern for others, a pattern sometimes referred to as callous-unemotional (CU) traits. Unlike the early conduct disorder risk factor, the opposite pole of the CU risk factor (care and concern for others) could serve as a promotive factor in working with a 16-year-old Panzram. Empathy training, along with cultivation of Pazram's perspective taking and listening skills, could help smooth over the rough edges of his callousness and seeming lack of concern, but overall prospects for significant change in this area are not good given how stable CU traits are, particularly once a child reaches adolescence (Frick et al., 2014). A non-protective interaction was obtained between CU traits and psychosocial maturity showing psychosocial maturity disproportionately lowering future offending in youth with few CU traits (Simmons et al., 2020). This denotes a stand-alone promotive effect. Another stand-alone promotive effect was recorded in a study where witnessing but not experiencing victimization mediated the relationship between CU traits and delinquency (Oberth et al., 2017). The results of this study indicate that witnessing violence can increase callousness to interpersonal injury and so shielding and buffering youth from such exposure could serve a promotive function and thereby support desistance.

Changing Identifications

When it comes to identifications that support Panzram's criminal lifestyle, the desire to be seen as the "meanest man on earth" is certainly the risk factor that should be looked into first. It is easy to see how this moniker could fuel antisocial and criminal behavior. Besides being antisocial, this title also seems rather grandiose, as would be the case for being the most of anything on earth. An antidote to this grandiose self-view would be a self-view as ordinary. Viewing oneself as ordinary has been found to support unassisted change in heroin addicts attempting to kick the habit on their own (Biernacki, 1986) and could serve as the opposite pole of the "meanest man on earth" risk factor. In contrast to the opposite pole promotive effect of viewing oneself as ordinary, reflected appraisals may serve as stand-alone promotive factors. Using data provided by 284 male respondents from the Marion County Youth Study, Walters (2020d) probed the relationship between adolescent reflected appraisals as a delinquent and desistance from crime between late adolescence and early adulthood. Results revealed that reflected appraisals as a delinquent impeded the adolescent-to-adult transition in desistance. Extrapolating from these results, one could argue that a reflected appraisal as a noncriminal is likely to aid desistance. Finally, high self-control may serve as a protective factor, according to the results of a study by Courey and Pare (2016). In this study, high self-control protected individuals with a criminogenic identity from engaging in the level of crime observed in men with a criminogenic identity and low self-control.

Changing Beliefs

Reactive criminal thinking may be an even stronger predictor of recidivism than PCT (Walters, 2020e; Walters & Lowenkamp, 2016). This might have something to do with the fact that impulsivity and disorganized thinking, key features of RCT, make it difficult for a person to avoid arrest and other legal entanglements. Such a relationship may be of particular relevance to someone like Panzram who spent the vast majority of his life, from mid-adolescence to his execution at age 39, in jail or prison. A review of Panzam's writings reveals evidence of both PCT and RCT, although RCT will be highlighted here. The promotive alternative to high RCT is low RCT. This can be achieved by challenging the rationality and functional utility of RCT. The challenge would begin with a trained therapist but then hopefully be internalized by the client, in this case, the 16-year-old Panzram. Stand-alone promotive factors for RCT include decreased substance use (Walters, 2012) and the Big Five personality trait of conscientiousness (Walters, 2018h). Caudy et al. (2015) witnessed an interaction between GCT and substance misuse in a sample of 337 jail inmates presenting with varying degrees of substance misuse, but the effect occurred at the low rather than high end of the risk dimension, once again indicating that it is more properly classified a stand-alone promotive effect than a protective factor. Treating substance abuse problems in those with minimal levels of criminal thinking should yield particularly strong dividends for programs designed to prevent offending.

CONCLUSION

The purpose of this chapter was to illustrate how criminality or a person's propensity to commit crime can be managed by building competencies. Introducing a change plan matrix that crossed four elements (involvements, commitments, identifications, and beliefs) with three competencies (opposite pole promotive factor, protective factor, stand-alone promotive factor), the current chapter demonstrates how it is possible to find and use competencies to reduce specific risk factors. A competency is a skill designed to reduce a risk. As a skill, it can be acquired through instruction. All of the competencies described in this chapter (e.g., peer resistance skills, prosocial peer relations, extended time horizon, emotion regulation skills, high self-efficacy for a conventional lifestyle, high negative outcome expectancies for crime) can be taught. And each provides either a promotive or protective effect. Promotive competencies reduce the risk of delinquency and crime by directly impinging on the antisocial outcome, whereas protective competencies reduce risk by interacting with risk factors and limiting their negative impact on the individual. As was evident throughout this chapter, there are several noticeable gaps in the literature on promotive and protective effects, particularly the latter. In the next chapter, we examine another way to manage criminality, this time by changing the environment.

Chapter 10

Managing Criminality

Part II. Reducing Risk by Changing Environments

"People Live and Function in Multiple Environments"

According to lifestyle theory, managing criminality or a person's propensity to commit crime is best achieved by identifying, targeting, and reducing risk. And reducing risk is usually accomplished in one of two ways. One way is to build competencies. These competencies assist the individual in resolving issues related to the risks that confront them, while helping them cope with problems that may not be so easily resolved. This was discussed in the previous chapter. A second way to reduce risk is to change environments. People function in multiple environments and their behavior is greatly influenced by these environments. Whether the environment is internal or external, social or physical, institutional or personal, it can have a lasting effect on the frequency, duration, and severity of problems an individual is likely to encounter over the course of a day, week, month, year, or lifetime. Before deliberating on how risk can be reduced by changing environments, it is imperative that we consider how lifestyle theory views desistance, starting with the question, is there a need for special theories of desistance separate and distinct from more general theories of crime? This is then followed by a second question, which asks how a person comes to realize that change is necessary. Answers to these two questions serve as springboards to a more in-depth analysis of how changing and altering environments can help reduce the risks that support criminality.

TWO QUESTIONS

Is There a Need for a Separate Theory of Desistance?

In chapter 9, we examined the two most frequently cited theories of desistance. One model of desistance comes from Sampson and Laub's (1993) age-graded theory and takes as its principal thesis the belief that desistance is a function of turning points in a person's life. The other major desistance theory comes from Paternoster and Bushway (2009). This is commonly referred to as the identity theory of desistance (ITD). Whereas turning points derive from Sampson and Laub's more general theory of crime, ITD was developed specifically to explain desistance. This raises the question, whether special theories of desistance, separate and distinct from more general theories of crime, are needed. I would argue that they are not, and that such specialization can encourage a view that desistance is somehow separate from crime, when, in fact, they are both part of the same process. This brings us back to the age-crime curve described in chapter 5 whereby criminality begins its ascent in late childhood/early adolescence, peaks in mid-adolescence, and then drop off in late adolescence/early adulthood. Desistance is embedded in that process—a process within a process, if you will—and to view the two legs of the process as separate is to create an artificial dichotomy. Hence, desistance should be studied as part of a larger theory of crime, not parceled out as if it were an entity unto itself but retained as a feature of criminality constructed from natural (unassisted) and unnatural (treatment) processes.

At What Point Does a Person Conclude That Change Is Necessary?

As indicated in chapter 9, the first branch of the attribution triad is a belief in the necessity of change. Each precondition for change is critical to the process, but a belief in the necessity of change is at the heart of the change process, based on the logic that if change is not necessary why bother. Change can be arduous, grueling, and time-consuming, not to mention scary; so why should someone put themselves through such an ordeal if they do not believe it is necessary? So, at what point does a person realize that change is necessary? According to lifestyle theory, a belief in the necessity of change sets in when a person perceives that the lifestyle is no longer working (i.e., the pain outweighs the pleasure). This is referred to in lifestyle theory as a crisis, examples of which are provided in table 10.1 broken down by source (internal, external) and motive (approach-oriented, avoidance-oriented). The therapist need not manufacture a crisis as is sometimes done in structural family therapy (Minuchin, 1974). Crises are a daily occurrence for someone engaged

Table 10.1 Sources and Motives for Crises

Motive	*Internal Source*	*External Source*
Approach-Oriented	• Desire to live a crime-free life • Interest in attending college	• Finding a meaningful and rewarding job • Parenthood
Avoidance-Oriented	• Fear of dying in prison • Disgust with life on the streets	• Shock of seeing crime partner killed • Stress and strain of recurrent trips to jail

Source: Table created by author.

in a drug or criminal lifestyle. An experienced therapist simply develops these naturally occurring crises in order to get the client to the point where they perceive that a change is necessary. Some youth who commit crime are believed to drift in and out of offending, usually in response to changes taking place in the environment (Matza, 1964). This is why changing environments, the centerpiece of the current chapter, is so important. In many cases, drifters may not need to develop a belief in the necessity of change because they had no commitment to the lifestyle to begin with. For non-drifters, even those with no more than a marginal commitment to a criminal lifestyle, a belief in the necessity of change is often required, though orchestrating changes in the environment can still be of assistance.

CHANGES TO THE EXTERNAL ENVIRONMENT

There are many parts of the external environment, both social and physical, that can be used to manage criminality and reduce risk. Changing these environments can bring about a change in individuals. The environments to be discussed in this section are the parenting environment, the sibling environment, the peer environment, the school environment, the neighborhood environment, the collective (societal) environment, and the physical environment.

Changing the Parenting Environment

The parenting environment has two principal functions: control and support. The control function is designed to provide the child with external control and discipline while the child learns to exert and internalize control and discipline over their thoughts, feelings, and behaviors. The support function, by contrast, is concerned primarily with providing the child with emotional support and nurturance. Changing the parenting environment by emphasizing control means improving a parent's ability to supervise, monitor, direct, and discipline the child. The hope is that the child will eventually internalize the external control and discipline provided by the parents and learn to exercise control and discipline over themselves. This is a competency-based approach similar to many of the techniques described in chapter 9, but now, instead of teaching competency skills to the child, it is the parents who are receiving competency training. By providing the child with a safe, consistent, and non-chaotic home environment, the parents are providing the child with increased opportunity for success while reducing opportunities for failure. Whether a child takes advantage of a positive home environment is a decision the child must make. But those who do take advantage of a positive home environment are in a much better position to manage the stress, freedoms, and responsibilities of everyday life and the risk factors that lead to crime than children who do not take advantage of a positive home environment.

Parent training is one of the more popular and effective ways of changing the parenting environment. The training provided is designed to improve parents' ability to control and discipline the child using rules that are clear, procedures that are consistent, and rewards and punishments that are reasonable and effective. Two relatively recent meta-analyses by Piquero and colleagues indicate that early family/parent training is an effective deterrent to future antisocial and delinquent behavior (Piquero et al., 2009, 2016). In the first meta-analysis, Piquero et al. (2009) calculated a weighted effect size (Cohen's *d*) of .35 for studies on children whose parents were enrolled in parent training or family education programs. The programs included in the meta-analysis ranged from parent effectiveness training to regular home visits from nurses and mental health professionals. Piquero et al. updated their meta-analysis in 2016 and found similar results and a weighted Cohen's *d* of .37. The majority of children in the Piquero et al. meta-analyses were of preschool or primary school age. Other studies have shown that parent training is also effective with chronically delinquent youth and their untargeted siblings, and that it appears to work by improving parenting skills and lowering the use of abusive parental discipline (Bank et al., 1991; Lundahl et al., 2006).

Parental support can be just as important as parental control in managing criminality and reducing risk. Parents who bond with their child provide a supportive environment in which a child can learn, grow, and prosper. Social control theory has long held that being attached to parents (Hirschi, 1969) and having a stake in conformity (Toby, 1957) can lead to lower levels of future criminality. Parental support in the form of physical affection, compassionate parenting, and open communication can play a critical role in promoting attachment and a child's stake in conformity. Moreover, a supportive relationship can be instrumental in internalizing parental control and warmth. A parent with whom a child has a close relationship will serve as a stronger role model and source of emulation than a parent with whom a child has a distant or weak relationship. Handy and colleagues (2008) correlated three dimensions of parenting (involvement, autonomy support, and structure) with internalization of moral values in a sample of 101 middle adolescents and discovered that all three correlated significantly with the adolescent offspring's internalization of moral values. Another aspect of parental support, a strong parent-child attachment relationship, has also been found to lead to internalization of moral beliefs from parent to child (Liable & Thompson, 2000).

Because parenting programs are usually more about parental control than they are about parental support, the emphasis of such programs is usually on teaching parents to set rules, monitor behavior, and properly dispense rewards and punishments. Even so, there are programs that focus at least partially on parental support. One such program is parent-child interaction therapy (PCIT: Eyberg, 1988). PCIT is designed for children 2–5 years of age who suffer from disruptive behavior problems like conduct disorder, attention deficit/hyperactivity disorder, and oppositional defiant disorder. Blending concepts from attachment and social learning theories, it is usually administered in 9–12 sessions of 60–90 minutes each under the supervision of a trained therapist. PCIT is taught in two phases. The first or child-directed phase centers around the development of a positive parent-child relationship through the medium of play. The second or parent-directed phase is geared primarily toward parental control and seeks to teach the parent how to guide the child's activities and apply consequences to discourage negative behavior. In a meta-analysis of 12 randomized control and pre-post studies, Ward et al. (2016) discovered that PCIT was an effective intervention for children with disruptive behavior disorders. As with interventions designed to improve parental control, interventions like PCIT, which are designed to improve parental support, are also effective in reducing a child's propensity for antisocial behavior.

Changing the Sibling Environment

As discussed in chapter 3, siblings can be an important source of information for a young child. Not only do children learn by observing and modeling the actions, thoughts, and feelings of siblings, they also learn through their interactions with siblings, whether those interactions are cooperative or conflictual. In a recent study, using data from the Illinois Study of Bullying and Sexual Violence, Walters and Espelage (2020a) determined that early aggression between adolescent-aged siblings contributed to school fighting one year later in a relationship mediated by hostility. These results indicate that having an aggressive relationship with a sibling can lead to an upsurge of hostility over a period of six months, and that an augmented level of hostility can give rise to escalating involvement in school aggression six months hence. In another study, this one using data from the Cambridge Study of Delinquent Development, Walters (2019j) tested a pathway composed of two consecutive mediators that began with exposure to older sibling delinquency at age 10/11 as the independent variable and ended with participant delinquency at age 16/17 as the dependent variable. The results of this study indicated that school problems at age 12/13 and peer delinquency at age 14/15 mediated the larger relationship between sibling delinquency at age 10/11 and participant delinquency at age 16/17. From these associations, it could be surmised that observing delinquency in an older sibling led to school problems, which then precipitated selection of a delinquent group, from whom the youth learned even more delinquent attitudes and behaviors.

One way to change the sibling environment is to change the parenting environment. This is based on research showing that parental rejection (Garcia et al., 2000), parental arrest (Fagan & Najman, 2003), and parental aggression (Ingram et al., 2020) all correlate with sibling conflict, violence, and delinquency. Differential parental treatment in which parents favor one child over another is an additional parenting behavior capable of creating sibling conflict and strong feelings of sibling rivalry. One way to minimize the negative impact of differential parental attention and sibling rivalry is to provide each child with confirmation, thereby recognizing each child as a unique and valuable human being (Phillips & Schrodt, 2015). Consequently, one of the chief ways in which the sibling environment is changed is by changing the parenting environment. There is also evidence that sibling relationships can be improved directly. One line of research is to use the competencies discussed in the previous chapter to change the sibling environment highlighted in the current chapter. In a study of 4-to-8-year-old siblings from 95 families, it was determined that teaching each sibling emotion regulation skills led to a significant improvement in the quality of the sibling relationship (Kennedy & Kramer, 2008). A meta-analysis by Buist et al. (2013) likewise revealed that with a rise in sibling warmth, a drop in sibling conflict, and less differential treatment from parents, siblings displayed fewer internalizing and externalizing problem behaviors.

Changing the Peer Environment

Two complementary processes can be used to transform the peer environment from one that supports delinquency and antisocial behavior to one that discourages delinquency and antisocial behavior. These complementary processes achieve their transformative power by countering criminogenic peer influences with prosocial peer influences. Parental supervision and knowledge are potential protective factors when it comes to reducing the criminogenic effect of delinquent and deviant peers on participant delinquent behavior. One study, in particular, Lu et al. (2020), identified a significant negative interaction between parental knowledge and deviant peer associations in their effect on participant delinquency. Further analysis revealed that the interaction was the result of a significant drop in participant delinquency as youth with high deviant peer associations were exposed to high parental knowledge. Earlier, Ray et al. (2017) discovered that parental monitoring attenuated the effect of callous-unemotional (CU) traits on peer delinquency, but only when parental warmth was also high. The results of both studies suggest that parental knowledge and monitoring protect against participant and peer delinquency by interacting with peer deviance and CU traits, respectively, and so are capable of creating a genuine protective effect.

Another change in the peer environment that may lower a person's propensity to commit crime entails elevating the prosocial component of the environment. Katz and Fox (2010) examined a number of risk factors for gang involvement in Trinidad and Tobago (perceived availability of firearms, residential mobility, parental support of antisocial behavior, early initiation of antisocial behavior, intention to use drugs, antisocial peers, and peers who use drugs) and discovered that the risk factors, as risk factors are apt to do, achieved a cumulative effect. The risk factors were opposed or balanced by a series of promotive factors (social skills, belief in moral order, and association with prosocial peers). Former gang members reported fewer contacts with prosocial peers and significantly weaker social skills than non-gang members. Prosocial peers, on the other hand, encouraged prosocial activities. Youth who associate with delinquent peers tend to engage in unstructured activities with minimal adult supervision (Walters, 2018m), whereas youth who associate with conventional or prosocial peers tend to engage in structured activities with maximum adult supervision (Albanesi et al., 2007). One way to reduce criminality, then, is to keep the child engaged in structured activities with prosocial peers.

A peer environment governed by delinquent peer associations is an environment ripe for victimization. Research on victim-offender overlap (Jennings et al., 2012) indicates that victims and perpetrators of crime are often one and the same. Becoming a victim of crime, particularly a violent crime, increases a person's odds of becoming a perpetrator of crime through the mediating effect of hostility and RCT (Walters, 2020f; Walters & Espelage, 2020b), whereas being a perpetrator of crime enhances one's odds of becoming a victim of crime through person proximity (Walters, 2020i, 2020s). Person proximity refers to the fact that being in close proximity to those who perpetrate delinquency, violence, or bullying increases one's odds of being victimized by these same associates. The most obvious solution to the self-perpetuating nature of the victim-offender relationship is to minimize the child's exposure to antisocial peers and maximize their exposure to prosocial peers. Beyond this, potential protective factors like positive childhood experiences (e.g., high parental education, parental warmth, two-parent family, high perceived socioeconomic status (SES), and prosocial peer support) have been found to be effective in limiting the impact of a negative peer environment on early childhood depression, oppositional defiant disorder, and conduct disorder (Zhang et al., 2021).

Changing the Neighborhood and Community Environments

Neighborhoods can also promote criminality. As discussed in chapter 3, crime is not equally distributed across communities, with some vicinities experiencing much higher rates of crime than other vicinities. One possible explanation for these variations in crime across neighborhoods is that crime is concentrated in the poorest sections of the city. Although there is a modest relationship between neighborhood wealth and crime (Friedson & Sharkey, 2015), this accounts for only a small portion of the neighborhood-crime relationship and does not explain why crime is sometimes elevated in the wealthier parts of the city and depressed in some of the poorest areas. What appears to be more important than simply the wealth or SES of a neighborhood is the overall level of neighborhood disorder, as characterized by physical deterioration and psychological disorganization. Physical deterioration plays a central role in broken windows theory (Wilson & Kelling, 1982). According to broken windows theory, physically dilapidated buildings and unkempt grounds are a signal to criminals that people in the neighborhood do not provide their community with adequate guardianship nor are they likely to call the police when crimes occur. Criminals therefore figure it is okay for them to set up operations in that neighborhood. Neighborhood disorganization and the criminology of place are characterized by low social capital, weak collective efficacy, fear of crime, and a general sense of anonymity, all of which allow crime to prosper (Sampson, 2013).

A community is threatened by forces both within and outside the neighborhood. The within neighborhood threats come from people living in the area, more often than not, neighborhood children who are not properly supervised, and who are engaged in various delinquent acts. Outside neighborhood threats come from people living outside the area who seek to invade the neighborhood and use it for their own criminal purposes. A neighborhood's crime rate is the sum of these two forces, and while both need to be addressed, they require different approaches. Within neighborhood effects are best managed by working to improve communication between neighbors. This entails knowing who lives in the neighborhood and providing informal social control to neighborhood children by letting them know they are being watched and reporting problem behavior to the parents when it occurs.

Outside neighborhood effects are best managed by developing a strong sense of collective efficacy and common purpose between neighbors and protecting the open areas of the neighborhood (i.e., streets, sidewalks, and parks). These open areas are vital to the security of a neighborhood because they are usually the areas criminal groups attempt to control before taking over a neighborhood. Solidarity can be achieved with periodic informal get-togethers like yard sales and neighborhood barbeques or through more formal procedures like neighborhood watches.

Changing the Collective (Societal) Environment

Attempting to make changes in the larger society in order to reduce the propensity to commit crime presents unique opportunities and challenges. Two of these macro-level opportunities are discussed here: social structure and general cultural ethos. Although there is no such thing as a classless society, most cultures have abandoned the rigid class structures of the eighteenth and nineteenth centuries in which social status was based almost entirely on inherited wealth and position. In some ways, the United States pioneered this reformulation of social class, yet even here individuals from the lower social classes did not have the same opportunities and access to the financial rewards of society as people in the upper and middle classes. In Merton's (1957) classic strain theory, lower and working-class individuals are postulated to be at higher risk for future criminality because of these blocked opportunities. Providing those in the lower and working classes with greater access to the financial rewards of society and effectively dealing with the problem of income inequality, which continues to rise in the United States and parts of Europe (Hoffmann et al., 2020), will require time. In the meanwhile, we might want to take a lesson from Latin America, one of the few areas where income inequality has decreased in recent years, with redistributive efforts being supported by public spending on education, revenue from personal income taxes, and a greater emphasis on social contributions (Clifton et al., 2020).

Classic strain theory is based on two arguments: a structural argument and a cultural argument. The structural argument, which was discussed in the previous paragraph, maintains that lower-class individuals are more likely to commit crime than middle- and upper-class individuals because of their limited access to legitimate means for achieving material wealth. The cultural argument is based on a cultural ethos of material success, which according to Merton (1957) is how American society defines personal success. This argument is discussed here. Walters (2021i) discovered that a free market cultural ethos measured at the macro (national) level interacted with criminal thinking and delinquency measured at the micro (individual) level. In effect, citizens from nations professing a strong free market cultural ethos displayed a more robust criminal thinking-delinquency relationship than citizens from countries holding to a weak free market cultural ethos. Changing a cultural ethos is neither quick nor easy. The first question that needs to be answered is whether the population is interested in changing its ethos. This is not like changing high schools to increase one's chances of being accepted by an elite college, in part because the cultural ethos is not something the average person is aware of or at least is able to articulate. There could, however, be a gradual change in priorities and perspective over the course of many years that leads to a transformation of the cultural ethos of a society, which, of course, would require changes in education, governance, and business practice.

Changing the Physical Environment

Up to this point, the focus has been on the social environment. The physical environment, however, can be just as important to criminality and risk as the social environment, although it is usually more difficult to change than the social environment. When it comes to violent crime, the physical environment, in the form of ambient temperature, plays a significant role in both criminality and crime. In chapter 3, a study was reviewed in which the RCT-violent offending relationship was found to be significantly stronger in countries with a higher rather than lower average ambient temperature (Walters, 2021a). Certain criminologists have attributed the tendency of southern states previously allied with the confederacy to have elevated homicide rates to a southern subculture of violence in which protecting one's honor can lead to violent conflicts (Gastil, 1971). A simpler explanation is that southern states have higher average ambient temperatures than northern states and that the discomfort of a high ambient temperature leads to violence. In fact, the average ambient temperature and the per capita homicide rate for all 50 U.S. states correlate highly ($r = .47$). Although alternate explanations for these results exist, differences in the average age of male residents, differences in urbanization, and the rate of nonviolent (property) offending cannot be considered among them given a partial correlation of .34 ($p < .05$) when these three variables are controlled.

It could be argued that because there is not much that can be done to lower high ambient temperatures, that we should just accept the situation and move on to topics that are more amenable to change. After observing a relationship between ambient temperature and daily shootings in Chicago, however, Reeping and Hemenway (2020) made several suggestions that may prove useful in reducing the number of daily shootings in Chicago and other cities. According to the results of their study, a 10-degree (C) higher temperature was associated with 34% more shootings on weekdays and 42%

more shootings on weekends and holidays. They offer several recommendations that might help reduce gun violence by mitigating the negative impact high ambient temperatures have on people's behavior. One recommendation is to increase the availability of air-conditioning during the summer months to lower-income residents, perhaps through some type of voucher system. The authors also recommend keeping adolescents occupied during the summer months by enrolling them in community programs and summer camps, providing them with internships, and altering the school schedule. The ambient temperature-interpersonal violence relationship illustrates how the physical environment can affect the social environment. An increase in interpersonal violence can also be added to the list of negative consequences of worldwide climate change, with ambient temperatures increasing at an alarming rate in all corners of the globe.

CHANGES TO THE INTERNAL ENVIRONMENT

Criminality is not only reduced by making changes to external environments; it can also be reduced by making changes in a person's internal environment. The internal environment consists of cognitive, emotional, and biological processes located within the person. Making changes in the cognitive and emotional environments in an effort to reduce risk and criminality were discussed in chapter 9 of this book and will be discussed again in chapter 11 as ways of preventing crime. There is no need, then, to discuss them here. The internal environments to be discussed in the current section are biologically based and involve the balancing of opposites in the central nervous system. First, we will examine the balance between the sympathetic and parasympathetic branches of the autonomic nervous system (ANS); this will then be followed by a review of the balance between two neurotransmitters, dopamine and serotonin.

Changing the Reactivity of the Autonomic Nervous System

Conditioning to punishment is an important step in teaching children the difference between right and wrong (moral model) and showing them how to control their behavior (control model). As was previously mentioned, some children do not condition well to punishment because of ANS abnormalities. The ANS, it should be noted, is composed of two parts or branches. The sympathetic branch of the ANS activates the cardiovascular system and other involuntary functions to provide the organism with the energy it needs to manage perceived threats, in what is commonly referred to as the "fight or flight" response. The parasympathetic branch of the ANS promotes a relaxation response designed to restore and preserve energy so that the organism is in a position to deal with future threats. Many individuals at risk for delinquency and crime have problems generating a strong sympathetic response, which then gives rise to weak sympathetic reactivity (El-Sheikh et al., 2011) and a low resting heart rate (Farrington & Bergstrøm, 2021). Because the individual has trouble generating a proper autonomic response to threat, they do not condition well to punishment and experience great difficulty in learning from their mistakes (Raine et al., 1997). In other words, punishments do not have the same corrective effect on an individual with an under-aroused ANS as they do on an individual with a fully functioning ANS.

Sometimes it is not the intensity of the autonomic response that is the problem but the fact that it does not map well onto the punishment. For instance, if the child's autonomic response is delayed so that there is a period during which the punishment is active but the child's autonomic response is absent, or if the child's autonomic response does not stop when the punishment stops, conditioning will be weak and largely ineffective. Hence, if the child's autonomic response to the punishment does not start right when the punishment starts or end right when the punishment ends, the child will have difficulty associating the stimulus targeted for punishment with the punishing response. One way to rectify this problem is to find a better balance between the sympathetic and parasympathetic branches of the ANS based on the notion that balance between opposites is a key to biological health. Because nearly all of the treatment studies that have addressed ANS imbalance have focused on reducing sympathetic dominance (i.e., stress and anxiety disorders), there is not a great deal currently known about how to increase sympathetic arousal or decrease parasympathetic activity. Clinicians have used aversion conditioning, also known as aversive therapy, to treat sex offending, but this has raised serious ethical concerns, particularly when used to "treat" homosexuality (Davison, 2021; Wardlaw, 1979). As a result, its use, even for the treatment of sex offending, has been largely curtailed.

Changing the Dopamine-Serotonin Balance

Dopamine and serotonin are neurotransmitters that play vital roles in the mammalian central nervous system. Where dopamine is an excitatory neurotransmitter, promoting feelings of pleasure and driving the individual toward appetitive goals, serotonin can have either an excitatory or inhibitory effect depending on where in the central nervous system it is located. In the areas of the central nervous system where serotonin and dopamine intersect, serotonin is primarily an inhibitory neurotransmitter. As previously stated, balance often signals a healthy biological system, of which equilibrium between dopamine and serotonin is a prime example. Pleasure-seeking behavior and risk-taking appear to be stimulated by dopamine and inhibited by serotonin (Cupaioli et al., 2021; Narvaes & de Almeida, 2014). While there is nothing wrong with seeking pleasure or taking risks, problems arise when these activities are pursued to the detriment of other important aspects of a person's life. Serotonin helps balance the dopaminergic drive for immediate gratification against various long-term considerations. The complex interplay of dopamine and serotonin gives rise to the life instinct upon which existential fear is based and from which all behavior is believed to emanate. We could address the imbalance either by blocking dopamine or enhancing serotonin. The latter appears more feasible given that the antipsychotic medications used to reduce dopamine have more serious side effects than those designed to increase serotonin.

Whereas imbalance in the ANS usually favors the sympathetic branch, imbalance in the dopamine-serotonin system usually favors dopamine. And as was previously mentioned, enhancing serotonin is considered safer than blocking dopamine. The treatment protocol, then, is to use specific serotonin reuptake inhibitors (SSRIs) like Prozac, Zoloft, Celexa, or Paxil to enhance the action of serotonin at the synapse. The SSRIs were originally designed to treat depression and have been approved by the Food and Drug Administration (FDA) for the treatment of both depression and obsessive-compulsive disorder. If serotonin does, in fact, modulate the effect of dopamine, as proposed by lifestyle theory, it should also assist with behavioral control. Although research on this issue is still in its infancy, SSRIs have been found to reduce anger and irritability (Romero-Martinez et al., 2019), aggression (Sohanpal et al., 2007), hostility (Kamarck et al., 2009), and impulsivity (Butler et al., 2010). It should also be noted that while all drugs have side effects, SSRIs are relatively safe compared to most other psychotropic medications. Stories based largely on media accounts from the late 1990s and early 2000s of large numbers of suicides and assaults associated with the use of several of the more popular SSRIs were found to be either non-credible or greatly exaggerated (Walsh & Dinan, 2001). Even so, use of these medications should be monitored by a licensed physician.

CHANGES TO INSTITUTIONAL ENVIRONMENTS

The criminal justice system is made up of three parts: the police, the courts, and corrections. Each individual part of the system has the capacity to affect the criminality of each individual citizen who comes into contact with it. Although usually not as central to a person's criminality as, say, a person's unique internal or external environment, these institutional environments are just as capable of shaping a person's thoughts, feelings, and actions as an internal or external stimulus. Consequently, each institution contributes an environment, which, while it may not be as crucial to a person's criminality as a personalized internal or external environment, could still be instrumental in altering the person's propensity to commit crime.

Changing the Policing Environment

There has been a great deal written about policing and the negative impact it can have on the community in the last several years. Although I do not subscribe to any of the more radical approaches to changing the policing environment, such as defunding the police, I do believe certain changes in the policing environment could contribute to a generalized reduction in people's propensity for crime. These changes can be organized around three themes: selection, training, and accountability.

Selection

Certain roles and patterns are incompatible with effective police work. Some of the roles that conflict with being a good police officer include the tough cop, the clean-beat crime fighter, and the cowboy or hot-dog, and some of the patterns that stand in the way of effective policing are personality disorders of the borderline, antisocial, avoidant, and dependent variety (Miller, 2004). These roles and patterns are normally assessed as part of the screening process for employment as a police officer. This process typically includes a pre-employment interview, a lie detector test, a physical exam, and psychological testing. The MMPI/MMPI-2 is the psychological test most often used to screen police applicants (Cochrane et al., 2003), and while it does a good job of identifying personality disorders, it is not particularly effective in assessing other areas of concern, such as power orientation, authoritarianism, and aggression. For instance, a measure of behavioral control did a much better job of predicting potentially aggressive officers than the MMPI-2 in a study by Koeplfer and colleagues (2012). Recently, Aita et al. (2018) followed a group of 1,536 newly hired police officers and identified 205 (base rate = 13.3%) who were classified as "bad hires" because they were arrested, had more than five misconduct reports, or were terminated for cause within five years of being hired. The "bad hires" were significantly more likely than the rest of the sample to have had a history of outpatient psychiatric treatment, a history of substance abuse treatment, a history of multiple physical altercations, a history of arrest or detention, and a history of job-related reprimands and suspensions. Historical items and behavioral measures may therefore be of some use in identifying candidates who are just not cut out for police work. Another way to improve selection is to increase diversity within the police force. The results of a recent study showed that minority and female officers were significantly less likely to use excessive force than white male officers (Ba et al., 2021).

Training

Just as the selection of police officers is more involved than most people think, so too is the training. Federal, state, and local police usually go through several months of intensive training in a police academy before starting work as a police officer, followed by on-the-job training under the watchful eyes of a veteran officer. The academy training covers a wide range of topics, a partial list of which includes classroom instruction in criminal law and procedure, scenarios dealing with the handling of arrested persons, firearms training and qualification, physical fitness and self-defense, patrol procedures, traffic control, vehicle code enforcement, crash investigations, criminal investigations, drug law enforcement, and emergency response training. Even with the training, there are some important areas that are not covered or covered only superficially by the academy curriculum. Two such areas are working with the mentally ill and the use of de-escalation techniques. The deinstitutionalization of the mentally ill, which began in the late 1960s, has created a mental health crisis in the United States. Treating as many of the mentally ill as possible in the community rather than in a state mental hospital sounded like a good idea when it was first proposed, but many of these individuals were never followed up after they were released to the community and so they wound up living on the streets for the police to deal with. Law enforcement is not in a position to solve the problems of the mentally ill homeless but must deal with problem as the criminal justice system's first point of contact for mentally ill individuals who violate the law. Therefore, teaching officers how to talk to the mentally ill and where to refer them, rather than simply locking them up in a jail cell, can help keep the problem from getting worse (Seo et al., 2021). Likewise, learning de-escalation techniques designed to defuse a situation, particularly a domestic disturbance situation, is something that can and should be emphasized in police training (Wolfe et al., 2020).

Accountability

Proper selection and training are designed to maximize the number of good police officers and minimize the number of bad police officers. Even with state-of-the-art selection and training procedures, however, there will be some individuals who slip through the cracks. This is where accountability comes into play. Policing can be a difficult, dangerous, and often thankless job. The rewards of the position often seem to be outweighed by the stresses, leaving those in the profession to experience high rates of burnout, suicide, alcoholism, and divorce (Martin & Martin, 2017). And because no one is perfect, mistakes happen. That said, when police officers abuse their authority or place their personal desire for power over the good of the people they are sworn to protect, this is a problem for which the officer needs to be held accountable. The movement to ensure police accountability, unlike the movement to defund the police, is not only reasonable, it is long overdue. For too long, police unions have protected bad police officers in the false belief that holding bad police officers accountable for their bad behavior will put good police officers at risk. I would argue just the opposite. Failing to hold bad police officers accountable shines a negative light on the entire police department, which then affects people's attitudes toward police legitimacy and their willingness to assist the police. Problems in the policing environment can have an adverse effect on the overall health of a community (Simckes et al., 2021), which, in turn, can lead to a rise in the propensity of some members of the community to commit crime. That is why changing police environments can be of some importance in managing criminality and reducing risk.

Changing the Court Environment

The courts are another institutional environment with the power to increase or decrease criminality in the general population. Two issues relating to the courts will be discussed in this section: simplifying the law and educating the public.

Simplifying the Law

One of Beccaria's principal arguments in his treatise, "On crimes and punishments," was that people must know and comprehend the law before they can obey it. The law can be complicated, cumbersome, and dense, but it must be made sufficiently understandable to the average person if it is to serve as a foundation for the orderly running of society. Some, particularly those working in the legal profession, might argue that simplifying the law could lead to its trivialization and misinterpretation, although a 2013 paper by Nyman-Metcalf and Täks finds that it may be possible to present the law in simpler terms without losing its impact or meaning. Reporting on how the European Union (EU) was attempting to transpose EU law into individual Member State law, Nyman-Metcalf and Täks (2013) discussed how the EU designed a broad strategy to simplify regulatory statutes by repealing unnecessary, irrelevant, and obsolete laws, amending and codifying laws that were inconsistent, conflicting, or nontransparent, and standardizing, as much as possible, regulations across the various Member States. The EU operates two websites that provide specialists and the general public with free access to EU law and which offer easy to understand charts that map out the similarities and differences between EU law and the laws of the individual countries that make up the EU.

Educating the Public

Another way to make the law more accessible to the average person is to educate the public about the role of law in maintaining order and protecting people's rights. Education on the law can and should occur at all ages but may be most effective when conducted in early to mid-adolescence. Kokka (2020) reports using a social justice pedagogy in mathematics with 10 privileged students enrolled in the sixth grade of an elite private school. Eight of the 10 students gained what Kokka referred to as critical mathematics consciousness as characterized by improved sociopolitical understanding, critical civic empathy, and strengthened mathematical skills. Instructing youth in civics is not simply a matter of teaching civic-related topics to a group of students, but entails presenting the topic in a way that is interesting and meaningful to the students being instructed. Özdemir et al. (2016) discovered that an engaging and inspirational teaching style was associated with student-initiated class discussions on civic-related topics and responsibilities in seventh- and tenth-grade students residing in Sweden. At this point in time, there is no way to determine exactly how civic-related learning in the classroom affects a child's propensity to commit crime but given the theoretical role civic-consciousness plays in supporting others and following the rule of law, the greater likelihood is that it should have a positive impact.

Changing the Correctional Environment

Corrections, the third component of the criminal justice system, also provides an environment that can either support or impede criminality. Three topics will be covered under corrections: reduced reliance on incarceration, increased emphasis on rehabilitation, and abolishing the death penalty.

Reduced Reliance on Incarceration

There are twice as many individuals on parole or probation in the United States as there are in jail or prison. This is a ratio that has decreased slightly in the past 40 years (having dropped from 2.5:1 prior to 2008; see figure 10.1) and which currently lags behind Western European countries like France (3:1), England (4:1), and the Netherlands (5:1). There are several reasons why the United States might want to reduce its reliance on jails and prisons as a way of managing society's lawbreakers. First, community supervision is much cheaper than incarceration. In 2012, it cost $28,948.00 to keep a single inmate in a Bureau of Prisons facility for one year (https://www.uscourts.gov/

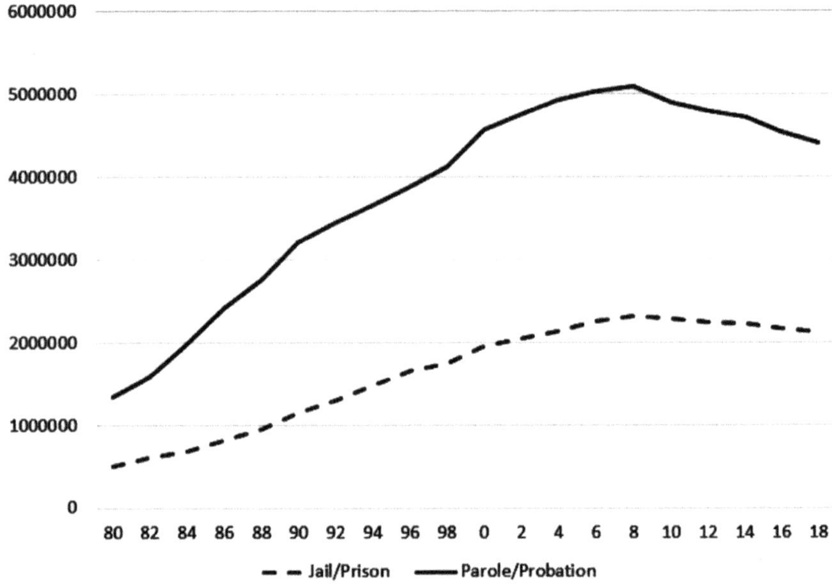

Figure 10.1 Number of Persons in the United States Who Were Incarcerated in Jail or Prison versus Supervised in the Community on Parole or on Probation between 1980 and 2018. *Source:* Bureau of Justice Statistics (2021).

news/2013/07/18). This is 8.6 times more costly than having them supervised in the community by a federal probation officer ($3,347.41). Second, prison can be criminogenic, particularly for individuals at low risk for criminality. Analyzing panel data from 46 states between 1974 and 2002, Vieraitis et al. (2007) discovered that a growing number of inmate releases from state prison predicted an increase in new criminal offenses, thereby showing a criminogenic trend for prison release. Third, programs conducted in the community tend to produce better results than programs conducted in prison. This has been ascribed to the fact that treatment in the community eliminates the need for reintegration given that the individual is already in the community and the observation that community programs employ more evidence-based practices than prison programs (Friedmann et al., 2007). Therefore, while there is a need for prison in the case of serious and dangerous felons, America could benefit from reducing its reliance on imprisonment in managing low- and medium-risk offenders.

Increased Emphasis on Rehabilitation

There are five functions that the correctional system serves: punishment, deterrence, incapacitation, rehabilitation, and reparation. In the United States, adult prison satisfies the punishment and incapacitation functions, whereas adult community supervision fulfills both the punishment and rehabilitation functions and juvenile justice is supposed to be directed toward the rehabilitation and reparation functions. Lifestyle theory holds that there should be as much emphasis on rehabilitation as there is on punishment and incapacitation in adult prisons, and that adult community supervision should stress rehabilitation and reparation on par with the juvenile justice system. First, rehabilitation works if done properly. When intervention is informed by assessment, goals and objectives are framed around RNR principles, treatment follows a cognitive-behavioral format, and follow-up and after-care sessions are included in the package, positive results often occur (Polaschek & Collie, 2004; Weisburd et al., 2017). One of the greatest impediments to research on rehabilitation is uncertainty as to how rehabilitation should be defined. Forsberg and Douglas (2020) address this issue by providing five different definitions: rehabilitation as anti-recidivism, rehabilitation as harm reduction, rehabilitation as therapy, rehabilitation as moral improvement, and rehabilitation as restoration. Three of these definitions (anti-recidivism, harm reduction, and moral improvement) relate directly to changing environments and a fourth (therapy) relates to building competencies. I reject the fifth definition (restoration) because it views rehabilitation as restoring the individual to a former positive state. With many serious offenders, there is no former positive state to which they can return.

Abolishing the Death Penalty

The United States is one of the few industrialized nations in the world that still uses capital punishment. The question of whether retention of the death penalty is based on a firm empirical rationale is therefore a pertinent one. Unfortunately, research on the death penalty has yielded mixed results and no clear conclusions. For instance, there is evidence both for and against capital punishment as a deterrent to homicide (Manski & Pepper, 2013). The studies that have been used to support a deterrent effect for the death penalty indicate that the effect is small and short-lived (Dezhbakhsh & Shepherd, 2006; Phillips, 1980). These studies are counterbalanced by investigations denoting that the death penalty may produce a brutalization effect in which violent crime actually goes up rather than down (Bailey, 1998; Land et al., 2012). There appears to be as much support for a deterrent effect as there is for a brutalization effect when it comes to capital punishment. Consequently, there is no empirical justification for or against a policy of capital punishment based on its alleged deterrent and brutalization effects. Any policy relating to the death penalty must therefore be based on a philosophy of retribution. The point of the present section is to demonstrate that if the institutional environment could be altered to make incarceration less prominent and rehabilitation more prominent, and if this environment could avoid the potential brutalization effects associated with a policy of capital punishment, then it may be possible to reduce criminality by enhancing the perceived legitimacy of the country's criminal justice system in the eyes of its citizens.

CARL PANZRAM AT AGE 11

I will close this chapter on managing risk by changing environments by revisiting Carl Panzram at age 11 years, right before he was sent to Red Wing reformatory for theft. This is done in an effort to understand how environments not only affect a child's development but also how they might be changed to reduce a child's propensity to engage in future offending.

Changing Panzram's External Environments

From all accounts, Panzram never had much use for people, a pattern that originated in the home. Based on his subsequent actions it seems likely that he never developed an emotional attachment to either parent. This may be where his lack of connection to people began, backed up by a paucity of empathy and minimal care and concern for others. Although a reasonable supposition, there is no evidence in the historical record to either confirm or refute this assertion. We do know that Panzram did not think much of either parent. We also know that his father abandoned the family when Panzram was 7 or 8 years old and that by age 11 he had been living in a one-parent home for 3 or 4 years. If there is any truth to the concept of an optimal period for emotional attachment to a parenting figure, then it is likely Panzram at age 11 missed it. Still, it may have been possible, even at age 11, to improve Panzram's relationship with his mother by encouraging Mrs. Panzram to provide more structure, discipline, and support to Carl. Of course, given her farming background and fact that she was raising a family of six on her own, she may not have had the time or inclination to follow through on these psychological recommendations designed to improve her relationship with her youngest son.

Panzram had no more of an emotional connection to his siblings than he did to his parents. He did, however, have several older brothers who could have potentially served as role models and several sisters who could have provided him with a portion of the nurturing he was apparently not getting from his mother. Reorganizing the sibling environment might well have been one of the better options with someone like Panzram. Associations outside the home were no better than associations within the home. Panzram mentions few if any positive relations he had after he left the family home for good at age

13 or 14. In fact, he views most interactions with others as opportunities for predation, which appears to be his principal means of interacting with others. The handful of non-predatory relationships he did have were with other criminals and these only lasted until he or his codefendant were caught and jailed. Getting 11-year-old Panzram involved in structured adult-supervised activities with more prosocial peers might be one way of reducing his propensity for crime by changing his peer environment. Of the three definitions of rehabilitation outlined by Forsberg and Douglas (2020) that relate to changing environments, rehabilitation as moral improvement is the definition most consistent with efforts to change Panzram's parenting, sibling, and peer environments.

Changing Panzram's Internal Environments

Panzram, like many violent criminals, probably suffered from an under-aroused ANS and inadequate sympathetic response to punishment, both of which were made worse by the abuse he received at Red Wing. Because a lower heart rate and decreased sympathetic activity are ordinarily associated with good health, people are not normally looking to increase their heart rate or sympathetic response. Rather than trying to elevate young Panzram's heart rate or stimulate his sympathetic nervous system, a more realistic and responsible approach would be to work on managing his behavior despite the ANS anomalies. This could perhaps be achieved by recommending that Panzram's mother and older siblings limit their use of physical punishment with Panzram and strive to be consistent in their application of whatever punishment they do use. In addition, they should offset the punishment with healthy doses of reinforcement for positive behavior. From what he has written, Panzram believed that the only attention he ever received from his family came in the form of abusive punishment, "Every time I looked cock-eyed or done anything that displeased anyone who was older and stronger and able to catch me and kick me around whenever they felt like it" (Panzram, 1928, p. 1). Just as there is imbalance in Panzram's ANS (parasympathetic activity dominating over sympathetic activity), so too is there imbalance in the dopamine-serotonin relationship. In consultation with Panzram's physician, a trial on an SSRI might be in order, given that SSRIs have been found to be safe and effective in the treatment of childhood depression and anxiety (Boydston et al., 2016). Because success in treating internal environments is likely to be no more than partial, rehabilitation in this case is perhaps best defined as harm reduction.

Changing Panzram's Institutional Environments

Despite being put to work on the family farm at a relatively young age, Panzram acknowledged that his mother made sure he attended school on a regular basis. His above-average intelligence is obvious from his autobiography, which demonstrates reasonably good writing style for someone who dropped out of school at age 13 or 14. We have no information on the content of Panzram's education or what issues were emphasized by his teachers, although if there had been a stronger emphasis on social justice and civic responsibility perhaps it would have had a small effect on his behavior. Panzram's attitude toward the policing environment was as negative as his attitude toward the social environment, the school environment, and society in general. To the extent that Panzram's hatred of the police is more than just an expression of his negative attitude toward authority figures, a change in the policing environment, like a change in the early educational environment or a change in the social environment, could have had a softening effect on some of Panzram's thoughts and actions, but it probably would not have been enough to divert him from a life of crime.

Corrections may be the most important institutional environment for altering a person's risk of criminality. Red Wing reformatory was Panzram's first real taste of the American correctional system and it didn't go down well. It is also where he experienced socially sanctioned institutional violence and abuse. This and subsequent trips to jails and prisons played an important role in shaping Panzram's negative and fatalistic world-view. One can only

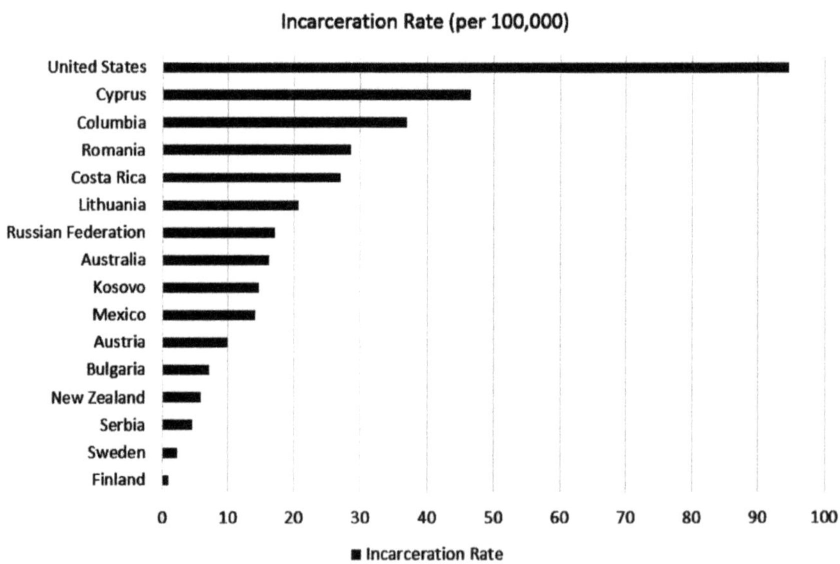

Figure 10.2 Number of Juveniles per 100,000 Population Incarcerated in the United States and 15 Other Countries in 2010. *Source:* United Nations Office on Drugs and Crime (2011).

imagine how Panzram might have responded had he been placed in a different correctional setting, one in which incarceration was less prominent and rehabilitation more available. Assigning Panzram to a juvenile probation officer instead of placing him in a reformatory where he was physically, psychologically, and sexually abused could have made a world of difference to an 11-year old. Although there is no way to know for sure what would have happened had things been different, research on juvenile justice indicates that juvenile probation is more effective and less criminogenic than incarceration (McCarthy et al., 2016). The United States incarcerates twice as many juveniles per capita as the next highest country, Cyprus, and many times more than countries like Sweden and Finland (see figure 10.2). Changing institutional environments like the police, the courts, and corrections falls under a definition of rehabilitation as anti-recidivism. That is because by changing these environments, particularly the correctional environment, we can reduce recidivism rather than increase it.

CONCLUSION

In this and the previous chapter, the focus has been on reducing criminality or a person's propensity to commit crime by building competencies (chapter 9) and changing environments (this chapter). Thus, while it is possible to reduce criminality by teaching moderate-to-high-risk individuals competency skills, it is also possible to reduce criminality by changing and altering environments, whether it be the social and physical external environments, the biological internal environment, or the criminal justice institutional environment. Protective and promotive factors were highlighted in chapter 9 but discussed only sparingly in the present chapter. This does not mean that risk, promotive, and protective factors play any less of a role in changing the environment than they do in building competencies. Each environment presents a certain level of risk. That risk can be reduced by changing the environment in one or more ways. Alterations to each environment, in fact, can be considered promotive and protective factors. Parental support and prosocial peers are not in and of themselves competencies (at least not with respect to the high-risk individual), but they could serve to promote positive outcomes and protect against risk factors by making the youth's social environment less compatible with future offending. As we move into the next chapter, there will be a shift in emphasis away from reducing risk and toward preventing specific crimes, although many of the principles described in this and the previous chapter will still apply, particularly the principles by which crime is prevented—namely, by building competencies in the targeted individual and changing environments.

Chapter 11

Crime Prevention

Limiting Opportunities, Altering Incentives, and Addressing Aggravating and Mitigating Conditions

"Preventing Crime, One Crime at a Time"

The decision to commit crime is based on several factors, among them—opportunity, incentive, and aggravating and mitigating conditions. These and other factors are responsible for criminal decision-making, but they can also be of assistance in preventing certain criminal events. Thus, while chapters 9 and 10 were designed to illustrate how criminality can be managed or a person's propensity to commit crime reduced, the current chapter's principal focus is on clarifying how specific crimes can be prevented. Obviously, when criminality is reduced, a certain percentage of crimes are prevented, but just as a comprehensive theory of criminology must attend to both criminality and crime, so too must a comprehensive approach to management and change pay close attention to propensity and decision-making. In the two previous chapters, effective management of criminality meant either building competencies or changing environments. The same goes for the preventive strategies described in the current chapter. As we proceed through the three stages of the decision-making model—opportunity, incentive, and aggravating/mitigating conditions—we will explore various strategies designed to prevent specific crimes from occurring by either building competencies or changing environments in ways that make crime less likely. We begin, then, with the competencies and environmental changes that may be used to limit perceived opportunities for crime.

PREVENTING CRIME BY LIMITING OPPORTUNITIES

Limiting or reducing opportunities for crime can be achieved by either changing the environment or building participant competencies. We examine both approaches in this section, starting with changing environments.

Changing Environments: Situational Crime Prevention

The 5 mechanisms and 25 techniques of Situational Crime Prevention (SCP) are listed here. This model is based on the pioneering work of Cornish and Clarke (2003) on the situational origins of criminal behavior. The model is grounded in the assumption that the 25 techniques are ways of reducing opportunities for crime. Based on how lifestyle theory views opportunities, however, only some of the techniques listed will primarily affect perceived opportunities for crime. Others are more apt to influence the incentive and mitigating/aggravating stages of the criminal decision-making process or exert a more generalized effect on several stages simultaneously. The seven SCP techniques most likely to exert a specific effect on a person's perceived opportunities for crime via a change in the environment are target hardening, target removal, target concealment, access control, extended guardianship, assisted natural surveillance, and strengthened formal surveillance. We begin this section, then, by discussing target hardening.

Increase Effort to Offender

- Target Hardening
- Access Control
- Screen Exits
- Deflect Offenders
- Control Tools and Weapons

Increase Risk to Offender

- Extend Guardianship
- Assist Natural Surveillance
- Reduce Anonymity
- Utilize Place Managers
- Strengthen Formal Surveillance

Decrease Benefits to Offender

- Conceal Targets
- Target Removal

- Property Identification
- Disrupt Markets
- Deny Benefits

Discourage Excuses

- Set Rules
- Post Instructions
- Alert Conscience
- Assist Compliance
- Control Drugs and Alcohol

Avoid Provocations

- Reduce Stress and Frustration
- Avoid Disputes
- Reduce Emotional Arousal
- Neutralize Peer Pressure
- Discourage Imitation

Target Hardening

Target hardening means making a target (person or object) less vulnerable to victimization by strengthening or reinforcing it in some way, shape, or fashion. Installing a hidden "kill switch" in a car's ignition system—thereby making it impossible to start the car without first turning off the switch—or providing a woman who has been violently victimized in the past with self-defense training are examples of target hardening. By making a potential target less vulnerable to theft or attack, we are reducing the actual and perceived opportunity for crime. Target hardening is often used to discourage property offending and has been found to produce small reductions in home burglaries when inexpensive target hardening programs have been tested (Johnson et al., 2017) and moderate reductions in car theft when somewhat more expensive target hardening programs are instituted (Bässmann, 2011). A home burglary study found that the modest effects attained by a relatively expensive target hardening initiative raised questions about the procedure's cost-effectiveness (Hirschfield et al., 2010).

Target Removal

Although target hardening is capable of reducing criminal opportunities, its effect does not end there. Target hardening can also produce an effect at the incentive stage, given that a potential car thief is unlikely to know that a car has a "kill switch" before trying to steal it and a potential rapist is unlikely to know that the woman they are stalking has had self-defense training. Once they find out, they are no longer at the opportunity stage of the decision-making process—now they are at the incentive stage. Target removal, on the other hand, is a pure opportunity stage intervention, for with the target removed, there is no longer an opportunity for crime. An example of target removal would be a detachable car stereo that the driver brings along with them when they go into a store or return home. Placing a victim of domestic violence in a woman's shelter would be another example of target removal. Research indicates that not only do these women benefit from the protection they receive at the shelter, but their well-being improves significantly as well (Allen et al., 2021). Perhaps the biggest drawback to the target removal technique is that there are only a limited number of situations where it is applicable.

Target Concealment

Target concealment, if not a pure opportunity stage environmental change technique, is close to it. Off-street parking, where an automobile is placed in a garage or carport is an example of target concealment. Research indicates that a car is much less likely to be stolen or vandalized if it is parked in an off-street area than if it is parked along the street. Analyzing data from the British Crime Survey, Clarke and Mayhew (1994) determined that parking in a domestic garage was 20 times safer than parking in a driveway or other private place, and 50 times safer than parking along a street near the person's home. The type of street can also make a difference. In a study conducted in Atlantic City, New Jersey, Levy and Tartaro (2010) discovered that a car parked along a two-way street was five times more likely to be stolen than a car parked along a one-way street, despite roughly equal numbers of one- and two-way streets in Atlantic City where parking is allowed. We might also consider locking the front and back doors of a house and hiding valuables in the trunk of a car as other commonsense ways of concealing valuable items. The bottom line with respect to target concealment is that items properly concealed provide minimal opportunity for crime.

Access Control

Using a password to open a laptop, or a phone to gain entry into an apartment complex are examples of access control. Unlike target removal, there is no guarantee that access control will eliminate a criminal opportunity, but in many cases, it will greatly curtail it. If the person has selected a strong password and staff at the apartment complex are sufficiently prudent, there is very little opportunity for a hacker to break into the laptop or an unwanted visitor to make it into the apartment complex. In an exploratory study of failed mass shootings in the United States, Silva and Greene-Colozzi (2021) noted that access control, target hardening, and several internal SCP procedures (lockdowns, place managers, and armed security) foiled a number of these planned mass shootings. Access control was part of a natural experiment made possible by the introduction of entry gates at 76 Dutch train stations which allowed only ticket holders access to the station. Monthly data collected between 2013 and 2018 revealed that there were 9% fewer crimes committed in the 76 train stations with entry gates compared to the 184 Dutch train stations without entry gates (Lindenbergh et al., 2020). The authors conclude that reduced access resulted in less crime because fewer individuals were able to "hang out" and get into trouble at the train stations with entry gates.

Extended Guardianship

The term "guardianship" comes from Cohen and Felson's (1979) routine activity theory. A guardian is a person or group whose presence prevents crime and whose absence makes crime more likely. When at home, a person serves as a guardian of their own property. When a group of neighbors start a neighborhood watch, they serve as guardians of their neighborhood. In a meta-analysis of 18 neighborhood watch programs, Bennett and colleagues (2006) determined that 15 of the studies showed a deterrent effect on crime (odds ratio > 1). Overall, the meta-analysis yielded a modest but significant pooled effect size (odds ratio = 1.19, 95% CI = 1.08, 1.31). A decade later, Kang (2015) compared participants and nonparticipants in neighborhood watch programs and discovered that residents who participated in neighborhood watch programs were older, had larger families, owned their own homes, and came from neighborhoods high in residential stability but with elevated rates of crime and higher than average levels of concentrated disadvantage.

Assisted Natural Surveillance

Natural surveillance attempts to prevent crime by modifying environmental design. By making the environment less hospitable to criminals, whether it be by increasing street lighting or building a home designed to maximize defensible space, it is possible to significantly reduce a neighborhood's or home's vulnerability to victimization. Supporting whistleblowers in the workplace would be another way to complement natural surveillance. In a study on crime that covered neighborhoods in Seattle, Washington, Sohn (2016) determined that neighborhood designs which increased surveillance by encouraging pedestrian activity enjoyed some of the lowest crime rates in the city. Besides defensible space, there is evidence that other forms of natural surveillance, like improved street lighting, have a modest to moderate deterrent effect on crime (Welsh et al., 2016).

Strengthened Formal Surveillance

Another way to prevent crime is to expand formal sources of surveillance like security guards, burglar alarms, and guard dogs. Like natural surveillance, formal surveillance works by reducing opportunities for crime, although like natural surveillance, it also affects incentives for crime by increasing an offender's risk of detection and apprehension. One area in which formal surveillance is used regularly is in retail stores as a way of deterring shoplifting. Lindblom and Kajalo (2011) surveyed store managers of a multinational fashion store chain in Sweden, Norway, and Finland and discovered that a well-trained employee is one of the best deterrents to retail theft. Of all the different categories of formal surveillance rated by the store managers, electronic alarm tags (classified as a screen exits strategy by SCP) were considered the most effective procedure for deterring shoplifting.

Building Competencies: Distinguishing between Opportunity and Incentive

It is not unusual for offenders and researchers to merge the first two stages of the decision-making model into a single stage. This is understandable given the minimal amount of time that normally separates these two stages and the speed with which most decisions are made. Still, it is vital that those at highest risk for engaging in crime learn to distinguish between a criminal opportunity and evaluation of that opportunity. The first stage of the criminal decision-making process is determining whether or not a criminal opportunity exists. As has been pointed out repeatedly in this book, criminal opportunity is a perception, not an objective "fact." Once the individual perceives a criminal opportunity, the next step is to evaluate the opportunity's likelihood of success. When the two stages are combined or treated as one, there is a tendency for the evaluation stage to be contaminated or overridden by the opportunity stage. This, in fact, could explain why many offender decisions are impulsive and irrational. By keeping the two stages separate, better decisions can be made. Before this can happen, however, the process must be slowed down, and before the process can be slowed down, the individual must possess the skills, qualities, and competencies required to slow down thinking that has become automatic.

The first competency that must be acquired in order to slow down the decision-making process is relaxation. The second competency is learning to give oneself sufficient time to assess and appraise the various options available in a particular situation. Relaxation techniques can be effective in counteracting a youth's natural inclination to think and act rashly. Those who acquire the relaxation competency make less impulsive decisions and may be better able to focus their attention on the task at hand (Cratty, 2004). Meditation, yoga, and mindfulness can often achieve similar results (Dienstmann, 2021). The second competency, inhibiting the natural tendency to react automatically to a criminal opportunity, can be learned through attention training. Mind-wandering is a common problem among adolescents. It can interfere with a youth's ability to remain focused on a topic, task, or idea by creating internal and external distractions (Smallwood et al., 2007). Attention training can be helpful in these situations. Although mind-wandering has been found to improve with age, along with a corollary increase in cognitive control (Maillet & Schacter, 2016), there are still adults who have problems staying focused. This is important because focus is required when evaluating options and making decisions. Mrazek et al. (2020) evaluated a program designed to reduce mind-wandering in high school students by teaching them mindfulness techniques in an on-line course called "Finding Focus." Results revealed that students participating in the course showed significant improvements in their ability to focus in class, avoid mind-wandering, and multitask.

PREVENTING CRIME BY ALTERING INCENTIVES

Incentives (pros and cons) for crime are used to assess the likely consequences of acting on a criminal opportunity. These incentives are the staple of the second stage of criminal decision-making. The two principal ways incentives can be altered to prevent crime is by changing environments using SCP techniques that either increase the risk or reduce the reward associated with committing a crime and improving on a person's ability to perform a cost-benefit analysis.

Changing Environments: Additional SCP Techniques

Previously, we discussed seven SCP techniques that appear to have the most to offer prevention efforts designed to limit criminal opportunities. In this section, we will review the five SCP techniques from the 25 listed by Cornish and Clarke (2003) that have the most to offer interventions designed to alter incentives for crime: disrupt markets, screen exits, utilize place managers, reduce anonymity, and deny benefits.

Disrupt Markets

One incentive-blunting preventive technique is to disrupt criminal markets where stolen property is pawned and resold. Monitoring of pawn shops by law enforcement is a prime example of how markets can be disrupted to reduce crime. Criminals looking to unload stolen property will avoid pawn shops they know are being monitored by the police. Hence, such monitoring changes the incentive for crime by both reducing the profit that an offender can anticipate receiving and increasing the offender's risk of detection and arrest. Disrupting drug markets using a police-only strategy, whether it be periodic raids or regular patrols has produced very little in the way of an effect, and any effects that have been observed have been small and short-lived. On the other hand, geographically focused strategies like problem-oriented policing and community-based approaches like police-community partnerships have been found to be effective in reducing neighborhood drug sales and corollary property and violent crimes (Mazerolle et al., 2007).

Screen Exits

To screen exits means requiring a person to show or have something before exiting an area, whether it be an exit ticket upon leaving a parking garage or removing an electronic merchandise tag in order to exit a department store with the merchandise. This SCP technique is also more of a second stage (incentive) than first stage (opportunity) strategy because it increases the risk to the offender. Sidebottom and colleagues (2017) reviewed eight quantitative studies on the use of merchandise tags as a deterrent to shoplifting and found evidence of a small deterrent effect in five out of the eight studies. From the small number of studies reviewed, however, it was not possible to determine whether this modest deterrent effect occurred because tagging increased risk, reduced reward, or increased the effort required to steal the item.

Utilize Place Managers

A place manager is a person (store clerk) or machine (closed circuit television: CCTV) that provides increased surveillance in an area where crime is likely to occur. Having two store clerks man a convenience store instead of one, hiring and training bouncers to deal with unruly patrons at a bar, and using a CCTV to monitor bullying on a school bus are all examples of how place managers can be used to prevent crime and antisocial behavior. Project Green Light began in 2016 with the installation of several hundred high-definition CCTV cameras in dozens of Detroit businesses. The images were sent to monitors in the business and to the Detroit Police Department's real-time crime center. Circo and McGarrell (2021) compared 87 businesses enrolled in Project Green Light with a matched group of 201 businesses that were not part of the Project and did not employ CCTV. The results revealed an increase in the reporting of minor offenses, but not in violent crime for businesses enrolled in Project Green Light. Over time, property crimes and disorder crimes decreased at a faster pace in businesses with CCTV than in businesses without CCTV.

Reduce Anonymity

It is no secret that neighborhoods with higher levels of anonymity often have higher rates of crime (Sampson, 2013). Reducing this anonymity could help prevent crime by increasing the risk of apprehension, decreasing the pleasure of committing a crime, and encouraging greater guardianship between familiar strangers. Repeat encounters with the same individual may help shape a person's perception of the environment as represented by the number of familiar strangers in that environment; a familiar stranger being someone the person recognizes but does not know personally (Milgram et al., 1992). Zahnow and colleagues (2021) studied this phenomenon at bus stops in Brisbane, Australia, the capital of Queensland and third largest city in Australia. Calculating the total number of station passengers who encountered a familiar stranger within a five-day work week or two consecutive weekends, Zahnow et al. wanted to know whether this information correlated with the total count of recorded theft, drug, and nuisance crimes occurring in the vicinity of the transit station. Findings from this study showed that stations with more familiar strangers had less of a problem with theft, drug offenses, and nuisance crimes.

Deny Benefits

To deny benefits means to minimize the amount of pleasure or reward an individual can anticipate from a particular criminal act. Two examples of how denial of benefits could discourage criminal behavior are provided by Cornish and Clarke (2003). These are graffiti cleanup and speed bumps. Making a group of juvenile gang members remove the graffiti they have just drawn or spray-painted onto a building or railroad trestle could certainly be construed as taking the fun out of vandalism. Similarly, a speed bump would in all likelihood take the fun out of speeding, not to mention the car's rear axil if the car was traveling at a high rate of speed. Denying the benefits of antisocial behavior prevents crime by reducing, limiting, and removing the rewards associated with the antisocial behavior. This is not simply a matter of pain and pleasure; it is also a matter of right and wrong. A recent study found that guilt over one's involvement in a recent criminal event reduced crime by easing crime-promoting attitudes like proactive criminal thinking (PCT) (Walters, 2020k).

Building Competencies: Cost-Benefit Analysis

The competency that is most useful in promoting prosocial outcomes for the incentive stage of the decision-making process is learning how to conduct a proper and thorough cost-benefit analysis. In theory, a cost-benefit analysis is simple, although in practice it has the potential to become rather complex. Jules Dupuit (1804–1866), an Italian-born French civil engineer, is credited with popularizing the cost-benefit or subjective utilities approach to problem-solving. Dupuit used it to solve engineering problems and economic conundrums. In fact, economists were one of the first professional groups to make use of the subjective utilities approach in solving problems related to the field. It was not long before other social scientists began using it as well. Whereas applying the subjective utilities approach to situations where a person is deciding whether to take advantage of a criminal opportunity is more complex than choosing an advertising campaign for a product that has just come out on the market or deciding whether to increase the price of a commodity that is selling better than had originally been anticipated, the overall objective is the same—to maximize pleasure (gains) and minimize pain (loses).

Shure and Spivak (1980) pioneered the use of interpersonal problem-solving training with pre- and early delinquent youth as a way of improving their ability to use the subjective utilities approach. They reasoned that teaching parents to instruct their children in the technique was more cost-effective than having a therapist do it. The results of several studies showed that parents were able to teach the technique to their children and that the children were able to use the technique to solve problems while reducing their antisocial and aggressive behaviors in the process (Shure, 1999). An early review of the interpersonal problem-solving literature on delinquent youth revealed that many youthful offenders suffered from problem-solving deficits and that training them in social skills—including interpersonal problem-solving skills—led to improved internal control, reduced aggression, and lower recidivism (Cunliffe, 1992). One limitation of research in this area is that interpersonal problem-solving is rarely evaluated in isolation, but rather, as part of a larger social skills package. Several school-based social skills programs that include an interpersonal problem-solving component were found to decrease future aggression and antisocial behavior in high-risk children (Crean & Johnson, 2013; Webster-Stratton & Reid, 2003). A study by van der Stouwe and colleagues (2016), on the other hand, revealed that delinquent youth exposed to social skills training displayed no improvement in their interpersonal problem-solving skills, although the 8- to 12-session format may have been too low impact to have had much effect on actively delinquent youth.

The utilitarian aspects of interpersonal problem-solving are fairly straightforward. Whether working with a child, adolescent, or adult, the key to success in teaching interpersonal problem-solving skills to those at risk for future antisocial and aggressive behavior and those currently involved in delinquent or criminal behavior is making the implicit, explicit. What I mean by this is that the person undergoing training should be encouraged to articulate the subjective utilities of the option or options being evaluated. This then entails, keeping the opportunity and incentive stages of the criminal decision-making process separate. Whether the individual simply lists the costs and benefits of acting on a criminal opportunity or assigns numbers to each individual cost and benefit, the process needs to be made more explicit. It also needs to be made more systematic in that the cost-benefit analysis portion of interpersonal problem-solving is composed of three steps: Step 1 listing the various costs and benefits of a particular course of action, Step 2 performing a formal (with numbers) or informal (without numbers) evaluation of these costs and benefits, and Step 3 selecting a course of action based on the results of Step 2. Time should also be considered in the evaluation. Crime tends to produce more short-term than long-term benefits and more long-term than short-term costs compared to prosocial activity. Offenders, as was previously noted, pay closer attention to the short-term consequences than to the long-term consequences (Wilson & Herrnstein, 1985). If interpersonal problem-solving training is to prove effective, then offenders need to find a better balance between short- and long-term consequences.

A cost-benefit analysis of a criminal opportunity requires that the subjective utility of committing a crime be compared to the subjective utility of not committing a crime. The decision to commit a crime is not the same as deciding which materials to include in a bridge or how many boxes of cereal a grocery store needs to order and then sell to realize a 5% profit. Unlike most economic decisions, moral considerations can be just as important as utilitarian concerns when it comes to appraising a criminal opportunity. From a moral standpoint, then, we must ask ourselves how our decision potentially affects others. Thus, when performing a cost-benefit analysis of a criminal opportunity, utilitarian concerns (pain and pleasure) should be balanced against moral concerns (right and wrong). This suggests that some "criminal" decisions may reflect higher moral reasoning than other "criminal" decisions. One of the scenarios Kohlberg (1969) used to assess moral reasoning was a hypothetical moral dilemma confronting a man named Heinz whose wife was near death from a special kind of cancer.

According to the scenario, a druggist living in the same town as Heinz had discovered a drug that doctors believed might save the woman's life. The druggist paid $200 for the ingredients to make the drug and was charging $2,000 for a single dose. Heinz could only scrape up $1,000 after emptying his life savings and going to family and friends. He offered to pay the druggist the other $1,000 later, but the druggist insisted on getting the full $2,000 up front. Heinz, desperate to save his wife, breaks into the druggist's store and steals the drug. Respondents are then asked to evaluate the morality of Heinz's behavior. Although someone functioning at a conventional or preconventional level of moral reasoning might view Heinz's behavior as wrong based on the fact that he broke into the druggist's store and stole the drug, persons functioning at a postconventional level of moral reasoning tend to view the situation differently. Someone functioning at a postconventional level of moral reasoning would take into account the relative value of human life versus man-made rules and indicate that Heinz's behavior reflects a belief in a social contract (protection of life: Stage 5 moral reasoning) or universal ethical principles (human life over financial profit: Stage 6 moral reasoning).

PREVENTING CRIME BY ADDRESSING AGGRAVATING AND MITIGATING CONDITIONS

The third stage of the decision-making model is made up of aggravating and mitigating circumstances and conditions. Like the risk and promotive factors that contribute to the criminality models described in chapters 6, 7, 9, and 10, aggravating and mitigating conditions sit at opposite ends of the same coin. Aggravating conditions push the decision in a direction that is favorable to the commission of a crime, whereas mitigating conditions pull the decision in a direction unfavorable to the commission of a crime. Multiple aggravating and mitigating conditions will often impinge on a single decision. As such, there is a cumulative weighting of factors before the decision is made, although the individual may not be aware of all or even most of these aggravating and mitigating conditions. For the sake of simplicity and ease of description, two examples of aggravating/mitigating conditions that pertain to changes in the environment and two examples of aggravating/mitigating conditions that call upon new competencies are discussed in this section.

Changing External Environments: Bystanders

Bystanders as an Aggravating Condition

Research conducted on street and barroom confrontations indicates that bystanders often assume a vital role in how these confrontations play out. Felson et al. (1984) reviewed the effect of third-party actors on homicide and assault and determined that perpetrators, ages 16–60, struck more blows when bystanders, usually family and friends, were supportive of violence than when bystanders were not supportive of violence. The effect was more pronounced in younger perpetrators. A later study showed that third parties were more apt to intervene when the barroom altercation was more serious than when it was less serious (Parks et al., 2013). This raises the possibility of a bidirectional relationship between combatants and bystanders; combatants demonstrating a greater tendency to become violent when bystanders support violence, and bystanders demonstrating a greater tendency to intervene both aggressively and nonaggressively when combatants are engaged in a more violent encounter. Keeping neighborhood or barroom conflict from spilling over into bodily injury or homicide therefore requires quick action on the part of police and security to keep these situations from escalating.

The antisocial spectrum behavioral pattern of bullying may also be subject to aggravation via bystander behavior. Bystanders normally assume one of three roles in a bullying situation: the outsider role, the defender role, and the reinforcer role. The outsider is a passive nonacting observer of the bullying situation, the defender intervenes in an attempt to stop the bullying, and the reinforcer promotes even more bullying by engaging in pro-bullying behaviors (Song & Oh, 2017). The reinforcer serves as an aggravating influence, not unlike the third-party reinforcers of non-bullying violence encountered in the Felson et al. (1984) study. By reinforcing aggressive behavior and sometimes joining in on the bullying, students who assume the reinforcer role make the negative consequences of the bullying situation that much worse (Sarmiento et al., 2019). Another study found that pro-bullying bystander behavior was associated with low levels of empathy and high levels of moral disengagement (Troop-Gordon et al., 2019). These aggravating conditions can be nullified to some extent by a school environment in which an authoritative teacher provides students with a warm, caring, supportive, controlled, challenging, and cohesive classroom experience (Thornberg et al., 2018).

Bystanders as a Mitigating Condition

In the previously reviewed Felson et al. (1984) study, while some bystanders exerted an aggravating influence over the conflict situation, other bystanders mitigated the situation by serving as negotiators and trying to calm one or more of the combatants. When bystanders served as a mitigating influence, perpetrators struck significantly fewer blows than when bystanders exerted an aggravating or neutral influence over a situation. This illustrates the bipolar nature of aggravating-mitigating conditions, with bystander behavior being capable of encouraging violence and producing a more serious outcome or discouraging violence and promoting a less serious outcome. In a thematic analysis of videotaped spectator violence at sporting events, Block and Lesneskie (2018) discovered that bystanders could sometimes reduce spectator violence with either a physical or verbal intervention. Physical interventions sometimes presented a risk to the bystander, although when they were performed by a friend or family member they were usually successful. Verbal interventions in which a bystander asked or insisted that the combatants stop fighting were safer for the bystander but rarely stopped the altercation.

A number of school programs have been developed to encourage bystanders to safely intervene when they observe bullying or other forms of interpersonal aggression. A study by Bauman et al. (2010) demonstrated that the two most effective bystander interventions for bullying were insisting the perpetrator stop or telling an adult. Storer et al. (2017) describe a "whole school" bystander intervention program designed to reduce dating violence and bullying. Using focus groups from three high schools in urban Washington state, the authors were able to identify several factors that students viewed as facilitating bystander intervention/reporting and several factors that impeded bystander intervention/reporting. Supports for intervening included a trusting relationship with teachers in general, encouragement and emotional support from a respected teacher, and modeling of good bystander behavior by one or more teachers. Barriers to intervention included lack of student power, pessimistic attitudes toward the possibility of change, ineffective school responses, lack of visibility of dating violence, and gender inequality in the school environment. What these results indicate is that school-student relationships are vital in encouraging student bystanders to intervene when they observe a fellow student being victimized.

Changing Internal Environments: Mental State

Mental State as an Aggravating Condition

Mental states can serve as aggravating conditions for crime by virtue of their ability to disrupt rational thinking. If the decision-making model is based on rational understanding, then a disturbed mental state brought on by intoxication or mental illness will likely make the decision progressively less rational. Intoxication on alcohol and other drugs is known to have an adverse effect on a person's decision-making abilities and impulse control. Even a blood alcohol concentration (BAC) level below the legal limit of 80 mg/100 ml has been shown to produce a noticeable reduction in a person's inhibitory control and a noticeable increase in their propensity for risky decision-making (Weafer & Fillmore, 2016). For someone with a BAC significantly above the limit, which is what you would expect to find in someone who is visibly intoxicated, the effects would be much more debilitating. Environmental manipulations may be modestly successful in managing this internal environment problem. Policies such as not serving alcohol during the last several innings or minutes of a sporting event and giving bartenders the responsibility of not serving alcohol to customers who are visibly intoxicated have been found to produce equivocal results (Elgán et al., 2021). Physical withdrawal from drugs or the anticipated loss of a drug a person has become physically or psychologically dependent upon could also serve as aggravating mental states capable of affecting a person's decision-making.

Before discussing serious or major mental illness as an aggravating internal environment capable of promoting crime, it is important that we acknowledge that the vast majority of seriously mentally ill individuals are not dangerous (Gottfried & Christopher, 2017). In fact, those who have been diagnosed with schizophrenia, bipolar disorder, or major depression are more likely to be the victims of violent crime than the perpetrators (Peay, 2009). That said, a fair number of individuals with major mental illness do wind up in jail. The question is why? I would submit that problems with cognitive and emotional control stemming from mental illness are behind the large number of mentally ill people in jail. As such, those with major mental health issues are at increased risk for violating the law and coming to jail for mostly minor, nuisance type crimes such as vagrancy, trespassing, drug possession, and public intoxication. For this reason, mental illness can be considered an internal environment capable of exerting an aggravating effect on one's likelihood of taking advantage of a criminal opportunity and committing a crime, usually a minor one. Psychotropic medication is currently the best way to control serious mental health symptoms, although it cannot cure mental illness, it can create serious side effects and it is not maximally effective with all individuals.

Mental State as a Mitigating Condition

Sobriety can be considered the mitigating condition that counterbalances the aggravating effect of intoxication. Although substance misuse is a risk factor and not misusing drugs is a promotive factor, sobriety is related to both, for if a person does not have a substance misuse problem, sobriety will be much more common than if they do have a substance misuse problem. Substance misuse often plays a leading role in a criminal lifestyle as evidenced by the drug-crime connection and Worst of Both Worlds (WBW) hypothesis. To reduce the aggravating effect of substance misuse on a person's life and promote the mitigating effect of sobriety, the best option may be to enroll those for whom intoxication has become a common experience in some form of substance abuse treatment. Research indicates that substance abuse treatment can bring about a reduction in both substance misuse and crime (Chandler et al., 2009). In addition, treatment availability has been found to impede financially motivated and violent crimes (Bondurant et al., 2018), whereas discontinuing treatment has been shown to increase a person's odds of committing a criminal offense and going to prison (Kaskela & Pitkäen, 2021). Cognitive-behavioral interventions, along with relapse prevention and therapeutic communities, are among the most effective treatment options available to clinicians wishing to intervene with cases of substance abuse and recurrent intoxication (McHugh et al., 2010; McMurran, 2009).

We previously discussed the importance of psychotropic medication in managing the aggravating effect of a disturbed mental state in persons with major mental illness. It may also be possible to prevent some of the serious mental health problems that lead to a disturbed mental state, although primary prevention of psychiatric disorders is still in its infancy. Areas that are currently being looked at include interventions designed to improve parental health, pre-school and early education programs, school-based mental health initiatives, promotion of healthy lifestyles, and efforts to remedy social inequities and enhance social cohesion (Trivedi et al., 2014). One particularly promising area with respect to preventing major mental illness is the identification and remediation of adverse childhood experiences (ACEs), such as childhood illnesses, physical or sexual victimization, and exposure to household violence and dysfunction. The total number of ACEs experienced by an individual has been found to correlate with mental illness in adults using both retrospective (Anda et al., 2006) and prospective (Stafford et al., 2015) data. ACEs are also more common in those who eventually develop problems with adult criminality and substance misuse (Goodard & Pooley, 2019). For a variety of reasons, limiting ACE's would appear to make a great deal of sense when it comes to working with substance abusing and non-substance abusing offenders, whether or not they have a history of major mental illness.

Building Cognitive Competencies: Criminal Thinking

Criminal Thinking as an Aggravating Condition

Over the past two decades, meta-analyses have clearly indicated that cognitive-behavior therapy is among the most effective interventions for delinquency and adult crime (Landenberger & Lipsey, 2005; Pearson & Lipton, 1999; Wilson et al., 2005). There is also evidence that offenders exposed to cognitive-behavior therapy experience a significant reduction in criminal thinking over the course of treatment (Lindblom et al., 2017; Morgan et al., 2014; Walters et al., 2002) and that higher scores on a criminal thinking measure like the Psychological Inventory of Criminal Thinking Styles (PICTS) accurately predict recidivism (Gonsalves et al., 2009; Palmer & Hollin, 2004; Walters & Lowenkamp, 2016). The larger question, however, is whether treatment-related changes on the PICTS predict future behavior. This was tested in two studies, the first of which disclosed that decreased reactive criminal thinking (RCT) in jail inmates enrolled in a self-administered intervention for criminal thinking predicted a drop in future disciplinary infractions while in jail (Folk et al., 2016). In the second study, Walters (2017c) discovered that reductions on the general criminal thinking (GCT) in a group of prison inmates enrolled in a 10-week cognitive-behavioral intervention preceded a drop in prison-based disciplinary infractions following completion of the 10-week intervention. Although these results suggest that there may be a relationship between participation in treatment, reduction in criminal thinking, and reduction in problematic in-jail and in-prison behavior, more research is required to determine whether these findings extend to recidivism in the community.

Procedures developed by Albert Ellis (1913–2007) and Aaron Beck (1921–2021) that are designed to challenge irrational beliefs have been incorporated into criminal lifestyle theory. This was accomplished, in part, by taking two assumptions central to Ellis (1962), Beck et al. (1979), and others' perspectives on cognitive-behavioral intervention and integrating them into the criminal lifestyle model of change. The first assumption is that criminal thinking, which is marked by false premises and faulty logic, is as irrational as the irrational beliefs upon which Ellis and Beck based their models. The second assumption that criminal lifestyle theory borrowed from the work of Ellis and Beck is that criminal thinking, like other forms of irrational thinking, is automatic. The fact that criminal thinking becomes fixed, entrenched, and automatic through repetition and reiteration makes it difficult to treat. It is therefore imperative when developing competencies to counteract the effects of criminal thinking that the criminal thinking be slowed down enough to be analyzed. This can be accomplished using some of the techniques described previously in a section of the chapter dealing with keeping the opportunity and incentive stages of the decision-making model separate. Two such techniques are relaxation training and attentional training. Charting thoughts and feelings is a cognitive-behavioral technique that could also be used to slow down criminal thinking so that it can be analyzed and dissected. I recommend a four-step procedure for clinicians and counselors working with offenders in a group setting and interested in challenging the criminal thinking that supports criminal behavior.

The first step of the procedure I use for criminal thinking is to educate clients about the nature, content, and purpose of criminal thinking. Didactic sessions and bibliotherapy are used to achieve this goal. Lifestyle theory assumes that is it easier and less threatening to observe criminal thinking in others than it is to observe it in oneself. Consequently, the second step in changing criminal thinking is providing clients with examples of such thinking. If the intervention is being conducted in a group setting then participants can serve as examples for each other, although it can even be more helpful to review videotaped interviews with famous criminals like Charles Manson and Ted Bundy. These taped interviews can be used as guides to the criminal thought process. The third step of the procedure is to help clients identify the thinking styles in themselves and achieve introspection. I will sometimes use a drill I call the "single pill exercise" to stimulate the introspection process.

I start by informing clients (tongue in cheek) that a gas that selectively kills people in the criminal lifestyle has been released into the room, and that I have a pill that will protect one group member from the gas. From here, I ask group members, who should get the pill. The resulting discussion will nearly always produce a rich flow of criminal thoughts. The fourth and final step of the procedure is teaching the client how to challenge criminal thoughts, once identified. This is achieved by instructing clients to test the rationality of their thinking by asking themselves two questions: (1) What evidence is there for the belief? (2) Will the belief get me what I want and make me feel the way I want to feel?

Low Criminal Thinking as a Mitigating Condition

Three scenario studies have explored the relationship between criminal thinking and the certainty of getting caught and punished for an antisocial act like cheating on a test or a criminal act like selling drugs. In all three investigations, participants achieving higher scores on the PICTS PCT, RCT, or GCT were significantly less likely than those scoring low on these scales of being dissuaded from acting on a criminal opportunity when the odds of getting caught were low (Walters & Morgan, 2019; Walters et al. 2019, 2021a). Across all three studies, however, participants achieving lower scores on one or more of the PICTS criminal thinking scales were significantly less likely to acknowledge an intention to act on a hypothetical antisocial/criminal opportunity than individuals earning higher scores on one or more of the PICTS criminal thinking style scales net the effects of certainty. This is an example of how low criminal thinking can serve as a mitigating condition in the criminal decision-making process.

Building Affective Competencies: Emotions Management

Emotional Dysregulation as an Aggravating Condition

Like criminal thinking, emotional dysregulation can be viewed as a stable dynamic risk factor for criminality and an aggravating condition for crime. To some researchers, particularly those interested in psychopathy, emotional dysregulation is one of two emotional patterns that lead to aggression and antisocial behavior. These two patterns are commonly referred to as deficit emotion (callous-unemotional [CU]) and dysfunctional emotion (emotional dysregulation). This bipartite breakdown is sometimes used to subclassify psychopathy into primary (deficit emotion) and secondary (dysfunctional emotion) subtypes (Newman et al., 2005). Raine (2019) postulates that while primary psychopathy is more closely aligned with proactive/instrumental aggression, secondary psychopathy is more closely tied to reactive/expressive aggression. It would therefore make sense for emotional and behavioral dysregulation to play a more salient role in reactive aggression than it does in proactive aggression, and while this is precisely what Card and Little (2006) found in a major meta-analysis, a more recent study by Garofalo et al. (2020) suggests that emotional dysregulation may contribute to both proactive and reactive aggression. Depending on the situation, a person finds themselves in, emotional dysregulation would appear to have the capacity to facilitate individual criminal events and as such should be addressed in treatment.

One competency that can be used to counter the crime-enhancing effects of emotional dysregulation is emotional control. Nancy Eisenberg, one of the world's leading experts on emotional dysregulation, recommends training in emotional/behavioral control for children with attention deficit/hyperactivity and other emotional dysregulation problems (Eisenberg et al., 2010). A way for children to learn the competency to control their emotions would be through Meichenbaum's (1977) self-instructional training (SIT) technique, a procedure that views attention as a skill that can be taught and learned. In the first of five phases, the therapist models speaking out loud as they perform a task the child has had trouble mastering in the past. This is then followed by a second phase in which the therapist vocalizes step-by-step instructions as the child performs the task. The third phase of SIT involves having the child vocalize their self-instructions as they go about performing the task. During the fourth phase, the child gradually reduces the volume of their vocalizations, speaking in a regular voice during the initial trials and lowering it to a whisper by the time they reach the final trials. The fifth phase of SIT entails having the child complete the task guided only by their subvocal self-statements in a process known as "covert self-instruction." Although SIT was original designed for children with attentional problems, it can also be used with criminal adults, although the tasks and self-statements will differ depending on client age.

Emotional Maturity as a Mitigating Condition

Learning to overcome weak emotional control through a competency-building technique like SIT is one way of coping with emotional dysregulation. Another way is to possess sufficient emotional maturity in the first place so that emotional dysregulation does not present a problem. Individuals with sufficient emotional maturity are less likely to take advantage of a criminal opportunity when such an opportunity presents itself because emotional maturity allows them to conduct a more thorough and less biased cost-benefit analysis of the criminal opportunity. There are many characteristics and attributes that parents both possess and impart to their children that have a bearing on a child's emotional maturity. Bridgett et al. (2015) discussed several of these in a review of the intergenerational transmission of self-regulation. The principal factor identified in the Bridgett et al. review was parental self-regulation, which when weak created a stressful and chaotic home environment for the child, and child genetic makeup, which then intersected with the stressful and chaotic environment created by weak parental self-regulation. These two factors affect the rearing behavior of parents, which when deficit, lead to weak child self-regulation and the intergenerational transmission of emotional dysregulation from parent to child. In situations where parental self-regulation is strong and child genetics resilient, the child has a much lower likelihood of choosing the criminal option when presented with a criminal opportunity.

PREVENTING THE MURDER OF LAUNDRY SUPERVISOR WARNKE

Whenever a serious incident occurs in prison it can usually be traced back to certain breakdowns in custody and control. And while it is easy to criticize and play Monday morning quarterback, it is still important to review these incidents so that the mistakes of the past can be avoided in the future. Even though Carl Panzram may have been hell-bent on murdering his supervisor, there are still environmental and competency-based interventions that could have perhaps been of some assistance in preventing this murder from happening in the first place.

Prevention through Changing Environments

The first question I would have if I was investigating the murder of Laundry Supervisor Warnke is why a 3-foot iron bar was so easily accessible to inmates? Normally, items that can be used to harm another person or affect an escape are placed under lock and key to be used only under the direct supervision of a staff member. This way, such items are not just lying around waiting for an inmate like Panzram to pick them up and use them against someone. Employing a technique from SCP discussed earlier in this chapter (limiting access) and another technique that was not discussed (controlling tools and weapons), the murder could perhaps have been prevented by keeping the iron bar locked up. Of course, as anyone who has ever worked in a correctional institution knows, not every item that could potentially be used to harm someone can be properly secured. After all, inmates have been known to make their own weapons from small items they find lying around or steal from their worksite. Still, a 3-foot iron bar is not a small item and greatly increases the odds of an assault turning fatal compared to a lock-in-the-sock or homemade shank. I have to assume that in the after-action report that always follows a homicide or major assault in prison, that this was mentioned and that greater protections were put into place in the form of new policies and procedures that stressed the necessity of keeping dangerous weapons out of the hands of inmates.

A second question I have regarding events leading up to the Warnke murder is why was Panzram still walking freely on the prison compound after making at least two specific threats against staff members. It is difficult to imagine an inmate not being locked up in segregation for investigation as soon as anyone got word that he had threatened a staff member. Several inmates reported that Panzam threatened to kill both Warnke and an officer named Watkins and one inmate even acknowledged that he informed Warnke of this just minutes before Warnke was murdered. In the letters and statements found in Borowski (2020), no one indicated that they had informed any other staff members about these threats. One inmate stated that Panzram was known for making non-specific threats against staff and other inmates but that this was the first time he knew of where Panzram threatened a specific person. If staff had known about these threats and not placed Panzram in segregation pending investigation, then they were grossly negligent. From the information provided, however, there is no evidence that this is what happened. In the landmark 1994 U.S. Supreme Court ruling *Farmer v. Brennan*, the court ruled that prison officials have an obligation to protect inmates when there is substantial risk of harm. One would hope that this also applies to prison staff. Even so, the Farmer decision postdates the Warnke murder by 65 years.

Prevention through Building Competencies

It is difficult to imagine much headway being made with Panzram on building competencies given his mindset during the time he was at USP Leavenworth. Still, everyone has the capacity to change, no matter how small that capacity might be. One of the better options in building competencies with Panzram would have been training in interpersonal problem-solving. There were no psychologists at Leavenworth in 1929 and interpersonal problem-solving training had not yet been invented. Yet, if Panzram had been willing to receive help and if he could have been taught the five steps of the full problem-solving model then perhaps it could have made a difference. In the first step of the problem-solving model the individual defines the problem (i.e., Mr. Warnke refuses to allow for a job change). The next step is to brainstorm possible solutions to the problem (e.g., ask Mr. Warnke again in another month, go to another supervisor or higher authority, remain in the job, refuse to go to work, assault or murder Mr. Warnke). The third step is to conduct a cost-benefit analysis of the options generated during the second step, considering both utilities and moral factors, the latter of which would have been difficult with Panzram. In completing the fourth step, Panzram should select the option that produced the greatest benefit-to-cost ratio. During the fifth and final step of the procedure, Panzram should implement the option he selected at Step 4 and after a reasonable period of time evaluate his circumstances to determine whether the problem has been resolved or whether there even is a problem (e.g., Panzram may decide he doesn't mind working in the laundry).

Another competency that might be of some assistance in reducing Panzram's likelihood of committing specific crimes would be increased emotional control. Panzram acknowledges that he is impulsive and often acts without forethought. He may therefore have been receptive to an intervention that gave him more control over his impulsivity. I can't help but think of the time Panzram, frustrated with his inability to understand Kant's critique, tore the book up into "10,000 pieces" and threw the pieces out under the door of his cell. Had it been possible to work with Panzram on this, perhaps we could have started by breaking the Critique down into smaller pieces and work bit by bit using an adult version of SIT. We would start by modeling appropriate behavior; a therapist reading a passage out loud to Panzram, explaining it, and including with the explanation, coping self-talk designed to keep Panzram calm and on-task. This would then be followed by Panzram explaining a passage that was read out loud by the therapist, with the therapist again adding calming self-talk. Eventually, Panzram would read a passage out loud, explain it, and keep himself calm with coping self-talk. We would continue in this vein while gradually reducing the vocalizations so that Panzram's readings, explanations, and self-talk became increasingly more covert. I already discussed how Panzram was capable of internalization, but that he just didn't do it enough. This would be an opportunity for him to practice and perfect internalized speech, a major feature of internalization.

CONCLUSION

In chapters 6, 7, and 8, we discussed how a comprehensive theory of criminology should explain both criminality (the propensity to engage in criminal activity) and crime (participation in a specific criminal act). Taking a glimpse at the practical side of this theory, chapters 9, 10, and the present chapter discussed ways by which criminality can be managed and crime prevented, namely, by building competencies and changing environments. Therefore, just as criminality is reduced by building certain skills and competencies and changing internal and external environments, so too is crime prevented by constructing competencies and altering internal and external environments.

One point I would like to make before closing this chapter is that there needs to be some degree of continuity and integration for these interventions to work. It makes no sense to treat an individual's substance abuse problem with a 12-step program and their criminal thinking with cognitive-behavior therapy. A cognitive-behavioral approach can and should be used with both. The need for an overarching theory under which the moral and control models of criminality and the decision-making model of crime can be organized, distinct from but related to competency-building and environment-altering interventions, brings us to the final chapter of this book in which we return to the forest and remind ourselves that everything that has been discussed thus far in this book fits into a larger framework.

Chapter 12

Returning to the Forest

"The Journey Continues"

This book ends as it began, trying to make sense of the forest and tree problem in criminology. We ran across a wide variety of trees in our journey through the criminal lifestyle forest. Let us briefly review how we got to this point. Following a brief excursion into the biological bases of antisocial behavior, we examined major social, cognitive, and developmental features of criminality and crime. Guided by the realization that these features are most useful when viewed in relationship to one another, discussion turned to salient variable relationships contained in triads and higher order variable clusters. Just as trees form groves, the individual features of a criminal lifestyle form triads and higher-order variable clusters, as exemplified by the moral and control models of criminality and the decision-making model of crime. These higher-order models, which began as vehicles of understanding, soon became vehicles for change as we set our sights on building competencies and changing environments as a means of assisting those with designs on exiting a criminal lifestyle. It would appear that we have come full circle, back to the forest we left 11 chapters ago. The current chapter can be viewed as the beginning of a new journey, a journey designed to understand how the different aspects or trees that filled chapters 1 through 11 can be considered part of a well-integrated and highly fruitful forest. That forest is described briefly in this the final chapter as a way of providing a larger context for the criminal lifestyle.

BIOLOGY AND LEARNING

Lifestyle theory postulates that biological systems evolved as a means of protecting an organism's survival and helping perpetuate the species. There is nothing new or particularly profound in that statement, for it echoes views expressed by Charles Darwin (1809–1882) more than a century and a half ago. According to Darwin's original theory of evolution, traits and predispositions that augment an organism's ability to compete, survive, and reproduce are the ones most likely to be passed on to the next generation. Through a process of natural selection, organisms that are most fit, survive, mate, and pass their advantage onto their offspring. By contrast, organisms that are least fit, are less likely to survive, mate, and pass their disadvantage onto the next generation. In some cases, that is because they do not survive to a child-bearing age, and in other cases it is because they cannot find a mate. As a result, biological systems most conducive to survival and mating end up being passed down in a population. Neo-Darwinists sought to improve on Darwin's original theory by synthesizing it with Mendelian genetics. In this revised version of evolutionary theory, it is argued that small genetic mutations are passed down from parent to child which may then act to increase fitness (Dawkins, 1976). In this model, genes serve as the unit of evolution, whereas natural selection serves as the mechanism of evolution.

When it comes to promoting organism survival, some of the most important genes are those that code for neurotransmitters like dopamine and serotonin. As a critical element of brain chemistry, dopamine produces a pleasurable sensation that the organism finds highly reinforcing. Drugs of abuse, regardless of their classification (i.e., stimulant, depressant, opiate, cannabis), achieve their euphoric effect in large part by stimulating the release of dopamine (NIDA, 2020). Aggressive behavior and conduct disorder may achieve a similar effect even though an external chemical is not being introduced into the brain as it is with drugs (Grigorenko et al., 2010). Dopamine has strong motivational properties and protects survival by encouraging the organism to approach appetitive stimuli, thereby providing it with the nourishment it needs to survive (Weng et al., 2013). It is also activated by novel stimuli, which, in turn, furnish the organism with new information capable of enhancing its survival (Tsuchimine et al., 2009). Serotonin, like dopamine, is a monoamine neurotransmitter, but unlike dopamine, which produces pleasure and strong motivation to approach appetitive stimuli, serotonin engenders a sense of calm, well-being, and cognitive control. It also helps with digestion and sleep (Di Giovanni et al., 2008).

Dopamine and serotonin may interact to form a balanced relationship capable of protecting the organism's survival. In this balanced relationship, dopamine supplies the drive and serotonin the control needed to safeguard the organism's biological viability. Research indicates that dopamine and serotonin interact in their effect on mood (Mitchell & Phillips, 2007), memory (González-Burgos & Feria-Velasco, 2008), learning (Olvera-Cortés et al., 2008), and cognition (Logue & Gould, 2014), so why not behavior? Dopamine supports survival by directing the organism toward appetite activities, creating excitement and energy, and exposing the organism to novel stimuli, thereby providing it with nourishment, vigor, and survival-relevant information on the environment. Serotonin supports survival by protecting and refurbishing energy stores and promoting sleep and relaxation. The two together form the life instinct, which in humans, confronted by a constantly changing environment, responds with existential fear. Neither dopamine nor serotonin alone can provide the level of protection required to facilitate the organism's survival, but both together can. Dopamine does its part by generating the pleasure that directs the organism toward activities designed to advance its survival, and serotonin does its part by providing the control and perspective necessary to keep the organism from overextending itself and inadvertently placing its survival in jeopardy.

It can be stated with some degree of authority that dopamine generates the pleasure and serotonin the pain (more accurately, the anticipation of pain) that the ancient Greeks first described, Beccaria and Bentham later emphasized, and behavioral psychology subsequently formalized as reinforcement and punishment. Learning plays a central role in the generation of existential fear and in the formation of lifestyles designed to cope with this fear. One of these lifestyles, the criminal lifestyle, has been the focus of this book. The life instinct, as was previously stated, is a biological construct that has evolved from the balance of two monoamine neurotransmitters—dopamine and serotonin. If survival is the ultimate goal, then instinct and learning are the ways by which this goal is achieved. Many threats to survival are handled instinctively, although learning assumes an increasingly more important role as one moves up the phylogenetic ladder. Learning, for instance, plays an especially salient role in human management of existential fear and threats to survival. In fact, learning based on the biology of existential fear, the ultimate motivator, is the foundation of most human behavior, criminal or otherwise. Regardless of whether one follows a respondent, operant, or social learning model, the individual learns how to maximize pleasure and minimize pain.

Balancing dopamine and serotonin in an effort to maximize pleasure and minimize pain and protect the organism's survival is how organisms capable of experiencing pain and pleasure guard their existence. Possessing the resources, instinctual and acquired (learning), to achieve this goal is referred to as adaptability. Because social solidarity is less instinctual in humans than it is in many other species (de Waal, 2014), moral values are viewed as being more important in defining adaptability in humans than it is in lower animals. The degree to which an organism is capable of adapting to a constantly changing environment can be considered a marker of how successful it is likely to be in achieving the long-term goal of personal sustainability. Diversity of skills and responses aids in this effort. The more diverse types of responses an organism is capable of producing, the better its chances of survival. In the previous three chapters, we discussed ways of reducing criminality and crime by building competencies and changing environments. Building competencies is a way of increasing diversity within an organism. Those organisms with more competencies (greater diversity) will be more adaptable and therefore be more likely to survive a constantly changing environment. We often think of adaptability and diversity as taking place in groups or species over millions of years, but it can also occur within one generation of a solitary organism.

NONLINEAR DYNAMICAL SYSTEMS THEORY

Nonlinear dynamical systems theory, alternately referred to as chaos theory, contains processes that may be capable of linking the biological, learning, and adaptive resources described in the preceding section with developmental issues and intervention strategies reviewed in earlier chapters. In fact, the principal emphasis of nonlinear dynamical systems theory is explaining how change occurs over time. Several of these processes provide a framework for understanding the specific models and constructs covered in this book. Five of these processes are reviewed here: iteration, sensitive dependence on initial condition, bifurcation, fractals, and self-organization.

Iteration

Iteration is repetition of a mathematical algorithm calculated with multiple replications in order to generate an outcome. It is also commonly viewed as a computational method for recording successive approximations designed to achieve a maximal level of accuracy, with each iteration building on the one it follows. As the system begins to unfold back onto itself, it grows in complexity. Chaos is not always complex, and complexity is not always chaotic, yet the two often accompany one another. The iterative process is used to demonstrate the chaotic nature of data relationships and illustrate how difficult it can be to predict future outcomes. Thus, while it is possible to predict within a range, the size of the range will vary depending on the topic and how much time has elapsed. From this, we can gather that absolute or perfect prediction is unattainable. One of the principal functions of iteration is to allow system growth and expansion (Williams & Arrigo, 2002).

Sensitive Dependence on Initial Conditions

According to the principle of sensitive dependence on initial conditions, a small change in the starting value of an iteration or the status of a variable can become amplified over time as the iterated points start to spread out from each other. A small proximal change will remain relatively stable and largely predictable when the patterns conform to a fixed point or limit cycle attractor but can become unstable and highly unpredictable in situations where the iterations conform to a strange attractor. These large shifts are most likely to occur in open systems where there is a free exchange of energy between the system and its surrounding environment. Lorenz's (1979) butterfly effect is an example of sensitive dependence on initial conditions in an open system. According to the analogy, a butterfly flapping its wings in one location will have virtually no effect on proximal weather patterns but could have a profound effect on the weather a month or two later in a different location. What this suggests is that there is a certain degree of uncertainty built into any relationship and sometimes the uncertainty can become very large and highly relevant.

Bifurcation

Bifurcation is the process by which a stable system opens itself up for change by moving toward an unstable or chaotic state. Technically, a bifurcation can be defined as an abrupt qualitative change in a dynamical system as a parameter is varied continuously. The sudden breakdown or disruption in the equilibrium of the system signals that this is the point at which the system is open or subject to change (Mathews et al., 1999). There are several different types of bifurcation: saddle-node bifurcation, pitchfork bifurcation, transcritical bifurcation, Hopf bifurcation, and period doubling bifurcation, to name just a few. Period doubling occurs when it takes twice as long for the numerical values of an iteration to repeat themselves or twice as many bifurcations are required to complete a cycle. Bifurcation would appear to be particularly helpful in identifying such things as motivation and readiness for change.

Fractals

Fractals are patterns that replicate and repeat themselves. This results in self-similarity between different levels or scales of a pattern or object (Mandelbrot, 1980). Examples from nature include snowflakes, coastlines, and trees. Starting with the trunk of the tree and working our way out to the main branches, and then to the secondary branches, and finally to the twigs, self-similarity between the different levels is clearly evident. Working our way up to the next level, groves capture many of the features of the individual tree and the forest, many of the features of the grove. Human evolution offers another example of a fractal. Certain characteristics and traits have been passed down from one generation to the next through natural selection as a way of dealing with a constantly changing environment. In a similar manner, individuals learn what does and does not work, retaining what works and discarding that which doesn't work. Adaptation, it would appear, supports survival over many generations or within a single generation.

Self-Organization

Although a closed system offers few opportunities for change, an open system is set up for change. Human behavior, the subject of the current book, is very much an open system and therefore a topic for research and change. In fact, the ability to create new forms is vital to the ongoing health and survival of an open system (Barton, 1994). Two types of change can occur with self-organization: first-order change and second-order change. Whereas first-order change is restricted principally to an exchange of energy with the surrounding environment and does not require much in the way of structural change within the system itself, second-order change entails both an exchange of energy with the environment and structural change within the system (Prigogine & Stengers, 1984). As a result, first-order change is usually slow and gradual, á la Popper (1999), whereas second-order change tends to be abrupt and rapid, and more in line with Kuhn (1962/2012). Self-organization may be particularly important in explaining developmental changes leading to delinquency onset and desistance (Saunders & Skar, 2001).

CRIMINAL THINKING: THE GLUE THAT HOLDS THE LIFESTYLE TOGETHER

I like to conceptualize criminal thinking, particularly criminal thought process, as the adhesive that binds the different parts of a criminal lifestyle together. Without this adhesive the lifestyle would certainly fall apart, which, of course, is the whole point of intervening with someone in a drug or criminal lifestyle. That is why it is so important to address antisocial cognition and criminal thinking when conducting interventions for substance abuse and crime. We have already discussed in some detail how proactive criminal thinking (PCT) and reactive criminal thinking (RCT) provide a link between crime and criminality, but the adhesive action of criminal thinking is at work in other areas as well. Antisocial cognition, for instance, adheres the criminal lifestyle to its developmental antecedents (bullying, animal cruelty, firesetting, and other impulse-control disorders). It is also responsible for crime continuity by way of psychological inertia, although this effect appears to be restricted to RCT. Macro- and micro-level variables may also be linked, as in the case of ambient temperature and violent crime, via RCT, whereas a free market cultural ethos and delinquency are linked by way of RCT and PCT. Finally, lifestyle theory assumes that drug relapse and criminal recidivism, even after seemingly successful treatment or several years of prison, are the result of remnants of PCT and RCT that were not adequately addressed by the treatment program or correctional institution. According to lifestyle theory, thought precedes action and so an individual is subject to relapse or recidivation by way of their thoughts.

DISTINGUISHING THE FOREST FROM THE TREES

In this, the final section of the final chapter of a book on criminality and crime, I would like to describe the overarching meta-theory under which criminal lifestyle theory, the moral model of lifestyle criminality, the control model of lifestyle criminality, and the decision-making model of crime all operate. Criminal lifestyle theory is broader than any of the models described in this book, yet it is not the overarching theory under which all other lifestyle constructs and models fall. That is because a criminal lifestyle is just one of several possible lifestyles a person could adopt in an effort to cope with the existential fear provoked by a constantly changing environment. An even broader theory in which biology (dopamine/serotonin balance) and learning (approaching pleasure/avoiding pain; differentiating between right and wrong) inform the neo-Darwinian concept of evolution as the natural selection of maximally adaptive genetic codes and where iterations, sensitive dependence on initial conditions, bifurcation, fractals, and self-organization account for human development and change, serves as a meta-theory for lifestyles that currently and potentially exist. It is a theory in which stability and change are all part of the same process. This, then, is the forest that houses all of the individual trees discussed in this book. The criminal lifestyle, however, is just one of many lifestyles a person can use to deny the reality of change. A fundamental assumption of the lifestyle mega-theory described in this chapter is that change not only occurs in the environment, where it generates existential fear, it also occurs within the person.

Change presents the human organism with an existential dilemma or crisis. To deny that the environment is constantly changing is to deny reality, and to fail to respond to a constantly changing environment is to place one's survival at risk. Lifestyles help structure a person's life and in so doing hold promise of eliminating existential fear. The promise is built on an illusion, however, because lifestyles provide only short-term respite from the problems of existence given that the stimulus for existential fear, environmental change, is eternal. The only real solution to existential fear is adaptation, which means acknowledging existential fear as an inherent part of the human condition and changing in response to an environment that is constantly changing. The objective, according to lifestyle theory, is to live a life free of lifestyles. This is more of a goal than a destination, an ideal that can be used to guide people toward more genuine living. Thus, while change may be the source of existential fear, it is also its remedy. By building competencies and modifying and changing the environment, people can learn to become less dependent on lifestyles to both structure their time and form their relationships and in the process become more genuine. It is the human capacity for learning that is both a source of and solution to existential fear. As was noted several times in this book, a criminal lifestyle is a function of things learned as well as things not learned. The same goes for any lifestyle, and the key to living free is learning that which helps us adapt to a constantly changing environment and unlearning that which makes us dependent on a lifestyle.

References

Abar, C. C., Jackson, K. M., & Wood, M. (2014). Reciprocal relations between perceived parental knowledge and adolescent substance use and delinquency: The moderating role of parent-teen relationship quality. *Developmental Psychology, 50*(9), 2176–2187.

Adams, M. S., Robertson, C. T., Gray-Ray, P., & Ray, M. C. (2003). Labeling and delinquency. *Adolescence, 38*(149), 171–186.

Adler, P. A. (1993). *Wheeling and dealing: An ethnography of an upper-level drug dealing and smuggling community* (2nd ed.). Columbia University Press.

Afzali, M., Stewart, S H., Séguin, J. R., & Conrod, P. (2020). The network constellation of personality and substance use: Evolution from early to late adolescence. *European Journal of Personality, 34*(6), 1109–1119.

Agnew, R. (1989). A longitudinal test of the revised strain theory. *Journal of Quantitative Criminology, 5*(4), 373–387.

Agnew, R. (1992). Foundation for a general strain theory. *Criminology, 30*(1), 47–87.

Agnew, R., Scheuerman, H., Grosholz, J., Isom, D., Watson, L., & Thaxton, S. (2011). Does victimization reduce self-control? A longitudinal analysis. *Journal of Criminal Justice, 39*(2), 169–174.

Ainsworth, M. S. (1989). Attachments beyond infancy. *American Psychologist, 44*(4), 709–716.

Aita, S. L., Hill, B. D., Musso, M. W., & Gouvier, W. D. (2018). Can we identify bad cops based on history? Base rates of historical markers in law enforcement pre-employment evaluations. *Journal of Police and Criminal Psychology, 33*(3), 201–208.

Akers, R. L. (1998). *Social learning and social structure: A general theory of crime and deviance*. Northeastern University Press.

Akers, R. L., Sellers, C. S., & Jennings, W. G. (2021). *Criminological theories: Introduction, evaluation, and application*. Oxford University Press.

Albanesi, C., Cicognani, E., & Zani, B. (2007). Sense of community, civic engagement and social well-being in Italian adolescents. *Journal of Community and Applied Social Psychology, 17*(5), 387–406.

Alexander, Q. T. (2018). Who am I? Criminal social identity as a mediator in the relationship between criminal peers and criminal attitudes within a sample of probationers/parolees. *Dissertations and Theses*. Paper 4479.

Allen, A. B., Robertson, E., & Patin, G. A. (2021). Improving emotional and cognitive outcomes for domestic violence survivors: The impact of shelter stay and self-compassion support groups. *Journal of Interpersonal Violence, 36*(1–2), NP598–624NP.

American Psychiatric Association. (2013). Diagnostic and statistical manual of mental disorders (5th ed). Author. https://doi.org/10.1176/appi.books.9780890425596

Amsel, A. (1958). The role of frustration nonreward in noncontinuous reward situations. *Psychological Bulletin, 55*(2), 102–119.

Anda, R. F., Felitti, V. J., Bremner, J. D., Walker, J. D., Whitfield, C., … Giles, W. H. (2006). The enduring effects of abuse and related adverse experiences in childhood: A convergence of evidence from neurobiology and epidemiology. *European Archives of Psychiatry and Clinical Neuroscience, 256*(3), 174–186.

Anderson, C. A. (1987). Temperature and aggression: Effects on quarterly, yearly, and city rates of violent and nonviolent crime. *Journal of Personality and Social Psychology, 52*(6), 1161–1173.

Anderson, C. A., & Anderson, D. C. (1984). Ambient temperature and violent crime: Tests of the linear and curvilinear hypotheses. *Journal of Personality and Social Psychology, 46*(1), 91–97.

Andrews, N. C. Z., Hanish, L. D., & Santos, C. E. (2017). Reciprocal associations between delinquent behavior and social network position during middle school. *Journal of Youth and Adolescence, 46*(9), 1981–1932.

Angie, A. D., Connelly, S., Waples, E. P., & Kligyte, V. (2011). The influence of discrete emotions on judgement and decision-making: A meta-analytic review. *Cognition and Emotion, 25*(8), 1393–1422.

Anstiss, B., Polaschek, D. L. L., & Wilson, M. (2011). A brief motivational interviewing intervention with prisoners: When you lead a horse to water, can it drink for itself? *Psychology, Crime and Law, 17*(8), 689–710.

Ariza, J. J. M., Cebulla, A., Aldridge, J., Shute, J., & Ross, A. (2014). Proximal adolescent outcomes of gang membership in England and Wales. *Journal of Research in Crime and Delinquency, 51*(2), 168–199.

Arsenio, W., Adams, E., & Gold, J. (2009). Social information processing, moral reasoning and emotion attributions: Relations with adolescents' reactive and proactive aggression. *Child Development, 80*(6), 1739–1755.

Augustyn, M. B., Ward, J. T., Krohn, M. D., & Dong, B. (2019). Criminal justice contact across generations: Assessing the intergenerational labeling hypothesis. *Journal of Developmental and Life-Course Criminology, 5*(2), 137–175.

Ayers, C. D., Williams, J. H., Hawkins, J. D., Peterson, P. L., Catalano, R. F., & Abbott, R. D. (1999). Assessing correlates of onset, escalation, deescalation, and desistance of delinquent behavior. *Journal of Quantitative Criminology, 15*(3), 277–306.

Ayers, R., Ingram, J., Rees, A., Neale, J., Beattie, A., & Telfer, M. (2014). Enhancing motivation within a rapid opioid substitution treatment feasibility RCT: A nested qualitative study. *Substance Abuse Treatment, Prevention, and Policy, 9*, 44.

Ba, B. A., Knox, D., Mummolo, J., & Rivera, R. (2021). The role of officer race and gender in police-civilian interactions in Chicago. *Science, 371*(6530), 696–702.

Bachman, R., Kerrison, E., Paternoster, R., O'Connell, D., & Smith, L. (2016). Desistance for a long-term drug-involved sample of adult offenders: The importance of identity transformation. *Criminal Justice and Behavior, 43*(2), 164–186.

Bailey, W. C. (1998). Deterrence, brutalization, and the death penalty: Another examination of Oklahoma's return to capital punishment. *Criminology, 36*(4), 711–733.

Bandura, A. (1978). The self system in reciprocal determinism. *American Psychologist, 33*(4), 344–358.

Bandura, A. (1986). *Social foundations of thought and action: A social cognitive theory*. Prentice Hall.

Bandura, A. (1989). Human agency in social cognitive theory. *American Psychologist, 44*(9), 1175–1184.

Bandura, A. (1994). Self-efficacy. In V. S. Ramachaudran (Ed.), *Encyclopedia of human behavior* (pp. 71–81). Academic Press.

Bandura, A., Barbaranelli, C., Caprara, G. V., & Pastorelli, C. (1996). Mechanisms of moral disengagement in the exercise of moral agency. *Journal of Personality and Social Psychology, 71*(2), 364–374.

Bandura, A., Caprara, G. V., Barbaranelli, C., Gerbino, M., & Pastorelli, C. (2003). Role of affective self-regulatory efficacy in diverse spheres of psychosocial functioning. *Child Development, 74*(3), 769–782.

Bandura, A., & Schunk, D. H. (1981). Cultivating competence, self-efficacy, and intrinsic interest through proximal self-motivation. *Journal of Personality and Social Psychology, 41*(3), 586–598.

Bank, L., Marlowe, H., Reid, J. B., Patterson, G. R., & Weinrott, M. R. (1991). A comparative evaluation of parent-training interventions for families of chronic delinquents. *Journal of Abnormal Child Psychology, 19*(1), 15–33.

Bank, L., Patterson, G. R., & Reid, J. B. (1996). Negative sibling interaction patterns as predictors of later adjustment problems in adolescent and young adult males. In G. H. Brody (Ed.), *Advances in applied developmental psychology: Sibling relationships* (pp. 197–229). Ablex.

Barbieri, N., Clipper, S. J., Narvey, C., Rude, A., Craig, J. M., & Piquero, N. L. (2019). Assessing strain theory and measures of victimization, 2002–2018. *Aggression and Violent Behavior*. Online first, https://doi.org/10.1016/j.avb.2019.06.005

Barnes, G. M., Hoffman, J. H., Welte, J. W., Farrell, M. P., & Dintcheff, B. A. (2006). Effects of parental monitoring and peer deviance on substance use and delinquency. *Journal of Marriage and Family, 68*(4), 1084–1104.

Barnes, J. C., Beaver, K. M., & Boutwell, B. B. (2011). Examining the genetic underpinnings to Moffitt's developmental taxonomy: A behavioral genetic analysis. *Criminology, 49*(4), 923–954.

Barrett, D. E., Katsiyannis, A., Zhang, D., & Zhang, D. (2014). Delinquency and recidivism: A multicohort, matched-control study of the role of early adverse experiences, mental health problems, and disabilities. *Journal of Emotional and Behavioral Disorders, 22*(1), 3–15.

Barriga, A. Q., Landau, J. R., Stinson, B. L., Liau, A. K., & Gibbs, J. C. (2000). Cognitive distortion and problem behaviors in adolescents. *Criminal Justice and Behavior, 27*(1), 36–56.

Barton, S. (1994). Chaos, self-organization, and psychology. *American Psychologist, 49*(1), 5–14.

Bartusch, D. J., & Matsueda, R. L. (1996). Gender, reflected appraisals, and labeling: A cross-group test of an interactionist theory of delinquency. *Social Forces, 75*(1), 145–177.

Bässmann, J. (2011). Vehicle theft reduction in Germany: The long-term effectiveness of electronic immobilization. *European Journal on Criminal Policy and Research, 17*(3), 221–246.

Batool, S., & Shehzad, S. (2019). Effect of parenting styles on moral development of secondary school students. *Journal of Research and Reflections in Education, 13*(2), 183–195.

Bauman, S., Yoon, J., Iurino, C., & Hackett, L. (2020). Experiences of adolescent witnesses to peer victimization: The bystander effect. *Journal of School Psychology, 80*, 1–14.

Beauregard, E., & Leclerc, B. (2007). An application of the rational choice approach to the offending process of sex offenders: A close look at the decision-making. *Sexual Abuse: A Journal of Research and Treatment, 19*(2), 115–133.

Beaver, K. M., Gibson, C. L., DeLisi, M., Vaughn, M. G., & Wright, J. P. (2012). The interaction between neighborhood disadvantage and genetic factors in the prediction of antisocial outcomes. *Youth Violence and Juvenile Justice, 10*(1), 25–40.

Beaver, K. M., Nedelec, J. L., da Silva Costa, C., & Vidal, M. M. (2015). The future of biosocial criminology. *Criminal Justice Studies, 28*(1), 6–17.

Beaver, K. M., Shutt, J. E., Boutwell, B. B., Ratchford, M., Roberts, K., & Barnes, J. C. (2009). Genetic and environmental influences on levels of self-control and delinquent peer affiliation: Results from a longitudinal sample of adolescent twins. *Criminal Justice and Behavior, 36*(1), 41–60.

Beaver, K. M., Wright, J. P., DeLisi, M., & Vaughn, M. G. (2008). Genetic influences on the stability of low self-control: Results from a longitudinal sample of twins. *Journal of Criminal Justice, 36*(6), 478–485.

Beccaria, C. (1995). *On crimes and punishments* (trans. R. Davies). Cambridge University Press. (original work published 1764)

Bechara, A. (2004). The role of emotion in decision-making: Evidence from neurological patients with orbitofrontal damage. *Brain and Cognition, 55*(1), 30–40.

Beck, A. T., Rush, A. J., Shaw, B. F., & Emery, G. (1979). *Cognitive therapy of depression*. Guilford.

Becker, H. S. (1963). *Outsiders: Studies in the sociology of deviance*. The Free Press.

Belenko, S., Knight, D., Wasserman, G. A., Dennis, M. L., Wiley, T., … Sales, J. (2017). The juvenile justice behavioral health services cascade: A new framework for measuring unmet substance use treatment services needs among adolescent offenders. *Journal of Substance Abuse Treatment, 74*, 80–91.

Bennett, T., Holloway, K., & Farrington, D. P. (2006). Does neighborhood watch reduce crime? A systematic review and meta-analysis. *Journal of Experimental Criminology, 2*(4), 437–458.

Benson, M. L., & Moore, E. (1992). Are white-collar and common offenders the same? An empirical and theoretical critique of a recently proposed general theory of crime. *Journal of Research in Crime and Delinquency, 29*(3), 251–272.

Berg, M. T., & Mulford, C. F. (2020). Reappraising and redirecting research on the victim-offender overlap. *Trauma, Violence and Abuse, 21*(1), 16–30.

Bernat, D. H., Oakes, M., Pettingell, S. L., & Resnick, M. (2012). Risk and direct protective factors for youth violence: Results from the National Longitudinal Study of Adolescent Health. *American Journal of Preventive Medicine, 43*(2S1), S57–S66.

Bernburg, J. G., Krohn, M. D., & Rivera, C. J. (2006). Official labeling, criminal embeddedness, and subsequent delinquency: A longitudinal test of labeling theory. *Journal of Research in Crime and Delinquency, 43*(1), 67–88.

Berridge, K. C. (2007). The debate over dopamine's role in rewards: The case for incentive salience. *Psychopharmacology, 191*(3), 391–431.

Bersani, B. E., & Chapple, C. L. (2007). School failure as an adolescent turning point. *Sociological Focus, 40*(4), 370–391.

Biernacki, P. (1986). *Pathways from heroin addiction: Recovery without treatment.* Temple University Press.

Blakemore, S.-J., & Robbins, T. W. (2012). Decision-making in the adolescent brain. *Nature Neuroscience, 15*(9), 1184–1191.

Blasius, J., & Friedrichs, J. (2007). Internal heterogeneity of a deprived urban area and its impact on residents' perception of deviance. *Housing Studies, 22*(5), 753–780.

Block, S., & Lesneskie, E. (2018). A thematic analysis of spectator violence at sporting events in North America. *Deviant Behavior, 39*(9), 1140–1152.

Boisvert, D., Wells, J., Armstrong, T. A., & Lewis, R. H. (2018). Serotonin and self-control. A genetically moderated stress sensitization effect. *Journal of Criminal Justice, 56*, 98–106.

Bondurant, S. R., Lindo, J. M., & Swensen, I. D. (2018). Substance abuse treatment centers and local crime. *Journal of Urban Economics, 104*, 124–133.

Bonta, J., & Andrews, D. (2017). *The psychology of criminal conduct* (6th ed.). Routledge.

Borowski, J. (2020). *Panzram at Leavenworth.* Waterfront Productions.

Bowlby, J. (1982). *Attachment and loss. Vol 1: Attachment* (2nd ed.). Basic Books. (original work published 1969)

Boydston, L., French, W. P., & Varley, C. K. (2016). A review on anxiety disorders in children and adolescents. *Journal of Alternative Medicine Research, 8*(4), 421–429.

Braga, A. A., Welsh, B. C., & Schnell, C. (2015). Can policing disorder reduce crime? A systematic review and meta-analysis. *Journal of Research in Crime and Delinquency, 52*(4), 567–588.

Branstetter, S. A., Low, S., & Furman, W. (2011). The influence of parents and friends on adolescent substance use: A multidimensional approach. *Journal of Substance Use, 16*(2), 150–160.

Brehm, J. W. (2007). A brief history of dissonance theory. *Social and Personality Psychology Compass, 1*(1), 381–391.

Bretherton, I., & Munholland, K. A. (2016). The internal working model construct in light of contemporary neuroimaging research. In J. Cassidy & P. R. Shaver (Eds.), *Handbook of attachment: Theory, research, and clinical applications* (3rd ed., pp. 63–88). Guilford.

Brezina, T., & Topalli, V. (2012). Criminal self-efficacy: Exploring the correlates and consequences of a "successful criminal" identity. *Criminal Justice and Behavior, 39*(8), 1042–1062.

Bridgett, N. M. B., Edwards, E. S., & Deater-Deckard, K. (2015). Intergenerational transmission of self-regulation: A multidisciplinary review and integrative conceptual framework. *Psychological Bulletin, 141*(3), 602–654.

Broidy, L. M. (2001). A test of general strain theory. *Criminology, 39*(1), 9–35.

Broidy, L. M., & Agnew, R. (1997). Gender and crime: A general strain theory perspective. *Journal of Research in Crime and Delinquency, 34*(3), 275–306.

Brook, D. W., Brook, J. S., Rubenstone, E., Zhang, C., & Saar, N. S. (2011). Developmental associations between externalizing behaviors, peer delinquency, drug use, perceived neighborhood crime, and violent behavior in urban communities. *Aggressive Behavior, 37*(4), 349–361.

Brown, B. B., & Bakken, J, P. (2011). Parenting and peer relationships: Reinvigorating research on family-peer linkages in adolescence. *Journal of Research on Adolescence, 21*(1), 153–165.

Brownfield, D., & Sorenson, A. M. (1994). Sibship size and sibling delinquency. *Deviant Behavior, 15*(1), 45–61.

Brownfield, D., & Thompson, K. (2005). Self-concept and delinquency: The effects of reflected appraisals by parent and peers. *Western Criminology Review, 6*(1), 22–29.

Brumback, T., Thompson, W., Cummins, K., Brown, S., & Tapert, S. (2021). Psychosocial predictors of substance use in adolescents and young adults: Longitudinal risk and protective factors. *Addictive Behaviors*. Online first, https://doi.org/10.1016/j.addbeh.2021.106985

Buckholtz, J. W., Treadway, M. T., Cowan, R. L., Woodward, N. D., Benning, S. D., … Zald, D. H. (2010). Mesolimbic dopamine reward system hypersensitivity in individuals with psychopathic traits. *Nature and Neuroscience, 13*(4), 419–421.

Buist, K. L., Deković, M., & Prinzie, P. (2013). Sibling relationship quality and psychopathology of children and adolescents: A meta-analysis. *Clinical Psychology Review, 33*(1), 97–106.

Buker, H. (2011). Formation of self-control: Gottfredson and Hirschi's general theory of crime and beyond. *Aggression and Violent Behavior, 16*(4), 265–276.

Bunch, J. M., Iratzoqui, A., & Watts, S. J. (2018). Child abuse, self-control, and delinquency: A general strain perspective. *Journal of Criminal Justice, 56*, 20–28.

Bureau of Justice Statistics. (2021, May 27). *Annual probation survey, annual parole survey, annual survey of jails, census of jails, and national prison statistics program, 1980–2018*. Author.

Burt, C. H., & Simons, R. L. (2014). Pulling back the curtain on heritability studies: Biosocial criminology in the postgenomic era. *Criminology, 52*(2), 223–262.

Burt, C. H., Simons, R. L., & Simons, L. G. (2006). A longitudinal test of the effects of parenting and the stability of self-control: Negative evidence for the general theory of crime. *Criminology, 44*(2), 353–396.

Bussey, K., & Bandura, A. (1984). Influence of gender constancy and social power on sex-linked modeling. *Journal of Personality and Social Psychology, 47*(6), 1292–1302.

Butković, A., & Bratko, D. (2003). Generation and sex differences in sensation seeking: Results of the family study. *Perceptual and Motor Skills, 97*(3), 965–970.

Butler, T., Schofield, P. W., Greenberg, D., Allnutt, S. H., Indig, D., … Ellis, A. (2010). Reducing impulsivity in repeat violent offenders: An open label trial of a selective serotonin reuptake inhibitor. *Australian and New Zealand Journal of Psychiatry, 44*(12), 1137–1143.

Bybee, J. (Ed.). (1998). *Guilt and children*. Academic Press.

Carbone-Lopez, K., & Lauritsen, J. (2013). Seasonal variation in violent victimization: Opportunity and the annual rhythm of the school calendar. *Journal of Quantitative Criminology, 29*(3), 399–422.

Card, N. A., & Little, T. D. (2006). Proactive and reactive aggression in childhood and adolescence: A meta-analysis of differential relations with psychosocial adjustment. *International Journal of Behavioral Development, 30*(5), 466–480.

Cassel, R. N., DeMoulin, D. F., Chow, P., & Heiger, R. C. (2001). Comparing the cognitive dissonance of 57 juvenile delinquent girls with that of 215 typical high school students. *Education, 121*(3), 454–458.

Catalano, R. F., & Hawkins, J. D. (1996). The social development model: A theory of antisocial behavior. In J. D. Hawkins (Ed.), *Delinquency and crime: Current theories* (pp. 149–197). Cambridge University Press.

Caudy, M. S., Folk, J. B., Stuewig, J. B., Wooditch, A., Martinez, A., … Taxman, F. S. (2015). Does substance misuse moderate the relationship between criminal thinking and recidivism? *Journal of Criminal Justice, 43*, 12–19.

Chambers, E. C., Fuster, D., Suglia, S. F., & Rosenbaum, E. (2015). Depressive symptomatology and hostile affect among Latinos using housing rental assistance: The AHOME study. *Journal of Urban Health: Bulletin of the New York Academy of Medicine, 92*(4), 611–621.

Chan, H. C., & Wong, R. W. Y. (2019). Childhood and adolescent animal cruelty and subsequent interpersonal violence in adulthood: A review of the literature. *Aggression and Violent Behavior, 48*, 83–93.

Chandler, R. K., Fletcher, B. W., & Volkow, N. D. (2009). Treating drug abuse and addiction in the criminal justice system: Improving public health and safety. *Journal of the American Medical Association, 301*(2), 183–190.

Chen, P., Voisin, D. R., & Jacobson, K. C. (2016). Community violence exposure and adolescent delinquency: Examining a spectrum of promotive factors. *Youth and Society, 48*(1), 33–57.

Cherbuin, N., Windsor, T. D., Anstey, K. J., Maller, J. J., Meslin, C., & Sachdeve, P. S. (2008). Hippocampal volume is positively associated with behavioural inhibition (BIS) in a large community-based sample of mid-life adults: The PATH through life study. *Social Cognitive and Affective Neuroscience, 3*(3), 262–269.

Cioffi, C. C., Griffin, A. M., Natsuaki, M. N., Shaw, D. S., Reiss, D., … Leve, L. D. (2021). The role of negative emotionality in the development of child executive function and language abilities form toddlerhood to first grade: An adoption study. *Developmental Psychology, 57*(3), 347–360.

Circo, G., & McGarrell, E. (2021). Estimating the impact of an integrated CCTV program on crime. *Journal of Experimental Criminology, 17*(1), 129–150.

Clair-Michaud, M., Martin, R. A., Stein, L. A. R., Bassett, S., Lebeau, R., & Golembeske, C. (2016). The impact of motivational interviewing on delinquent behaviors in incarcerated adolescents. *Journal of Substance Abuse Treatment, 65*, 13–19.

Clarke, R. V. (2004). Technology, criminology, and crime science. *European Journal on Criminal Policy and Research, 10*(1), 55–63.

Clarke, R. V., & Cornish, D. B. (1985). Modeling offenders' decisions: A framework for research and policy. *Crime and Justice, 6*, 147–185.

Clarke, R. V., & Mayhew, P. (1994). Parking patterns and car theft risks: Policy relevant findings from the British crime survey. In R. V. Clarke (Series Ed.) & J. E. Eck & D. Weisburd (Vol. Eds.), *Crime prevention studies* (Vol. 4, pp. 91–107). Criminal Justice Press.

Clifton, J., Diaz-Fuentes, D., & Revuelta, J. (2020). Falling inequality in Latin America: The role of fiscal policy. *Journal of Latin American Studies, 52*(2), 317–341.

Clinkinbeard, S. S. (2014). What lies ahead: An exploration of future orientation, self-control, and delinquency. *Criminal Justice Review, 39*(1), 19–36.

Cloward, R. A., & Ohlin, L. E. (1960). *Delinquency and opportunity: A theory of delinquent gangs.* Free Press.

Cochrane, R. E., Tett, R. P., & Vandecreek, L. (2003). Psychological testing and selection of police officers. *Criminal Justice and Behavior, 30*(5), 511–537.

Cohen, L., & Felson, M. (1979). Social change and crime rate trends: A routine activity approach. *American Sociological Review, 44*(4), 588–608.

Coleman, J. S. (1988). Social capital in the creation of human capital. *American Journal of Sociology, 94*, S95–S120.

Conger, A. J. (1974). A revised definition for suppressor variables: A guide to their identification and interpretation. *Educational and Psychological Measurement, 34*, 35–46.

Connolly, E. J., Cooke, E. M., Beaver, K. M., & Brown, W. (2020). Do developmental changes in impulsivity and sensation seeking uniquely predict violent victimization? A test of the dual systems model. *Journal of Criminal Justice*. Online first, https://doi.org/10.1016/j.jcrimjus.2019.101639

Cooke, J. E., Kochendorfer, L. B., Stuart-Parrigon, K. L., Koehn, A. J., & Kerns, K. A. (2019). Parent–child attachment and children's experience and regulation of emotion: A meta-analytic review. *Emotion, 19*(6), 1103–1126.

Cornish, D., & Clarke, R. (2003). Opportunities, precipitators, and criminal decisions: A reply to Wortley's critique of situational crime prevention. In M. Smith & D. Cornish (Eds.), *Theory for practice in situational crime prevention* (pp. 41–96). Criminal Justice Press.

Cotton, J. L. (1986). Ambient temperature and violent crime. *Journal of Applied Social Psychology, 16*(9), 786–801.

Courey, M., & Pare, P.-P. (2016). A closer look at the relationship between low self-control and delinquency: The effects of identity styles. *Crime and Delinquency, 62*(3), 368–396.

Coyle, B. (2019). What the f**k is maturity?: Young adulthood, subjective maturity and desistance from crime. *British Journal of Criminology, 59*(5), 1178–1198.

Cratty, B. J. (2004). Adapted physical education: Self-control and attention. *Focus on Exceptional Children, 37*(3), 1–8.

Crean, H. F., & Johnson, D. B. (2013). Promoting alternative thinking strategies (PATHS) and elementary school aged children's aggression: Results from a cluster randomized trial. *American Journal of Community Psychology, 52*(1/2), 56–72.

Criss, M. M., & Shaw, D. S. (2005). Sibling relationships as contexts for delinquency training in low-income families. *Journal of Family Psychology, 19*(4), 592–600.

Cuff, B. M. P., Brown, S. J., Taylor, L., & Howat, D. J. (2016). Empathy: A review of the concept. *Emotion Review, 8*(2), 144–153.

Cullen, F. T. (1983). *Rethinking crime and deviance theory: The emergence of a structuring tradition*. Rowman & Littlefield.

Cunliffe, T. (1992). Arresting youth crime: A review of social skills training with young offenders. *Adolescence, 27*(108), 891–900.

Cupaioli, F. A., Zucca, F. A., Caporale, C., Lesch, K.-P., Passamonti, L., & Zecca, L. (2021). The neurobiology of human aggressive behavior: Neuroimaging, genetic, and neurochemical aspects. *Progress in Neuropsychopharmacology & Biological Psychiatry*. Online first, https://doi.org/10.1016/j.pnpbp.2020.110059

Cusson, M., & Pinsonneault, P. (1986). The decision to give up crime. In D. B. Cornish & R. V. Clarke (Eds.), *The reasoning criminal: Rational choice perspective on offending* (pp. 72–82). Springer.

Damasio, A. (1994). *Descartes' error: Emotion, reason, and the human brain.* Putnam.

D'Amico, E. J., Edelen, M. O., Miles, J. N. V., & Morral, A. R. (2008). The longitudinal association between substance use and delinquency among high-risk youth. *Drug and Alcohol Dependence, 93*(1), 85–92.

Davison, K. (2021). Cold war Pavlov: Homosexual aversion therapy in the 1960s. *History of the Human Sciences, 34*(1), 89–119.

Dawkins, R. (1976). *The selfish gene.* Oxford University Press.

De Buck, A., & Pauwels, L. J. R. (2019). Are impulsive adolescents differentially vulnerable to normative or situational peer influences? A partial replication study. *Journal of Contemporary Criminal Justice, 35*(4), 461–483.

De Coster, S., & Lutz, J. (2018). Reconsidering labels and primary deviance: False appraisals, reflected appraisals, and delinquency onset. *Journal of Research in Crime and Delinquency, 55*(5), 609–648.

Defoe, I. N., Dubas, J. S., Dalmaijer, E. S., & van Aken, M. A. G. (2020). Is the peer presence effect on heightened adolescent risky decision-making only present in males? *Journal of Youth and Adolescence, 49*(3), 693–705.

Defoe, I. N., Keijsers, L., Hawk, S. T., Branje, S., Dubas, J. S., … Meeus, W. (2013). Siblings versus parents and friends: Longitudinal linkages to adolescent externalizing problems. *Journal of Child Psychology and Psychiatry, 54*(8), 881–889.

DeLisi, M., Beaver, K. M., Vaughn, M. G., & Wright, J. P. (2009). All in the family: Gene x environment interaction between DRD2 and criminal father is associated with five antisocial phenotypes. *Criminal Justice and Behavior, 36*(11), 1187–1197.

de Vries, S. L. A., Hoeve, M., Stams, G. J. J. M., & Asscher, J. J. (2016). Adolescent-parent attachment and externalizing behavior: The mediating role of individual and social factors. *Journal of Abnormal Child Psychology, 44*(2), 283–294.

de Waal, F. B. M. (2014). Natural normativity: The "is" and "ought" of animal behavior. *Behaviour, 151*(2/3), 185–204.

Dezhbakhsh, H., Rubin, P. H., & Shepherd, J. M. (2003). Does capital punishment have a deterrent effect? New evidence from postmoratorium panel data. *American Law and Economics Review, 5*(2), 344–376.

Dezhbakhsh, H., & Shepherd, J. M. (2006). The deterrent effect of capital punishment: Evidence from a "judicial experiment." *Economic Inquiry, 44*(3), 512–535.

Di Chiara, G., & Imperato, A. (1988). Drugs abused by humans preferentially increase synaptic dopamine concentrations in the mesolimbic system of freely moving rats. *Proceedings of the National Academy of Sciences, 85*(14), 5274–5278.

Dienstmann, G. (2021). *Mindful self-discipline: Living with purpose and achieving your goals in a world of distractions*. Live and Dare Publications.

Di Giovanni, G., Di Matteo, V., & Esposito, E. (Eds.). (2008). *Progress in brain research* (Vol. 172). Elsevier.

Dijkstra, J. K., Cillessen, A. H. N., & Borch, C. (2013). Popularity and adolescent friendship networks: Selection and influence dynamics. *Developmental Psychology, 49*(7), 1242–1252.

Di Lieto, M. C., Pecini, C., Castro, E., Inguaggiato, E., Cecchi, F., … Sgandurra, G. (2020). Empowering executive functions in 5- and 6-year old typically developing children through educational robotics: An RCT study. *Frontiers in Psychology, 10*, 3084.

Dodge, K. A. (2006). Translational science in action: Hostile attributional style and the development of aggressive behavior problems. *Development and Psychopathology, 18*(3), 791–814.

Doherty, E. E., & Bersani, B. E. (2018). Mapping the age of official desistance for adult offenders: Implications for research and policy. *Journal of Developmental and Life-Course Criminology, 4*(4), 516–551.

Dolan, M., McEwan, T. E., Doley, R., & Fritzon, K. (2011). Risk factors and risk assessment in juvenile fire-setting. *Psychiatry, Psychology and Law, 18*(3), 378–394.

Donner, C. M., Marcum, C. D., Jennings, W. G., Higgins, G. E., & Banfield, J. (2014). Low self-control and cybercrime: Exploring the utility of the general theory of crime beyond digital piracy. *Computers in Human Behavior, 34*, 165–172.

dos Santos, M. A., de Freitas e Castro, J. M., & de Freitas Lino Pinto Cardoso, C. S. (2020). The moral emotions of guilt and shame in children: Relationship with parenting and temperament. *Journal of Child and Family Studies, 29*(10), 2759–2769.

Dow-Edwards, D., MacMaster, F. P., Peterson, B. S., Niesink, R., Andersen, S., & Braams, B. R. (2019). Experience during adolescence shapes brain development: From synapses and networks to normal and pathological behavior. *Neurotoxicology and Teratology*. Online first, https://doi.org/10.1016/j.ntt.2019.106834

Drozda, C. (2006). Juveniles performing auto theft: An exploratory study into a deviant leisure lifestyle. *Leisure, 30*(1), 111–132.

Earman, J. (Ed.). (1984). *Testing scientific theories: Minnesota studies in the philosophy of science* (Vol. 10). University of Minnesota Press.

Eisenberg, M. J., Van Horn, J. E., Dekker, J. M., Assink, M., Van Der Put, C. E., … Stams, G. J. J. M. (2019). Static and dynamic predictors of general and violent criminal offense recidivism in the forensic outpatient population: A meta-analysis. *Criminal Justice and Behavior, 46*(5), 732–750.

Eisenberg, N., Spinrad, T. L., & Eggum, N. D. (2010). Emotion-related self-regulation and its relation to children's maladjustment. *Annual Review of Clinical Psychology, 6*, 495–525.

Elgán, T. H., Durbeej, N., Holder, H. D., & Gripenberg, J. (2021). Effects of a multi-component alcohol prevention intervention at sporting events: A quasi-experimental control group study. *Addiction*. Online first, https://doi.org/10.1111/add.15461

Ellis, A. (1962). *Reason and emotion in psychotherapy*. Lyle Stuart.

El-Sheikh, M., Hinnant, B., & Erath, S. (2011). Developmental trajectories of delinquency symptoms in childhood: The role of marital conflict and autonomic nervous system activity. *Journal of Abnormal Psychology, 120*(1), 16–32.

Elwert, F., & Winship, C. (2014). Endogenous selection bias: The problem of conditioning on a collider variable. *Annual Review of Sociology, 40*(1), 31–53.

Eme, R. (2020). Life course persistent antisocial behavior silver anniversary. *Aggression and Violent Behavior*. Online first, https://doi.org/10.1061/j.avb.2019.101344

Evans, D. W., & Marsh, H. L. (2017). A brief introduction to early forms of non-verbal social cognition. *Infant Behavior and Development, 48*, 2–4.

Evans, T. D., Cullen, F. T., Burton, V. S., Dunaway, R. G., & Benson, M. L. (1997). The social consequences of self-control: Testing the general theory of crime. *Criminology, 35*(3), 475–504.

Eyberg, S. (1988). Parent–child interaction therapy: Integration of traditional and behavioral concerns. *Child and Family Behavior Therapy, 10*(1), 33–46.

Fagan, A. A., & Najman, J. M. (2003). Sibling influences on adolescent delinquent behaviour: An Australian longitudinal study. *Journal of Adolescence, 26*(5), 546–558.

Farnworth, M., & Leiber, M. J. (1989). Strain theory revisited: Economic goals, educational means, and delinquency. *American Sociological Review, 54*(2), 263–274.

Farrell, A. D., Thompson, E. L., & Mehari, K. R. (2017). Dimensions of peer influences and their relationship to adolescents' aggression, other problem behaviors and prosocial behavior. *Journal of Youth and Adolescence, 46*(6), 1351–1369.

Farrell, A. H., & Vaillancourt, T. (2020). Adolescent empathic concern and perspective taking: Heterogeneous developmental trajectories and childhood social and psychological factors. *Journal of Personality*. Online first, https://doi.org/10.1111/jopy.12607

Farrington, D. P. (1998). Youth crime and antisocial behavior. In A. Campbell & S. Muncer (Eds.), *The social child* (pp. 353–392). Taylor & Francis.

Farrington, D. P. (2005). Cambridge study in delinquent development [Great Britain]. Inter-university Consortium for Political and Social Research [distributor]. https://doi.org/10.3886/ICPSR08488.v2

Farrington, D. P., & Bergstrøm, H. (2021). High resting heart rate protects against childhood risk factors in predicting adult psychopathy. *Journal of Criminal Psychology*. Online first, https://doi.org/10.1108/JCP-01-2021-0003

Farrington, D. P., Jolliffe, D., Hawkins, J. D., Catalano, R. F., Hill, K. G., & Kosterman, R. (2003). Comparing delinquency careers in court records and self-reports. *Criminology, 41*(3), 933–958.

Farrington, D. P., Ttofi, M. M., & Piquero, A. R. (2016). Risk, promotive, and protective factors in youth offending. Results from the Cambridge study in delinquent development. *Journal of Criminal Justice, 45*, 63–70.

Feinberg, M. E., Solmeyer, A. R., Hostetler, M. L., Sakuma, K.-L., Jones, D., & McHale, S. M. (2013). Siblings are special: Initial test of a new approach to preventing youth behavior problems. *Journal of Adolescent Health, 53*, 166–173.

Feldman, J. S., & Olson, S. L. (2021). Supportive maternal and paternal caregiving and the children's emerging effortful control abilities. *Journal of Child and Family Studies, 30*(4), 894–904.

Felson, J. (2014). What can we learn from twin studies? A comprehensive evaluation of the equal environments assumption. *Social Science Research, 43*, 184–199.

Felson, R. B., Osgood, D. W., Cundiff, P. R., & Wiernik, C. (2019). Life in the fast lane: Drugs, hedonistic lifestyles, and economic crime. *Crime and Delinquency, 65*(9), 1292–1318.

Felson, R. B., Ribner, S. A., & Siegel, M. S. (1984). Age and the effect of third parties during criminal violence. *Sociology and Social Research, 68*(4), 452–462.

Festinger, L. (1957). *A theory of cognitive dissonance*. Stanford University Press.

Fiddick, L. (2011). There is more than the amygdala: Potential threat assessment in the cingulate cortex. *Neuroscience and Biobehavioral Reviews, 35*(4), 1007–1018.

Flanagan, I. M. L., Auty, K. M., & Farrington, D. P. (2019). Parental supervision and later offending: A systematic review of longitudinal studies. *Aggression and Violent Behavior, 47*, 215–229.

Fleming, C. B., Catalano, R. F., Mazza, J. J., Brown, E. C., Haggerty, K. P., & Harachi, T. W. (2008). After-school activities, misbehavior in school, and delinquency from the end of elementary school through the beginning of high school: A test of social development model hypotheses. *Journal of Early Adolescence, 28*(2), 277–303.

Folk, J. B., Disabato, D. J., Daylor, J. M., Tangney, J. P., Barboza, S., ... Holwager, J. (2016). Effectiveness of a self-administered intervention for criminal thinking: Taking a chance on change. *Psychological Services, 13*(3), 272–282.

Forsberg, L., & Douglas, T. (2020). What is criminal rehabilitation? *Criminal Law and Philosophy*. Online first, https://doi.org/10.1007/s11572-020-09547-4

Forth, A. E., Kosson, D., & Hare, R. D. (2003). *Psychopathy checklist: Youth version technical manual*. Multi-Health Systems.

Frankl, V. E. (2000). *Man's search for ultimate meaning*. Barnes & Noble.

Freijy, T., & Kothe, E. J. (2013). Dissonance-based interventions for health behaviour change: A systematic review. *British Journal of Health Psychology, 18*(2), 310–337.

Frick, P. J., Ray, J. V., Thornton, L. C., & Kahn, R. E. (2014). Annual research review: A developmental psychopathology approach to understanding callous-unemotional traits in children and adolescents with serious conduct problems. *Journal of Child Psychology and Psychiatry, 55*(6), 532–548.

Frick, P. J., & Viding, E. (2009). Antisocial behavior from a developmental psychopathology perspective. *Development and Psychopathology, 21*(4), 1111–1131.

Friedmann, P. D., Taxman, F. S., & Henderson, C. E. (2007). Evidence-based practices for drug-involved adults in the criminal justice system. *Journal of Substance Abuse Treatment, 32*(3), 267–277.

Friedson, M., & Sharkey, P. (2015). Violence and neighborhood disadvantage after the crime decline. *Annals of the American Academy of Political and Social Science, 660*, 341–358.

Gallupe, O., McLevey, J., & Brown, S. (2019). Selection and influence: A meta-analysis of the association between peer and personal offending. *Journal of Quantitative Criminology, 35*(2), 313–335.

Gannon, T. A. (2016). Forensic psychologists should use the behavioral experiment to facilitate cognitive change in clients who have offended. *Aggression and Violent Behavior, 27*, 130–141.

Gantiva, C., Cendales, R., Diaz, M., & González, Y. (2021). Is there really a relationship between empathy and aggression? Evidence from physiological and self-report measures. *Journal of Interpersonal Violence, 36*(7–8), 3438–3458.

Gao, Y., & Wong, D. S. W. (2018). Strains and delinquency of migrant adolescents in China: An investigation from the perspective of general strain theory. *Youth and Society, 50*(4), 506–528.

Garcia, M. M., Shaw, D. S., Winslow, E. B., & Yaggi, K. E. (2000). Destructive sibling conflict and the development of conduct problems in young boys. *Developmental Psychology, 36*(1), 44–53.

Garofalo, C., Neumann, C. S., & Velotti, P. (2020). Psychopathy and aggression: The role of emotion dysregulation. *Journal of Interpersonal Violence*. Online first, https://doi.org/10.1177/0886260519900946

Gastil, R. D. (1971). Homicide and a regional culture of violence. *American Sociological Review, 36*(3), 412–427.

Gatti, U., & Verde, A. (2012). Cesare Lombroso: Methodological ambiguities and brilliant intuitions. *International Journal of Law and Psychiatry, 35*(1), 19–26.

Gearhart, M. C., & Tucker, R. (2020). Criminogenic risk, criminogenic need, collective efficacy, and juvenile delinquency. *Criminal Justice and Behavior, 47*(9), 1116–1135.

Gendreau, P., Grant, B. A., Leipciger, M., & Collins, S. (1979). Norms and recidivism rates for the MMPI and selected experimental scales on a Canadian delinquent sample. *Canadian Journal of Behavioural Science, 11*(1), 21–31.

Gendreau, P., Little, T., & Goggin, C. (1996). A meta-analysis of the predictors of adult offender recidivism: What works! *Criminology, 34*(1), 575–607.

Gibson, M. (2002). *Born to crime: Cesare Lombroso and the origins of biological criminology*. Praeger.

Gifford-Smith, M., Dodge, K. A., Dishion, T. J., & McCord, J. (2005). Peer influence in children and adolescents: Crossing the bridge from developmental to intervention science. *Journal of Abnormal Child Psychology, 33*(3), 255–265.

Giordano, P. C., Cernkovich, S. A., & Rudolph, J. L. (2002). Gender, crime, and desistance: Toward a theory of cognitive transformation. *American Journal of Sociology, 107*(4), 990–1064.

Glenn, A. L., Raine, A., Venables, P. H., & Mednick, S. A. (2007). Early temperament and psychophysiological precursors of adult psychopathic personality. *Journal of Abnormal Psychology, 116*(3), 508–518.

Goddard, H. H. (1972). *Feeblemindedness: Its causes and consequences*. Macmillan. (original work published 1914)

Goddard, T., & Pooley, J. A. (2019). The impact of childhood abuse on adult male prisoners: A systematic review. *Journal of Police and Criminal Psychology, 34*(2), 215–230.

Goldberg, S. (2000). *Attachment and development*. Oxford University Press.

Gonsalves, V. M., Scalora, M. J., & Huss, M. T. (2009). Prediction of recidivism using the Psychopathy Checklist–Revised and the Psychological Inventory of Criminal Thinking Styles within a forensic sample. *Criminal Justice and Behavior, 36*(1), 741–756.

González-Burgos, I., & Feria-Velasco, A. (2008). Serotonin/dopamine interaction in memory formation. In G. Di Giovanni, V. Di Matteo, & E. Esposito (Eds.), *Progress in brain research* (Vol. 172, pp. 603–623). Elsevier.

Goring, C. (1913). *The English convict: A statistical study*. Darling & son.

Gottfredson, M., & Hirschi, T. (1987). The methodological adequacy of longitudinal research on crime. *Criminology, 25*(3), 581–614.

Gottfredson, M. R., & Hirschi, T. (1990). *A general theory of crime*. Stanford University Press.

Gottfried, E. D., & Christopher, S. C. (2017). Mental disorders among criminal offenders: A review of the literature. *Journal of Correctional Health Care, 23*(3), 336–346.

Graham, E. E. (2003). Dialectic contradictions in postmarital relationships. *Journal of Family Communication, 3*(4), 193–214.

Grasmick, H. G., & Bryjak, G. J. (1980). The deterrent effect of perceived severity of punishment. *Social Forces, 59*(2), 471–491.

Grasmick, H. G., Tittle, C. R., Bursik, R. J., Jr., & Arneklev, B. K. (1993). Testing the core empirical implications of Gottfredson and Hirschi's general theory of crime. *Journal of Research in Crime and Delinquency, 30*(1), 5–29.

Green, K. M., Doherty, E. E., Sifat, M. S., & Ensminger, M. E. (2019). Explaining continuity in substance use: The role of criminal justice system involvement over the life course of an urban African American prospective cohort. *Drug and Alcohol Dependence, 195*, 74–81.

Grigorenko, E. L., DeYoung, C. G., Eastman, M., Gretchell, M., Haeffel, G. J., ... Yrigollen, C. M. (2010). Aggressive behavior, related conduct problems, and variation in genes affecting dopamine turnover. *Aggressive Behavior, 36*(3), 158–176.

Guerette, R. T., & Bowers, K. J. (2009). Assessing the extent of crime displacement and diffusion of benefits: A review of situational crime prevention evaluations. *Criminology, 47*(4), 1331–1368.

Ha, O. K., & Beauregard, E. (2016). Sex offending and low self-control: An extension and test of the general theory of crime. *Journal of Criminal Justice, 47*, 62–73.

Hammond, C. (2014). *Cellular and molecular neurophysiology*. Academic Press.

Hanson, R. K., & Bussière, M. T. (1998). Predicting relapse: A meta-analysis of sexual offender recidivism studies. *Journal of Consulting and Clinical Psychology, 66*(2), 348–362.

Hanson, R. K., & Morton-Bourgon, K. E. (2005). The characteristics of persistent sexual offenders: A meta-analysis of recidivism studies. *Journal of Consulting and Clinical Psychology, 73*(6), 1154–1163.

Harden, K. P., Quinn, P. D., & Tucker-Drob, E. M. (2012). Genetically influenced change in sensation seeking drives the rise of delinquent behavior during adolescence. *Developmental Science, 15*(1), 150–163.

Hardy, S. A., Padilla-Walker, L. M., & Carlo, G. (2008). Parenting dimensions and adolescents' internalization of moral values. *Journal of Moral Education, 37*(2), 205–223.

Hare, R. D. (1993). *Without conscience: The disturbing world of the psychopaths among us*. Guilford.

Harris, J. W., & Jones, M. S. (2020). Shaping youths' perceptions and attitudes toward the police: Differences in direct and vicarious encounters with police. *Journal of Criminal Justice*. Online first, https://doi.org/10.1016/j.jcrimjus.2020.101674

Hartley, C. A., & Somerville, L. H. (2015). The neuroscience of adolescent decision-making. *Current Opinion in Behavioral Sciences, 5*, 108–115.

Haslam, N., McGrath, M. J., Viechtbauer, W., & Kuppens, P. (2020). Dimensions over categories: A meta-analysis of taxometric research. *Psychological Medicine, 50*(9), 1418–1432.

Hatcher, R. M., & Roberts, A. L. I. (2019). Can completers, non-completers, and non-starts of community-based offending behavior programs be differentiated by internal treatment readiness factors? *International Journal of Offender Therapy and Comparative Criminology, 63*(7), 1066–1081.

Hawk, S. T., Hale, W. W., Raaijmakers, Q. A. W., & Meeus, W. (2008). Adolescents' perceptions of privacy invasion in reaction to parental solicitation and control. *Journal of Early Adolescence, 28*(4), 583–608.

Hayes, A. F. (2018). *Introduction to mediation, moderation, and conditional process analysis: A regression-based approach* (2nd ed.). Guilford.

Haynie, D. L., & Osgood, D. W. (2005). Reconsidering peers and delinquency: How do peers matter? *Social Forces, 84*(2), 1109–1130.

Hayward, K. (2007). Situational crime prevention and its discontents: Rational choice theory versus the "culture of now." *Social Policy and Administration, 41*(3), 232–250.

Healy, D. (2010). Betwixt and between: The role of psychosocial factors in the early stages of desistance. *Journal of Research in Crime and Delinquency, 47*(4), 419–438.

Heilbrun, K. (2003). Violence risk: From prediction to management. In D. Carson & R. Bull (Eds.), *Handbook of psychology in legal contexts* (pp. 127–143). Wiley.

Heilmann, K., Kahn, M. E., & Tang, C. K. (2021). The urban crime and heat gradient in high and low poverty areas. *Journal of Public Economics*. Online first, https://doi.org/10.1016/j.jpubeco.2021.104408

Henggeler, S. W., Schoenwald, S. K., Borduin, C. M., Rowland, M. D., & Cunningham, P. B. (1998). *Multisystemic treatment of antisocial behavior in children and adolescents*. Guilford.

Hill, J. M., Blokland, A. A. J., & van der Geest, V. R. (2018). Risk factors for self-reported delinquency in emerging adulthood. *European Journal of Criminology, 15*(5), 544–566.

Hindelang, M. J., Gottfredson, M. R., & Garofalo, J. (1978). *Victims of personal crime: An empirical foundation for a theory of personal victimization.* Ballinger.

Hirschfield, A., Newton, A., & Rogerson, M. (2010). Linking burglary and target hardening at the property level: New insights into victimization and burglary protection. *Criminal Justice Policy Review, 21*(3), 319–337.

Hirschi, T. (1969). *Causes of delinquency*. University of California Press.

Hirschi, T. (1979). Separate and unequal is better. *Journal of Research in Crime and Delinquency, 16*(1), 34–38.

Hirschi, T., & Gottfredson, M. (1983). Age and the explanation of crime. *American Journal of Sociology, 89*(3), 552–584.

Hirschi, T., & Gottfredson, M. (1993). Commentary: Testing the general theory of crime. *Journal of Research in Crime and Delinquency, 30*(1), 47–54.

Hirtenlehner, H. (2020). The interaction between self-control and perceived sanction risk; An analysis from the viewpoint of different theories. *Criminal Justice Review, 45*(1), 104–128.

Hochstetler, A. (2001). Opportunities and decisions: Interactional dynamics in robbery and burglary groups. *Criminology, 39*(3), 737–763.

Hochstetler, A. (2002). Sprees and runs: Opportunity construction and criminal episodes. *Deviant Behavior, 23*(1), 45–73.

Hoeben, E. M., Meldrum, R. C., Walker, D., & Young, J. T. N. (2016). The role of peer delinquency and unstructured socializing in explaining delinquency and substance use: A state-of-the-art review. *Journal of Criminal Justice, 47*, 108–122.

Hoeben, E. M., & Thomas, K. J. (2019). Peer and offender decision-making. *Criminology and Public Policy, 18*(4), 759–784.

Hoeve, M., Dubas, J. S., Eichelsheim, V. I., van der Laan, P. H., Smeenk, W., & Gerris, J. R. M. (2009). The relationship between parenting and delinquency: A meta-analysis. *Journal of Abnormal Child Psychology, 37*(6), 749–775.

Hoffmann, F., Lee, D. S., & Lemieux, T. (2020). Growing income inequality in the United States and other advanced economies. *Journal of Economic Perspectives, 34*(4), 52–78.

Hollis-Peel, M. E., Reynald, D. M., van Bavel, M., Elffers, H., & Welsh, B. C. (2011). Guardianship for crime prevention: A critical review of the literature. *Crime, Law and Social Change, 56*(1), 53–70.

Holmes, A. J., Hollinshead, M. O., Roffman, J. L., Smoller, J. W., & Buckner, R. L. (2016). Individual differences in cognitive control circuit anatomy link sensation seeking, impulsivity, and substance use. *Journal of Neuroscience, 36*(14), 4038–4049.

Holodynski, M. (2013). The internalization theory of emotions: A cultural historical approach to the development of emotions. *Mind, Culture, and Activity, 20*(1), 4–38.

Hoogerheide, V., van Wermeskerken, M., Loyens, S. M. M., & van Gog, T. (2016). Learning from video modeling examples: Content kept equal, adults are more effective models than peers. *Learning and Instruction, 44*, 22–30.

Huizinga, D., Esbensen, F.-A., & Weiher, A. W. (1991). Are there multiple paths to delinquency? *Journal of Criminal Law and Criminology, 89*(1), 83–117.

Huizinga, D., & Jakob-Chen, C. (1998). Contemporaneous co-occurrence of serious and violent juvenile offending and other problem behaviors. In R. Loeber & D. P. Farington (Eds.), *Serious and violent juvenile offenders: Risk factors and successful interventions* (pp. 47–67). Sage.

Imai, K., Keele, L., & Yamamoto, T. (2010). Identification, inference, and sensitivity analysis for causal mediation effects. *Statistical Science, 25*(1), 51–71.

Ingram, K. M., Espelage, D. L., Davis, J. P., & Merrin, G. J. (2020). Family violence, sibling, and peer aggression during adolescence: Associations with behavioral health outcomes. *Frontiers in Psychiatry, 11*, Article 26.

Intavia, J., Wolff, K. T., & Piquero, A. R. (2018). Investigating the effects of media consumption on attitudes toward police legitimacy. *Deviant Behavior, 39*(8), 963–980.

Javakhishvili, M., & Vazsonyi, A. T. (2021). Empathy, self-control, callous-unemotionality, and delinquency: Unique and shared developmental antecedents. *Child Psychiatry and Human Development*. Online first, https://doi.org/10.1007/s10578-021-01137-2

Jennings, W. G., Piquero, A. R., & Reingle, J. M. (2012). On the overlap between victimization and offending: A review of the literature. *Aggression and Violent Behavior, 17*(1), 16–26.

Jennings, W. G., & Reingle, J. M. (2012). On the number and shape of developmental/life-course violence, aggression, and delinquent trajectories: A state-of-the-art review. *Journal of Criminal Justice, 40*(6), 472–489.

Jessor, R., & Jessor, S. L. (1977). *Problem behavior and psychosocial development: A longitudinal study of youth*. Academic Press.

Joe, G. W., Simpson, D. D., Dansereau, D. F., & Rowan-Szal, G. A. (2001). Relationships between counseling rapport and drug abuse treatment outcomes. *Psychiatric Services, 52*(9), 1223–1229.

Johnson, S. D., Davies, T., Murray, A., Ditta, P., Belur, J., & Bowers, K. (2017). Evaluation of operation swordfish: A near-repeat target-hardening strategy. *Journal of Experimental Criminology, 13*(4), 505–525.

Johnson, W. L., Giordano, P. C., Longmore, M. A., & Manning, W. D. (2016). Parents, identities, and trajectories of antisocial behavior from adolescence to young adulthood. *Journal of Developmental and Life-Course Criminology, 2*(4), 442–465.

Jolliffe, D., & Farrington, D. P. (2004). Empathy and offending: A systematic review and meta-analysis. *Aggression and Violent Behavior, 9*(5), 441–476.

Jones, S. E., Miller, J. D., & Lynam, D. R. (2011). Personality, antisocial behavior, and aggression: A meta-analytic review. *Journal of Criminal Justice, 39*(4), 329–337.

Joo, Y. S., & Lee, W. K. (2020). Does living in a chaotic home predict adolescent delinquency? A moderated mediation model of impulsivity and school connectedness. *Children and Youth Services*. Online first, https://doi.org/10.1016/j.childyouth.2020.105617

Jose, R., Hipp, J. R., Butts, C. T., Wang, C., & Lakon, C. M. (2016). Network structure, influence, selection, and adolescent delinquent behavior: Unpacking a dynamic process. *Criminal Justice and Behavior, 43*(1), 264–284.

Kaiser, A. J., Davis, H. A., Milich, R., Smith, G. T., & Charnigo, R. (2018). Bidirectional relations of impulsive personality and alcohol across three waves of data collection. *Substance Use and Misuse, 53*(14), 2386–2393.

Kamarck, T. W., Haskett, R. F., Muldoon, M., Flory, J. D., Anderson, B., … Manuck, S. B. (2009). Citalopram intervention for hostility: Results of a randomized clinical trial. *Journal of Consulting and Clinical Psychology, 77*(1), 174–188.

Kang, J. H. (2015). Participation in the community social control, the neighborhood watch groups: Individual- and neighborhood-related factors. *Crime and Delinquency, 61*(2), 188–212.

Kapetanovic, S., Boele, S., & Skoog, T. (2019). Parent-adolescent communication and adolescent delinquency: Unraveling within-family processes from between-family differences. *Journal of Youth and Adolescence, 48*(9), 1707–1723.

Karabanova, O. A., Kovaleva, G. S., Loginova, O. B., & Molcanov, S. V. (2014). Moral orientation on norms of mutual help and responsibility in middle childhood. *Procedia: Social and Behavioral Sciences, 146*, 175–180.

Karaman, N. G. (2013). Predicting the problem behavior in adolescents. *Eurasian Journal of Educational Research, 52*, 137–154.

Karstedt, S., & Farrall, S. (2006). The moral economy of everyday crime. *British Journal of Criminology, 46*(6), 1011–1036.

Kaskela, T., & Pitkänen, T. (2021). Association between the discontinuation of substance use inpatient treatment and the risk of committing a crime leading to imprisonment: A Finnish registry-based 5-year follow-up. *Criminal Behaviour and Mental Health, 31*(3), 171–182.

Katz, C. M., & Fox, A. M. (2010). Risk and protective factors associated with gang-involved youth in Trinidad and Tobago. *Pan American Journal of Public Health, 27*(3), 187–202.

Kennedy, D. E., & Kramer, L. (2008). Improving emotion regulation and sibling relationship quality: The More Fun with Sisters and Brothers program. *Family Relations, 57*(5), 567–578.

Kenny, D. A. (2013). *Mediation: Sensitivity analysis* [webinar]. Retrieved from http://davidakenny.net/webinars/Mediation/Sensitivity/Sensitivity.html.

Kenny, D. A., & Judd, C. M. (2014). Power anomalies in testing mediation. *Psychological Science, 25*(2), 334–339.

Kerr, K. L., Avery, J. A., Barcalow, J. C., Moseman, S. E., Bodurka, J., … Simmons, W. K. (2015). Trait impulsivity is related to ventral ACC and amygdala activity during primary reward anticipation. *Social Affective and Cognitive Neuroscience, 10*(1), 36–42.

Kerr, M., & Stattin, H. (2000). What parents know, how they know it, and several forms of adolescent adjustment: Further support for a reinterpretation of monitoring. *Developmental Psychology, 36*(3), 366–380.

Kerr, M., Stattin, H., & Burk, W. J. (2010). A reinterpretation of parental monitoring in longitudinal perspective. *Journal of Research on Adolescence, 20*(1), 39–64.

Kiesner, J., Poulin, F., & Nicotra, E. (2003). Peer relations across contexts: Individual-network homophily and network inclusion in and after school. *Child Development, 74*(5), 1328–1343.

Kim, J. J., & Jung, M. W. (2006). Neural circuits and mechanisms involved in Pavlovian fear conditioning: A critical review. *Neuroscience and Biobehavioral Reviews, 30*(2), 188–202.

Klein Tuente, S., Bogaerts, S., & Veling, W. (2019). Hostile attribution bias and aggression in adults – A systematic review. *Aggression and Violent Behavior, 46*, 66–81.

Knight, K., Garner, B. R., Simpson, D. D., Morey, J. T., & Flynn, P. M. (2006). An assessment for criminal thinking. *Crime and Delinquency, 52*(1), 159–177.

Knudsen, E. I. (2004). Sensitive periods in the development of the brain and behavior. *Journal of Cognitive Neuroscience, 16*(8), 1412–1425.

Koepfler, J., Brewster, J., Stoloff, M., & Saville, B. (2012). Predicting police aggression: Comparing traditional and non-traditional prediction models. *Journal of Police and Criminal Psychology, 27*(2), 141–149.

Kogler, L., Müller, V. I., Werminghausen, E., Eickhoff, S. B., & Derntl, B. (2020). Do I feel or do I know? Neuroimaging meta-analyses on the multiple facets of empathy. *Cortex, 129*, 341–355.

Kohlberg, L. (1981). *The philosophy of moral development: Moral stages and the idea of justice*. Harper & Row.

Kokka, K. (2020). Social justice pedagogy for whom? Developing privileged students' critical mathematics consciousness. *Urban Review, 52*(4), 778–803.

Kolko, D. J., & Kazdin, A. E. (1991). Aggression and psychopathology in matchplaying and firesetting children: A replication and extension. *Journal of Clinical Child Psychology, 20*(2), 191–201.

Kornhauser, R. R. (1978). *Social sources of delinquency: An appraisal of analytic models*. University of Chicago Press.

Kovandzic, T. V., Sloan, J. J., & Vieraitis, L. M. (2004). "Striking out" as crime reduction policy: The impact of "three strikes" laws on crime rates in U.S. cities. *Justice Quarterly, 21*(2), 207–239.

Kramer-Kuhn, A. M., & Farrell, A. D. (2016). The promotive and protective effects of family factors in the context of peer and community risks for aggression. *Journal of Youth and Adolescence, 45*(4), 793–811.

Krebs, M.-C., Schüler, A., & Scheiter, K. (2019). Just follow my eyes: The influence of model-observer similarity on eye movement modeling examples. *Learning and Instruction, 61*, 126–137.

Kroner, D. G., & Mills, J. F. (2001). The accuracy of five risk appraisal instruments in predicting institutional misconduct and new convictions. *Criminal Justice and Behavior, 28*(4), 471–489.

Krueger, R. F., Hicks, B. M., Patrick, C., Carlson, S. R., Iacono, W. G., & McGue, M. (2002). Etiological connections among substance dependence, antisocial behavior, and personality: Modeling the externalizing spectrum. *Journal of Abnormal Psychology, 111*(3), 411–424.

Krueger, R. F., Markon, K. E., Patrick, C. J., Benning, S. D., & Kramer, M. D. (2007). Linking antisocial behavior, substance use, and personality: An integrative quantitative model of the adult externalizing spectrum. *Journal of Abnormal Psychology, 116*(4), 645–666.

Kubrin, C. E. (2000). Racial heterogeneity and crime: Measuring static and dynamic effects. *Research in Community Sociology, 10*, 189–218.

Kuhn, T. S. (2012). *The structure of scientific revolutions* (4th ed.). University of Chicago Press. (original work published 1962)

Kurtz, D. L., & Zavala, E. (2017). The importance of social support and coercion to risk of impulsivity and juvenile offending. *Crime and Delinquency, 63*(4), 1838–1860.

Lahey, B. B., Hinton, K. E., Burgess, L., Meyer, F. C., Landman, B. A., … Zald, D. H. (2021). Dispositional negative emotionality in childhood and adolescence predicts structural variation in the amygdala and caudal anterior cingulate during early adulthood: Theoretically and empirically based tests. *Research on Child and Adolescent Psychopathology*. Online first, https://doi.org/10.1007/s10802-021-00811-2

Lahey, B. B., Van Hulle, C. A., D'Onofrio, B. M., Rodgers, J. E., & Waldman, I. D. (2008). Is parental knowledge of their adolescent offspring's whereabouts and peer associations spuriously associated with offspring delinquency? *Journal of Abnormal Child Psychology, 36*(6), 807–823.

Laible, D. J., & Thompson, R. A. (2000). Mother-child discourse, attachment security, shared positive affect, and early conscience development. *Child Development, 71*(5), 1424–1440.

Laird, R. D., Zeringue, M. M., & Lambert, E. S. (2018). Negative reactions to monitoring: Do they undermine the ability of monitoring to protect adolescents? *Journal of Adolescence, 63*, 75–84.

Land, K. C., Teske, R. H. C., & Zheng, H. (2012). The differential short-term impacts of executions on felony and non-felony homicides. *Criminology and Public Policy, 11*(3), 541–563.

Landenberger, N. A., & Lipsey, M. W. (2005). The positive effects of cognitive-behavioral programs for offenders: A meta-analysis of factors associated with effective treatment. *Journal of Experimental Criminology, 1*(4), 451–476.

Langevin, R. (2003). A study of the psychosexual characteristics of sex killers: Can we identify them before it is too late? *International Journal of Offender Therapy and Comparative Criminology, 47*(4), 366–382.

LaSpada, N., Delker, E., East, P., Blanco, E., Delva, J., … Gahagan, S. (2020). Risk taking, sensation seeking and personality as related to changes in substance use from adolescence to young adulthood. *Journal of Adolescence, 82*, 23–31.

Lauritsen, J. L. (1993). Sibling resemblance in juvenile delinquency: Findings from the national youth survey. *Criminology, 31*(3), 387–409.

Leaw, J. N., Ang, R. P., Huan, V. S, Chan, W. T., & Cheong, S. A. (2015). Re-examining of Moffitt's theory of delinquency through agent based modeling. *PLoS ONE, 10*(6). https://doi.10.1371/journal.pone.0126752

Le Blanc, M., McDuff, P., & Kaspy, N. (1998). Family and early adolescent delinquency: A comprehensive sequential family control model. *Early Child Development and Care, 142*(1), 63–91.

Lemert, E. M. (1967). *Human deviance, social problems, and social control*. Prentice Hall.

Leung, R. K., Toumbourou, J. W., & Hemphill, S. A. (2014). The effect of peer influence and selection processes on adolescent alcohol use: A systematic review of longitudinal studies. *Health Psychology Review, 8*(4), 426–457.

Leve, L. D., & Chamberlain, P. (2004). Female juvenile offenders: Defining an early-onset pathway for delinquency. *Journal of Child and Family Studies, 13*(4), 439–452.

Levy, M. P., & Tartaro, C. (2010). Repeat victimization: A study of auto theft in Atlantic City using the WALLS variables to measure environmental indicators. *Criminal Justice Policy Review, 21*(3), 296–318.

Li, H., Penzo, M. A., Taniguchi, H., Kopec, C. D., Huang, J., & Li, B. (2013). Experience-dependent modification of a central amygdala fear circuit. *Nature Neuroscience, 16*(3), 332–341.

Li, X., & Ang, R. P. (2019). Parental arrest and adolescent delinquency in Singapore: The moderating roles of narcissism, callous-unemotional traits, and impulsivity. *Journal of Child and Family Studies, 28*(3), 776–783.

Lin, B., Liew, J., & Perez, M. (2019). Measurement of self-regulation in early childhood: Relations between laboratory and performance-based measures of effortful control and executive functioning. *Early Childhood Research Quarterly, 47*, 1–8.

Lindblom, A., & Kajalo, S. (2011). The use and effectiveness of formal and informal surveillance in reducing shoplifting: A survey in Sweden, Norway and Finland. *International Review of Retail, Distribution and Consumer Research, 21*(2), 111–128.

Lindblom, S., Eriksson, L., & Hiltunen, A. J. (2017). Evaluation of the cognitive intervention programme "A New Direction" targeting young offenders in Sweden. *Journal of Scandinavian Studies in Criminology and Crime Prevention, 18*(2), 176–190.

Lindegaard, M. R., Bernasco, W., Jacques, S., & Zenebergen, B. (2014). Posterior gains and immediate pains: Offender emotions before, during and after robberies. In J.-L. Van Gelder, H. Elffers, D. Reynald, & D. Nagin (Eds.), *Affect and cognition in criminal decision-making* (pp. 58–76). Routledge.

Lindenbergh, V. M., Kleemans, E. R., & Ferwerda, J. (2020). Activities, access control, and crime: A quasi-experimental study regarding entry gates at train stations in the Netherlands. *European Journal on Criminal Policy and Research*. Online first, https://doi.org/10.1007/s10610-020-09472-1

Lippold, M. A., Coffman, D. L., & Greenberg, M. T. (2014). Investigating the potential causal relationship between parental knowledge and youth risky behavior: A propensity score analysis. *Prevention Science, 15*(6), 869–878.

Liu, L., & Bachman, R. (2021). Self-identity and persistent offending: A quantitative test of identity theory of desistance. *Journal of Offender Rehabilitation*. Online first, https://doi.org/10.1080/10509674.2021.1931623

Ljubin-Golub, T., Vrselja, I., & Pandžić, M. (2017). The contribution of sensation seeking and the big five personality factors to different types of delinquency. *Criminal Justice and Behavior, 44*(11), 1518–1536.

Logue, S. F., & Gould, T. J. (2014). The neural and genetic basis of executive function: Attention, cognitive flexibility, and response inhibition. *Pharmacology, Biochemistry and Behavior, 123*, 45–54.

Lombroso, C. (2008). *Criminal man* (transl., M. Gibson & N. H. Rafter). Duke University Press. (original work published 1876)

Lonardo, R. A., Giordano, P. C., Longmore, M. A., & Manning, W. D. (2009). Parents, friends, and romantic partners: Enmeshment in deviant networks and adolescent delinquency involvement. *Journal of Youth and Adolescence, 38*(3), 367–383.

Lonczak, H. S., Huang, B., Catalano, R. F., Hawkins, J. D., Hill, K. G., … Kosterman, R. (2001). The social predictors of adolescent alcohol misuse: A test of the social development model. *Journal of Studies on Alcohol, 62*, 179–189.

Longobardi, C., & Badenes-Ribera, L. (2019). The relationship between animal cruelty in children and adolescent and interpersonal violence: A systematic review. *Aggression and Violent Behavior, 46*, 201–211.

LoParo, D., & Waldman, I. (2014). Twins' rearing environment similarity and childhood externalizing disorders: A test of the equal environments assumption. *Behavior Genetics, 44*(6), 606–613.

Lorenz, E. (1979). *Predictability: Does the flap of a butterfly's wings in Brazil set off a tornado in Texas?* Paper presented at the annual meeting of the American Association for the Advancement of Science, Washington, DC.

Lösel, F., & Bender, D. (2014). Aggressive, delinquent, and violent outcomes of school bullying: Do family and individual factors have a protective function? *Journal of School Violence, 13*(1), 59–79.

Lott, J. R. (1998). *More guns, less crime: Understanding crime and gun control laws.* University of Chicago Press.

Lu, H., Chen, Q., Xie, C., Liang, Q., Wang, L., ... Wang, J. (2020). Interparental conflict and delinquency among Chinese adolescents: Parental knowledge as a mediator and deviant peer affiliation as a moderator. *Frontiers in Psychology, 11*, Article 1775.

Lundahl, B. W., Nimer, J., & Parsons, B. (2006). Preventing child abuse: A meta-analysis of parent training programs. *Research on Social Work Practice, 16*(3), 251–262.

Ly, T., Fedoroff, J. P., & Briken, P. (2019). A narrative review of research on clinical responses to the problem of sexual offenses in the last decade. *Behavioral Sciences and the Law, 38*(2), 117–134.

Lykken, D. T. (1957). A study of anxiety in the sociopathic personality. *Journal of Abnormal and Social Psychology, 55*(1), 6–10.

Lynne-Landsman, S. D., Graber, J. A., Nichols, T. R., & Botvin, G. J. (2011). Is sensation seeking a stable trait or does it change over time? *Journal of Youth and Adolescence, 40*(1), 48–58.

Maassen, G. H., & Bakker, A. B. (2001). Suppressor variables in path models: Definitions and interpretations. *Sociological Methods and Research, 30*(2), 241–270.

Macdonald, J. M. (1961). *The murderer and his victim.* Charles C Thomas.

Magill, M., Colby, S. M., Orchowski, L., Murphy, J. G., Hoadley, A., ... Barnett, N. P. (2017). How does brief motivational intervention change heavy drinking and harm among underage young adult drinkers? *Journal of Consulting and Clinical Psychology, 85*(5), 447–458.

Maglinte, J. A., Reyes, M. E. S., & Balajadia, H. A. (2016). "I choked her but I did not punch her": Constructions of intimate partner violence among men in the Philippines. *Psychological Studies, 61*(4), 321–330.

Maillet, D., & Schacter, D. L. (2016). From mind wandering to involuntary retrieval: Age-related differences in spontaneous cognitive processes. *Neuropsychologia, 80*, 142–156.

Malmberg, M., Kleinjan, M., Overbeek, G., Vermulst, A. A., Lammers, J., & Engels, R. C. M. E. (2013). Are there reciprocal relationships between substance use risk personality profiles and alcohol or tobacco use in early adolescence? *Addictive Behaviors, 38*(12), 2851–2859.

Malti, T., Keller, M., & Buchmann, M. (2012). Do moral choices make us feel good? The development of adolescents' emotions following moral decision making. *Journal of Research on Adolescence, 23*(2), 389–397.

Mandelbröt, B. (1990). Fractals—A geometry of nature. *New Scientist, 15,* 38–43.

Mandracchia, J. T., & Morgan, R. D. (2011). Understanding criminals' thinking: Further examination of the Measure of Offender Thinking Styles–Revised. *Assessment, 18*(4), 442–452.

Mann, F. D., Patterson, M. W., Grotzinger, A. D., Kretsch, N., Tackett, J. L., … Harden, P. (2016). Sensation seeking, peer deviance, and genetic influences on adolescent delinquency: Evidence for person-environment correlation and interaction. *Journal of Abnormal Psychology, 125*(5), 679–691.

Manski, C. F., & Pepper, J. V. (2013). Deterrence and the death penalty: Partial identification analysis using repeated cross sections. *Journal of Quantitative Criminology, 29*(1), 123–141.

Martin, G., Bergen, H. A., Richardson, A. S., Roeger, L., & Allison, S. (2004). Correlates of firesetting in a community sample of young adolescents. *Australian and New Zealand Journal of Psychiatry, 38*(3), 148–154.

Martin, L. N., & Delgado, M. R. (2011). The influence of emotion regulation on decision-making under risk. *Journal of Cognitive Neuroscience, 23*(9), 2569–2581.

Martin, T. K., & Martin, R. H. (2017). Police suicide and PTSD: Connection, prevention, and trends. *Law Enforcement Executive Forum, 17*(2), 27–42.

Martinelli, A., Ackermann, K., Bernhard, A., Freitag, C. M., & Schwenck, C. (2018). Hostile attribution bias and aggression in children and adolescents: A systematic literature review on the influence of aggression subtype and gender. *Aggression and Violent Behavior, 39*, 25–32.

Maruna, S. (2001). *Making good: How ex-convicts reform and build their lives.* American Psychological Association.

Maruna, S. (2004). Desistance and explanatory style: A new direction in the psychology of reform. *Journal of Contemporary Criminal Justice, 20*(2), 184–200.

Maruna, S., & Copes, H. (2005). What have we learned from five decades of neutralization research? *Crime and Justice, 32*, 221–320.

Matsueda, R. L. (1992). Reflected appraisals, parental labeling, and delinquency: Specifying a symbolic interactionist theory. *American Journal of Sociology, 97*(6), 1577–1611.

Matthews, K. M., White, M. C., & Long, R. G. (1999). Why study the complexity sciences in the social sciences? *Human Relations, 52*(4), 439–462.

Matza, D. (1964). *Delinquency and drift.* Wiley.

Maume, M. O., & Lee, M. R. (2003). Social institutions and violence: A sub-national test of institutional anomie theory. *Criminology, 41*(4), 1137–1172.

Mazerolle, L., Soole, D. W., & Rombouts, S. (2007). *Crime prevention research reviews No. 1: Disrupting street-level drug markets.* U. S. Department of Justice Office of Community Oriented Policing Services.

McAlaney, J., Helmer, S. M., Stock, C., Vriesacker, B., Van Hal, G., … Mikolajczyk, R. (2015). Personal and perceived peer use of and attitudes toward alcohol among

university and college students in seven EU countries: Project SNIPE. *Journal of Studies on Alcohol and Drugs, 76*(3), 430–438.
McCartan, L. M., & Gunnison, E. (2007). Examining the origins and influence of low self-control. *Journal of Crime and Justice, 30*(1), 35–60.
McCarthy, P., Schiraldi, V., & Shark, M. (2016, October). The future of youth justice: A community-based alternative to the youth prison model. *New thinking in community corrections*. National Institute of Justice.
McClelland, G. H., & Judd, C. M. (1993). Statistical difficulties of detecting interactions and moderator effects. *Psychological Bulletin, 114*(2), 376–390.
McCord, J., & Ensminger, M. E. (1997). Multiple risks and comorbidity in an African-American population. *Criminal Behaviour and Mental Health, 7*(4), 339–352.
McCoy, S. S., Dimler, L. M., Samuels, D. V., & Natsuaki, M. N. (2019). Adolescent susceptibility to deviant peer pressure: Does gender matter? *Adolescent Research Review, 4*(1), 59–71.
McCuish, E., Lussier, P., & Corrado, R. (2018). Incarceration as a turning point? The impact of custody experiences and identity change on community reentry. *Journal of Developmental and Life-Course Criminology, 4*(4), 427–448.
McCulloch, A., & McMurran, M. (2008). Evaluation of a treatment programme for alcohol-related aggression. *Criminal Behaviour and Mental Health, 18*(4), 224–231.
McGloin, J. M., Sullivan, C. J., Piquero, A. R., Blokland, A., & Nieuwbeerta, P. (2011). Marriage and offending specialization: Expanding the impact of turning points and the process of desistance. *European Journal of Criminology, 8*(5), 361–376.
McGloin, J. M., & Thomas, K. J. (2019). Peer influence and delinquency. *Annual Review of Criminology, 2*, 241–264.
McHugh, R. K., Hearon, B. A., & Otto, M. W. (2010). Cognitive-behavioral therapy for substance use disorders. *Psychiatric Clinics of North America, 33*(3), 511–525.
McMurran, M. (1994). *The psychology of addiction*. Taylor & Francis.
McMurran, M. (2007). What works in substance misuse treatments for offenders? *Criminal Behaviour and Mental Health, 17*(4), 225–233.
McMurran, M. (2009). Motivational interviewing with offenders: A systematic review. *Legal and Criminological Psychology, 14*(1), 83–100.
McMurran, M., & Delight, S. (2017). Processes of change in an offender personality disorder pathway prison progression unit. *Criminal Behaviour and Mental Health, 27*(3), 254–264.
McPhedran, S. (2009). A review of the evidence for associations between empathy, violence, and animal cruelty. *Aggression and Violent Behavior, 14*(1), 1–4.
Mead, G. H. (1934). *Mind, self, and society*. University of Chicago Press.
Mednick, S. A., Gabrielli, W. F., & Hutchings, B. (1984). Genetic influences in criminal convictions: Evidence from an adoption study. *Science, 224*(4651), 891–894.
Meehl, P. E. (1989). Schizotaxia revisited. *Archives of General Psychiatry, 46*, 935–944.
Meehl, P. E. (2004). What's in a taxon? *Journal of Abnormal Psychology, 113*(1), 39–43.

Megens, K. C. I. M., & Weerman, F. M. (2012). The social transmission of delinquency: Effects of peer attitudes and behavior revisited. *Journal of Research in Crime and Delinquency, 49*(3), 420–443.

Meichenbaum, D. H. (1977). *Cognitive behavior modification: An integrative approach.* Plenum.

Meldrum, R. C. (2008). Beyond parenting: An examination of the etiology of self-control. *Journal of Criminal Justice, 36*(3), 244–251.

Merton, R. (1957). *Social theory and social structure*. Free Press.

Messner, S. F., & Rosenfeld, R. (1994). *Crime and the American dream*. Wadsworth.

Micalizzi, L., Sokolovsky, A. W., Janssen, T., & Jackson, K. M. (2019). Parental social support and sources of knowledge interact to predict children's externalizing behavior over time. *Journal of Youth and Adolescence, 48*(3), 484–494.

Mikkonen, J., Savolainen, J., Aaltonen, M., & Martikainen, P. (2020). Using age difference and sex similarity to detect evidence of sibling influence on criminal offending. *Psychological Medicine*. Online first, https://doi.org/10.1017/S0033291720003724

Milaniak, I., & Widom, C. S. (2015). Does child abuse and neglect increase risk for perpetration of violence inside and outside the home? *Psychology of Violence, 5*(3), 246–255.

Milgram, S., Sabini, J. E., & Silver, M. E. (1992). *The individual in a social world: Essays and experiments*. McGraw-Hill.

Miller, J., & Davis, R. C. (2008). Unpacking public attitudes to the police: Contrasting perceptions of misconduct with traditional measures of satisfaction. *International Journal of Police Science and Management, 10*(1), 9–22.

Miller, L. (2004). Good cop – bad cop: Problem officers, law enforcement culture, and strategies for success. *Journal of Police and Criminal Psychology, 19*(2), 30–48.

Miller, W. R., & Rollnick, S. (1991). *Motivational interviewing: Preparing people to change addictive behavior*. Guilford.

Mills, J. F., Kroner, D. G., & Forth, A. E. (2002). Measures of criminal attitudes and associates (MCAA): Development, factor structure, reliability, and validity. *Assessment, 9*(3), 240–253.

Mitchell, D., & Tafrate, R. C. (2012). Conceptualization and measurement of criminal thinking: Initial validation of the criminogenic thinking profile. *International Journal of Offender Therapy and Comparative Criminology, 56*(7), 1080–1102.

Mitchell, R. L. C., & Phillips, L. H. (2007). The psychological, neurochemical and functional neuroanatomical mediators of effects of positive and negative mood on executive functions. *Neuropsychologist, 45*(4), 617–629.

Moffitt, T. E. (1993). Adolescence-limited and life-course-persistent antisocial behavior: A developmental taxonomy. *Psychological Review, 100*(4), 674–701.

Monahan, K. C., Steinberg, L., Cauffman, E., & Mulvey, E. P. (2009). Trajectories of antisocial behavior and psychosocial maturity from adolescence to young adulthood. *Developmental Psychology, 45*(6), 1654–1668.

Morgan, R. D., Kroner, D. G., Mills, J. F., Bauer, R. L., & Serna, C. (2014). Treating justice involved persons with mental illness: Preliminary evaluation of a comprehensive treatment program. *Criminal Justice and Behavior, 41*(7), 902–916.

Morris, R. G., & Copes, H. (2012). Exploring the temporal dynamics of the neutralization/delinquency relationship. *Criminal Justice Review, 37*(4), 442–460.

Mrazek, A. J., Mrazek, M. D., Carr, P. C., Delegard, A. M., Ding, M. G., ... Schooler, J. W. (2020). The feasibility of attention training for reducing mind-wandering and digital multitasking in high schools. *Education Sciences, 10*, Article 201.

Muftić, L. R., Finn, M. A., & Marsh, E. A. (2015). The victim-offender overlap, intimate partner violence, and sex: Assessing differences among victims, offenders, and victim-offenders. *Crime and Delinquency, 61*(7), 899–926.

Muftić, L. R., & Updegrove, A. H. (2018). The mediating effect of self-control on parenting and delinquency: A gendered approach with a multinational sample. *International Journal of Offender Therapy ad Comparative Criminology, 62*(10), 3058–3076.

Mulford, C. F., Blachman-Demner, D. R., Pitzer, L., Schubert, C. A., Piquero, A. R., & Mulvey, E. P. (2018). Victim offender overlap: Dual trajectory examination of victimization and offending among young felony offenders over seven years. *Victims and Offenders, 13*(1), 1–27.

Mulvey, E. P. (2012, November). *The pathways to desistance study: Design and methods.* Paper presented at the American Society of Criminology Annual Meeting, Chicago, IL. Retrieved on 06-03-2013 from http://citation.allacademic.com/meta/p574246_index.html

Murray, J., & Farrington, D. P. (2005). Parental imprisonment: Effects on boys' antisocial behaviour and delinquency through the life-course. *Journal of Child Psychology and Psychiatry, 46*(12), 1269–1278.

Murray, J., & Farrington, D. P. (2010). Risk factors for conduct disorder and delinquency: Key findings from longitudinal studies. *Canadian Journal of Psychiatry, 55*(10), 633–642.

Mustaine, E. E., & Tewksbury, R. (2000). Comparing the lifestyles of victims, offenders, and victim-offenders: A routine activity theory assessment of similarities and differences for criminal incident participants. *Sociological Focus, 33*(3), 339–362.

Nagin, D. S. (2013). Deterrence in the twenty-first century: A review of the evidence. *Crime and Justice, 42*(1), 199–263.

Nagin, D., & Paternoster, R. (2000). Population heterogeneity and state dependence: State of the evidence and directions for future research. *Journal of Quantitative Criminology, 16*(2), 117–144.

Narvaes, R., & de Almeida, R. M. M. (2014). Aggressive behavior and three neurotransmitters: Dopamine, GABA, and serotonin—A review of the last 10 years. *Psychology and Neuroscience, 7*(4), 601–607.

Narvaez, D. (2005). The neo-Kohlbergian tradition and beyond: Schemas, expertise and character. In C. Pope-Edwards & G. Carlo (Eds.), *Nebraska symposium on motivation, Vol. 51: Moral motivation through the lifespan* (pp. 119–163). University of Nebraska Press.

National Institute on Drug Abuse (NIDA). (2020, June). *Drugs, brains, and behavior: The science of addiction*. Author.

Newman, J. P., MacCoon, D. G., Vaughn, L. J., & Sadeh, N. (2005). Validating a distinction between primary and secondary psychopathy with measures of Gray's BIS and BAS constructs. *Journal of Abnormal Psychology, 114*(2), 319–323.

Nickoletti, P., & Taussig, H. N. (2006). Outcome expectancies and risk behaviors in maltreated adolescents. *Journal of Research on Adolescence, 16*(2), 217–228.

Novak, K. B., & Crawford, L. A. (2010). Routine activities as determinants of gender determinants of gender differences in delinquency. *Journal of Criminal Justice, 38*(5), 913–920.

Nye, F. I. (1958). *Family relationships and delinquent behavior.* Wiley.

Nyman-Metcalf, K., & Täks, E. (2013). Simplifying the law—can ICT help us? *International Journal of Law and Information Technology, 21*(3), 239–268.

Oberth, C., Zheng, Y., & McMahon, R. J. (2017). Violence exposure subtypes differentially mediate the relation between callous-unemotional traits and adolescent delinquency. *Journal of Abnormal Child Psychology, 45*(8), 1565–1575.

Okuda, M., Martins, S. S., Wall, M. W., Chen, C., Santaella-Tenorio, J. … Duarte, C. S. (2019). Do parenting behaviors modify the way sensation seeking influences antisocial behaviors? *Journal of Child Psychology and Psychiatry, 60*(2), 169–177.

Olvera-Cortés, M. E., Anguiano-Rodriguez, P., López-Vázquez, M. A., & Alfaro, J. M. C. (2008). Serotonin/dopamine interaction in learning. In G. Di Giovanni, V. Di Matteo, & E. Esposito (Eds.), *Progress in brain research* (Vol. 172, pp. 567–602). Elsevier.

Osgood, D. W., Wilson, J. K., O'Malley, P. M., Bachman, J. G., & Johnston, L. D. (1996). Routine activities and individual deviant behavior. *American Sociological Review, 61*(4), 635–655.

Özdemir, S. B., Stattin, H., & Özdemir, M. (2016). Youth's initiations of civic and political discussions in class: Do youth's perceptions of teachers' behaviors matter and why? *Journal of Youth and Adolescence, 45*(11), 2233–2245.

Padilla-Walker, L. M., & Son, D. (2019). Longitudinal associations among routine disclosure, the parent-child relationship, and adolescents' prosocial and delinquent behaviors. *Journal of Social and Personal Relationships, 36*(6), 1853–1871.

Palmer, E. J. (2003). An overview of the relationship between moral reasoning and offending. *Australian Psychologist, 38*(3), 165–174.

Palmer, E. J., & Hollin, C. R. (2004). Predicting reconviction using the Psychological Inventory of Criminal Thinking Styles with English prisoners. *Legal and Criminological Psychology, 9*(1), 57–68.

Panayioutou, G., Fanti, K. A., & Lazarou, C. (2015). Fearful victims and fearless bullies? Subjective reactions to emotional imagery scenes of children involved in school aggression. *Personality and Individual Differences, 78*, 29–33.

Panzram, C. (1928, November). *Typescript of Panzram manuscript: Part I, section 1.* Special Collection at San Diego State University (Henry Lesser, donor).

Pardini, D. (2016). Empirically based strategies for preventing juvenile delinquency. *Child and Adolescent Psychiatric Clinics of North America, 25*(2), 257–268.

Park, J.-H. (2006). Aggressor/victim subtypes and teacher factors in first grade as risk factors for later mental health symptoms and school functioning. *Asia Pacific Education Review, 7*(1), 108–119.

Parks, M. J., Osgood, D. W., Felson, R. B., Wells, S., & Graham, K. (2013). Third party involvement in barroom conflicts. *Aggressive Behavior, 39*(4), 257–268.

Paternoster, R. (2010). How much do we really know about criminal deterrence? *Journal of Criminal Law and Criminology, 100*(3), 765–823.

Paternoster, R., & Bushway, S. (2009). Desistance and the "feared self": Toward an identity theory of criminal desistance. *Journal of Criminal Law and Criminology, 99*(4), 1103–1156.

Paulus, M. P., & Yu, A. J. (2012). Emotion and decision-making: Affect-driven belief systems in anxiety and depression. *Trends in Cognitive Sciences, 16*(9), 476–483.

Pavlov, I. P. (1927). *Conditioned reflexes: An investigation of the physiological activity of the cerebral cortex.* Oxford University Press.

Pearson, F. S., & Lipton, D. S. (1999). A meta-analytic review of the effectiveness of corrections-based treatments for drug abuse. *The Prison Journal, 79*(4), 384–410.

Peay, J. (2009). Mental illness, dangerousness and protecting society. *Psychiatry, 8*(12), 490–492.

Petrich, D. M., Liu, H., & Nedelec, J. L. (2020). The longitudinal associations between motivation, self-regulatory capacities, and future-oriented cognition and behavior among serious young offenders. *Law and Human Behavior, 44*(5), 424–436.

Phelps, E. A., O'Connor, K. J., Gatenby, C., Gore, J. C., Grillon, C., & Davis, M. (2001). Activation of the left amygdala to a cognitive representation of fear. *Nature Neuroscience, 4*(4), 437–441.

Phillips, D. P. (1980). The deterrent effect of capital punishment: New evidence on an old controversy. *American Journal of Sociology, 86*(1), 139–148.

Phillips, K. E., & Schrodt, P. (2015). Sibling confirmation as a moderator of rivalries and relational outcomes in sibling relationships. *Journal of Family Communication, 15*(1), 58–74.

Piaget, J. (1932). *The moral judgment of the child.* The Free Press.

Piaget, J. (1954). *The construction of reality in the child.* Basic Books.

Piotrowski, A. (2019). Relation of inmates' entitlement to identification with criminal groups, narcissism and readiness for self-improvement. *Current Issues in Personality Psychology, 7*(3), 252–263.

Piquero, A. R., Farrington, D. P., Welsh, B. C., Tremblay, R., & Jennings, W. G. (2009). Effects of early family/parent training programs on antisocial behavior and delinquency. *Journal of Experimental Criminology, 5*(2), 83–120.

Piquero, A. R., Jennings, W. G., Diamond, B., Farrington, D. P., Tremblay, R. E., … Reingle Gonzalez, J. M. (2016). A meta-analysis update on the effects of early family/parent training programs on antisocial behavior and delinquency. *Journal of Experimental Criminology, 12*(2), 229–248.

Pittelkow, M.-M., aan het Rot, M., Seidel, L. J., Feyel, N., & Roest, A. M. (2021). Social anxiety and empathy: A systematic review and meta-analysis. *Journal of Anxiety Disorders.* Online first, https://doi.org/10.1016/j.janxdis.2021.102357

Plomin, R., Willerman, L., & Loehlin, J. C. (1976). Resemblance in appearance and the equal environments assumption in twin studies of personality traits. *Behavior Genetics, 6*(1) 43–52.

Polaschek, D. L., & Collie, R. M. (2004). Rehabilitating serious violent adult offenders: An empirical and theoretical stocktake. *Psychology, Crime and Law, 10*(3), 321–334.

Polaschek, D. L. L., & Ross, E. C. (2010). Do early therapeutic alliance, motivation, and stages of change predict therapy change for high-risk, psychopathic violent prisoners? *Criminal Behaviour and Mental Health, 20*(2), 100–111.

Popper, K. R. (1999). *The logic of scientific discovery* (rev. ed.). Routledge.

Pornari, C. D., & Wood, J. (2010). Peer and cyber aggression in secondary school students: The role of moral disengagement, hostile attribution bias, and outcome expectancies. *Aggressive Behavior, 36*(2), 81–94.

Pratt, T. C., & Cullen, F. T. (2000). The empirical status of Gottfredson and Hirschi's general theory of crime: A meta-analysis. *Criminology, 38*(3), 931–964.

Pratt, T. C., Cullen, F. T., Sellers, C. S., Winfree, T., Madensen, T. D., … Gau, J. M. (2010). The empirical status of social learning theory: A meta-analysis. *Justice Quarterly, 27*(6), 766–802.

Pratt, T. C., & Turanovic, J. J. (2018). Celerity and deterrence. In D. S. Nagin, F. T. Cullen, & C. L. Jonson (Eds.), *Deterrence, choice, and crime: Contemporary perspectives—Advances in criminological theory* (Vol. 23, pp. 187–210). Routledge.

Pratt, T. C., Turner, M. G., & Piquero, A. R. (2004). Parental socialization and community context: A longitudinal analysis of the structural sources of low self-control. *Journal of Research in Crime and Delinquency, 41*(3), 219–243.

Prigogine, I., & Stengers, I. (1984). *Order out of chaos*. Bantam Books.

Prins, E. H. (2008). "Maturing out" and the dynamics of the biographical trajectories of hard drug addicts. *Forum: Qualitative Social Research, 9*(1), Article 30.

Prochaska, J. O., & DiClemente, C. C. (2005). The transtheoretical approach. In J. C. Norcross & M. R. Goldfried (Eds.), *Handbook of psychotherapy integration* (pp. 147–171). Oxford University Press.

Racz, S. J., & McMahon, R. J. (2011). The relationship between parental knowledge and monitoring and child and adolescent conduct problems: A 10-year update. *Clinical Child and Family Psychology Review, 14*(4), 377–398.

Raine, A. (2019). The neuromoral theory of antisocial, violent, and psychopathic behavior. *Psychiatry Research, 277*, 64–69.

Raine, A., Venables, P. H., & Mednick, S. A. (1997). Low resting heart rate at age 3 years predisposes to aggression at age 11 years: Evidence from the Mauritius child health project. *Journal of the American Academy of Child and Adolescent Psychiatry, 36*(10), 1457–1464.

Ray, J. V., Frick, P. J., Thornton, L. C., Myers, T. D. W., Steinberg, L., & Cauffman, E. (2017). Callous-unemotional traits predict self-reported offending in adolescent boys: The mediating role of delinquent peers and the moderating role of parenting practices. *Developmental Psychology, 53*(2), 319–328.

Rebocho, M. F., & Silva, P. (2014). Target selection in rapists: The role of environmental and contextual factors. *Aggression and Violent Behavior, 19*(1), 42–49.

Reeping, P. M., & Hemenway, D. (2020). The association between weather and the number of daily shootings in Chicago (2012–2016). *Injury Epidemiology, 7*, 1.

Reiss, A. J. (1951). Delinquency as the failure of personal and social controls. *American Sociological Review, 16*(2), 196–207.

Reiss, A. J., & Farrington, D. P. (1991). Advancing knowledge about co-offending: Results from a prospective longitudinal survey of London males. *Journal of Criminal Law and Criminology, 82*(2), 360–395.

Ren, L., Zhao, J. S., & He, N. P. (2019). Broken windows theory and citizen engagement in crime prevention. *Justice Quarterly, 36*(1), 1–30.

Reppetto, T. A. (1976). Crime prevention and the displacement phenomenon. *Crime and Delinquency, 22*, 166–177.

Rest, J. R., Narvaez, D., Thoma, S. J., & Bebeau, M. J. (2000). A neo-Kohlbergian approach to morality research. *Journal of Moral Education, 29*(4), 381–395.

Restivo, E., & Lanier, M. M. (2015). Measuring the contextual effects and mitigating factors of labeling theory. *Justice Quarterly, 32*(1), 116–141.

Reyes, H. L. M., Foshee, V. A., Gottfredson, N. C., Ennett, S. T., & Chen, M. S. (2020). Codevelopment of delinquency, alcohol use, and aggression toward peers and dates: Multitrajectory patterns and predictors. *Journal of Research on Adolescence, 30*(4), 1025–1038.

Rhee, S. H., & Waldman, I. D. (2002). Genetic and environmental influences on antisocial behavior: A meta-analysis of twin and adoption studies. *Psychological Bulletin, 128*(3), 490–529.

Rhineberger-Dunn, G., Mack, K. Y., & Baker, K. M. (2017). Comparing demographic factors, background characteristics, and workplace perceptions as predictors of burnout among community corrections officers. *Criminal Justice and Behavior, 44*(2), 205–225.

Ridenour, T. A., Caldwell, L. L., Coatsworth, D., & Gold, M. A. (2011). Directionality between tolerance of deviance and deviant behavior is age-moderated in chronically stressed youth. *Journal of Child and Adolescent Substance Abuse, 20*(2), 184–204.

Riggs Romaine, C. L. (2019). Psychosocial maturity and risk-taking in emerging adults: Extending our understanding beyond delinquency. *Emerging Adulthood, 7*(4), 243–257.

Rioux, C., Castellanos-Ryan, N., Parent, S., & Séguin, J. R. (2016). The interaction between temperament and the family environment in adolescent substance use and externalizing behaviors: Support for diathesis–stress or differential susceptibility? *Developmental Review, 40*, 117–150.

Roberts, P., & Stewart, B. A. (2018). Defining the "generalist specialist" niche for Pleistocene Homo sapiens. *Nature Human Behaviour, 2*, 542–550.

Rocheleau, G. C., & Chavez, J. M. (2015). Guilt by association: The relationship between deviant peers and deviant labels. *Deviant Behavior, 36*(3), 167–186.

Rocque, M. (2017). *Desistance from crime: New advances in theory and research.* Palgrave Macmillan.

Rocque, M., Posick, C., & Paternoster, R. (2016). Identities through time: An exploration of identity as a cause of desistance. *Justice Quarterly, 33*(1), 45–72.

Rolls, E. T. (2015). Limbic systems for emotion and for memory, but no single limbic system. *Cortex, 62*, 119–157.

Romer, D., Reyna, V. F., & Satterthwaite, T. D. (2017). Beyond the stereotypes of adolescent risk taking: Placing the adolescent brain in developmental context. *Developmental Cognitive Neuroscience, 27*, 19–34.

Romeral, L. F., Fernández, J. S., & Fraguela, J. A. G. (2018). Moral reasoning in adolescent offenders: A meta-analytic review. *Psicothema, 30*(3), 289–294.

Romero-Martinez, A., Murciano-Marti, S., & Moya-Albiol, L. (2019). Is sertraline a good pharmacological strategy to control anger? Results of a systematic review. *Behavioral Sciences, 9*(5), Article 57.

Rowe, D. C., & Farrington, D. P. (1997). The familial transmission of criminal convictions. *Criminology, 35*(1), 177–201.

Rowe, D. C., & Gulley, B. L. (1992). Sibling effects on substance use and delinquency. *Criminology, 30*(2), 217–233.

Ruiz, M. A., Pincus, A. L., & Schinka, J. A. (2008). Externalizing pathology and the five-factor model: A meta-analysis of personality traits associated with antisocial personality disorder, substance use disorder, and their co-occurrence. *Journal of Personality Disorders, 22*(4), 365–388.

Ruscio, J., Walters, G. D., Marcus, D. K., & Kaczetow, W. (2010). Comparing the relative fit of categorical and dimensional latent variable models using consistency tests. *Psychological Assessment, 22*(1), 10–19.

Sacchetti, B., Scelfo, B., & Strata, P. (2005). The cerebellum: Synaptic changes and fear conditioning. *Neuroscientist, 11*(3), 217–227.

Sah, P., Faber, E. S. L., Lopez de Armentia, M., & Power, J. (2003). The amygdaloid complex: Anatomy and physiology. *Physiology Reviews, 83*(3), 803–834.

Salcido, C. G., Ray, J. V., Caudy, M., Viglione, J., & Walter, R. J. (2019). Associations between psychopathic traits and readiness for change: An exploratory analysis. *Personality and Individual Differences, 141*, 86–91.

Sampson, R. J., & Groves, W. B. (1989). Community structure and crime: Testing social-disorganization theory. *American Journal of Sociology, 94*(4), 774–802.

Sampson, R. J., & Laub, J. H. (1993). *Crime in the making: Pathways and turning points through life.* Harvard University Press.

Sampson, R. J., & Laub, J. H. (2003). Life-course desisters? Trajectories of crime among delinquent boys followed to age 70. *Criminology, 41*(3), 555–592.

Sampson, R. J., & Laub, J. H. (2016). Turning points and the future of life-course criminology: Reflections on the 1986 criminal careers report. *Journal of Research in Crime and Delinquency, 53*(3), 321–335.

Sampson, R. J., Raudenbush, S. W., & Earls, F. (1997). Neighborhoods and violent crime: A multilevel study of collective efficacy. *Science, 277*, 918–924.

Sandstrom, H., & Huerta, S. (2013, September). *The negative effects of instability on child development: A research synthesis*. Urban Institute.

Saner, H., & Ellickson, P. (1996). Concurrent risk factors for adolescent violence. *Journal of Adolescent Health, 19*(2), 94–103.

Sarmiento, A., Herrera-López, M., & Zych, I. (2019). Is cyberbullying a group process? Online and offline bystanders of cyberbullying act as defenders, reinforcers and outsiders. *Computers in Human Behavior, 99*, 328–334.

Saunders, P., & Skar, P. (2001). Archetypes, complexes and self-organization. *Journal of Analytical Psychology, 46*(2), 305–323.

Savolainen, J. (2000). Inequality, welfare state, and homicide: Further support for the institutional anomie theory. *Criminology, 38*(4), 1021–1042.

Schalkwijk, F., Stams, G. J., Stegge, H., Dekker, J., & Peen, J. (2016). The conscience as a regulatory function: Empathy, shame, pride, guilt, and moral orientation in delinquent adolescents. *International Journal of Offender Therapy and Comparative Criminology, 60*(6), 675–693.

Schmidt, S. N. L., Hass, J., Kirsch, P., & Mier, D. (2021). The human mirror neuron system—A common neural basis for social cognition? *Psychophysiology*. Online first, https://doi.org/10.1111/psyp.13781

Schurz, M., R., Radua, J., Tholen, M. G., Maliske, L., Margulies, D. S., … Kanske, P. (2020). Toward a hierarchical model of social cognition: A neuroimaging meta-analysis and integrative review of empathy and theory of mind. *Psychological Bulletin*. Online first, http://dx.doi.org/10.1037/bul0000303

Schwind, C., Buder, J., Cress, U., & Hesse, F. W. (2012). Preference-inconsistent recommendations: An effective approach for reducing confirmation bias and stimulating divergent thinking? *Computers and Education, 58*(2), 787–796.

Sellier, A.-L., Scopelliti, I., & Morewedge, C. K. (2019). Debiasing training improves decision making in the field. *Psychological Science, 30*(9), 1371–1379.

Seo, C., Kim, B., & Kruis, N. E. (2021). Variation across police response models for handling encounters with people with mental illnesses: A systematic review and meta-analysis. *Journal of Criminal Justice*. Online first, https://doi.org/10.1016/j.jcrimjus.2020.101752

Seo, D., Patrick, C. J., & Kennealy, P. J. (2008). Role of serotonin and dopamine system interactions in the neurobiology of impulsive aggression and its comorbidity with other clinical disorders. *Aggression and Violent Behavior, 13*(5), 383–395.

Sharma, L., Markon, K. E., & Clark, L. A. (2014). Toward a theory of distinct types of "impulsive" behaviors: A meta-analysis of self-report and behavioral measures. *Psychological Bulletin, 140*(2), 374–408.

Shaw, C. R., & McKay, H. (1942). *Juvenile delinquency and urban areas*. University of Chicago Press.

Shechner, T., Hong, M., Britton, J. C., Pine, D. S., & Fox, N. A. (2014). Fear conditioning and extinction across development: Evidence from human studies and animal models. *Biological Psychology, 100*, 1–12.

Sherman, L. W., & Berk, R. A. (1984). The specific deterrent effects of arrest for domestic assault. *American Sociological Review, 49*(2), 261–272.

Shover, N. (1983). The later stages of ordinary property offender careers. *Social Problems, 31*(2), 208–218.

Shure, M. B. (1999, April). Preventing violence the problem-solving way. *Juvenile Justice Bulletin*. U.S. Department of Justice.

Shure, M. B., & Spivack, G. (1980). Interpersonal problem solving as a mediator of behavioral adjustment in preschool and kindergarten children. *Journal of Applied Developmental Psychology, 1*(1), 29–43.

Sidebottom, A., Thornton, A., Tompson, L., Belur, J., Tilley, N., & Bowers, K. (2017). A systematic review of tagging as a method to reduce theft in retail environments. *Crime Science, 6*, Article 7.

Siegfried, C., & Woessner, G. (2016). The explanatory power of the general theory of crime: A comparative analysis of a general population and serious offender sample. *Deviant Behavior, 37*(5), 509–524.

Silva, J. R., & Greene-Colozzi, E. A. (2021). An exploratory study of failed mass shootings in America. *Security Journal*. Online first, https://doi.org/10.1057/s41284-020-00281-z

Simckes, M., Willits, D., McFarland, M., McFarland, C., Rowhani-Rahbar, A., & Hajat, A. (2021). The adverse effects of policing on population health: A conceptual model. *Social Science and Medicine*. Online first, https://doi.org/10.1016/j.socscimed.2021.114103

Simmons, C., Fine, A., Knowles, A., Frick, P. J., Steinberg, L., & Cauffman, E. (2020). The relation between callous-unemotional traits, psychosocial maturity, and delinquent behavior among justice-involved youth. *Child Development, 91*(1), e120–e133.

Simon, H. A. (1982). *Models of bounded rationality*. MIT Press.

Simonen, J., Kataja, K., Pirskanen, H., Holmila, M., & Tigerstedt, C. (2017). Trusting and misleading. Parents' and children's communication and negotiation about alcohol as described by teenagers. *Addiction Research and Theory, 25*(4), 342–348.

Simourd, D. J. (1997). The Criminal Sentiments Scale-Modified and Pride in Delinquency Scale: Psychometric properties and construct validity of two measures of criminal attitudes. *Criminal Justice and Behavior, 24*(1), 52–70.

Skardhamar, T., Monsbakken, C. W., & Lyngstad, T. H. (2014). Crime and the transition to marriage: The role of the spouse's criminal involvement. *British Journal of Criminology, 54*(3), 411–427.

Skardhamar, T., & Savolainen, J. (2014). Changes in criminal offending around the time of job entry: A study of employment and desistance. *Criminology, 52*(2), 263–291.

Skinner, B. F. (1938). *The behavior of organisms: An experimental analysis*. Appleton-Century-Crofts.

Smallwood, J., Fishman, D. J., & Schooler, J. W. (2007). Counting the cost of an absent mind: Mind wandering as an underrecognized influence on educational performance. *Psychonomic Bulletin and Review, 14*(2), 230–236.

Sobel, D. M., & Legare, C. H. (2014). Causal learning in children. *WIREs: Cognitive Science, 5*(4), 413–427.

Sohn, D.-W. (2016). Residential crimes and neighbourhood built environment: Assessing the effectiveness of crime prevention through environmental design (CPTED). *Cities, 52*, 86–93.

Soleimani, M., Yousefi, & Ghazanfarianpour, S. (2020). The role of intelligence profiles and executive functions (selective attention and switching) in predicting creativity components. *Journal of Modern Rehabilitation, 14*(3), 177–190.

Sommer, M., Meinhardt, J., Rothmar, C., Döhnel, K., Hajak, G., … Sodian, B. (2014). Me or you? Neural correlates of moral reasoning in everyday conflict situations in adolescents and adults. *Social Neuroscience, 9*(5), 452–470.

Song, J., & Oh, I. (2017). Investigation of the bystander effect in school bullying: Comparison of experiential, psychological and situational factors. *School Psychology International, 38*(3), 319–336.

Sparkes, A. C., & Day, J. (2016). Aging bodies and desistance from crime: Insights from the life stories of offenders. *Journal of Aging Studies, 36*, 47–58.

Spruit, A., Schalkwijk, F., van Vugt, E., & Stams, G. J. (2016). The relationship between self-conscious emotions and delinquency: A meta-analysis. *Aggression and Violent Behavior, 28*, 12–20.

Stafford, M., Gale, C. R., Mishra, G., Richards, M., Black, S., & Kuh, D. L. (2015). Childhood environment and mental wellbeing at age 60–64 years: Prospective evidence from the MRC national survey of health and development. *PLoS ONE,* 10(6). https://doi.org/10.1371/journal.pone.0126683

Stafford, M. C., & Warr, M. (1993). A reconceptualization of general and specific deterrence. *Journal of Research in Crime and Delinquency, 30*(2), 123–135.

Stefan, C. A., & Avram, J. (2019). Investigating attachment status effects on preschoolers' empathic perspective taking. *Child and Youth Care Forum, 48*(5), 663–675.

Stein, L. A. R., Martin, R., Clair-Michaud, M., Lebeau, R., Hurlbur, W., … Rohsenow, D. (2020). A randomized clinical trial of motivational interviewing plus skills training vs. relaxation plus education and 12-steps for substance using incarcerated youth: Effects on alcohol, marijuana, and crimes of aggression. *Drug and Alcohol Dependence*. Online first, https://doi.org/10.1016/j.drugalcdep.2019.107774

Steinberg, L. (2008). A social neuroscience perspective on adolescent risk-taking. *Developmental Review, 28*(1), 78–106.

Stephenson, L. J., Edwards, S. G., & Bayliss, A. P. (2021). From gaze perception to social cognition: The shared-attention system. *Perspectives on Psychological Science*. Online first, https://doi.org/10.1177/1745691620953773

Stern, J. A., & Cassidy, J. (2018). Empathy from infancy to adolescence: An attachment perspective on the development of individual differences. *Developmental Review, 47*, 1–22.

Storer, H. L., Casey, E. A., & Herrenkohl, T. I. (2017). Developing "whole school" bystander interventions: The role of school-settings in influencing adolescents responses to dating violence and bullying. *Children and Youth Services Review, 74*, 87–95.

Stylianou, I., Charalampous, K., & Stavrinides, P. (2019). Psychopathic traits and adolescents' delinquency: A short-term longitudinal study. *European Journal of Developmental Psychology, 16*(4), 417–432.

Sutherland, E. H. (1947). *Principles of criminology* (4th ed.). J.B. Lippincott.

Sykes, G. M., & Matza, D. (1957). Techniques of neutralization: A theory of delinquency. *American Sociological Review, 22*(6), 664–670.

Szpak, M., & Bialecka-Pikul, M. (2020). Links between attachment and theory of mind in childhood: Meta-analytic review. *Social Development, 29*(3), 653–673.

Takahashi, A., Shimamoto, A., Boyson, C. O., De Bold, J. F., & Miczek, K. A. (2010). GABAB receptor modulation of serotonin neurons in the dorsal raphé nucleus and escalation of aggression in mice. *Journal of Neuroscience, 30*(35), 11771–11780.

Tan, J. X., & Fajardo, M. L. R. (2017). Efficacy of multisystemic therapy in youths ages 10–17 with severe antisocial behaviour and emotional disorders: Systematic review. *London Journal of Primary Care, 9*(6), 95–103.

Tangney, J. P., Stuewig, J., Furukawa, E., Kopelovich, S., Meyer, P. J., & Cosby, B. (2012). Reliability, validity, and predictive utility of the 25-item Criminogenic Cognitions Scale (CCS). *Criminal Justice and Behavior, 39*(10), 1340–1360.

Tannenbaum, F. (1938). *Crime and the community*. Ginn & Company.

Tarter, R. E., Kirisci, L., Habeych, M., Reynolds, M., & Vanyukov, M. (2004). Neurobehavior disinhibition in childhood predisposes boys to substance use disorder by young adulthood: Direct and mediated etiologic pathways. *Drug and Alcohol Dependence, 73*(2), 121–132.

Taxman, F. S., Rhodes, A. G., & Dumenci, L. (2011). Construct and predictive validity of criminal thinking scales. *Criminal Justice and Behavior, 38*(2), 174–187.

Tehrani, H. D., & Yamini, S. (2020). Parenting practices, self-control and anti-social behavior: Meta-analytic structural equation modeling. *Journal of Criminal Justice*. Online first, https://doi.org/10.1061/j.jcrimjust.2020.101687

Teixeira, S. (2016). Beyond broken windows: Youth perspectives on housing abandonment and its impact on individual and community well-being. *Child Indicators Research, 9*(3), 581–607.

Thomas, K. (2018). Revisiting delinquent attitudes: Measurement, dimensionality and behavioral effects. *Journal of Quantitative Criminology, 34*(1), 313–341.

Thornberg, R., Wänström, L., & Jungert, T. (2018). Authoritative classroom climate and its relations to bullying victimization and bystander behaviors. *School Psychology International, 39*(6), 663–680.

Thornberry, T. P. (1987). Toward an interactional theory of delinquency. *Criminology, 25*(4), 863–892.

Tiihonen, J., Halonen, P., Tiihonen, L., Kautiainen, H., Storvik, M., & Callaway, J. (2017). The association of ambient temperature and violent crime. *Scientific Reports, 7*(1), 6543.

Timmer, A., Antonaccio, O., & French, M. T. (2020). Hot or cold processing? Adolescent decision-making and delinquency. *Justice Quarterly*. Online first, https://doi.org/10.1080/07418825.2020.1730424

Toby, J. (1957). Social disorganization and stake in conformity: Complementary factors in the predatory behavior of hoodlums. *Journal of Criminal Law and Criminology, 48*(1), 12–17.

Tonry, M. (2008). Learning from the limitations of deterrence research. *Crime and Justice, 37*(1), 279–311.

Topalli, V., Higgins, G. E., & Copes, H. (2014). A causal model of neutralization acceptance and delinquency: Making the case for an individual difference model. *Criminal Justice and Behavior, 41*(5), 553–573.

Torry, Z. D., & Billick, S. B. (2011). Implications of antisocial parents. *Psychiatric Quarterly, 82*(4), 275–285.

Tracy, J. L., & Robins, R. W. (2004). Putting the self into self-conscious emotions: A theoretical model. *Psychological Inquiry, 15*(2), 103–125.

Trivedi, J. K., Tripathi, A., Dhanasekaran, S., & Moussaoui, D. (2014). Preventive psychiatry: Concept appraisal and future directions. *International Journal of Social Psychiatry, 60*(4), 321–329.

Trivedi-Bateman, N. (2019). The combined roles of moral emotion and moral rules in explaining acts of violence using a situational action theory approach. *Journal of Interpersonal Violence*. Online first, https://doi.org/10.1177/0886260519852634

Troop-Gordon, W., Frosch, C. A., Wienke Totura, C. M., Bailey, A. N., Jackson, J. D., & Dvorak, R. D. (2019). Predicting the development of pro-bullying bystander behavior: A short-term longitudinal analysis. *Journal of School Psychology, 77*, 77–89.

Trucco, E. M., Colder, C. R., & Wieczorek, W. F. (2011). Vulnerability to peer influence: A moderated mediation study of early adolescent alcohol use initiation. *Addictive Behaviors, 36*(7), 729–736.

Tsuchimine, S., Yasui-Furukori, N., Kaneda, A., Saito, M., Sugawara, N., & Kaneko, S. (2009). Minor genetic variants of the dopamine D4 receptor (DRD4) polymorphism are associated with novelty seeking in healthy Japanese subjects. *Genetic Progress in Neuro-Psychopharmacology & Biological Psychiatry, 33*(7), 1232–1235.

Ttofi, M. M., Farrington, D. P., Lösel, F., & Loeber, R. (2011). The predictive efficacy of school bullying versus later offending: A systematic/meta-analytic review of longitudinal studies. *Criminal Behaviour and Mental Health, 21*(2), 80–89.

Ullman, S. E., & Knight, R. A. (1992). Fighting back: Women's resistance to rape. *Journal of Interpersonal Violence, 7*(1), 31–43.

United Nations Office on Drugs and Crime. (2011). *United Nations crime trends survey (2010)*. Author.

Vachon, D. D., Lynam, D. R., & Johnson, J. A. (2014). The (non)relation between empathy and aggression: Surprising results from a meta-analysis. *Psychological Bulletin, 140*(3), 751–773.

Valasik, M., & Barton, M. S. (2018). The George Wilson effect: Does intergenerational closure and collective efficacy reduce juvenile delinquency in a neighborhood? *Deviant Behavior, 39*(12), 1658–1671.

van der Stouwe, T., Asscher, J. J., Hoeve, M., van der Laan, P. H., & Stams, G. J. J. M. (2016). Social skills training for juvenile delinquents: Post-treatment changes. *Journal of Experimental Criminology, 12*(4), 515–536.

van Dijk, A., de Castro, B. O., Thomaes, S., & Poorthuis, A. M. G. (2018). Was it meant to be mean? Young children's hostile attributional bias and intent attribution skills. *Social Development, 27*(4), 683–698.

Varghese, F. P., Charlton, S. R., Wood, M., & Trower, E. (2014). Temporal discounting and criminal thinking: Understanding cognitive processes to align services. *Psychological Services, 11*(2), 171–178.

Vaughn, M. G., Fu, Q., Beaver, K. M., DeLisi, M., Perron, B. E., & Howard, M. O. (2011). Effects of childhood adversity on bullying and cruelty to animals in the United States: Findings from a national sample. *Journal of Interpersonal Violence, 26*(17), 3509–3525.

Veltri, C. O., Sellbom, M., Graham, J. R., Ben-Porath, Y. S., Forbey, J. D., & White, R. S. (2014). Distinguishing personality psychopathology five (PSY-5) characteristics associated with violent and nonviolent juvenile delinquency. *Journal of Personality Assessment, 96*(2), 158–165.

Venables, N. C., Foell, J., Yancey, J. R., Beaver, K. M., Iacono, W. G., & Patrick, C. J. (2018). Integrating criminological and mental health perspectives on low self-control: A multi-domain analysis. *Journal of Criminal Justice, 56*, 2–10.

Vieraitis, L. M., Kovandzic, T. V., & Marvell, T. B. (2007). The criminogenic effects of imprisonment: Evidence from state panel data, 1974–2002. *Criminology and Public Policy, 6*(3), 589–622.

Vowell, P. R., & May, D. C. (2000). Another look at classic strain theory: Poverty status, perceived blocked opportunity, and gang membership as predictors of adolescent violent behavior. *Sociological Inquiry, 70*(1), 42–60.

Wahlstrom, D., White, T., & Luciana, M. (2010). Neurobehavioral evidence for change in dopamine system activity during adolescence. *Neuroscience and Biobehavioral Reviews, 34*(5), 631–648.

Wainwright, L., Nee, C., & Vrij, A. (2018). "I don't know how, but I'll figure it out somehow": Future possible selves and aspirations in "at-risk" early adolescents. *International Journal of Offender Therapy and Comparative Criminology, 62*(2), 504–523.

Walsh, A., & Wright, J. P. (2015). Biosocial criminology and its discontents: A critical realist philosophical analysis. *Criminal Justice Studies, 28*(1), 124–140.

Walsh, M.-T., & Dinan, T. G. (2001). Selective serotonin reuptake inhibitors and violence: A review of the available evidence. *Acta Psychiatrica Scandinavica, 104*(2), 84–91.

Walters, G. D. (1990). *The criminal lifestyle: Patterns of serious criminal conduct.* Sage.

Walters, G. D. (1992a). Drug-seeking behavior: Disease or lifestyle? *Professional Psychology: Research and Practice, 23*(2), 139–145.

Walters, G. D. (1992b). A meta-analysis of the gene-crime relationship. *Criminology, 30*(4), 595–613.

Walters, G. D. (1995). The Psychological Inventory of Criminal Thinking Styles: Part 1: Reliability and preliminary validity. *Criminal Justice and Behavior, 22*(3), 307–325.

Walters, G. D. (1997a). A confirmatory factor analysis of the Lifestyle Criminality Screening Form. *Criminal Justice and Behavior, 24*(2), 294–308.

Walters, G. D. (1997b). Predicting short-term release outcome using the LCSF and PICTS. *Journal of Mental Health in Corrections Consortium, 43*, 18–25.

Walters, G. D. (1998a). The Lifestyle Criminality Screening Form: Psychometric properties and practical utility. *Journal of Offender Rehabilitation, 27*(3–4), 9–23.

Walters, G. D. (1998b). Planning for change: An alternative to treatment planning with sexual offenders. *Journal of Sex and Marital Therapy, 24*(3), 217–229.

Walters, G. D. (2000). Spontaneous remission from alcohol, tobacco, and other drug abuse: Seeking quantitative answers to qualitative questions. *American Journal of Drug and Alcohol Abuse, 26*(3), 443–460.

Walters, G. D. (2001a). Development of a Fear-of-Change Scale for the Psychological Inventory of Criminal Thinking Styles (PICTS). *Journal of Offender Rehabilitation, 34*(1), 1–8.

Walters, G. D. (2001b). The shaman effect in counseling clients with alcohol problems. *Alcoholism Treatment Quarterly, 19*(3), 31–43.

Walters, G. D. (2002). The heritability of alcohol abuse and dependence: A meta-analysis of behavior genetic research. *American Journal of Drug and Alcohol Abuse, 28*(3), 557–584.

Walters, G. D. (2003a). Changes in criminal thinking and identity in novice and experienced inmates: Prisonization revisited. *Criminal Justice and Behavior, 30*(4), 399–421.

Walters, G. D. (2003b). Changes in outcome expectancies and criminal thinking following a brief course of psychoeducation. *Personality and Individual Differences, 35*(3), 691–701.

Walters, G. D. (2004). Changes in positive and negative crime expectancies in inmates exposed to a brief psychoeducational intervention: Further data. *Personality and Individual Differences, 37*(3), 505–512.

Walters, G. D. (2005). Predicting institutional adjustment with the Lifestyle Criminality Screening Form and Psychological Inventory of Criminal Thinking Styles. *International Journal of Forensic Mental Health, 4*(1), 63–70.

Walters, G. D. (2006a). *Lifestyle theory: Past, present, and future.* Nova Science Publishers.

Walters, G. D. (2006b). *The PICTS composite scales and recidivism: Predicting release outcome in inmates previously enrolled in psychological programming.* Unpublished manuscript.

Walters, G. D. (2007a). Correlations between the Psychological Inventory of Criminal Thinking Styles and World-View Rating Scale in male federal prisoners. *Criminal Behaviour and Mental Health, 17*(1), 184–188.

Walters, G. D. (2007b). Measuring proactive and reactive criminal thinking with the PICTS: Correlations with outcome expectancies and hostile attribution biases. *Journal of Interpersonal Violence, 22*(4), 371–385.

Walters, G. D. (2007c). Predicting institutional adjustment with the Lifestyle Criminality Screening Form and the Antisocial Features and Aggression scales of the PAI. *Journal of Personality Assessment, 88*(1), 9–105.

Walters, G. D. (2008). Self-report measures of psychopathy, antisocial personality, and criminal lifestyle: Testing and validating a two-dimensional model. *Criminal Justice and Behavior, 35*(12), 1459–1483.

Walters, G. D. (2011a). The latent structure of life-course-persistent antisocial behavior: Is Moffitt's developmental taxonomy a true taxonomy? *Journal of Consulting and Clinical Psychology, 79*(1), 96–105.

Walters, G. D. (2011b). Taking the next step: Combining incrementally valid indicators to improve recidivism prediction. *Assessment, 18*(2), 227–233.

Walters, G. D. (2012). Substance abuse and criminal thinking: Testing the countervailing, mediation, and specificity hypotheses. *Law and Human Behavior, 36*(6), 506–512.

Walters, G. D. (2013). Testing the specificity postulate of the violence graduation hypothesis: Meta-analyses of the animal cruelty-offending relationship. *Aggression and Violent Behavior, 18*(6), 797–802.

Walters, G. D. (2014a). Crime and substance misuse in adjudicated delinquent youth: The worst of both worlds. *Law and Human Behavior, 38*(2), 139–150.

Walters, G. D. (2014b). An item response theory analysis of the Psychological Inventory of Criminal Thinking Styles: Comparing male and female probationers and prisoners. *Psychological Assessment, 26*(3), 1050–1055.

Walters, G. D. (2014c). Relationships among race, education, criminal thinking, and recidivism: Moderator and mediator effects. *Assessment, 21*(1), 82–91.

Walters, G. D. (2014d). Testing the direct, indirect, and moderated effects of childhood animal cruelty on future aggressive and non-aggressive offending. *Aggressive Behavior, 40*(3), 238–249.

Walters, G. D. (2015a). Cognitive mediation of crime continuity: A causal mediation analysis of the past crime–future crime relationship. *Crime and Delinquency, 61*(9), 1234–1256.

Walters, G. D. (2015b). Criminal and substance involvement from adolescence to adulthood: Precursors, mediators, and long-term effects. *Justice Quarterly, 32*(4), 729–747.

Walters, G. D. (2015c). The decision to commit crime: Rational or nonrational? *Criminology, Criminal Justice Law, and Society, 16*(3), 1–18.

Walters, G. D. (2015d). Parental attitude toward deviance as a predictor of delinquency: Making the connection via perception and cognition. *Journal of Adolescence, 39*, 27–35.

Walters, G. D. (2015e). Proactive criminal thinking and the transmission of differential association: A cross-lagged multi-wave path analysis. *Criminal Justice and Behavior, 42*(11), 1128–1144.

Walters, G. D. (2015f). Recidivism and the Worst of Both Worlds hypothesis: Do substance misuse and crime interact or accumulate? *Criminal Justice and Behavior, 42*(4), 435–451.

Walters, G. D. (2016a). Age of crime/substance onset and crime/drug versatility as dimensions of the "Worst of Both Worlds" effect. *Criminal Justice Policy Review, 27*(7), 668–683.

Walters, G. D. (2016b). Breaking the cycle demonstration project: Using a quasi-experimental analysis to test the "Worst of Both Worlds" hypothesis and risk principle. *Journal of Experimental Criminology, 12*(1), 127–141.

Walters, G. D. (2016c). Criminal thought content and criminal thought process as mediators of peer influence: Combined versus individual effects. *Criminal Justice Review, 41*(3), 318–334.

Walters, G. D. (2016d). Friends, cognition, and delinquency: Proactive and reactive criminal thinking as mediators of the peer influence and peer selection effects among male delinquents. *Justice Quarterly, 33*(6), 1055–1079.

Walters, G. D. (2016e). Low self-control, peer rejection, reactive criminal thinking, and delinquent peer associations: Connecting the pieces of the crime puzzle. *Journal of Developmental and Life-Course Criminology, 2*(2), 209–231.

Walters, G. D. (2016f). Mediating the distal crime-drug relationship with proximal reactive criminal thinking. *Psychology of Addictive Behaviors, 30*(1), 128–137.

Walters, G. D. (2016g). The parent-peer interface: Does inductive parenting reduce the criminogenic effect of delinquent peers. *Youth Violence and Juvenile Justice, 14*(4), 411–425.

Walters, G. D. (2016h). Proactive and reactive criminal thinking, psychological inertia, and the crime continuity conundrum. *Journal of Criminal Justice, 46*, 45–51.

Walters, G. D. (2016i). Proactive criminal thinking, cold heartedness, and counselor rapport in correctional clients participating in substance abuse treatment. *Personality and Individual Differences, 98*, 239–243.

Walters, G. D. (2016j). Reflected appraisals and self-view in delinquency development: An analysis of retrospective accounts from members of the Racine birth cohorts. *Journal of Criminal Justice, 47*, 100–107.

Walters, G. D. (2016k). Working alliance between substance abusing offenders and their parole officers and counselors: Its impact on outcome and role as a mediator. *Journal of Criminal Justice, 39*(3), 421–437.

Walters, G. D. (2017a). Animal cruelty and firesetting as behavioral markers of fearlessness and disinhibition: Putting two-thirds of Macdonald's triad to work: *Journal of Forensic Psychiatry and Psychology, 28*(1), 10–23.

Walters, G. D. (2017b). The drug-crime connection in adolescent and adult respondents: Interaction versus addition. *Journal of Drug Issues, 47*(2), 205–216.

Walters, G. D. (2017c). Effect of a brief cognitive behavioural intervention on criminal thinking and prison misconduct in male inmates: Variable-oriented and person-oriented analyses. *Criminal Behaviour and Mental Health, 27*(5), 457–469.

Walters, G. D. (2017d). Measuring low self-control and reactive criminal thinking in the NLSY–Child Sample: One construct or two? *American Journal of Criminal Justice, 42*(2), 314–328.

Walters, G. D. (2017e). *Modelling the criminal lifestyle: Theorizing at the edge of chaos*. Palgrave Macmillan.

Walters, G. D. (2017f). Proactive criminal thinking and deviant identity as mediators of the peer influence effect. *Youth Violence and Juvenile Justice, 15*(3), 281–298.

Walters, G. D. (2017g). Reactive criminal thinking as a consequence of low self-control and prior offending. *Deviant Behavior, 38*(2), 119–129.

Walters, G. D. (2018a). Callous-unemotional traits and moral disengagement as antecedents to the peer influence effect: Moderation or mediation? *Journal of Crime and Justice, 41*(3), 259–275.

Walters, G. D. (2018b). Change in the perceived certainty of punishment as an inhibitor of post-juvenile offending in serious delinquents: Deterrence at the adult transition. *Crime and Delinquency, 64*(10), 1306–1325.

Walters, G. D. (2018c). Child and adolescent maltreatment as a mediator of continuity in callous-unemotional traits and low self-control. *Children and Youth Services Review, 84*, 26–34.

Walters, G. D. (2018d). College as a turning point: Crime deceleration as a function of college attendance and improved cognitive control. *Emerging Adulthood, 6*(5), 336–346.

Walters, G. D. (2018e). Does drug use inhibit crime deceleration or does crime inhibit drug use deceleration? A test of the reciprocal risk postulate of the Worst of Both Worlds hypothesis. *Substance Use and Misuse, 53*(10), 1681–1687.

Walters, G. D. (2018f). Getting specific about psychological inertia: Mediating the past crime–future crime relationship with self-efficacy for a conventional lifestyle. *Criminal Justice Review, 43*(2), 186–201.

Walters, G. D. (2018g). Mediating the relationship between parental control/support and offspring delinquency: Self-efficacy for a conventional lifestyle versus self-efficacy for deviance. *Crime and Delinquency, 64*(5), 606–624.

Walters, G. D. (2018h). Personality and crime: Mediating the agreeableness-offending and conscientiousness-offending relationships with proactive and reactive criminal thinking. *Personality and Individual Differences, 129*, 166–170.

Walters, G. D. (2018i). Positive and negative social influences and crime acceleration during the transition from childhood to adolescence: The interplay of risk and protective factors. *Criminal Behaviour and Mental Health, 28*(5), 414–423.

Walters, G. D. (2018j). Procedural justice, legitimacy beliefs, and moral disengagement in emerging adulthood: Explaining continuity and desistance in the moral model of criminal lifestyle development. *Law and Human Behavior, 42*(1), 37–49.

Walters, G. D. (2018k). Resistance to peer influence and crime desistance in emerging adulthood: A moderated mediation analysis. *Law and Human Behavior, 42*(6), 520–530.

Walters, G. D. (2018l). Sibling delinquency as a risk factor for future offending: An exploratory analysis. *Youth Violence and Juvenile Justice, 16*(4), 343–357.

Walters, G. D. (2018m). Unsupervised routine activities as a mediator of the parental knowledge-delinquency relationship. *Justice Quarterly, 35*(5), 871–894.

Walters, G. D. (2019a). Animal cruelty and bullying: Behavioral markers of delinquency risk or causal antecedents of delinquent behavior. *International Journal of Law and Psychiatry, 62*, 77–84.

Walters, G. D. (2019b). Are the effects of parental control/support and peer delinquency on future offending cumulative or interactive? A multiple group analysis of 10 longitudinal studies. *Journal of Criminal Justice, 60*, 13–24.

Walters, G. D. (2019c). Early attachment and narcissistic entitlement: Tracing the roots of adolescent proactive criminal thinking. *Journal of Developmental and Life-Course Criminology, 5*(2), 266–285.

Walters, G. D. (2019d). Gang influence: Mediating the gang-delinquency relationship with proactive criminal thinking. *Criminal Justice and Behavior, 46*(7), 1044–1062.

Walters, G. D. (2019e). Maturing out of delinquency: Unpacking the effects of identity achievement and future orientation on crime desistance. *Self and Identity, 18*(3), 267–283.

Walters, G. D. (2019f). Peer influence or projection bias? Predicting respondent delinquency with perceptual measures of peer delinquency in 22 samples. *Journal of Adolescence, 70*, 1–12.

Walters, G. D. (2019g). Predicting early adolescent offending with criminal victimization and delinquent peer associations by way of negative attitudes toward the police. *Law and Human Behavior, 43*(6), 517–526.

Walters, G. D. (2019h). Psychological inertia revisited: Replicating and extending the differential effect of proactive and reactive criminal thinking on crime continuity. *Deviant Behavior, 40*(2), 156–170.

Walters, G. D. (2019i). Social control versus social learning: Self-efficacy for future academic success and peer delinquency as mediators of the parental support-delinquency relationship. *Criminal Justice Review, 44*(2), 101–118.

Walters, G. D. (2019j). Tracing the delinquency acquisition sequence from older siblings, to friends, to self: A mediation analysis. *Journal of Adolescence, 75*, 113–122.

Walters, G. D. (2020a). *Closing the integration gap in criminology: The case for criminal thinking*. Routledge.

Walters, G. D. (2020b). Crime and social cognition: A meta-analytic review of the developmental roots of adult criminal thinking. *Journal of Experimental Criminology*. Online first, https://doi.org/10.1007/s11292-020-09435-w

Walters, G. D. (2020c). Criminal thinking as a moderator of the perceived certainty-offending relationship: Age variations. *Psychology, Crime and Law, 26*(3), 267–286.

Walters, G. D. (2020d). Desistance and identity: Do reflected appraisals as a delinquent impede the crime-reducing effects of the adolescent-to-adult transition? *Criminal Justice Review, 45*(3), 303–318.

Walters, G. D. (2020e). Desisting from crime: In-prison behaviour and cognition as predictors of post-release success. *Canadian Journal of Criminology and Criminal Justice, 62*(3), 11–28.

Walters, G. D. (2020f). Hostility and reactive criminal thinking as mediators of the violent victimization-violent offending relationship: Affect before cognition? *Criminal Justice Studies, 33*(4), 316–336.

Walters, G. D. (2020g). Mediating the mediator: The indirect effect of short-term hostility on the past reactive criminal thinking–future reactive criminal thinking relationship. *Deviant Behavior, 41*(9), 1157–1175.

Walters, G. D. (2020h). Mediating the peer influence effect with facets of criminal thought process and content in a group of early adolescents: Replication and extension. *Journal of Police and Criminal Psychology, 35*(2), 207–218.

Walters, G. D. (2020i). Mediating the victim-offender overlap with delinquent peer associations: A preliminary test of the person proximity hypothesis. *Criminal Justice Studies, 33*(4), 297–315.

Walters, G. D. (2020j). Moral disengagement as a mediator of the co-offending–delinquency relationship in serious juvenile offenders. *Law and Human Behavior, 44*(5), 437–448.

Walters, G. D. (2020k). Neutralization, moral disengagement, and delinquency in adolescence: Testing the reciprocal effects of proactive criminal thinking and guilt on future offending. *Justice Quarterly, 37*(2), 210–230.

Walters, G. D. (2020l). Parental control as a stimulus for youth control: Mediating the parental knowledge-child delinquency relationship with cognitive impulsivity. *Crime and Delinquency*. Online first, https://doi.org/10.1177/0011128720962449

Walters, G. D. (2020m). Perceived peer delinquency, proactive criminal thinking, neighborhood disorder, and serious offending: Moderated mediation and theoretical integration. *Journal of Crime and Justice, 43*(4), 467–485.
Walters, G. D. (2020n). Positive peers—The neglected stepchildren of social influence theories of crime. *Journal of Abnormal Child Psychology, 48*(5), 719–732.
Walters, G. D. (2020o). Predicting future intimate partner violence with past intimate partner violence: The moderating role of proactive and reactive criminal thinking. *Criminal Justice and Behavior, 47*(8), 943–955.
Walters, G. D. (2020p). Prosocial peers as risk, protective, and promotive factors for the prevention of delinquency and drug use. *Journal of Youth and Adolescence, 49*(3), 618–630.
Walters, G. D. (2020q). School-age bullying victimization and perpetration: A meta-analysis of prospective studies and research. *Trauma, Violence and Abuse*. Online first, https://doi.org/10.1177/1524838020906513
Walters, G. D. (2020r). The sibling effect for delinquency: Mediation by proactive criminal thinking and moderation by age. *International Journal of Offender Therapy and Comparative Criminology, 64*(2–3), 265–288.
Walters, G. D. (2020s). Unraveling the bidirectional relationship between bullying victimization and perpetration: A test of mechanisms from opportunity and general strain theories. *Youth Violence and Juvenile Justice, 18*(4), 395–411.
Walters, G. D. (2021a). Ambient temperature as a moderator of the reactive criminal thinking–violent offending relationship: A multilevel analysis. *Journal of Criminological Research Policy and Practice*. Online first, https://doi.org/10.1108/JCRPP-10-2020-0067
Walters, G. D. (2021b). The certainty–offending relationship as a function of a nation's free market cultural ethos. *European Journal of Criminology*. Online first, https://doi.org/10.1177/14773708211039644
Walters, G. D. (2021c). Criminal thinking and gang affiliation: Antecedents and consequences. *Journal of Criminological Research Policy and Practice, 7*(2), 150–163.
Walters, G. D. (2021d). Delinquency as a consequence of parental warmth and self-efficacy: Total sample and individual male and female mediation analyses. *Journal of Adolescence, 89*, 137–148.
Walters, G. D. (2021e). Explaining the drug-crime connection with peers, proactive criminal thinking and victimization: Systemic, cognitive social learning, and person proximity mechanisms. *Psychology of Addictive Behaviors, 35*(3), 366–376.
Walters, G. D. (2021f). Extending the "Worst of Both Worlds" hypothesis to the developmental antecedents of crime and substance use: School bullying and alcohol experimentation. *European Child and Adolescent Psychiatry*. Online first, https://doi.org/10.1007/s00787-021-01771-0
Walters, G. D. (2021g). In search of a mechanism: Mediating the perceived parental support-delinquency relationship with child empathy. *Journal of Moral Education*. Online first, https://doi.org/10.1080/03057240.2021.1872511
Walters, G. D. (2021h). Mitigating bullying–delinquency risk with parental support and knowledge: Testing a three-way interaction, *Psychology, Crime & Law*. Online first, https://doi.org/10.1080/1068316X.2021.1876052

Walters, G. D. (2021i). Moderating the criminal thinking-delinquency relationship with a free market cultural ethos: Integrating micro- and macro-level concepts in criminology. *European Journal of Criminal Policy and Research*. Online first, https://doi.org/10.1007/s10610-021-09480-9

Walters, G. D. (2021j). Parents and best friends perceived reaction to participant deviance and self-reported delinquency: Moderation by sex and mediation by youth attitude toward deviance in mid- to late adolescence. *Criminal Justice Review*. Online first, https://doi.org/10.1177/07340168211015728

Walters, G. D. (2021k). Predicting short-term parole outcome in substance abusing offenders with the Lifestyle Criminality Screening Form. *International Journal of Forensic Mental Health, 20*(3), 253–264.

Walters, G. D. (2021l). Protecting against delinquency in early adolescence with nonverbal intelligence and neighborhood social capital. *Journal of Early Adolescence*. Online first, https://doi.org/10.1177/02724316211020362

Walters, G. D. (2021m). Trajectories of bullying victimization and perpetration in Australian school children and their relationship to future delinquency and conduct problems. *Psychology of Violence, 11*(1), 19–27.

Walters, G. D. (2022a). Changes in criminal thinking from mid-adolescence to early adulthood: Does trajectory direction matter? *Law and Human Behavior*. https://doi.org/10.1037/

Walters, G. D. (2022b). Does adolescent drug use belong on the antisocial spectrum? Mediating the drug-crime connection with cognitive impulsivity. *International Journal of Law and Psychiatry*, 80, 101761.

Walters, G. D., & Chlumsky, M. L. (1993). The Lifestyle Criminality Screening Form and antisocial personality disorder: Predicting release outcome in a state prison sample. *Behavioral Sciences & the Law, 11*(1), 111–115.

Walters, G. D., & DeLisi, M. (2015). Psychopathy and violence: Does antisocial cognition mediate the relationship between the PCL: YV factor scores and violent criminality? *Law and Human Behavior, 39*(4), 350–359.

Walters, G. D., Deming, A., & Casbon, T. (2015). Predicting recidivism in sex offenders with the Psychological Inventory of Criminal Thinking Styles (PICTS). *Assessment, 22*(2), 167–177.

Walters, G. D., & Elliott, W. N. (1999). Predicting release and disciplinary outcome with the Psychological Inventory of Criminal Thinking Styles: Female data. *Legal and Criminological Psychology, 4*(1), 15–21.

Walters, G. D., & Espelage, D. L. (2017). Mediating the bullying victimization-delinquency relationship with anger and cognitive impulsivity: A test of general strain and criminal lifestyle theories. *Journal of Criminal Justice, 53*, 66–73.

Walters, G. D., & Espelage, D. L. (2018a). Cognitive insensitivity and cognitive impulsivity as mediators of bullying continuity: Extending the psychological inertia construct to bullying behavior. *School Psychology Quarterly, 33*(4), 527–536.

Walters, G. D., & Espelage, D. L. (2018b). From victim to victimizer: Hostility, anger, and depression as mediators of the bullying victimization-bullying perpetration association. *Journal of School Psychology, 68*, 73–83.

Walters, G. D., & Espelage, D. L. (2018c). Resurrecting the empathy–bullying relationship with a pro-bullying attitudes mediator: The Lazarus Effect in mediation research. *Journal of Abnormal Child Psychology, 46*(6), 1229–1239.

Walters, G. D., & Espelage, D. L. (2019). Bullying perpetration and subsequent delinquency: A regression-based analysis of early adolescent schoolchildren. *Journal of Early Adolescence, 39*(5), 669–688.

Walters, G. D., & Espelage, D. L. (2020a). Hostility, anger, and dominance as mediators of the sibling aggression-school fighting relationship: Mechanisms of violence generalization. *Psychology of Violence, 10*(1), 48–57.

Walters, G. D., & Espelage, D. L. (2020b). Peer victimization, antisocial cognition, and delinquency in early adolescent schoolchildren: A test of the person-situation interface. *Journal of School Violence, 19*(4), 512–524.

Walters, G. D., & Espelage, D. L. (2021). Reciprocity of cognitive and emotional antecedents to bullying: Bidirectional relations between cognitive impulsivity and anger. *Youth and Society*. Online first, https://doi.org/10.1177/0044118X211053025

Walters, G. D., Frederick, A. A., & Schlauch, C. (2007). Postdicting arrests for proactive and reactive aggression with the PICTS proactive and reactive composite scales. *Journal of Interpersonal Violence, 22*(11), 1415–1430.

Walters, G. D., & Geyer, M. D. (2007). The PICTS Fear-of-Change scale: Construct and predictive validity. *The Prison Journal, 87*(2), 211–226.

Walters, G. D., Hagman, B. T., & Cohn, A. M. (2011). Toward a hierarchical model of criminal thinking: Evidence from item response theory and confirmatory factor analysis. *Psychological Assessment, 23*(4), 925–936.

Walters, G. D., & Kiehl, K. A. (2015). Limbic correlates of fearlessness and disinhibition in incarcerated youth: Exploring the brain–behavior relationship with the Hare Psychopathy Checklist: Youth Version. *Psychiatry Research, 230*(2), 205–210.

Walters, G. D., Kremser, J., & Runell, L. (2020). Moderating the bullying perpetration-delinquency relationship with parental support and knowledge: A prospective analysis of middle school students. *Aggressive Behavior, 46*(3), 244–253.

Walters, G. D., & Lowenkamp, C. T. (2016). Predicting recidivism with the Psychological Inventory of Criminal Thinking Styles (PICTS) in community-supervised male and female federal offenders. *Psychological Assessment, 28*(6), 652–659.

Walters, G. D., & Magaletta, P. R. (2015). Comorbid antisocial and substance misuse proclivity and mental health service utilization by female inmates: Testing the Worst of Both Worlds hypothesis with the PAI. *Psychological Services, 12*(1), 28–36.

Walters, G. D., & McDonough, J. R. (1998). The Lifestyle Criminality Screening Form as a predictor of federal parole/probation/supervised release outcome: A 3-year follow-up. *Legal and Criminological Psychology, 3*(2), 173–181.

Walters, G. D., & Morgan, R. D. (2018). Assessing criminal thought content: Preliminary validation of the Criminal Thought Content Inventory (CTCI). *Psychology, Crime and Law, 24*(6), 603–620.

Walters, G. D., & Morgan, R. D. (2019). Certainty of punishment and criminal thinking: Do the rational and non-rational parameters of a student's decision to cheat on an exam interact? *Journal of Criminal Justice Education, 30*(2), 276–295.

Walters, G. D., Morgan, R. D., & Scanlon, F. (2019). The moderating effect of criminal thinking on certainty of apprehension in decisions to engage in antisocial behavior: Replication and extension. *Journal of Forensic Sciences, 64*(3), 805–813.

Walters, G. D., & Noon, A. (2015). Family context and externalizing correlates of childhood animal cruelty in adjudicated delinquents. *Journal of Interpersonal Violence, 30*(8), 1369–1386.

Walters, G. D., Ponce, R., Piñero, M. A., & Ernest, K. D. (2021a). Criminal thinking, certainty of apprehension, and the decision to engage in antisocial behavior: A study of day treatment program clients. *Journal of Forensic Sciences, 66*(2), 636–645.

Walters, G. D., Revella, L., & Baltrusaitis, W. J. (1990). Predicting parole/probation outcome with the aid of the Lifestyle Criminality Screening Form. *Psychological Assessment, 2*(3), 313–316.

Walters, G. D., Runell, L., & Kremser, J. (2021b). Drifters and delinquents: Commitment and neutralization in low- and high-rate offending early adolescents. *Crime and Delinquency*. Online first, https://doi.org/10.1177/00111287211039992

Walters, G. D., & Ruscio, J. (2013). Trajectories of youthful antisocial behavior: Categories or continua? *Journal of Abnormal Child Psychology, 41*(4), 653–666.

Walters, G. D., Trgovac, M., Rychlec, M., DiFazio, R., & Olson, J. R. (2002). Assessing change with the Psychological Inventory of Criminal Thinking Styles: A controlled analysis and multisite cross-validation. *Criminal Justice and Behavior, 29*(3), 208–331.

Walters, G. D., & White, T. W. (1989a). Heredity and crime: Bad genes or bad research? *Criminology, 27*(3), 455–485.

Walters, G. D., & White, T. W. (1989b). The thinking criminal: A cognitive model of lifestyle criminality. *Criminal Justice Research Bulletin, 4*(4), 1–10.

Walters, G. D., White, T. W., & Denney, D. (1991). The Lifestyle Criminality Screening Form: Preliminary data. *Criminal Justice and Behavior, 18*(4), 406–418.

Wang, X., Lei, L., Liu, D., & Hu, H. (2016). Moderating effects of moral reasoning and gender on the relation between moral disengagement and cyberbullying in adolescents. *Personality and Individual Differences, 98*, 244–249.

Wang, Y.-J., & Xia, L.-X. (2019). The longitudinal relationships of interpersonal openness trait, hostility, and hostile attribution bias. *Aggressive Behavior, 45*(6), 682–690.

Ward, M. A., Theule, J., & Cheung, K. (2016). Parent–child interaction therapy for child disruptive behaviour disorders: A meta-analysis. *Child Youth Care Forum, 45*(5), 675–690.

Wardlaw, G. R. (1979). Aversion therapy: Technical, ethical, and safety issues. *Australian and New Zealand Journal of Criminology, 12*(2), 43–54.

Warner, C., Conley, T., & Murphy, R. (2018). Criminal thinking shifts among male prisoners participating in a cognitive-based education programme. *Criminal Behaviour and Mental Health, 28*(2), 152–157.

Warr, M. (2002). *Companions in crime: The social aspects of criminal conduct.* Cambridge University Press.

Wason, P. C. (1960). On the failure to eliminate hypotheses in a conceptual task. *Quarterly Journal of Experimental Psychology, 12*(PT 3), 129–140.

Weafer, J., & Fillmore, M. T. (2016). Low-dose alcohol effects on measures of inhibitory control, delay discounting, and risk-taking. *Current Addiction Reports, 3*(1), 75–84.

Webster-Stratton, C., & Reid, M. J. (2003). Treating conduct problems and strengthening social and emotional competence in young children: The Dina Dinosaur treatment program. *Journal of Emotional and Behavioral Disorders, 11*(3), 130–143.

Wegrzyn, M., Westphal, S., & Kissler, J. (2017). In your face: The biased judgement of fear-anger expressions in violent offenders. *BMC Psychology, 5*, 16.

Weisburd, D., Farrington, D. P., & Gill, C. (2018). What works in crime prevention and rehabilitation: An assessment of systematic reviews. *Criminology and Public Policy, 16*(2), 415–449.

Weisburd, D., Wyckoff, L. A., Ready, J., Eck, J. E., Hinkle, J. C., & Gajewski, F. (2006). Does crime just move around the corner? A controlled study of spatial displacement and diffusion of crime control benefits. *Criminology, 44*(3), 549–592.

Weld, D., & Roche, S. P. (2017). A matter of time: A partial test of institutional anomie theory using cross-national time use data. *Journal of Quantitative Criminology, 33*(2), 371–395.

Welsh, B. C., Farrington, D. P., & Taheri, S. A. (2015). Effectiveness and social costs of public area surveillance for crime prevention. *Annual Review of Law and Social Science, 11*, 111–130.

Welte, J. W., Barnes, G. M., Hoffman, J. H., Wieczorek, W. F., & Zhang, L. (2005). Substance involvement and the trajectory of criminal offending in young males. *American Journal of Drug and Alcohol Abuse, 31*(2), 267–284.

Weng, J., Paslaski, S., Daly, J., VanDam, C., & Brown, J. (2013). Modulation for emergent networks: Serotonin and dopamine. *Neural Networks, 41*, 225–239.

White, H. R., Bates, M. E., & Buyske, S. (2001). Adolescence-limited versus persistent delinquency: Extending Moffitt's hypothesis into adulthood. *Journal of Abnormal Psychology, 110*(4), 600–609.

White, J. L., Moffitt, T. E., Caspi, A., Bartusch, D. J., Needles, D. J., & Stouthamer-Loeber, M. (1994). Measuring impulsivity and examining its relationship to delinquency. *Journal of Abnormal Psychology, 103*(2), 192–205.

Whited, W. H., Wagar, L., Mandracchia, J. T., & Morgan, R. D. (2017). Partners or partners in crime? The relationship between criminal associates and criminogenic thinking. *International Journal of Offender Therapy and Comparative Criminology, 61*(5), 491–507.

Whiteman, S. D., McHale, S. M., & Crouter, A. C. (2007). Explaining sibling similarities: Perceptions of sibling influences. *Journal of Youth and Adolescence, 36*(7), 963–972.

Widmer, E. D., & Weiss, C. C. (2000). Do older siblings make a difference? The effects of older sibling support and older sibling adjustment on the adjustment of socially disadvantaged adolescents. *Journal of Research on Adolescence, 10*(1), 1–27.

Wikström, P.-O. H. (2006). Individuals, settings, and acts of crime: Situational mechanisms and the explanation of crime. In P.-O. H. Wikström & R. Sampson (Eds.), *The explanation of crime: Context, mechanisms, and development* (pp. 61–107). Cambridge University Press.

Wikström, P.-O., Oberwittler, D., Treiber, K., & Hardie, B. (2012). *Breaking rules: The social and situational dynamics of young people's urban crime.* Oxford University Press.

Williams, C. R., & Arrigo, B. A. (2002). *Law, psychology, and justice: Chaos theory and the new disorder.* SUNY Press.

Wilson, D. B., Bouffard, L. A., & Mackenzie, D. L. (2005). A quantitative review of structured, group-oriented, cognitive-behavioral programs for offenders. *Criminal Justice and Behavior, 32*(2), 172–204.

Wilson, J. Q., & Herrnstein, R. J. (1985). *Crime and human nature: The definitive study of the causes of crime.* Simon & Schuster.

Wilson, J. Q., & Kelling, G. (1982). The police and neighborhood safety: Broken windows. *Atlantic Monthly, 127*, 29–38.

Wilson, S., Malone, S. M., Venable, N. C., McGue, M., & Iacono, W. G. (2021). Multimodal indicators of risk for and consequences of substance use disorders: Executive functions and trait disconstraint assessed from preadolescence into early adulthood. *International Journal of Psychophysiology, 163*, 47–57.

Wojciechowski, T. W. (2021). Snares or turning points? Examining the relevance of fatherhood entry timing and number of children for offending in adulthood. *Criminal Justice Review, 46*(1), 5–19.

Wolfe, S., Rojek, J., McLean, K., & Alpert, G. (2020). Social interaction training to reduce police use of force. *Annals of the American Academy of Political and Social Science, 687*(1), 124–145.

Wolff, K. T., & Baglivio, M. T. (2017). Adverse childhood experiences, negative emotionality, and pathways to juvenile recidivism. *Crime and Delinquency, 63*(12), 1495–1521.

Wolfgang, M. E. (1961). Pioneers in criminology: Cesare Lombroso (1835–1909). *Journal of Criminal Law, Criminology, and Police Science, 52*(4), 361–391.

Wolfgang, M. E., & Ferracuti, F. (1967). *The subculture of violence: Towards an integrated theory in criminology.* Tavistock Publications.

Wong, D. F. K., Ip, P. S. Y., Chan, M. H., & Zhuag, X. Y. (2018). A preliminary study on cognitive-behavior interventions for Hong Kong Chinese delinquent youth. *Research on Social Work Practice, 28*(7), 838–847.

Wright, J. P., & Beaver, K. M. (2005). Do parents matter in creating self-control in their children? A genetically informed test of Gottfredson and Hirschi's theory of low self-control. *Criminology, 43*(4), 1169–1202.

Wright, V. (2010, November). *Deterrence in criminal justice: Evaluating certainty vs severity of punishment.* The Sentencing Project.

Yochelson, S., & Samenow, S. E. (1976). *The criminal personality: Vol. 1. A profile for change.* Aronson.

Yoo, J. A. (2017). Developmental changes in the bidirectional relationships between parental monitoring and child delinquency. *Children and Youth Services Review, 73*, 360–367.

Young, J. T. N., Rebellon, C. J., Barnes, J. C., & Weerman, F. M. (2013). Unpacking the black box of peer similarity in deviance: Understanding the mechanisms linking personal behavior, peer behavior, and perceptions. *Criminology, 52*(1), 60–86.

Yousuf, H., Ehlers, V. L., Sehgal, M., Song, G., & Moyer, J. R. (2020). Modulation of intrinsic excitability as a function of learning within the fear conditioning circuit. *Neurobiology of Learning and Memory*. Online first, https://doi.org/10.1016/j.nlm.2019.107132

Zafirovski, M. (2012). Beneath rational choice: Elements of "irrational choice theory." *Current Sociology, 61*(1), 3–21.

Zahnow, R., Zhang, M., & Corcoran, J. (2021). The girl on the bus: Familiar faces in daily travel and their implications for crime protection. *Annals of the American Association of Geographers, 111*(5), 1367–1384.

Zald, D. H., Cowan, R. L., Riccardi, P., Baldwin, R. M., Ansari, M. S., … Kessler, R. M. (2009). Midbrain dopamine receptor availability is inversely associated with novelty-seeking traits in humans. *Journal of Neuroscience, 28*(53), 14372–14378.

Zhang, J., Lee, S-K., Piehler, T. F., Gewitz, A. H., & August, G. J. (2020). Bidirectional relations between parenting practices and child externalizing behaviors in formerly homeless families: A random-intercept cross-lagged panel analysis. *Parenting, 20*(3), 177–199.

Zhang, L., Fang, J., Zhang, D., Wan, Y., Gong, C., … Sun, Y. (2021). Polyvictimization and psychopathological symptoms in adolescence: Examining the potential buffering effect of positive childhood experiences. *Journal of Affective Disorders, 282*, 1308–1314.

Zhang, L., Wieczorek, W. F., & Welte, J. W. (2011). Early onset delinquency and trajectory of alcohol-impaired driving among young males. *Addictive Behaviors, 36*(12), 1154–1159.

Index

access control, 224, 226–27
adolescence-limited pattern, 7–9
age-crime curve, 80–82, 84, 85, 200
ambient temperature, 33, 53, 142, 167, 208–9, 253
anger, 15, 43, 76–78, 137, 138, 144, 165, 170, 211
animal cruelty, 1, 16, 17, 66, 95–97, 252
antisocial spectrum, 1, 16–18, 27, 28, 31, 37, 39, 40, 49, 53, 54, 59, 94, 107, 136, 145
assisted natural surveillance, 224, 227
attachment, 10, 39, 51, 70, 73, 74, 88, 106–8, 119, 123, 134, 146, 202, 203, 218
attribution triad, 181–82, 195, 200

Beccaria, Cesare, 2, 6, 154, 249
behavioral impulsivity. *See* low self-control
Bentham, Jeremy, 2, 6, 92, 93, 127, 153, 249
bidirectional effects, 9–15, 37, 49, 77, 95, 110, 128, 129, 131, 143, 153, 162, 234
bifurcation, 251
bounded rationality, 157–59, 161
bullying, 1, 12, 15–17, 27, 39, 40, 49, 66, 74, 75, 78, 83, 94–96, 107, 136, 143, 148, 178, 205, 230, 235, 236, 252
butterfly effect. *See* sensitive dependence on initial conditions
bystanders, 234–36

callous-unemotional (CU) traits, 18, 66, 113, 196, 197, 205, 240
causal mediation analysis. *See* mediation
change plan, 183–84
chaos theory. *See* nonlinear dynamical systems theory
cognitive-behavioral inconsistency, 182–84
cognitive impulsivity, 7, 15, 17, 37, 49, 64, 77, 83, 87, 88, 95, 96, 135, 143, 145
cognitive indolence, 60–62, 86, 99, 148, 179, 180, 183
cognitive insensitivity, 14, 17, 64, 83, 87, 88, 95, 96, 143
collective efficacy, 50, 206, 207
collider effect, 13–14
community. *See* neighborhood watch; schools
competencies, 175, 176, 184, 187, 189, 190, 194–96, 198, 199, 204, 217, 221, 223, 224, 228, 231, 234, 238–40, 243, 244, 247, 250, 254;

changing beliefs, 191–92; changing commitments, 188–90; changing identifications, 190–91; changing involvements, 187–88
confounding variables, 12–13
conscience. *See* emotions, self-conscious; empathy; moral reasoning
control model of lifestyle criminality, 70, 114, 115, 119, 120, 127–29, 138–44, 148, 151, 161, 171–72, 209, 245, 247, 253
cost-benefit analysis, 155–57, 233–34
courts: educating the public, 215; simplifying the law, 214–15
crime, definition of, 6, 21–23
crime continuity, 66, 74, 82–85, 95, 140, 143–44, 179, 253
criminality, definition of, 6, 21–23
criminal lifestyle: behavioral styles, 85–86; definition of, 15–16; function of, 89–94; stages of, 86–89
Criminal Sentiments Scale-Modified (CSS-M), 63
criminal thought content, 45, 59–61, 63, 64, 67, 73, 75, 76, 115–17
criminal thought content inventory (CTCI), 63–65, 75, 76
criminal thought process, 45, 59, 60, 62–64, 67, 72, 73, 76, 77, 98, 99, 110, 113, 117, 135, 171, 239, 252
Criminogenic Cognitions Scale (CCS), 63
criminogenic thinking profile (CTP), 63
cutoff, 59–62, 86, 99, 147, 148, 179
cyberbullying, 112

death penalty, 147, 154, 155, 157, 217–18
decision-making model of crime, 70, 103, 149, 160–68, 171–72, 223, 228, 234, 236, 245, 247, 253; aggravating/mitigating conditions, 22, 23, 46, 159, 162, 166–67, 175, 209, 223, 224, 234–41; incentive/deterrence, 112, 161–66, 175, 228, 229
deny benefits, 225, 229, 231
depression, 132, 137, 142, 160, 166, 206, 211, 219, 237
deterrence theory, 6, 22, 69, 153–57, 186
developmental taxonomy, 7–9, 130, 146
differential association. *See* learning theory, social
discontinuity, 60–62, 86, 99, 148, 179, 180, 183
disinhibition, 17, 28, 29, 83, 97, 130–31, 133, 139, 145, 146
disrupt markets, 225, 229–30
dopamine (DA), 30–31, 93–94, 109, 131, 165, 179, 209–11, 219, 248–49, 253
drugs. *See* substance use/misuse
Dupuit, Jule, 231

emotional: dysregulation, 240–41; maturity, 179, 241–42
emotions, self-conscious, 10, 14, 38, 39, 73, 74, 77, 78, 105, 108–10, 112, 117, 123, 134, 153, 161, 165, 171, 231
empathy, 38, 39, 48, 66, 73, 74, 95, 96, 99, 105–7, 112, 113, 123, 125, 165, 196–97, 215, 218, 235
entitlement, 60–62, 70, 77, 86, 99, 123
environments, 175, 176, 199, 201, 206, 209, 211, 214, 217–19, 221, 223, 224, 229, 234, 236, 242, 244, 247, 250
equal environments assumption, 25, 26
existentialism, 152
expectancies for change, 181–82, 184
extended guardianship, 224, 227

false premise: defense, 61, 62; denial, 61, 62

falsifiability, 5
fearlessness, 17, 28, 29, 95–97, 109, 110, 133
fear of change, 88, 90, 91, 178–80, 184, 194
fear of crime, 206
fractals, 251–52
free market cultural ethos, 52–54, 137, 142, 207, 208, 253

γ-Aminobutyric acid (GABA), 31
general criminal thinking (gct), 59, 63, 64, 69–72, 75, 76, 137, 142, 145, 192, 198, 238
general theory of crime, 6–7, 9, 36, 37, 49, 82, 83, 135, 163, 166, 200
genetics, 25–26, 40, 54, 73, 82, 146, 242, 248, 253
guilt. *See* emotions, self-conscious

hedonistic: belief system, 164–65; emotion, 165, 167, 172; expectancies, 165, 170, 172
hierarchy: horizontal, 17; vertical, 59, 61, 63
homophily. *See* peer
hostile attribution biases, 45, 60, 64, 71, 98, 138, 144
hostility, 43, 49, 76, 95–97, 103, 137–40, 143, 144, 148, 167, 203, 205, 211
How I Think (HIT), 63
human agency, 152–53

identity, criminal, 61, 64, 65, 73, 75, 115–18, 124, 125, 128, 190, 197
identity theory of desistance (ITD), 185–87, 200
identity transformation, 113, 116, 118, 186
incarceration, 73, 120, 121, 215–16, 218, 221
institutional anomie theory (IAT), 52, 136
internalization, 66, 67, 75, 99, 111, 113, 134, 147, 182, 195, 203, 244

iteration, 250

joint attention, 73, 106

Kuhn, Thomas, 5, 252

labeling, 15, 40, 83, 114, 117–18
learning theory, social, 10, 22, 33, 34, 37, 39–42, 44, 49, 57–59, 73, 74, 114, 124, 127, 134, 146, 149, 164, 172, 203, 210, 213, 248–50
life-course persistent pattern, 7–9, 130, 146
life instinct, 29–31, 93, 211, 249
lifestyle criminality screening form (LCSF), 15, 16, 85–86, 120
limbic system, 28–30, 93, 109, 131, 158
Lombroso, Cesare, 2, 6, 23–24
low self-control, 6–7, 9, 17, 18, 25, 36, 59, 83, 84, 129–36, 139–41, 145, 146, 149, 166, 197

Measure of Offender Thinking Styles-Revised (MOTS-R), 63
Measures of Criminal Attitudes and Associates (MCAA), 63
mediation, 11–12, 66–67
mental state, 236–38
moderation, 11–12, 68–69
mollification, 60–62, 77, 86, 98, 99, 123
moral: belief system, 165; emotion, 160, 165, 167, 172; expectancies, 172
moral disengagement, 14, 17, 45, 59, 64, 65, 72, 98, 112, 115, 119, 188, 235
moral integrity, 73, 112, 113, 115, 123–25, 128, 129, 134, 139
moral model of lifestyle criminality, 70, 84, 103, 104, 113–20, 123, 124, 127, 128, 139, 171, 209, 253
moral reasoning, 38, 39, 73, 74, 77, 105, 110–13, 134, 165, 233, 234
moral relativism, 103–5
moral universality, 103–5

motivational interviewing (MI), 179–81, 184
motivation for change, 178–81

negative emotionality/affect, 40, 49, 90, 130, 132–33, 139, 145, 146
neighborhood: anonymity, 206, 224, 229, 231; crime, 49–51, 134, 177, 206–7, 227; disorder, 68, 115, 167, 206
neighborhood watch, 227
neutralization, 10, 14, 45, 58, 59, 64, 65, 74, 76, 77, 98, 107, 112, 115, 136
nonlinear dynamical systems theory, 250–52

opportunity, 6, 8, 9, 24, 41, 53, 79, 84, 93, 134, 155, 156, 159, 161–64, 166, 170, 178, 202, 223, 225, 226, 228–30, 232, 233, 237, 239–42, 244
outcome expectancies, 59, 60, 64, 65, 88, 98, 115, 119, 192, 198

paradigm shift, 5, 252
parental: control, 6, 35–39, 46, 65, 74, 82, 94, 109, 131, 133, 134, 146, 177, 202, 203; deviance, 39–40, 204; knowledge, 36, 37, 39, 46, 94, 205; support, 36–39, 74, 106, 119, 131, 133, 178, 191, 202, 203, 205, 206, 221
peer: delinquency, 10, 14, 25, 37, 38, 42, 44–46, 66, 67, 69, 70, 74, 76, 94, 95, 113–17, 119, 124, 139–44, 185, 187–88, 192, 204–6, 219; influence, 10, 44–46, 66, 67, 73, 74, 76, 114–17, 141, 159, 187–88, 205; pressure, 11–12, 22, 134, 167, 225; rejection, 141–42; resistance, 14, 69, 188, 189, 192, 198; selection, 10, 44–46, 66, 74, 75, 140–41, 187–88
person proximity, 49, 95, 143, 205
perspective taking, 73, 99, 105, 197
police: accountability, 213–14; selection, 212–13; training, 213
Popper, Karl, 5, 252
population heterogeneity, 83, 84
power orientation, 60–62, 77, 86, 99, 123, 212
proactive criminal thinking (PCT), 17, 43, 45, 53, 59–65, 67–78, 83, 84, 87, 88, 95, 99, 107, 110, 112, 114–16, 119, 120, 123, 124, 128, 129, 135–44, 160, 167, 168, 170, 171, 188, 192, 197, 198, 231, 240, 252, 253
promotive factors, 22, 23, 26–28, 34–35, 37, 54, 132, 177, 184, 193, 198–99
prosocial peers, 47–48, 74, 84, 167, 188, 198, 205, 221
protective factors, 22, 23, 26–28, 34–35, 37, 46, 54, 184, 189, 193, 206
psychological inertia, 17, 27, 83–85, 95, 143, 178–80, 183, 184, 194, 253
Psychological Inventory of Criminal Thinking Styles (PICTS), 62, 63, 91, 238

Quetelet, Adolphe, 90

rational choice theory, 22, 154–57; limitations, 157–59
reactive criminal thinking, 17, 45, 49, 53, 59–65, 67–78, 83, 87, 88, 95, 98–100, 112, 114–16, 119, 120, 128, 129, 135–45, 148, 160, 167, 168, 170, 171, 179, 192, 197, 198, 205, 208, 238, 240, 252, 253
reciprocal risk, 27, 145
reduce anonymity, 224, 229, 231
reflected appraisals, 58, 65, 67, 75, 89, 90, 116, 118, 125, 197
rehabilitation, 216–17
risk: management, 176–78; prediction, 176–77
risk factors, 22, 23, 26–27, 31, 33, 38, 42, 84, 131, 176–78, 184, 187–88, 196, 205, 221
routine activity theory, 8–9, 156, 172, 227

schools, 50–52, 70
screen exits, 224, 228–30
secondary deviance. *See* labeling
self-efficacy, 39, 64, 65, 84, 88, 114, 115, 118–19, 152, 180–82, 184, 190, 191, 195, 198
self-organization, 252
self-view, 64, 75, 89, 90, 197
sensation seeking, 64, 65, 131–33, 139, 145, 146, 166
sensitive dependence on initial conditions, 251
sentimentality, 86, 112–13, 123
serotonin (5-HT), 30–31, 93, 109, 133, 165, 179, 209–10, 219, 248–49, 253
sibling effects: negative, 42–43; positive, 41–42
sibling relations, 40–44, 47, 73, 74, 87, 112, 116, 149, 202–4, 218, 219
situational action theory, 165, 166, 172
situational crime prevention, 224–28
social cognitive theory. *See* learning theory, social
social control theory, 19, 22, 37, 41, 74, 127, 149, 202, 206
social structure: macro, 51–54, 207–8
state dependence, 83
strain, 52, 79, 136–37, 139–45, 148, 201
strain theory: classic, 22, 51, 52, 136, 207; general, 22, 49, 52, 77, 136, 166, 172
strengthened formal surveillance, 224, 228
subjective utilities, 232
substance use/misuse, 16, 27, 29, 68, 85, 131, 132, 136, 139, 140, 143–45, 176, 198
superoptimism, 59–62, 77, 86, 99, 124, 167
suppressor variables, 13–14

target concealment, 224, 226
target hardening, 224, 225, 227
target removal, 224–26
Texas Christian University Criminal Thinking Scales (TCU CTS), 63, 68
theory of mind, 73, 99, 106, 158
therapeutic alliance, 179–89, 192, 194
three C's, 153
thrill-seeking. *See* sensation seeking
triads, 9, 11, 12, 59, 65, 68–70, 73, 78, 97
turning points, 185–86

utility, 161, 233
utilize place managers, 224, 229, 230

victimization, 12, 37, 48–49, 66, 94, 95, 116, 124, 142–44, 147, 148, 159, 163, 205, 225, 227

world-view, 89, 90, 92, 220
"Worst of both worlds" (WBW) hypothesis, 27, 144–45, 237

About the Author

Glenn D. Walters received his PhD in counseling psychology from Texas Tech University in 1982 and completed a one-year internship in clinical psychology at Dwight David Eisenhower Army Medical Center in Fort Gordon, Georgia, that same year. He has spent the last 11 years in the Department of Criminal Justice at Kutztown University where he currently holds the rank of full professor. His teaching responsibilities include classes in corrections, criminology, research methods, and substance abuse and crime. Prior to this, he spent 29 years working as a psychologist in the United States Disciplinary Barracks at Fort Leavenworth, Kansas, United States Penitentiary at Leavenworth, Kansas, Federal Correctional Institution at Fairton, New Jersey, and Federal Correctional Institution at Schuylkill, Pennsylvania. Dr. Walters's current research interests include development and validation of the Psychological Inventory of Criminal Thinking Styles (PICTS), delinquency development, moderation and mediation analysis, and creation of an overarching psychological theory of criminal behavior.

www.ingramcontent.com/pod-product-compliance
Ingram Content Group UK Ltd.
Pitfield, Milton Keynes, MK11 3LW, UK
UKHW020839290926
15470UKWH00004B/1437

9 781666 904420